Working With Black Young People

Edited by
Momodou Sallah
and
Carlton Howson

First published in 2007 by:
Russell House Publishing Ltd.
4 St. George's House
Uplyme Road
Lyme Regis
Dorset DT7 3LS

Tel: 01297-443948
Fax: 01297-442722
e-mail: help@russellhouse.co.uk
www.russellhouse.co.uk

British Library Cataloguing-in-publication Data:

A catalogue record for this book is available from the British Library.

ISBN: 978-1-905541-14-0

Typeset by TW Typesetting, Plymouth, Devon

Printed by ??

Contents

Dedication

To Pa Cherno Sallah and Haddy Fofana Sallah symbolising all mums and dads
who work day and night to bring up their children
into people society will be proud of.
To Kodou, for all her support.
And to Abdoulie and Sulayman who inspire me.

Momodou

To all those who have gone before; those who have died in struggle,
those from whom I have taken inspiration.
It is a testament of how the past connects the present with the future.
In particular Catherine, who conceived and gave birth to Annie,
who gave birth to Carlton who is the father of Akil and Aisha;
who are two Black young people who inspire and give me hope.

Carlton

Foreword

Learning from the past: work with Black young people

Those who have worked with Black young people in Britain over the past half century have observed dramatic generational changes, which all young people have experienced during a period of economic, social, political and cultural shifts. Many of those workers who faced up to those challenges have now either moved on, or moved away or passed away.

The late 1950s – through to 1965, was a period in which the acceptability of racism was to a large extent taken on the chin. Being called a 'wog' or 'coon' was common place, often said with a smile. However, also common place were the signs which advertised rooms to let and job vacancies but boldly stated: 'No Blacks, no Coloureds, no Irish need apply'.

The removal of the colour bar in 1965 did not remove discrimination, racism or prejudice. Mass unemployment was already a plague among Black young adults in places such as Brixton, Tottenham, Handsworth, Bristol and Toxteth, long before the Manpower Services Commission was created to tackle a similar phenomenon affecting the white community.

Thus, the defining years for an emergent dominant image of Black youth in Great Britain were the late 1960s through to the mid-1990s. The public image then of Black youth, which persists currently, was that of an unemployed and unemployable cohort, who were criminally inclined, not prepared to accept authoritative guidance (including parental direction) and operating in a sub-culture regarded as alien and oppositional to mainstream British values. Although this description is an over-generalisation and only had a genuine and relevant application to a small proportion of Black young people, the analysed annual ethnic statistics for criminal involvement, educational under-achievement, school exclusions, unemployment and the growing prison population tells its own story of the challenges faced during those three decades. Two generations of Black young people were adversely affected by the challenges facing them in British society, many arising simply from their impoverished environment, the colour of their skin and the barriers placed in their way to benefit from available educational and employment opportunities for self-development and success. Among the most serious difficulties faced were those of low self-esteem and the low expectations held of them by teachers, lecturers, employers and law enforcers.

As someone who personally experienced the devastating application of the 'Sus' laws during the 1970s, especially when wrongfully and innocently arrested simply for being Black, wearing a sheepskin coat and working in Brixton, I can solemnly testify to the incarceration which took place at that time. It is not surprising that deep alienation developed and at the heart of conflict was the policing of communities, especially Black communities. The uprisings of the 1980s bear testament to the struggle for fair and non-oppressive policing which now in the 21st century is more sensitive and respectful unless, of course, you are suspected of being a 'terrorist'.

A significant period for Black young people was the period of the civil rights movement in the USA and the Black Power demands which led to great Black assertiveness and challenges to racism and the status quo. It was a defining moment in the late 1960s when Black youth decided it would no longer put up with oppressive policing, racist attacks, extreme racist organisations or what they described as the low-grade 'shit' jobs which no-one else wanted to do but someone has to!

What is most heart warming today, is how many Black young people survive and thrive, in spite of the struggles and obstacles. It is also uplifting to see more Black young men succeeding, alongside their sisters who have been relatively more successful in all aspects of modern life. This optimism owes much to many from all communities, illustrating greater sensitivity and knowledge in challenging racism and exclusion and recognising the values and benefits of respect and fair treatment for everyone. It is also due to the recognition on the part of some Black young people that they have to take responsibility for self-development. However, there are still far too many immersed in poverty, exclusion and alienation, as well as detained at 'Her Majesty's pleasure'.

The insights in this book about working with Black young people are based on real life experiences. There are many people in Great Britain, working at a local level with young people from all backgrounds with a view to helping them realise their aspirations, hopes and dreams. In so doing they are contributing to a modern, multi-cultural society in which everyone, hopefully, can learn, live, work and socialise with others, free from exclusion, prejudice, discrimination, harassment and violence. It is a huge challenge but one worthy of our efforts for the future generations of all our young people. It is especially crucial for all those working with Black young people as youth workers, community workers, counsellors, mentors, leaders, law enforcers, educators and managers, to ensure that they use all their knowledge, experiences and skills to persuade Black young people to make the most of all the opportunities available for learning and personal and professional development, something that all young people should be encouraged and helped to do.

Lord Herman Ouseley

Introduction

This introduction seeks to explain the rationale for the book, provide a summary of the chapters and give a general indication of who the book is for and why it might be useful to them. *Working with Black Young People* aims to enable readers to gain a deeper appreciation of issues that confront Black young people and to consider strategies for change. We use Black in its political context and there is ample evidence (Hofstede, 1984; Small, 1986; Ahmad, 1990; Rattansi, 1992; Robinson, 1998; Sallah, 2005) to show that a lot of Black young people hold a different concept of reality to the dominant Eurocentric one and this needs to be given greater attention by all who work with Black young people. We concede that the term Black is highly contested and can appear 'meaningless' in locating specific groups within the Black community; however we use it deliberately because of their shared experiences of oppression, immigration history and discrimination; where relevant, specific sections of the Black community will be referred to.

Rationale for the book

There is a negative overrepresentation of Black young people in most aspects of life including education, criminal justice, housing and health care (Brown, 1984; Lakey, 1997; Barn et al., 1997; PSI, 1997; CRE, 1998; Barn, 2001; National Statistics Online, 2004; Cabinet Office Strategy Unit Report, 2003; Dacombe and Sallah, 2006), surely this cannot be the accepted status quo. The book challenges this as well as propose ways forward.

In addition there is a dearth of empiric literature (Stevenson, 1998) in the field of work with Black young people; a review reveals that the limited literature available is mainly geared towards young people in the child protection system (Barn, 2001; Thorburn, 2005). Therefore a book of this nature, which is able to bring together the different dimensions and perspectives on work with Black young people, provides invaluable information to academics, policy makers and practitioners.

Momodou and Carlton (Chapters 1 and 2) chart the shifting nature of British social policy responses within a historical context; from recruitment, restriction, repatriation, multiculturalism and now mainly integration as heralded by the establishment of the Commission for Integration and Cohesion in August 2006. Before any meaningful work around integration and cohesion can begin (given the racial tensions that have been a growing concern; 2001 Oldham, Burnley and Bradford, the aftermath of 7 July 2005 and Birmingham, 21–23 October 2005), there must be greater understanding of the various contexts in which work with Black young people takes place, the 'realities' they face; not only from the dominant mainstream but also from a minority perspective as well as a possible further Black youth subculture and we hope this book will be the catalyst.

There are many diverging, yet converging fields of work with Black young people: youth offending, social work, youth and community work, education and probation; *Working with Black Young People* puts the reader in touch with these issues and their impact on Black young people. It attempts to do this by drawing together practitioners, academics, and students, all of whom have drawn on their experiences in an attempt to explore a number of current issues. This book, in bringing all the different angles and perspectives together is highly desirable and long overdue.

Summary of chapters

This book asserts that many of those charged with working with Black young people will do so whilst keeping their 'eyes on a prize' that has very little to do with Black liberation. Effective work with Black young people must have at its core an agenda, a strategy that seeks to emancipate Black young people both at a physical and mental level.

Chapter 1 takes the reader on a journey; engaging in an exploration of historical factors, giving rise to current challenges. In this, it asserts that if workers are going to be effective in working with Black young people, then policy makers, practitioners and agencies must have an understanding of the geography, the politics, the economics, the faith, the desire, the determination, the racism and the triumphs that Black people face in working towards their liberation. Having set the context by presenting some theoretical and historical discussion, the book moves through to a number of discourses based on research and practice. These include a consideration of how government policy has sought to keep Black young people out and maintained state sanctioned racism.

Following on from Chapter 1, Chapter 2 correlates historical, immigration and social policy responses to service provision for Black young people and explores issues such as 'relativism and dogmatism in praxis', which raises awareness of the importance of culture in the formation of reality. Chapter 3 takes a critical look at the formation of Black identity and argues the differences between the African and African Caribbean identity formation in the UK and how service provision often disregards this using examples from looked after young people in placements. Chapter 4 explodes the myth of 'hard to reach' and 'invisible' Black young people and challenges service providers to re-examine their stereotypes of these Black young people. Chapter 5 explores the role of the Black voluntary sector; detailing the historical and cultural metamorphosis of this group. Chapter 6 critically explores racial harassment as well as policy responses in schools in relation to Black young people. Building on this, Chapter 7 looks at how practitioners who have all intentions of working in an anti-oppressive state often end up being the custodians and implementers of oppressive legislation and the case of refugees and asylum seekers is used to illustrate this. Chapter 8 expands on the theme of refugees and asylum seekers; reporting on a participatory action research carried out with young refugees and asylum seekers on their health needs. Chapter 9 examines the British uprisings, more generally the role of Black youths in protesting against the status quo but more specifically strategies for Muslim youth work. Chapter 10 asks the question 'Can white youth workers effectively meet the needs of Black young people?' From a practitioner's perspective, it explores the dilemmas white workers face in meeting the needs of their Black clients. Chapter 11 explores the issue of forced marriages which is very different from arranged marriages, and which applies not only to women but also to men. It looks at relevant legislation as well as suggests strategies forward. Chapter 12 poses the question as to whether Black young people matter at all in the provision of universal services; it engages in an analysis of national, regional and local policies and initiatives in answering this question. Chapter 13 examines how youth services work with Black young people, the issues they confront and how praxis can be improved. Chapter 14 looks at the impact of formal education on the African Caribbean child; it is argued that formal education continues to fail the young African Caribbean and proposes how informal education can counter and complement this. Chapter 15 discusses the learning from a mentoring project in Manchester with specific relevance to African Caribbean young men and draws on lessons to be learned. Finally, the last chapter, but by no means the least, takes a critical look at Black young people in the criminal justice system and explores strategies for better practice.

Who is the book for?

Essentially this publication will be an invaluable asset for those who work with Black young people; it will be immensely popular with students of social work, politics, humanities, youth and community workers, crime and justice and education practitioners, who are in search of a publication that forms a foundation from which they can build. It will also be of interest to those who are just curious.

Momodou and Carlton
April 2007

About the Authors

The Editors

Momodou Sallah has been working in the field of Youth and Community Work for the past fifteen years at the local, national and international levels. He has served as the National Youth Director of the Gambia Red Cross Society and has worked as a detached youth worker, youth and community worker, community youth tutor and a senior youth worker in various locations in the UK. Momodou is now a senior lecturer at the Youth and Community Division, De Montfort University and has engaged Black young people throughout his career in some capacity. He has conducted research around Black children and discipline and his research interests include diversity, globalisation and participation in relation to young people.

Carlton Howson has worked within the field of youth and community work for over twenty years. He has a keen interest in research and practice and retains his sensitivity to issues through practical work with communities and his commitment to racial justice. He has worked with De Montfort University since 1990 as a Senior Lecturer. His main teaching areas include social policy, Black perspectives and managing race and diversity. He has undertaken research in the growth of violence with weapons in Nottingham. He is currently involved in research (PhD) about the student experience with a particular focus on the experience of Black students in higher education.

The Contributors

Shahid Ashrif set up and managed Strathclyde's multi-agency Ethnic Minorities Project in 1986. He moved to Rochdale Local Authority as Race, and Community Education Adviser. HMI and the CRE have used his expertise in racial equality and youth and community work. His publications cover anti-racist science, science investigations, Islamophobia, racism and Black history. Shahid also worked as an education adviser in London and Coventry. In 2000, he was a part-time lecturer at De Montfort University, co-ordinating the mandatory 'Anti-oppressive Practice' module for the MA in Community Education and has been a regular contributor to the Black Perspectives module. Between February 2004 and December 2005, he was Equalities Adviser for Derby Homes.

Harjeet Chakira has a BA (Hons) in Criminology and MSc in Clinical Criminology. Her postgraduate research looked into the impact of stringent immigration legislation on women marrying UK nationals and later becoming subjected to domestic violence. Since completing her educational career Harjeet has worked within the sector of domestic violence with Asian women and children experiencing domestic violence. Previously as a refuge worker, then as an outreach worker, Harjeet is currently working for a voluntary organisation as a floating support worker where she advocates, advises and empowers survivors of abuse to live independently. Harjeet has had personal as well as professional experience dealing with issues related to gender and family violence and it is this experience which drives her passion and commitment in this area of work.

Rod Dacombe is a Research Fellow at Warwick Business School, Warwick University. His research interests include issues around the voluntary sector, urban politics and racism. He is currently awaiting confirmation of his DPhil in Social Policy from Oxford University.

Tony Graham has been actively involved in community development work within Nottingham's most disadvantaged communities for the past 25 years. He started out as a qualified electrician but since then he has had a variety of roles including being a youth worker; project manager; African Caribbean outreach worker; community service supervisor for the Nottinghamshire Probation Service; FE lecturer, trainer; local area partnership development co-ordinator and since 2002 as Operations Director for Connexions Nottinghamshire. His work within the area of community development and empowerment started when he became involved in Nottingham's first cultural exchange to Jamaica, in 1983. Since that time, the voluntary and community sector remains a passion; he is a firm believer in strong and active communities and as such has founded a number of key local groups. Tony's current role provides him with a great opportunity to continue to lobby and influence so that young people in Nottingham feel that it is a vibrant and exciting city to live in.

Jennifer Izekor is Director for Children and Learners at the Government Office for London where she has strategic responsibility for ensuring the implementation of the government's *Every Child Matters* agenda across London. Since the beginning of her career, she has been committed to developing services for young people having worked at the Probation Service, Centre Point, Alone in London charity and as a training and development consultant developing innovative services for vulnerable young people across London. As Head of Infrastructure Development for the National Council for Voluntary Youth Services, she spearheaded the national drive to develop infrastructure provision for the voluntary and community sector working closely with local, regional and national networks to prepare the sector for the emerging Connexions agenda. Immediately prior to becoming the Director for Children and Learners at the Government Office for London, Jennifer was Chief Executive of London East Connexions Partnership, one of the two largest partnerships in England spanning 10 London boroughs. Jennifer lives in Essex with her daughter.

Darren Johnson has worked in youth justice and children services for 24 years; he is a former Head of a Youth Offending Service. He leads for the Association of Youth Offending Team Managers on Diversity. He is a committee member of the NAYJ and Black Youth Justice Forum. He has contributed to a number of Home Office and Youth Justice Board working groups on race and diversity. He is currently a senior management consultant and trainer for Holland House and Proactive Partnership Ltd. He has written articles and contributes regularly to news and radio programmes on a range of youth justice related issues.

Richard Kennedy is 32 and married with three young children. From the age of 17, he has worked with children and young people in a variety of statutory settings. These include play, family and community development work in a neighbourhood family centre; youth offending work; one to one mentoring; residential care work; Connexions adviser, youth work. More recently Richard has worked for Lincolnshire Children's Services Youth Service and manages a large purpose built centre on a deprived estate in Lincoln. He also manages provision for asylum seekers and refuges in the Lincoln area.

Ann Marie Lawson worked in finance for over 20 years during which time she became involved in sessional youth work in her local community. She became passionate about youth work and decided to change career three years ago to take up full time youth work. She was employed by Northamptonshire County Council as an externally funded youth worker on a crime and anti-social behaviour partnership. During this time she built good relationships with other agencies and was awarded an Unsung Hero Award from Northamptonshire Police Authority for services to the community. She was promoted to area youth worker in 2004 with responsibility for a diverse range of projects. She has recently taken up a post with Groundwork North Northamptonshire as a youth development officer where one of her priorities is breaking down the barriers between the Eastern European and white British communities.

Chester Morrison has worked in a number of situations in youth and community work. His wide experience has seen him occupy such positions as community education officer in Derby, commissioning officer in Leicestershire, Principal Education Officer in Liverpool and he was for nine years an additional inspector with Ofsted. In the field of diversity he has worked for the Race Equality Council, Wolverhampton and is the independent chair of Race Equality Partnership, Wolverhampton. He is a Fellow of the Royal Society for the Arts and an associate of the European Research Project – UP2Youth. He was a main contributor to the Urbact Young Citizens Project that was concerned with improving young people's participation in civil society.

Raksha Pandya is a 26-year-old British-Indian woman who grew up in Leicester. Raksha has over 10-years health and social care experience in the field of learning disability, homelessness, drug and alcohol treatment and HIV. Currently Raksha has completed and published her second piece of research. The first piece investigated substance use in young refugee and asylum-seeking communities in the Northwest of Leicestershire and the second piece explored the support needs of HIV positive mothers with uninfected children. Throughout her career Raksha has worked to understand taboos and barriers which create un-equal access to health and social care. Having graduated at the University of Central England (Birmingham) with a BSc degree in Health Studies, she is currently completing her MA in Health and Community Development at De Montfort University.

Mandeep Rupra is an independent consultant, trainer, facilitator and researcher. She is the Principal Consultant of MRC, a practice that works with voluntary, community and statutory sector organisations. Mandeep's strong background in teaching has served as the catalyst for her committed work within the fields of race equality, anti-bullying and diversity. Her work with young people and practitioners has taken her into schools and youth settings across the UK and USA. She is also the author of The Race Equality Centre's award winning toolkit '*I Ain't Racist But . . . .*'

Alice Sawyerr is a full-time lecturer at Royal Holloway University of London, lecturing in psychology and mental health. She is also a clinician and an honorary consultant systemic psychotherapist at the Marlborough Family Service, CNWL Mental Health NHS Trust, in St John's Wood, London. She is a member of the British Psychological Society, The Association for Child Psychology and Psychiatry, a registered social care practitioner with GSCC and a UKCP registered family therapist. Her research and clinical interests include the development of positive identity, ethnicity, resilience, and good mental health in Black children and families throughout the lifespan.

Manuel Souto Otero is a DPhil. candidate at the Department of Social Policy and Social Work of the University of Oxford. His interests include social policy (in particular education and training policies) and industrial relations.

Dawn Summers has been a youth and community worker for more than 25 years and has worked for both the voluntary and statutory sector in providing services for young people. Direct experience of work with young people includes working with those affected by homelessness, substance abuse, HIV issues, poverty and deprivation, physical and sexual abuse, looked after young people and those whose lives have been limited by immigration policy and practice. The latter provided the impetus for her MA dissertation and the passion behind her writing and lecturing on the subject. More recently Dawn has been involved in the teaching and training of youth and community workers and runs her own training organisation. Academically, Dawn is currently involved in developing research concerning the role of young people in civil war, conflict and peace and reconciliation processes.

Diane Watt is a lecturer in youth and community work at Manchester Metropolitan University. For a number of years she co-ordinated the City College Manchester Mentor Service and was instrumental in the development of the School Mentor Project. She has also undertaken post-graduate research on the impact of Black role models in influencing the educational and professional aspiration of inner city school pupils.

Leona White-Simmonds has worked as a full time youth worker for the last 13 years. She is currently employed by Leicester City Council as a senior youth worker. Her role is to develop and facilitate a range of informal programmes with secondary schools across Leicester city. Throughout Leona's career she has actively been involved in both research and work with Black young people. Her particular interest is in the underachievement of Black young men within the British education system and how professionals can actively work towards combating this growing concern. Leona has an MA in Race and Ethnic Studies.

Adam Whitworth is a research officer at the Social Disadvantage Research Centre, Oxford University. He is particularly interested in issues relating to lone parents, poverty and social exclusion, area based interventions, and quantitative methodologies. He is also currently awaiting confirmation of his DPhil in Social Policy from Oxford University.

CHAPTER 1

Working with Black Young People: The Development of Black Consciousness in an Oppressive Climate

Carlton Howson

Introduction

We are at war, we are at war wit terrorism, we are at war wit racism, but most of all, we are at war wit ourselves.

Kanye West (2004)

This chapter arises out of a concern about the plight of Black young people. It is informed by my experiences of working with Black young people for a period that spans 25 years.

This chapter attempts to set the context for work with Black young people. It will conclude by asserting that historical factors will become manifest in current realities because of the changed 'climate' in which much of our work takes place and the inability of many graduates and practitioners to understand what is required to make a difference. One key or crucial aspect of working with Black young people is the necessity to have an understanding of the past, present and future; that is how the past informs the present and how the future will reflect aspects of the present. Moreover, successful work with Black young people must be grounded in the eradication of injustice and the exposure and dismantling of White supremacy ideology and practices designed to perpetuate it.

In writing this piece at this time I make three assertions: the plight of Black young people is not about to change in a positive sense; that the origins of some current challenges of work with Black young people can be found in a social policy determined to both control and marginalise Black communities whilst perpetuating a normalisation based on White supremacy (Gillborn, 2006) and many of those 'professionally' qualified workers lack the ability, skills, knowledge and understanding to make effective change or a difference for those Black young people with whom they work. Furthermore this lack of ability of workers is as a consequence of government policy (Sharif, 2001; Gillborn, 2006).

In this chapter I will argue that the inability (impotence) is as a consequence of a number of factors such as the limitations as a result of policy, the impact of history and the aspirations to do well and succeed in capitalism.

In order to make sense of the current conflicts and consider why working with Black young people presents a challenge today we need to review history. Peter Fryer (1984) provided an in-depth account charting the journey of the arrival of Black people in Britain. His accounts along with those of Paxman (1998) enable us to appreciate that the very idea of England as being a place for White people is derisible. England can best be described as a 'mongrel nation' (Izzard, 2003 Online) a place in which many forces have interacted to give rise to the current splendour or nightmare. Moreover it can be argued that the rich and diverse nature of Britain is linked to the search for refuge. Rattray (1928) noted that the impact of imperialism and colonialism left the souls of peoples, whom our civilisation has robbed of their heritages, to 'seek a lonely and unhonoured refuge'. Also Curruthers (1995) suggests that one has to be cautious when examining the European historiography. He infers that European historiography is comprised of the 'nomad' going from place to place and claiming aspects of that history as their own. Broomfield (1930: 516) went further and suggested that:

> ... *no race or nation may claim that its own attainments ... can exhaust the possibilities of human accomplishment ... each nation and race has its own special contribution to make.*

Thus the world that we know today has evolved over many centuries and Britain continues to be transformed by virtue of its interaction with other nations. Internally Britain's Black communities are growing faster than its White counterpart and there is an expectation that by the time of the next census, the Black population will form the majority in places, like Leicester, Bradford, Birmingham and some districts in the capital.

Historical influences

In recent years there has been much discussion about notions of multiculturalism, integration and diversity. These discussions often infer that there is a problem and that the problem is related to the inability of immigrants to conform to the British way of life and accept its norms and values. Stephen Small (1994: 2) noted that 'What is revealed by this ongoing discourse is that racial discrimination and inequality remain widespread in housing, employment, education and social services' (p.2). The discourse reveals a 'vague understanding of historical origins of such problems'. Moreover Small (1994) argues that a discourse based on the idea of newly arrived migrants or on forced repatriation 'blind us to the fact that there have been settlements in Britain for several hundred years'. Many of the people that have been referred to in recent discourses about terrorism (Sharif, 2001) were born and raised here, so the question of 'where are you from' is insulting and incorrect. It presupposes that if it can be determined where you are from it is possible to repatriate you.

In fact Fryer (1984) indicates that Black people have lived in England since Roman times. It is known that some were members of the army and held command positions. Although it is difficult to gain an accurate number Fryer (1984) reveals that by 1555 significant numbers of people from Africa and Asia were present and working in various jobs in England. By 1596 it is claimed that Queen Elizabeth 1 had issued a proclamation demanding the extradition of 'coloured' people because they were 'infidels' and because the country was facing economic pressures. (Fryer, 1984; Saggar, 1992; Ramdin, 1987, 1999). However the proclamation by Queen Elizabeth I in 1596 can be seen as evidence of state sanctioned racism.

Patterns of migration took a number of phases; this included those who were here prior to the colonial period as indicated above, and others who came during the colonial period either voluntarily or enforced as cargo or slaves. The periods during World Wars I and II led to another phase of migration: Britain encouraged people from its colonies to support them against the attack on the empire and her allies. People came from all parts of the empire to assist. In addition many people also arrived who were fleeing from persecution (from places such as Poland, Hungary, Italy and Germany). Following the wars some 'economic migrants' came initially with some encouragement to support the 'motherland' with a view of staying only a short time but they were unprepared for the treatment that they received; such was the level of poverty that many of those who initially came as 'economic migrants' or 'guest workers' became 'settlers' (Rex, and Tomlinson, 1979; Taylor, 1981). This phase developed over a number of years and coincided with the determination of many countries – said to be part of the empire – to seek their independence. This challenge to self-govern, created conflicts due to divide and rule strategies utilised by colonials. High levels of deprivation and the lack of an infrastructure to develop these countries led to underdevelopment and major internal conflicts in a number of these countries. Rodney (1972) spoke about aspects of underdevelopment with reference to the impact that Europe had on Africa; conflicts arose within some of these countries as different groups attempted to assert their authority or where political parties were established to represent the views of different factions. Some groups were simply acting in accordance with the previous administration and this would be perceived as insolent for those people who had fought for change. Sivanandan (1990) looked at Sri Lanka as a case study; he argued that by the time the British left Ceylon in 1948, the country had been divided for the 'purposes of political control'. He argued that the main reason behind the divisions was in order to rule and exploit. These conditions gave rise to the Tamil, a group that has consistently opposed the government and struggled for the right to self-determination in a hostile environment. This forced many people to flee persecution or war zones ('refugees and asylum seekers'). The ongoing conflict in places such as Afghanistan, Iraq and Palestine has meant that we have been in this current phase for about 30 years with far greater intensity during the last 20 years as a result of conflicts in Bosnia, Kosovo, Afghanistan, Iraq, Iran, Zimbabwe, Sri Lanka, Somalia, Sudan, and Eritrea to name a few. The increased demand for 'safe haven' is a direct result of the footprint or interventions by the 'civilised' world.

This movement (migration) was simply an extension of the relationships that had existed in one form or another and was established during periods of invasion and perfected during imperialism and colonialism. Brah (1985: 6) explored aspects of this relationship in India and concluded that:

> *Economic exploitation of a country cannot proceed for long without an ideology coming to the fore which serves to legitimate the system through which it operates.*

Following World War I and II Great Britain and indeed much of Europe needed to rebuild their cities and towns; cities that had been decimated by the conflict (Figueroa, 1985; National Archives, 2006 Online). These countries needed young people fit and able to assist in the rebuilding process. Once again Britain like its European counterparts turned to their colonies. People from the colonies were willing to contribute; they considered it their duty to assist the 'mother country' (Figueroa, 1985; Sharif, 2001; National Archives, 2006 Online). Walvin (1973: 212) noted:

When economic need demanded black labour, Britain was eager to house black workers; once the need had passed Britain was unwilling to contemplate the full consequences.

The 1950–1970s saw the process by which many of the lands previously occupied by invading forces were claiming their independence. The Lands occupied were widespread and included, India, Sri Lanka (Ceylon), many of the islands in the Caribbean, including: Grenada, Haiti, Martinique, Barbados and Jamaica. Countries in Central and South America included, Guyana, Venezuela, Belize, Panama, and Nicaragua. In Africa countries included: Nigeria, Sierra Leone, Tanganyika, Cameroon, Uganda, and Zimbabwe. Other areas colonised included Canada, Ireland, New Zealand, Australia, and Hong Kong. It can be seen from the above, that colonialism was a global enterprise. The coloniser was the epitome of European capitalist expansion and included countries such as Germany, Belgium, France, Britain, Italy, Portugal, Spain, Netherlands and USA. Some regarded this process as little more than symbolic in that the major control of these countries was retained by 'off shore governments' or other business interests (Sivanandan, 2004). Moreover, so depleted were many of these countries following the withdrawal of the colonialists that with the exception of a few, the major export was tourism (Sivanandan, 2004). These countries remained the 'entertainment' centres, the playground for the descendants of the invaders. Some of the Black politicians considered the quest for independence as a means toward Black self-determination (Clarke, 1991) but they were deluded. Many ('leaders') are now cast in the role of the 'emperor' – standing naked and exposed, whilst the descendants of the invaders scornfully look on, asking with disdain are they not ashamed. Others who gain some insight turn their scorn into guilt as they learn about the legacy of invasion.

What is most tragic are the lessons that our Black leaders come away with; far too many of our leaders aspired to be just like the White man (Fanon, 1986). Thus as the White man removed himself from the seat of government, he was replaced by a Black man who in most instances simply replicated the systems that he found in place (Louis Farrakhan, date unknown). Our leaders allowed power and greed to corrupt them and within a relatively short period of time the White man's shadow was cast wide and he could sit back and relax knowing he had created the means that would lead to our demise and destruction (Brah, 1985). His plan would have been successful were it not for the fact that Black people have withstood the most ferocious attacks, yet they have been resilient, they have a history of fighting and prevailing against the odds. Black people have been persecuted and attempts at their annihilation have been thwarted (Mothe, 1993). Their persecutors have sought to hide this but in the process of hiding the evidence, the persecutors have deluded themselves and have become somewhat intoxicated by their own sense of power. They believed in their deceit, and their own rhetoric. Their Generals and commanding officers convinced the masses (those bystanders, refusing to acknowledge that the emperor was indeed naked) that they would be 'surgical' and that they simply have to amass their armies, kill several thousand people of colour and declare 'mission accomplished'. This has now become symbolic as it was a statement made by President Bush (1st May 2003) signalling a successful campaign (Think Progress, 2006 Online). It haunts Bush, Blair and their co-conspirators in their on-going conflict in Iraq where the current debate aligns this crusade to other failures, such as Vietnam, Ethiopia and the Suez Canal.

There are those who refuse to acknowledge the atrocities, the massive destruction of life and the war crimes that have been committed. There are those who seek to absolve themselves of any responsibility by claiming that they were unaware. Moreover whilst there is widespread acknowledgement of the Jewish holocaust, there is an ongoing refusal to acknowledge that there ever was a Black holocaust. Benjamin Zephaniah (2004) used a poem called *War Crimes* to draw attention to the Black holocaust. He said that 'this holocaust involved the biggest transportation of people ever' and what is even more alarming is that we do not know the full extent of the actual figures. Why? Because they refuse to count how many Black lives have been destroyed. It is this history that has been kept hidden, it is this story that both Black and White communities need to be aware of. One of the consequences of not having your own story tellers is that others tell you the story that they wish you to know. In so doing they glorify themselves (Woodson, 1933; Addai-Sebo and Wong, 1988; Yosef ben-Jochannan and Clarke, 1991; Browder, 1992; Khamit-Kush, 1993; Richardson, 2005).

This too is a part of what it means to have a dysfunctional educational system; it is dysfunctional from the perspective of Black people because such a system does not only fail Black young people in relation to the actual qualification that they receive but it also fails them in relation to the utility of the knowledge that they acquire. It does not teach them about the world or their place in it. Rather it teaches them about the world and their place in it as subservient; it is located within White supremacist ideology. This system is also dysfunctional because not only does it fail Black young people, it also fails White young people because they come to accept their normality (Gregory, 1964; Gillborn, 2006). It is for this reason that Black perspectives are a crucial part of any provision that seeks to recognise and respond to the needs of Black young people. Black perspectives offer both Black and White young people a framework for the analysis of the distorted perspective.

Many of these countries were in the process of freeing themselves and the journey toward independence was now taking place in Africa, India and the Caribbean. The process proved to be destabilising and many people would lose their lives. As a consequence many people from the colonies now seeing themselves as 'at risk' began to exercise the limited rights that they had and which the British government was desperately seeking to remove to enter the UK (Sivanandan, 1982; Macdonald, 1983; Miles and Phizacklea, 1984).

The process of colonisation and imperialism had left many of these countries as 'dependent territories', they were dependent because of the impact of policies introduced into those countries by the Europeans (Rodney, 1972; Zephaniah, 2004). Philippa Gregory speaking about the British Empire and slavery in particular (in a film documentary exploring the reason why Benjamin Zephaniah refused to accept the OBE in 2004) said that it was one of the 'greatest crimes against humanity that has ever happened'. Ahmed Sekou Toure (1962) noted that:

> The relationship between the degree of destitution of peoples of Africa and the length and nature of the exploitation they had to endure is evident. Africa remains marked by the crimes of the slave-traders: up to now.

(in Rodney, 1972: 95)

Post war migration

It could be argued that the education process was very effective in that so many young people saw migration as *their duty*; it could also be argued that some of the people leaving their families at this time did so under an assumption that they would be leaving for a short period of time, just long enough to earn enough money to enable them to provide what was perceived as a better quality of life for their loved ones (Thomas-Hope, 1980).

Upon arrival many of the migrants experienced immediate rejection; they found themselves occupying the lowest strata possible. This was a shock as many of the young people were highly skilled and from backgrounds where the 'work ethic' was essential to their survival, there was no 'welfare' and even now I can remember comments that were expressed to me when I was a young child; one such being 'if you don't work you don't eat'. This was not a matter for debate, a discourse; it was the way it was/is. The early arrivals (migrants) soon found that their competition was with the rats as they sought places to live, work, shelter, eat and sleep. Many of these Black migrants were astonished. They felt deceived and perplexed because far from experiencing the welcome and riches or rewards that they had anticipated many of these people were now relegated in terms of the social standing that they were familiar with (Husband, 1982).

The presence of these newly arrived Black migrants invoked tension among the White indigenous community. However it soon became evident that all things were possible for some and the tension between Black and White young people was now manifesting itself openly on the streets (Sharif, 2001, Ramamurthy, 2006). Thus within a relatively short period of time the British government would issue a number of stringent immigration policies in 1962, 1965, 1968 and 1971 aimed at appeasing the White population whilst simultaneously consigning Black people to a status of second class citizens. The state was in actual fact legitimising racism (Sivanandan, 1976, 1978, 1982, 2006; Layton-Henry, 1992)

Ironically it could be argued that the state's attempt to keep Britain White contributed to what some regarded as an influx of Black people from countries that had been destabilised as an impact of the European footprint. The European footprint caused mass devastation in many countries and Britain boasted about the fact that 'the sun never set on its empire' thus was the extent of its footprint. Now the children of the empire were coming home, staking a claim to what they perceived as their heritage. Unfortunately Britain and its people were arrogant; the government dismissed the claims and attempted to absolve themselves of any responsibility (to the children of the empire) by reducing the rights of Black people within its former colonies to settlement in Britain.

The crisis begins: developing a Black consciousness

During the early 1980s Ellis Cashmore and Barry Troyna (1982) edited a book called *Black Youth in Crisis* in which they attempted to raise concerns about the situation that confronted Black young people. Prior to them a number of other (now well renowned) academics, authors, social commentators and activists were highlighting major concerns that confronted Black young people in Britain. The concerns that they raised ranged from the way in which the police were targeting Black young people, through to issues of mental health, education, housing, employment and immigration. These concerns gave rise to the immigration policies mentioned above, all designed to restrict or control the number of Black people entering the UK (Pryce, 1979; Hall, 1978; John, 1971, 1984; Sivanandan, 1976, 1978, 1982; Solomos, 1983; Gilroy, 1982; Lawrence 1982). Many of these writers were at the time focusing attention on 'Black youth', those Black young people who were disillusioned with British society (Ben-Tovim and Gabriel, 1982). They had experienced the disappointment of the dreams of their parents, dreams that remained unfulfilled (Tajfel, 1982). Some people talked about it as a dissonance brought about by differing expectations, values linked to what was perceived as a 'generation gap' (Tajfel, 1982). Others suggested that 'second generation' children were being assimilated into the British culture (way of life) and this was a cause of conflict with their parents and wider society (other people both Black and White and the systems that sought to socialise them) as it was deemed that these Black young people were losing respect and the values of their parents.

Our parents, our ancestors were far too busy creating the possibility for the realisation of the dream envisaged by Martin Luther King Jr. and many others. They took us to the brink, we were on the verge but instead of pushing forward we retreated, we lacked the courage, we were not ready to accept responsibility. Thus we took our examples from a system, a people that had raped us, brutalised us, killed us, desensitised and drugged us: now we are doing it all to ourselves, to each other. Many of us are intoxicated as we aspire, intoxicated and preoccupied in our aspiration to be like them as they wallow in their materialism, the means by which they value their self worth has now become our yard stick. It does seem ironic that nearly two hundred years later Willie Lynch (2006, Online) has achieved his objective because we have remained captive.

In his book *Nigger*, Gregory (1964) spoke of the notion of 'tomming' as a necessary strategy employed by some of our forebears but he also argued that there is an urgent necessity to move away from this. However some of our leaders were seduced and it can be argued that this is also one of the factors that precipitated the current crisis. Gregory (1964) related 'tomming' to the idea of being an 'Uncle Tom', where Black people tried their utmost to comply with the dictates of White people. They hoped that they would gain favour and preferential treatment by being loyal to the extent of circumventing efforts made by other Black people who were attempting to free themselves from the shackles of White supremacy.

The period from the late 1950s through to 2006 can be analysed in relation to the significance that this has had for Black young people. 1950s to the late 1960s ushered in the period of 'assimilation'. This can be described as the initial encounter; it was a period in which our parents initially responded to a call to support the redevelopment of the country. Britain was perceived as a prosperous place to go and earn some money, provide some assistance in the reconstruction of the 'motherland' and return home. There was *not* a great expectation that they would stay. Many of the migrants at this time saw themselves as economic migrants who were here as guest workers on a temporary basis. However it was the realisation that the 'promise' would remain unfulfilled and that many of those migrants were barely surviving and living in conditions well below their expectations. Confronted with this reality, the realisation of returning home and living the 'good life' can best be described as an aspiration or a myth (Anwar, 1979).

Within a relatively short period of time Britons were objecting to migrants coming into the country and taking 'their' jobs, it was not mentioned that Black people could not possibly take a job unless it was vacant and the jobs that were vacant tended to be the jobs that White indigenous people were refusing to take. Great Britain was a tolerant place where landlords and some employers felt able to display signs that said 'Blacks were not welcome' (Figueroa, 1985). Black people were used as scapegoats for the failure of the economy, and there were hostilities between Black and White people. I remember having a conversation with a man who was still actively involved in the struggle. He introduced himself to me by telling me that he started the first riots in Nottingham 1958, indicating that he was willing to do this again if the circumstances were necessary. I was also told about the spirit of family (especially the extended family), the camaraderie and alliances that existed between Black people arriving from different parts of the Caribbean.

This sense of family/community was also evident among the South Asian and African communities (Ramamurthy, 2006). Sivanandan (2004 Online) said:

> The unity that informed West Indian and Asian struggles during the '50s and '60s is, I think, the most significant legacy that has come down to us. It was a unity that sprang not so much from the assumed virtues of our politics as from our common experience of colonialism, our common experience of class (most of us were in working-class jobs) and most importantly of all, our common experience of an undifferentiating racism that debased and dehumanised West Indian and Asian and African alike.

In some respects it could be argued that this sense of 'family', this bonding was linked to security and the loss of the extended family. Akyigyina (2006: 23) recounted his memory of growing up in Britain:

> I lived amongst Black people for years, I spent a lot of time with Black people whilst I gradually got to know other people this focus was important, as just being with other Black people was making up for the loss of my extended family which had been the focus of my life . . . I might not have had anything in common with them, I still felt a sense of belonging as they were Black.

The feeling of loss and a sense of belonging that was found among Black people or indeed other 'displaced' people facilitated some groups in setting aside differences. This enabled some cooperation between different groups. The idea of unity among Black communities took some time to be established, but a movement had begun that was to establish 'Black' as more than a description or the colour of a person's skin. 'Black' was being transformed as an idea, a movement, a concept that denoted our identity, our resilience, our struggle, our politics and our place in it:

> That unity was inspired by the revolutionary struggles . . . the connections -between Third World struggles and anti-racist struggles, between Africans, West Indians and Asians, between the class and the community? . . . are unique to the history of black people in Britain – and it is a history we must recall if we are to contest the racist imperialism of the global era.
>
> (Sivanandan, 2006, online)

Initially it was a concept in which we took some pride. At this time we were all said to be the same, we were all Pakis, wogs, coons, blackies, niggers, darkies in fact we were everything that White people were not (that is everything negative).

More than one hundred years earlier Fredrick Douglas said that equality is only achieved through struggle. Now people on every continent would struggle for the realisation of the dreams that people such as Martin Luther King Jr, Malcolm X, Ghandi, Sojourner Truth, Nyerere, Gregory and many, many others before and after were imploring us to take control of our destiny. This was echoed by Stokely Carmichael in a manner that sent a chill through White America. The close relationship that Britain shared gave them cause for concern in that, after the establishment of the Black Panthers and the continued brutalisation of Black communities, Carmichael called for 'Black power'. This resonated with Black young people, they identified with this idea as they were just fed up and could not see the dream envisaged by King unless they took a far more proactive stance, in so doing they embraced the words of Ghandi when he said 'be the change you wish to see in the world', and brother Malcolm when he said 'by any means necessary'.

The multi-culturalism period, 1970–1980

By the 70s Black young people were now significant in some major cities, yet there was no social provision made. When one examines this, it is clear to see that from the perspective of policy makers that Black people were not expected to be a permanent feature of British life, so there was no point in extending the public purse. This was a further example of institutional racism, because the state was not prepared to take steps that sought to improve the situation for the Black community. The decision not to support the Black community at this time may have been based on a rationalisation that asserted that if there was a 'problem' it would be reduced and even disappear the more Black people (now euphemistically referred to as those from the New Commonwealth and Pakistan) assimilated into the culture of British society; there was even a suggestion that these Black people could or should be repatriated. In the view of the government and policy makers, the issue had to do with Black people and their inability to cope with the English language and the norms and values of British society. Provision was made under Section 11 of the Local Government Act 1966 for teaching English, the provision of interpreters and the possibility of recruiting staff to work specifically with Black communities. It was regarded as a solution to a temporary concern; there was no attempt made to acknowledge or respond to the endemic racism and how the discrimination that exudes from this, poisoned all those that it touched.

Thus Black young people would spend their days 'hanging' around on the streets, doing the kind of things that most young people did. Those that had jobs would work, those that were at school age would attend unless they were excluded. The Black community had began to organise itself in terms of support groups; for entertainment they would have house parties or hire a club. In some respects the lack of adequate provision served as a catalyst for the community in that many of the 'first generation' migrants had formed their own confederations to support each other in relation to their welfare, security and finding accommodation. They would now extend this initiative to all aspects of their lives as entrepreneurs, social, youth and community and welfare workers.

By the end of the 1970s there were significant numbers of Black young people who had been educated in this country; there were no 'language' issues that could be levelled against them. With the exception of some South Asian young people who had arrived in the UK in the early 1970s following policies introduced in Uganda by President Amin. These young people were now beginning to demand that which their parents did not feel able to demand. These young people did not see themselves as guest workers, many of them were born here and yet they were denied access to the same opportunities as their White counterparts. Many realised that colour was significant in determining the opportunities available. I was often told that in this country 'it was not enough to be as good as the White man; you had to be better than him in every thing that you do'. This proved to be another significant awakening, for there were those Black young people who perceived themselves as wanting to be like White people, even envious about what they enjoyed on account of their colour and the more the Black person became conscious of what was denied the more attractive and desirable they became (Hacker, 1995, Sharif 2001).

These were confusing times for the people living through them and for social commentators, some Black people were being encouraged to hate themselves, and to love all things White. However a process was taking place where some Black people were being encouraged to love themselves, there was a celebration of Blackness, emanating from across the USA, Alex Haley's Roots was on the television, several films depicted Black people as heroes. Shaft, and artists such as James Brown, Sam Cooke, Mohammed Ali, Millie, Marvin Gaye, and Curtis Mayfield were all making headlines in their opposition to the White status quo. Their stance was now inspiring others, some experienced dissonance as they attempted to reconcile their desire for the opportunities that they observed as being available to their White counterparts, whilst simultaneously seeking to embrace an evolving consciousness about their identity. Wherever you looked the relationship between Black and White people both at home and abroad was becoming perturbed and ambiguous.

The desire to be fully integrated and have opportunities that were apparently available to White people yet denied to Black people tormented them, this in turn fermented and increased the progression toward a different ideology; an ideology based on a consciousness of difference, a consciousness that brought together both beauty and the beast. It can be argued that Black consciousness was forming or had already existed, but that it took on a particular significance as a reaction to the treatment that Black people were receiving on the basis of their colour (Hacker, 1995) . Thus some Black people embraced their beauty and sought to find other positive aspects of their identity to celebrate. Many Black people might have felt uneasy as they sought to reconcile the apparent contradiction, however, in reality there was no contradiction, there was in fact a 'duality'.

It could be argued that this period gave rise to the 'rude boy/girl' image or the 'ragamuffin'. This was manifest by the 'style and fashion' now on the streets, the emergence of the Rasta, Cooley, 'afro hair' and 'dread locks'. This 'rude boy/girl' image became the perception on which the state and the racist media chose to focus, thus policies were designed for the interest of the policy makers and the constituencies they represented. These policy makers took one aspect of a minority of Black young people and devised a programme to destroy them. The programme may have been based on a perception or a construction of deviant and out of control Black young people. The main difficulty here is that this conception was often based on an isolated act. This type of reaction suggests an irrational fear of Black people. The behaviour is perceived as representative of the totality of Black young people; Black young people were now homonogised, and classified as bad and policies invoked which would seek to address this problem.

White young people were going through their own metamorphism in terms of drugs, knives, gangs, pubs and so on. Black young people had simply developed their own brand; it is debateable whether this 'rude boy/girl' image was a reaction to the exclusion experienced at this time. However it is well known that music, 'Black style and fashion' was a brand pirated by a number of White artists including Elvis Presley. The 'rude boy/girl' was symbolic; where some Black young people were acting in accordance with the negative labels that were attached or associated with them. Yet the reaction of the state demonstrated a misunderstanding by both those who make policies and others who work with Black young people. For as indicated above the social policies that emerged were at best an attempt to control Black young people through 'welfare' inducements and at worst a cynical attempt to destroy Black young people. During this period the British press concerned itself in representing Black young people as pimps, prostitutes, thieves, drug dealers and muggers; they demanded that their streets be returned to them. This gave the police the licence to invoke 'Sus' policies whereby they (the police) simply needed to think that you were about to commit a crime to arrest you. I was growing up at this time and can vividly remember being arrested three to four times a week. I remember on one occasion being accused of stealing my own car, when I refused to leave the car. The police called for 'back up' and within minutes I was surrounded by three patrol cars and a 'paddy wagon', I spent the night in a police cell because I did not have my papers with me. Throughout this time I insisted that if they would look at their own reports they would know who I was since I was constantly given 'producers' (a ticket that required you to produce your driving documents within five days).

What was perceived as state sanctioned harassment and an attack on Black young people culminated in a ferocious backlash vented against the police who were regarded as a tool utilised by the state. Many of the major cities were brought to a standstill as the fires burned in places like Brixton, St. Paul's, Lozells/Handsworth, Toxeth, Moss side and Leicester. The government attempted to dismiss the street disturbances of the early 80s as a criminal act (Benyon, 1984) but many people saw this as a turning point in the management of 'race' relations (Fryer, 1984; Saggar, 1992; Sivanandan, 1985; 2006). Until now Black young people had accepted their position: some even accepted the labels about their condition as being inferior, educationally subnormal, schizophrenic etc. but the riots invoked a sense of pride even among law abiding citizens which the vast majority of Black people are. They tended to be conservative; but now they were becoming politicised. Black young people in the UK were becoming aware of the significance of struggle, they had witnessed how the American state had kept Black people on the margins, and moreover they could see the graphic hostility vented against Black young people in South Africa under the apartheid system. As a young person I recall seeing children on the streets being beaten and killed but many others were fighting back against an armed force that they had little hope of defeating. Yet they continued to fight the repression sanctioned by the state. Their struggle became our struggle and we were encouraged to fight and use 'what ever means necessary' to reclaim our dignity, our right to determine who we are as a people and work towards a more humane society.

The 1980s–1990s, anti-racist

The impact of the street disturbances of the early 1980s sped up the introduction of facilities for Black young people. Politicians were aware of many of the issues because activists were in negotiations or had been raising concerns with local and central government for several years. Furthermore, the government argued that it had started to respond to many of the issues raised through initiatives such as urban aid programmes. However the term 'inner city' was a euphemism for Black people; the inner cities were regarded as the sprawling ghettoes where Black people lived (Harrison, 1985). Some indigenous White people accused Black people of turning their wonderful quaint cities into ghettoes. They failed to appreciate the fact that Black people moved into particular districts or areas because they were neglected, abandoned by White residents and condemned by local housing authorities, as unfit for human habitation as they were lacking in basic amenities. These areas were a living hell, a place 'where all our social ills come together, the place where all our sins are paid for' (Harrison, 1985: 21). Paul Harrison noted that:

> . . . the inner city is the social antipodes of middle-class Britain, a universe apart, an alien world devoid of almost every feature of an ideal environment.
>
> (Harrison, 1985: 21)

He argued that many intractable social problems existed: within the inner cities you would be confronted with a:

> . . . concentration of the worse housing, the highest unemployment, the greatest density of poor people, the highest crime rates and the most serious threat posed to law and order.
>
> (Harrison, 1985: 21)

Thus Black communities were at this time campaigning for support and resources to assist them in changing the crippling and corrosive impact of poverty and neglect as a feature of the inner cities. In addition to the above Black young people had to live with the nightmare caused by racism and discrimination. The campaigns by Black young people were frowned upon and there were often battles fought between Black young people and groups such as the National Front, who argued that Black people were responsible for their own condition and that 'they should go back to their country'. Many of these racists were unaware of the legacy of their grandparents.

The apparent allocation of resources at this time was little more than a cynical attempt to derail the momentum of the struggle. The summer of 1981 witnessed the birth of many voluntary groups; most of these were given resources to respond to the needs of their communities. This strategy of giving funds to groups with little or no experience of managing budgets, little understanding of the 'terms and conditions', left a legacy that now bewitches the Black community and some funding agencies. In that as a result of the lack of accountability, knowledge and skills, some funds were said to be 'mismanaged' or 'misappropriated'. It could be argued that the government at this time saw an opportunity to split and divide the Black community by giving funds to particular individuals, groups and communities. Some of those who received funding were expected to 'control' the activities of their community and the continuation of funding was linked to their capacity to maintain control over their communities.

However the struggle against oppression became a struggle for buildings and accommodation within a system determined to both marginalise and eliminate them. The government achieved this by publicly giving funds to some groups, (creating animosity, and envy) whilst privately cutting the funding from others including in some instances those groups that they (the government) had publicly declared their commitment to fund (Sivanadan, 1985; Hall, 1989). Thus under the gaze of the media and other groups the government would announce that it was allocating a certain amount of money to a particular community or group'. However these groups often did not receive these funds. Most lost funding altogether or they were forced to operate on reduced budgets making it difficult to address some of the issues that they were set up to address. Within this context it could be argued that solving the intractable problems of life in the inner city amplified by racism was a mission impossible (Sharif, 2001; Webb, 2001). In other words the vast majority of these groups were set up to fail and the failure of these groups provided the state with its justification for the withdrawal of resources. Moreover, because the state was 'invisible' to those communities (the benefactors) it meant that community activist and community management groups would be held responsible for the failure to tackle the many problems that adversely impacted on these communities.

A further aspect of this control and 'divide and rule' strategy was creating a competitive bidding process in which groups had to compete for resources, but often those judging or making decisions about which projects were deserving of support were not from the communities of interest and perhaps they had very little understanding of the issues. Moreover, fundraising is a skill that is considerably different from that of the 'delivery of a service' to a community that has to a large extent been disenfranchised:

> . . . *ethnic politicking began to replace anti-racist politics – and the term black, which had defined the politics of anti-racism, went out with it.*

> (Sivanandan, 2004, online)

In particular some groups realised that two factors were important in making a successful grant application. Your aims had to be those approved by your sponsor or you had to be a threat to stability; therefore some groups would set out to be the ugliest, the most decrepit, the most disadvantage, the most hideous or they would adopt an informant or surveillance role. The very thought of the 'delivery of a service' denotes 'them' and 'us' in that there is now a power relationship in place; a situation in which we now have 'clients', 'service users' or 'consumers'. This raises the question in what sense can this be seen as community development or indeed the empowerment or the transformation of a situation in which the benefactor becomes central in changing the conditions of their lives with assistance and guidance.

It is somewhat ironic to think about the idea of assimilation and values given many of the current/recent discourse about integration and values (Younge, 2006 online) Moreover, one might go as far as to suggest that many of the current conflicts with Black young people arise from an adoption of a 'British way of life' and the adoption of 'western (British) values' (Sivanandan, 2006).

The state's current obsession with values, morals and integration needs to be analysed in context; for if one explores this obsession, it can be seen that the state has once again moved against one of the most vulnerable groups in society; vulnerable in the sense that pathologising and demonising a group of people allows others to 'legitimately' target them, (Younge, 2006 online). The state using instruments such as the mass media, social services, police, education and the Crown Prosecution Service has pathologised and demonised Black young people. Ben-Tovim and Gabriel (1982: 146) agreed with other commentators of the time when they concluded that:

> *The dominant consensus on immigration has had catastrophic effects on the black communities in Britain, subjecting them to insecurity and harassment from state agencies.*

Moreover recent policies that have emerged from the government include the Race Relations (Amendment) Act 2000. The passing of this followed the successful campaign by the Lawrence family following the murder of their son Stephen. The Stephen Lawrence Inquiry was set up in 1997 and reported in 1999, (Home Office, 2006 Online). The report made shocking reading and claimed that many of the mistakes made during the investigation can be linked to what Macpherson called institutional racism, a term previously used by Stokely Carmichael (now known as Kwame Ture) back in 1967. The Every Child Matters Green paper was launched in 2003 following the formal response to the report into the death of Victoria Climbie, a young Black girl who was 'horrifically abused' even though she was known to local social services. This paved the way for the Children's Act 2004 (DfES, 2006 Online). Community Cohesion followed the disturbances in the north of England in 2001; Cantle chaired a committee that produced a report indicating that much more needed to be done in attempts at greater community cohesion (Home Office, 2001). The events of 11th September 2001 might have diverted attention but these were reignited recently with the London bombings on 7th July 2005 and the alleged further attempts shortly after. In this light, the rising tide of Islamophobia and the government's attempts to manage the crisis of 'race relations' they have set up a new Directorate entitled Race, Cohesion and Faith, formally launched on the 5th May 2006. What these policies reveal is the extent to which the government is seeking to pacify both Black and White communities whilst surreptitiously trying to find a way to persuade Black communities to accept an iniquitous situation. Within a period of five decades 'race relations' in Britain has gone from the assimilation policies present in the post war period of the nineteen fifties and sixties to the assimilation policies of today and in this current phase of managing 'race and diversity' there is no space for multiculturalism and ethnicity. There is 'no such thing as Black British or Asian British anymore, only British British. And to be British was to adhere to core British values' (Sivanandan, 2004 Online).

These efforts by the government have done very little to stem the tide of racism, racial violence, harassment, murder and social exclusion. Sivanandan (2006) argues that some of these policies negated the struggle or gave it 'the kiss of death' as the state sought to incorporate Black struggle into mainstream policy. This also had an impact of 'domesticating' some of our community 'leaders' as they settled for crumbs. Further I would argue that with respect to social policy and social welfare, all of the services geared toward 'well being' have failed. Thus Black young people have begun to look at other means to self advancement. The strategies employed vary in relation to ethnicity.

In India the British justified their presence on the grounds that it brought 'law and order', they were bringing 'civilisation' to what they perceived to be an 'uncivilised', backward and 'barbaric' people (Brah, 1985). One sadness that I have discovered is how little we actually know or indeed care about history; we lack a local perspective and seem to be totally unaware of the significance of issues as they impact on us and our neighbours. We have settled for the 'Macdonaldisation' of life whereby we want it now, and don't want to have to think about it. It would appear that life today is just like the 'fast food' outlets, the 'franchise' that promotes, the idea of immediate gratification, in which there is very little demand for critical thinking. Thus we fail to critique news; we rarely stop to analyse and think about the perspectives that are presented and their implications. Have we become so preoccupied that lives have truly become worthless? Perhaps it was this realisation that prompted Ghandi to reply that 'it would be a good thing' when asked about what he thought about British civilisation. Furthermore, an appreciation of our histories would enable us to see that some of the reasons given for the invasion of Iraq and Afghanistan are spurious and not dissimilar to those offered throughout the period of invasion of other countries in pursuance of 'democracy', when in actual fact they were motivated by greed (Parrish, 2006 Online).

Those who see past this and who become critical of the government's policy are regarded as 'radicals' to be culled or absorbed into a system that weakens their resolve to struggle (Sivanadan, 1985). What this country; and those who work with Black young people, need to appreciate is that the policies of this country have demonised its own young people; therefore, we can expect that it will be merciless and ruthless in its attempts to consolidate its programme and reassert itself as the force that all others must fear. If the state is willing to invoke such fear and calamity among its own people, we must expect that it would also unleash unimaginable horrors on those who are regarded as 'other' (Black young people) and in so doing re-establish its global domination:

> National security is also the ploy that the government has used to engender a politics of fear that would cower the nation into conformity and subservience – not just through state-sponsored lies and rumours . . . but through statutory enactments like the Anti-terrorism Crime and Security Act of 2001.
>
> (Sivanandan, 2004)

The question of relevance

In addition to the lack of understanding of how the social, economic, political, cultural, environmental and historical factors impact on Black young people we need to give some consideration to those who actually undertake the work. In so doing it is worth asking the question of how you assess your relevance to the group with whom you work; who do you work for and what is their sphere of influence on your work? What is your understanding of the needs of the groups with whom you work and how was this understanding acquired?

Identifying the accomplices education

One of the assertions that I proposed at the start of this chapter is that there are far too many professionally qualified people who lack the most basic of skills, knowledge and experience for working with people within a rapidly changing health and welfare agenda in which the ideology has shifted from care to control. With respect to 'race' relations the emphasis has remained consistently focused on control (Sharif, 2001). There is not the scope within this chapter to explore the intricacies of this discourse, though I recognise that it is a crucial debate as it directly relates to both policy and practice. However suffice to say that the significant point that I wish to note here is the emphasis on control using a range of punitive penal, welfare, and economic measures. Most fundamentally the government has shifted in two important ways:

- It has resorted to a market liberalist approach to welfare, in which the market determines the level of care available based essentially on ones ability to pay.
- With respect to Black young people in the post 9/11, and 7/7 era it has sought to invoke draconian measures to control: in so doing it has reduced all our civil liberties.

However, the impact is most profoundly experienced by Black young people especially Muslim young people. With respect to the impact on Black communities Sivanandan (2004 online) concludes that the state is acting on 'two trajectories' namely 'the war on asylum and the war on terror'. He goes on to say that these have:

> . . . *converged to produce a racism which cannot tell a settler from an immigrant, an immigrant from an asylum seeker, an asylum seeker from a Muslim, a Muslim from a terrorist.*

If today's racism 'is embedded and shaped by globalisation', where globalisation needs 'to rationalise and justify the treatment of refugees and asylum seekers' and to 'rationalise and justify the imperial project needed to remove unfriendly regimes that stand in the way of its expansion and penetration' (Sivanandan, 2004). Then it will be necessary for those who work with Black communities to be conversant with these issues and be able to facilitate young Black people in reigniting the spirit of insurgency that challenges the perpetuation of White supremacy.

The lack of skills, knowledge and experience render these professionals impotent. Some of these practitioners are victims not only of what Thompson (2001) refers to as levels or encounters with discrimination. Thompson asserts that discrimination is present at the personal, cultural, social (PCS) level and that all of these interact with each other to compound the discrimination experienced by particular social groups. He proposes a model that can be used in analysing discrimination in relation to gender, 'race', disability, class and sexuality. They are also victims of inadequate preparation; they have not been endowed with an education that enables them to work effectively or constructively with Black young people in a manner that is transformative, rather their preparation is for the perpetuation of White supremacy (Gillborn, 2006) as such questions must be raised about their relevance with respect to liberating people and connecting them to the struggle.

If we engage our effort not only with the poor in our attempts to treat their chronic illness, if we focus some attention on the causes of this illness and if we worked to alter the very foundation on which inequality is based I am apt to believe that then we are worthy of the title teacher or educator. For it is my contention that an educator is someone who works for change, someone who seeks to discover and explain, someone who works not for the purpose of their own glory or ego but people who through their words and actions stimulate others with a desire to be part of the change. I would argue that many practitioners today have been neutralised by the state and by their own ambitions. They are accommodated within capitalism: rather than practitioners who learn negativity, such practitioners are assimilated into the capitalist system and they have no real desire to uncoil themselves. It has been argued that to make a slave servile and contented, it is necessary to make them thoughtless and to 'darken the moral and mental vision and, as far as possible, to annihilate the power of reason' (Douglas, 1986 Online; Woodson, 1933).

Conclusion

One of the main problems facing both Black and White people in Britain is that they do not know their own history, and how Black people have contributed to the development of the country. This lack of knowledge often leads to mistaken assumptions and misguided conclusions. Both groups need to be more informed about the realities of racial and cultural diversity in British history: changes in the teaching of history can go some way to achieving this. It is important to appreciate that many of the current or recent problems which Black people face cannot be reduced to an argument that they just needs to adjust to the British way of life. Racism and discrimination is enduring, there needs to be a vigorous attempt at identifying and eradicating it, replacing it with justice and decency.

> *Racism, then, is not a given. It never stays still. It changes its shape, size, contours, purpose, function with changes in the economy, in the social structure, the political culture, the system – and above all it challenges, the resistance to that system. Today's racism is embedded and shaped by globalisation.*
>
> (Sivanandan, 2004, online)

In this chapter I have not sought to be objective for as Fanon (1986: 86) notes it would be 'dishonest for it is not possible to be objective'. I see the struggle or the problem of power and the relationships between Black and White people as my problem. Therefore I have sought to connect both Black and White people by illustrating the consequence of working from an ideology of White supremacy that does not give sufficient regard to the needs and aspirations of Black young people in their quest for self determination, or if not self determination then at least a transformed situation in which a person's value is not determined by the colour of their skin or their 'ethnicity':

> *To look at imperialism without relating it to globalisation and racism is not just to accept the notion that regime change and pre-emptive strikes . . . It is also to accept the . . . bringing civilisation and enlightenment to the lesser breeds, freeing them from tyranny, forcing them to be free if necessary, bombing them into freedom and democracy. Except that the underlying theme this time is not that of a superior race but of a superior civilisation. Hence the real war . . . is not between civilisations . . . but against the enforced hegemony of western civilisation.*
>
> (Sivanandan, 2004, online)

In 2001 Lord Herman Ouseley chaired the Bradford Report. After noting the many challenges that confronted practitioners, he went on to say that one of the most inspiring things that he observed:

> *. . . was the great desire among younger people for better education, more social and cultural interaction and commitment to contribute and achieve personal success. Some young people have pleaded desperately for this to overcome the negativity that they feel is blighting their lives.*

Working with Black young people requires more than a cognisance of power, inequality, capitalism and globalisation; it demands that we connect with struggle. Working with Black young people demands that we work with the desires of young people, but we locate our work within the everyday struggles so that our work is responsive and takes account of the context of White supremacy and its attempts to neutralise the efforts that Black people are making in redefining the terms on which they are recognised. An understanding of the past enables us to draw inspiration from the efforts of those who have gone before as we commit ourselves to transformation.

References

Addai-Sebo, A. and Wong, A. (Eds.) (1988) *Our Story: A Handbook of African History and Contemporary Issues,* London Strategic Policy Unit/London Borough of Haringay.

Akyigyina, E. (2006) *The Housing Needs of Refugees in Leicester.* Unpublished M.A. Thesis, Submitted to De Montfort University.

Anwar, M. (1979) *The Myth of Return: Pakistanis in Britain.* London: Heinemann Educational.

Ashrif, A. (2001) Charting The Development of Multi-Ethnic Britain. *Multicultural Teaching,* May 2001.

Ben-Jochannan, Y. and Clarke, J.H. (Eds.) (1991) *New Dimensions in African History.* New Jersey: African World Press.

Ben-Tovim, G. and Gabriel, J. (1982) The Politics of Race in Britain, 1962–79: A Review of Major Trends and Recent Debates. In Husband, C. (Ed.) *Race in Britain: Continuity and Change,* London: Hutchinson.

Benyon, J. (Ed.) (1984) *Scarman and After: Essays Reflecting on Lord Scarman's Report, The Riots and Their Aftermath.* London: Pargamon.

Brah, A. (1985) *Cultural Encounter During The Raj: Minority Experience in Ethnic Minorities and Community Relations.* Milton Keynes: Open University Press.

Broomfield, G.W. (1930) The Development of Swahili Language. *Africa,* 3: 4.

Browder, A.T. (1992) *Nile Valley Contributions to Civilization: Exploding The Myths Vol.1,* Washington: The Institute of Karmic Guidance.

Carmichael, S. and Hamilton, C. (1967) *Black Power: The Politics of Liberation in America.* New York: Vintage Books.

Cashmore, E. and Troyna, B. (Eds.) (1982) *Black Youth in Crisis.* London: Allen and Unwin.

Clarke, J.H. (1991) *African World Revolution: African at The Crossroads.* Trenton NJ: African Worlds Press.

DfES (2006) *Every Child Matters* [cited 24th October 2006]. http://www.everychildmatters.gov.uk/aims/background/.

Douglas, F. (1986) Introduction to The 1986 Penguin Edition of *Narrative of The Life of Frederick Douglas* [cited 24th October 06]. http://en.wikipedia.org/wiki/fredrick_douglas̓famous_quotes

Fanon, F. (1986) *Black Skin, White Masks.* London: Pluto Press.

Farrakhan, L. (Date Unknown) Audio Tape of a Talk Given on His Visit to Jamaica.

Figueroa, P. (1985) *Post-War Immigration: Minority Experience in Ethnic Minorities and Community Relations.* Milton Keynes: Open University Press.

Ghandi, M. (2006) [cited 24th October 06]. http://en.wikipedia.org/wiki/ghandi,

Gillborn, D. (2006) Rethinking White Supremacy: Who Counts in 'White World. *Sage Abstracts,* 6: 3, 318–40.

Gilroy, P. (1982) Police and Thieves. In Centre for Contemporary Cultural Studies, *The Empire Strikes Back.* London: Hutchinson.

Gregory, D. (1964) *Nigger: An Autobiography.* With Robert Lipsyte, New York: Pocket Books.

Hacker, A. (1995) *Two Nations: Black and White, Separate, Hostile, Unequal.* New York: Ballantine Books.

Hall, S. (1989) *The Voluntary Sector Under Attack?* Address given at the AGM of Islington Voluntary Action Council, 3rd Nov. 1988. London: Islington Voluntary Action Council.

Harrison, P. (1985) *Inside The Inner City.* London: Penguin.

Home Office (2001) *Community Cohesion a Report of the Independent Review Team Chaired by Ted Cantle.*

Home Office (2006) *Race Relations (Amendment) Act 2000, New Laws for Successful Multi-Racial Britain* [cited 2nd October 2006]. http://www.homeoffice.gov.uk/documents/cons-2001-race-relations/?version = 1

Home Office (2006) *Race, Cohesion and Faith*, [cited 15th October 2006]. http://www.communities.gov.uk/index.asp?id=1500185

Houston, A. and Baker, Jr. Introduction to The 1986 Penguin Edition of *Narrative of The Life of Frederick Douglas* [cited 24th October 06]. http://en.wikipedia.org/wiki/fredrick_douglas#famous_quotes

Husband, C. (Ed) (1982) *'Race' in Britain Continuity and Change*, London: Hutchinson.

Izzard, E. *Mongrel Nation*. Discovery Channel, [cited 16th June 2003]. http://discoverychannel.co.uk/mongrelnation/feature/feature5.shtml

John, G. (1971) *Because They're Black*. Harmondsworth: Penguin.

John, G. and Parkes, N. (1984) *Working With Black Youth: Complementary or Competing Perspectives?* Leicester: National Youth Bureau.

Khamit-Kush, I. (1993) *The Missing Pages of 'His-Story': Highlights in Black Achievement*. New York: D and J Books.

Lawrence, E. (1982) Just Plain Commonsense: The Roots of Racism. In Centre for Contemporary Cultural Studies, *The Empire Strikes Back*. London: Hutchinson.

Layton-Henry, Z. (1992) *The Politics of Immigration: Immigration, 'Race' and 'Race' Relations in Post War Britain'*. Oxford: Blackwell.

Lynch, W. (2006) [cited 24th October 06]. http://www.msu.edu/leonr/willielynch.htm

Macdonald, I. (1983) *Immigration Law and Practice in The United Kingdom*. London: Butterworths.

Malcolm X. (2006) [cited 24th October 06]. http://en.wikipedia.org/wiki/malcolm_x,

Miles, R. and Phizacklea, A. (1984) *Racism and Political Action in Britain*. London: Routledge.

Mothe, G. De La. (1993) *Reconstructing The Black Image*. Stoke-on-Trent: Trentham Books.

Mullard, C. (1985) *Race, Power and Resistance*. London: Routledge and Kegan Paul.

National Archives (2006) *Post War Migration*, [cited 10th October 2006]. http://www.nationalarchives.gov.uk/pathways/citizenship/brave_new_world/immigration.htm

Ouseley, H. (2001) *Pride Not Prejudice. The Bradford Report* London: HMSO.

Parrish, G. (2006) *Chomsky: 'There is No War on Terror'*, Alternet, Posted 14/01/2006, [cited 29th October 2006]. http://www.alternet.org/story/30487?comments=viewandcid=74932andpid=74912c74932

Paxman, J. (1998) *The English A Portrait of A People*, England: Penguin.

Peter, F. (1984) *Staying Power: The History of Black People in Britain*. Pluto.

Pryce, K. (1979) *Endless Pressure: A Study of West Indian Life-Styles in Bristol*. Harmondsworth: Penguin.

Ramamurthy, A. (2006) The Politics of Britain's Asian Youth Movements. *Race and Class,* 48: 38–60.

Ramdin, R (1999) *Reimaging Britain: 500 Years of Black and Asian History*. London: Pluto Press.

Ramdin, R. (1987) *The Making of The Black Working Class in Britain*. Hampshire: Wildwood House.

Rattray, R.S. (1928) Anthropology and Christian Missions. *Africa*, 1:1.

Rex, J. and Tomlinson, S. (1979) *Colonial Immigrants in a British City: Class Analysis*. London: Routledge and Kegan Paul.

Richardson, B. (Ed.) (2005) *Tell It Like it is: How Our Schools Fail Black Children*. London: Trentham Books.

Rodney, W. (1972) *How Europe Underdeveloped Africa*. Zimbabwe: Zimbabwe Publishing House.

Saggar, S. (1992) *Race and Politics in Britain*. London: Wheatsheaf.

Sivanandan, A (1990) *Communities of Resistance: Writings on Black Struggles For Socialism*. London: Verso.

Sivanandan, A. (1976) Race, Class and The State: The Black Experience in Britain. *Race and Class,* 27: 4, Spring.

Sivanandan, A. (1978) From Immigration Control to 'Induced Repatriation'. *Race and Class,* 2: 1, Summer.

Sivanandan, A. (1982) *A Different Hunger: Writings on Black Resistance*. London: Pluto.

Sivanandan, A. (2004) *Racism in The Age of Globalisation*. Speaking at The Third Claudia Jones Memorial Lecture on 28 October 2004 Organised by The National Union of Journalist's Black Members Council [cited 29th October 2004]. http://www.irr.org.uk/2004/october/ha000024.html

Sivanandan, A. (2006) Attacks on Multicultural Britain Pave The Way for Enforced Assimilation. *Guardian*, Sep. 13. [cited 12th October 2006]. http://www.guardian.co.uk/comment/story/0,,1870907,00.html

Sivanandan, A. RAT and the Degradation of Black Struggle. *Race and Class*, XXVI: 4.

Small, S. (1994) *Black People in Britain. Sociology Review*, Apr.

Solomos, J. (1983) *The Politics of Black Youth Unemployment: A Critical Analysis of Official Ideologies and Policies*. Birmingham: Research Unit on Ethnic Relations, Social Science Research Council.

Stuart, H. et al. (1978) *Policing The Crisis: Mugging, The State, and Law and Order*. London: Macmillan.

Tajfel, H. (1982) The Social Psychology of Minorities. In Husband, C. (Ed.) *'Race' in Britain: Continuity and Change*. London: Hutchinson.

Taylor, M.J. (1981) *Caught Between: A Review of Research Into Education of Pupils of West Indian Origin*. Windsor: NFER.

Think Progress (2006) *Mission Accomplished* [cited 24th October 06]. http://thinkprogress.org/2006/05/01/mission-accomplished-by-the-numbers/

Thomas-Hope, E. (1980) Hopes and Reality in The West Indian Migration to Britain. *Oral History*, 8: 1, 35–42.

Thompson, N. (2001) *Anti-Discriminatory Practice*. Basingstoke: Palgrave.

Walvin, J. (1973) *Black and White: The Negro in English Society, 1555–1945*. London: Allen Lane.

Webb, M. (2001) Black Young People. In Factor, F., Chauhan, V. and Pitts, J. (Eds.) *The RHP Companion to Working With Young People*. Lyme Regis: Russell House Publishing.

West, K. (2004) Jesus Walks. *The School Dropout*, Audio CD, Original Release Date: February 10, 2004 Label: Roc-A-Fella Asin: B0001ap12g.

Woodson, C.G. (1933) *The Mis-Education of The Negro*. New Jersey: African World Press.

Younge, G. (2006) Let's Have an Open and Honest Discussion About White People. *The Guardian*, Oct. 2, [cited 6th October 2006]. http://www.guardian.co.uk/columnists/column/0,,1885282,00.html

Zephaniah, B. (2004) Documentary About Why He Refused to Accept The OBE, Screened on The BBC Actual Date Unknown. (Director: Giovanni Ulleri).

CHAPTER 2

Service Provision for Black Young People: Linking the Historical Policy Response to Praxis

Momodou Sallah

Introduction

Across most of Western Europe today, contemporary discourse around immigration is inextricably linked to race; the first policy prerogative is to fortify the borders and restrict, if not snuff out, the flow of immigrants, and the second is the management of established or emerging immigrant populations who are mostly perceived as different from the indigenous population and this often means difference in 'race', colour, culture and religion. This chapter is mainly concerned with service provision in relation to those of South Asian, African and Caribbean heritage in Britain. While we are led to believe that, in democracies, all those who live within the state have access to equal opportunities regardless of their 'race', nationality, religion or any other strata of differentiation; sadly this is a dream whose realisation remains an elusive mirage for a great number of Black people in Britain; a microcosm of the situation across Europe. What is the correlation between historical responses to immigration and service delivery to young Black people? Are the services being offered in the fields of education, social welfare, criminal justice and all other facets of life fit for purpose? Are the policies and legislations being implemented dogmatic, relativist or culturally competent? Are practitioners at the forefront of public services able to manage these tensions?

Political definition of Black

The term Black can be described as generic and at best be defined as a fluctuating social construct whose boundaries are extended and contracted according to various interests. Hooks (1990: 54) states that in contemporary writing, race is divided by 'otherness that is not white, it is Black, brown, yellow or purple even.' These words echo in Banton's argument that 'up to the 1970s, the British classified other people as either white or coloured' (Banton, 1988: 2). This simplistic definition of Black as 'otherness' to white presents complex problems, as the racial equation goes beyond a simple matter of Black people of 'Negroid stock' from Africa with woolly hair and flat noses as opposed to white people of 'Aryan descent' with blond hair and blue eyes.

Both the Metropolitan Identity Code (Skellington et al., 1992) and 2001 Census provide interesting examples in that, although both use nationality (e.g. Pakistani or Somali) as a means of definition, they take different approaches with the Metropolitan Identity Code partly emphasising skin pigmentation as in 'dark skinned' European and the census on countries of origin. Therefore analysing the various definitions of Black, lends weight to the idea that racial definitions are socially constructed and dynamic. They are not static because there are always a variety of social forces and interests defining their remit of operation at any given time. Aware of the many pitfalls in tying oneself down to a definition, it is pertinent at this stage to take a historical glance where:

> *The meaning of Black before the sixteenth century included 'deeply stained' with dirt, soiled, dirty, foul . . . Black was an emotionally partisan colour, the handmaid and symbol of baseness and evil, a sign of danger and repulsion.*
>
> (Jordan, 1974: 6)

Williams (1964), Kloss (1979), Dominelli (1988) and Howitt and Owusu-Bempah (1994) have all demonstrated the negative association of the word Black with evil. This condemning definition of Black has partly been attributed to the Bible in Genesis IX, where Noah was said to have cursed his son, a curse that has been turned by writers of the 16th and 17th centuries into a 'Curse of Blackness' (Chouhan et al., 1996: 94).

Political context

From these negative historical conceptions of Black, the term has been re-invented and given a new meaning that replaced more negative appellations such as 'coloured' (Banton, 1988). Having earlier established that the term under discussion is a fluctuating social construct, Tizard and Phoenix (2002) contend that the term is no more in fashion as it is growingly being resisted by certain sections of the 'Black community':

> *In Britain, the term 'Black' has changed from excluding, to including and then excluding again people of Asian descent.*
>
> (Tizard and Phoenix, 2002: 7)

Legitimate concerns about the homogeneity of 'Black' have been expressed: Macey (1995) Katz (1996) and Thoburn et al. (2000). Modood (1988, 1990) calls the political postulation of 'Black' 'a coercive ideological fantasy' that subjectively defines ethnic minority communities. However, contrary to the logic he espouses, Modood defines people of Indian, Pakistani and Bangladeshi origin as South Asians; doesn't he duplicate his own subjective logic by the same token? Patel and Chouhan (1998) postulate that this political definition is a definition about unequal power relationships between the Black and white communities and serves as a uniting force to the Black community. Barn and Harman further argue that '. . . it is being advocated as a tool for strength and solidarity in the face of oppression' (2005: 10). They also criticise the opponents of the Black perspective for 'failing to understand structural power relations in society, and the relative social and economic positions of different racial/ethnic groups in society' (p. 11). The reasons for using Black in its political context are on the basis of racial discrimination and a shared context of colonialism and imperialism (Robinson, 1998).

Chouhan et al. (1996) note that the use of the term under discussion to cover Asian and African people may be contested in some quarters. However, for them it is inclusively and radically used in an age of multiple identities and it does not mean relinquishing other identities, to the contrary it 'is a rallying call for radical action for those people who wish

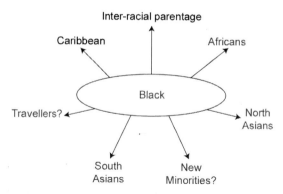

Figure 2.1 Political definition of Black people in UK

to stand behind it and who recognise its loaded historical meaning' (Chouhan et al., 1996: 104–5).

If we insist on calling the Black community 'ethnic minorities', then what about the white minorities like Jews, Irish and travellers? Garrett (2002) argues that in British social work, there is an institutionalised 'misrecognition' of an Irish dimension with regards to race. What term shall we use then? As earlier demonstrated, the use of the political term Black has the potential to brew a lot of controversy but we will use it cautiously yet deliberately because of Black people's shared history of immigration, discrimination and oppression in British society. What unites them is stronger than what divides them.

In this chapter therefore, Black will be used to represent people of African, African Caribbean and South Asian origin as well as children of inter-racial parentage from any of the earlier mentioned ethnicities. We acknowledge that the inclusion or non inclusion of inter-racial parentage children in the political definition of Black is intensely contested; this chapter does not have the scope to cover this but refers the reader elsewhere for extensive coverage (Prevatt-Goldstein, 2002; Okitikpi, 2005; Barn and Harman, 2005). North Asians – sometimes referred to as Chinese or Japanese – will not be included in the definition for historical and contemporary reasons. Where applicable and relevant, individual differences between the various Black communities will be noted. However it must be made clear from the outset that the focus is on the factors that unite Black people rather than what divides them.

A socio-economic picture of Black people

The growing visibility of Black people in Britain cannot be attributed only to their skin pigmentation and physical features, but also to their growth in numbers and the political influence that accompanies such numerical presence. The latest census (2001) puts the number of Black people at 7.9 per cent of the UK population amounting to 4.6 million. This has seen an increase of 53 per cent between the 1991 and the 2001 census from 3 million (Office of National Statistics, 2001). The 2001 census breaks down the Black population as follows: African (0.8 per cent) Caribbean (1 per cent) Black Mixed Parentage (1.2 per cent) Bangladeshi (0.5 per cent) Indian (1.8 per cent) Pakistani (1.3

per cent) Chinese (0.4 per cent) Other Asian (0.4 per cent) Other Ethnic Group (0.4 per cent) and Black Other (0.2 per cent).

The Black population in Britain, it can be argued, does not enjoy the same privileges as most of the rest of the White population. This could be attributed to the daunting historical process leading to the exodus of Black people into Babylon (Babylon refers to the West and specifically Britain in this context) with the resultant institutionalisation of racism as detailed in the Stephen Lawrence Inquiry (Macpherson, 1999). Therefore discriminatory practices, sanctioned by law, are carried out within a legal framework that militates against the holistic development of Black people from the cradle to the grave. Evidence shows people from the Black community continue to be disproportionately represented in the Criminal Justice System. For example, Black people are just over six times more likely to be stopped and searched, three times more likely to be arrested, and seven times more likely to be in prison than White people (Home Office, 2005: iv).

Constituting 7.9 per cent of the population, Black people formed 23 per cent of those stopped and searched in 2003/4 and 15 per cent of notifiable offences in the same year (Home Office, 2005). Why is this so? Why is it that Black people who constituted such a small percentage of the population have been negatively over-represented in the above quoted statistics especially given that Black young people 'between 10 and 25 years are no more or less likely to commit crime than their White counterparts' (Crime and Justice Survey in the Home Office, 2005: iv).

Continuing on this trend, it is worthwhile to note that on average, only 38 per cent of Asians and 23 per cent of Black people (African and Caribbean) achieved five or more GCSE or higher grades as compared to 45 per cent of white pupils in 1996 (CRE Fact sheets, *Young People in Britain*, 1998). It is further pertinent to note that Black people are less likely to have formal qualifications. This is true for 47 per cent of those of Bangladeshi and Pakistani origin as compared to 18 per cent of white people (CRE Fact sheets, *Education and Training in Britain*, 1998). The picture beginning to emerge is that Black people are more educationally disadvantaged than the rest of the British population. The following quote still remains relevant:

Ethnic minority pupils, who made up 11 per cent of all 5–15 year olds in compulsory schooling, accounted for 17 per cent of all permanent exclusions. Black children (African and Caribbean) forming 3 per cent of all 5–15 year-olds in 1995/96, but 11 per cent of permanently excluded pupils were disproportionately affected by exclusion . . . Black Caribbean pupils were five times more likely to face permanent exclusion in 1995/96 than white pupils.

(CRE, *Education and Training in Britain*, 1998)

The DfES report *Getting it Right* (BBC, 2007 online) confirms how teachers and educational establishments continue to fail especially Black Carribean young people as they are still more likely to be significantly excluded, more likely to be picked on for behaviour, disproportionately put in bottom sets, more likely to be punished and less likely to be praised.

On the economic and employment front, it remains the same for Black people; in the spring of 1997, 11 per cent of Black people (African and Caribbean) and 6 per cent of Asians with degrees were unemployed compared with only 3 per cent of white degree holders whilst 34 per cent of Black people without formal qualifications were unemployed compared to only 13 per cent of the white population (CRE, Education and Training in Britain, 1998). The CRE goes further to state that in 1995/96, the unemployment rate among ethnic minorities was 18 per cent compared to only 8 per cent of the white population. The statistics further went on to indicate 'nearly four in ten young Black women were unemployed in 1995/96 compared with just one in ten young white women' (CRE, *Employment and Unemployment Fact Sheet*, 1998). Again it should be noted that in the spring of 1997, 'The unemployment rate among young Black people was 35 per cent compared with 13 per cent among young white people' (CRE, *Fact Sheet on Young People in Britain*, 1998).

When it comes to housing, the trend continues, Black people tend to live in older, inner city accommodation which tends to be overcrowded, lacks basic amenities and are more at risk of associated environmental problems (Butt and Mirza, 1996; PSI, 1997). Brown (1984), Phillips (1987) and Lakey (1997) have argued that Black people are more vulnerable to poor housing due to institutional discrimination. Black people are more likely to live in deprived areas, more likely to experience over crowding: 7 per cent for Indians, 9 per cent for African and Carribean, 23 per cent for Bangladeshi and Pakistani as compared to 2 per cent for Whites. Black households are three times more likely than White households to be in a poor neighbourhood. Additionally the 44 most deprived areas in all local authorities have proportionally four times as many people from Black communities (Cabinet Office, 2000; Office of the Deputy Prime Minister, 2003; Harrison and Phillips, 2003). Black people are a lot more likely to be the victims of racially motivated incidents; 2.2 per cent for African and Caribbean, 4.6 per cent for Bangladeshi and Pakistani, 3.6 for Indian as opposed to 0.3 per cent for white people (National Statistics Online, 2004). It is interesting to note that 41 per cent of African Caribbean, 45 per cent of Indians, 82 per cent of Pakistani and 84 per cent of people of Bangladeshi origins have incomes that are less than the national average in comparison to only 28 per cent of white people! (Cabinet Office Strategy Unit Report, 2003).

Given the nature of the above quoted statistics, we cannot but conclude that Black people are more likely to be unemployed, less likely to have formal qualifications, more likely to be excluded from school and are disproportionately represented in the criminal justice system. That these statistics are there for all to see should not be a bone of contention, why this is so should probably provoke more passionate and academic reasoning from social scientists. This bleak picture of Black people in Britain, which in reality translates to economic disadvantage, social exclusion and institutionalised discrimi-nation, has left many unanswered questions. Is it a question of race that brought about such a situation? Is it self-inflicted and are we to accept that Black people are generally lazy and genetically less endowed? Is it the economic, social and political structures of society? In the end, is it the age-old intellectual debate of man or society? There are many answers to these questions but I stand convinced that the greatest damage is caused by the very structures of society that oppress given the construction of the British welfare state; translated and implemented by practitioners on the frontline like teachers, social workers, youth workers and criminal justice workers who manage a great many tensions; on some occasions relatively, other times dogmatically, with cultural competency as the ideal state to achieve.

Recruitment, restriction, repatriation and now integration

Before delving into the tensions that confront practitioners, it is necessary to explain the mechanics of the present situation; Black people were not meant to stay in Britain in large numbers, they were meant to satisfy post World War Two labour shortage only; they were not meant to 'swamp' (Thatcher, 1978) the mainland but they did and this created a 'social problem' for Britain.

It is pivotal to remember how the end of the Second World War culminated in massive labour shortage for Britain resulting in the recruitment of 'coloured' labour. However a couple of things shifted the recruitment or what Sivanandan (1982) calls 'laissez faire' British policy towards immigration to a restrictionist one. Saggar (1992) and Jacobs (1986) put a case that the 1958 'race riots' in Notting Hill were to usher in a new dawn of immigration policy and push the agenda from economic prerogative to social order. Sivanandan (1982) paints the background against which immigrant legislature was to follow shortly:

> *Within the space of a few years, from the early 1960s on, the terms of the debate on 'race' in Britain had been set, a common language developed in which that debate was conducted, and its fundamental assumptions established. Blacks were the problem; fewer Blacks make for better race relations; immigration control was the answer; social control would follow.*
>
> (Sivanandan, 1982: 99)

Saggar (1992) goes one step further by listing other factors responsible for the change in British policy towards 'coloured immigration'. He suggests that the failure of Britain to control the Suez Canal against Egyptian nationalisation and nationalism as well as the 'wind of change' resulting in the agitation for nationhood from British colonies cracked open the mighty British Empire. At the end, the question being asked was that if the colonies wanted independence from the motherland and were now considered surplus to the needs of the economy, especially given that the post war labour shortage was addressed, then the rationale went: wherein lies the wisdom in continually importing 'coloured' labour especially given the just concluded explosive 'race riots' in 1958? The 1962 Immigration Act did just that and restricted the entry of 'coloured' people through the voucher system. That it was aimed at 'coloured people' is no bone of contention as an ex-Tory minister involved in drafting the act confessed:

> *The restrictions were applied to coloured and white citizens . . . though everybody recognised that immigration from Canada, Australia and New Zealand formed no part of the problem.*
>
> (Deedes, 1968, cited in Saggar, 1992)

Other factors could be said to be the physical presence of 'coloured' people which for the general populace evoked images of 'being swamped' or dominated. Charles Collet, a then Conservative Councillor writing in the *Birmingham Evening Dispatch* captured this widespread view at the time, 'what a foolish race we are to tolerate the uncontrolled, unhealthy influx of colour immigrants' (*Birmingham Evening Standard*, cited in Miles and Phizacklea, 1984).

This view held by many among the general public was to be translated into policy, and abetted by the media-generated hysteria that, to some extent, influenced the 1965 elections. What we can draw so far from the above scenario is that British immigration policy shifted from one of recruitment to one of restriction for a number of reasons. With the passing of the 1971 Immigration Act that policy became one of control. Until this time 'coloured' people were not seen as a permanent feature in the British social and political landscape. Therefore the delivery of services did not necessarily take their needs into consideration. The passage of the 1971 Act was meant to shut the door of immigration once and for all, but events led elsewhere as the 1972 Asian Ugandan crisis resulting in the expulsion of Asian Ugandans holding British passports and the 1976 Malawi Asian crisis were to make the Tories retreat from their 1970 electoral promise, and admit more British passport holders from these countries (Saggar, 1992). Coupled with the economic depression of the 1970s, this resulted in another change of policy: the attempt to repatriate immigrants, or what Sivanandan (1982, 1990) calls 'induced repatriation'.

There were two approaches. The first, mainly propagated by the Conservative MP, Enoch Powell and his associates, called for the repatriation of 'coloured' immigrants in the interest of the British people (Saggar, 1992). This did not happen, but the idea influenced both Conservative and Labour policy towards 'coloured' immigration. A more subtle policy process used by the governments in the 1970s and 1980s was 'induced' repatriation. Sivanandan (1982, 1990) defines this as the application of measures and practices that made it almost impossible for 'coloured' immigrants to stay in the UK.

A clear ideological shift to the right by the Conservative party (Miles and Phizacklea, 1984) was to sanctify the discriminatory and exclusionary practices as a direct or indirect consequence of their policies. Cataloguing these practices is beyond the scope of this chapter. However, understanding that exclusionary practices affecting first and second-generation immigrants alienated them and resulted in the delivery of unresponsive services is essential for the arguments I will later put forward. As has been earlier demonstrated, the race debate has become synonymous with 'problematised' 'coloured' immigration; pigmentation has been the basis of discrimination and the question begs to be asked, how do you differentiate between the legal and illegal immigrant? Between the citizen and non-citizen? This resulted in the application of blanket discriminatory policies and practices across the board to the detriment of Black people, the virgin tests in 1979 where female partners were subjected to the inhumane and degrading gynaecological examination at their arrival from countries of origin in South Asia is a case in point (Saggar, 1992). This inhumane treatment, sanctioned by law, was implemented in the name of the British people. Another aspect was the X-ray examinations to which pregnant women and other vulnerable groups like children from Bangladesh were subjected to determine their age even though the inaccuracy of such by a number of years has been confirmed by experts (Saggar, 1992). The dispersal policies and practices from the mid 1960s constitutes another point in hand; a DES Circular in 1965 stated that no more than 30 per cent of pupils in any school should be composed of immigrant children because of the 'serious strain' it would cause. In addition, the 'one-in-six' housing allocation rule practiced in places like Birmingham (Flett, Herderson and Brown, 1979, cited in Williams, 1989) bear witness to discrimination officially carried out under the auspices of the law. Some people argue that these are ethics of the past but stop and search cloaked in anti-terrorism legislation and the threat to take away children of failed asylum seekers are present examples most of us choose to ignore.

With the agitation of anti-immigration lobbyists like Enoch Powell calling for total repatriation of Black people and the 'inducement' of Black immigrants through officially sanctioned discriminatory practices, and attempted Tory policy of voluntary repatriation to abdicate their newfound homeland; how could equitable distribution of social services be ensured? It could not because although the basis of discrimination was said to be colour and culture; the application of the discriminatory practices was one of power, the power of the majority over a minority who were often seen as melting Black hailstones tarnishing the snowy white British landscape, not permanent gems that decorate the British social landscape.

I contend that Black people do not have the power or influence to practice prejudice at the institutional level, whereas whiteness is accompanied by a degree of power without which racism would have little political or social impact. Given this scenario how did the British political body respond? Most British policy on race and immigration has been ad hoc and largely wary of public opinion. However, it should also be recognised that successive Labour and Tory governments attempted to deal with the 'social problems' that were perceived to result from Black immigration. Section 11 of the Local Government Act of 1966, the Local Government Grants (Social Needs) Act 1969, the 1976 Race Relations Act and the Inner Urban Areas Act 1978 (Lewis, 2000) were to an extent geared towards addressing the gaping social unrest which was a by-product of the socially inequitable environment of the 1960s and 1970s. The problem, however, was that the very premise on which the approach was built appears misguided. It was built on identification of Black people as:

> . . . *producers of problems. Here Black people are represented as the cause of problems because of the cultural and social disorganisation they are purported to induce as a result of their 'otherness'. The association of problems with Black people is pervasive . . .*

> (Lewis, 2000: 46)

Brixton uprisings and the aftermath

What is apparent is that this basic foundation of British social policy was flawed as the policy drive and movement from recruitment in the 1950s, restriction in the 60s and repatriation in the 1970s was to be shattered by the Brixton riots (uprisings) of 1981; spontaneous riots by mainly Black youths disaffected with the system. Lord Scarman, who led the inquiry into the riots, was to come out with many interesting findings and one of the most significant was the disengagement of Black youths and the discriminatory practices meted out to them by the police. This was to lead to a re-examination of policy towards Black people (Scarman, 1981).

The description and events leading to the uprising has been given sufficient coverage elsewhere (Scarman, 1981; Benyon, 1984). However, two reasons for the uprising are important to take note of: oppressive policing, especially the implementation of the 'sus' laws and the second, as identified by Scarman, was that it:

. . . was a protest against society by people, deeply frustrated and deprived, who saw in a violent attack upon the forces of law and order their one opportunity of compelling public attention to their grievances.

(Scarman, 1981: 14)

The Scarman Report was to generate tension, with some saying that the very holding of the Scarman inquiry itself tacitly endorsed the criminal behaviour of Black people during the riots. In contrast, it may be said that it brought the issue of race to the fore of public attention, thereby opening up the unspoken sore at the heart of British society: racism.

One of the major differences between the Scarman and Stephen Lawrence (Macpherson, 1999) inquiries is that the Stephen Lawrence Inquiry accepted the existence of institutional racism whilst the Scarman inquiry did not, even though the latter recognised that public bodies as well as private individuals were guilty of gross acts of discrimination. What could be more institutionally racist, and therefore more discriminatory, than when the very acts of public institutions discriminate against one group over another on the basis of 'race'? One would have assumed that the recommendations made by the Scarman Report, reports after the Handsworth, Brixton and Toxteth uprisings in 1985 would have drastically changed the continued racial disadvantage of the Black community. However, this did not happen, instead it was more a term of 'urban regeneration'; the nomenclature that came to replace 'race' as its mere mention had the tendency to drive people hypersensitive. The Stephen Lawrence Inquiry (1999) showed further that one of the major fault lines in British society is that of race and that it is conducted through 'institutional racism'. This has taken a new dimension that is shifting the perceived differences from biological to cultural (Smith, 1994). Smith recognises the many guises that racism can take. Racism cannot be solved by a few Black faces in the parliament or by pumping regeneration money into Black community organisations. This does not absolve the government from the responsibility of tackling and addressing institutional and structural racism. The injection of the term 'new minorities' to refer to Eastern Europeans and Turks reveals another dimension to the discourse.

A critical observation would reveal that to the contrary, not effectively tackling racism in all its manifestations has resulted in the growing polarisation of cultures and communities in the UK, and the Cantle Report (2001) went further to state that this disparity, especially contextualised after the Oldham, Burnley and Bradford unrest in the summer of 2001, denotes a trend of two parallel cultures in Britain.

We use the incidents that happened in Bradford, Burnley and Oldham in the summer of 2001 as examples because they are the latest in terms of a major conflict between White and Black communities since 1985 (there actually was the Birmingham disturbances between South Asian and African Caribbean communities in October 2005) and demonstrate the depth of division between various communities and it demonstrates as well the epitome of the latest government polices towards racial disadvantage through its key policy of *Community Cohesion*. But is this doing the job? Are they moving away from institutional racism as earlier insinuated by Scarman (1981) and stated by the Stephen Lawrence Inquiry (1999)? Again the policy drive appears misguided as Cantle (2001) argues that the programmes introduced in response seem to institutionalise the problems and brew further division based on perceived unfairness.

Also reminiscent of the Scarman Report (1981), the Cantle Report (2001) suggests that the opportunities being enjoyed by the various groups in the UK are dissimilar when it points out that: 'Opportunities are also far from equal, with many differences in real terms, in respect of housing, employment and education.' (Cantle, 2001: 10). However there have been some critics of the Cantle Report who argue that the consequences of racial disadvantage were not given a thoroughly in-depth look and therefore the extent to which socio-economic factors influenced the inflammatory riots partly misdiagnosed (Bodi, 2002).

Social policy response to the Black presence

The political debate on what to do with post war immigrants that took place between the 1960s to the 1980s was underpinned by notions of assimilation and integration; this approach was meant to ignore ideas of separateness and differences and in consequence adopted the 'colour blind' approach which was bent on treating everyone as the same (Phillips, 2002). This meant that the base lines of cultural, social, racial and economic differences were ignored or given little prominence.

The 1981 uprising shattered the mirage of assimilation and ushered in multiculturalism which recognised that the assimilationist and colour blind approaches had failed Black communities. The premise of multiculturalism being that the basis of racism is cultural ignorance and that by reorienting people's ignorance, then racism would be conquered and discrimination decimated. Multiculturalism, which saw the solution of racism as cultural education and attitudinal change, has been criticised by many as a tokenistic gesture merely trying to appease, whilst anti-racism on the other hand demanded fundamental policy and political changes. In addition multiculturalism has been seen by many local authorities as a safer option to the anti-racism approach, as the latter was a political hot potato that few politicians wanted to meddle with. (Phillips, 2002).

The present Labour Government, and a greater percentage of the establishment, would want us to believe that Britain is a multicultural society based on the values of cultural pluralism, but the policies and its results, as demonstrated earlier, paint a different picture, a real picture of the people in the streets, not some wishful thinking of a bureaucrat in Whitehall. That the polarised communities exist as a result of government policy or inaction, spanning over a 50 year period, has been demonstrated from the policies of recruitment, restriction, repatriation to present attempts at community cohesion and integration but the question begs to be asked; what does it mean to live in multicultural Britain? How do we develop values of 'Britishness'? What is this whole debate about assimilation, integration and multiculturalism? It could be noted that by the time of the Brixton uprisings (riots) the debate had also long moved from 'race relations' and 'integration' to multiculturalism. What was to follow then was an attempt in the 1980s to the present, to ply the 'multicultural' and 'cultural pluralism' approach and recognise Black people as a permanent feature of the British landscape in contrast to the previous policies, which sought to recruit, restrict and repatriate with the premise that Black people are the problem. It can be said that some positive steps have been taken especially given recent community tensions in Oldham, Bradford and Burnley culminating in the present government's policy drive of 'community cohesion' whose focus is the 'need for allegiance, loyalty and a meaningful concept of citizenship' (Allen, 2003: 28).

But the multicultural debate goes on, and not only in Britain but in many parts of the western world, where second, third and fourth generation immigrants struggle to be accepted into various societies on the basis of their ethnic origin. Holland, France and Sweden are very good examples. The fundamental question often boils down to the fact that there is often a struggle to accommodate them and the question is often asked as to whether to assimilate, integrate or *multiculturate*. Kundnani captures this mood when he succinctly exposes the naked assimilation attempts in France, Netherlands and Denmark:

> *Across Europe, hysteria has gripped the political classes. The questions of what to do about desperate immigrants and angry Muslims have coalesced into 'the integration debate'. In France, the official answer is forced assimilation, symbolised by the ban on the hijab in state schools and public buildings. In the Netherlands, a mass expulsion of 26,000 asylum seekers has been approved, while Rotterdam Council has told Muslims that mosques must be built in a more westernised style. In Denmark, immigrants have been told they cannot marry a foreign national under the age of 23 and, even then, must pay a deposit of £3,000 for the privilege. Across the continent, multiculturalism is out and 'integration' is in.*

(Kundnani, 2004, online)

This could be described as a very hash account of events but it highlights that the debate about integration and multiculturalism is not only limited to Britain but takes place at a global level. The present Labour Government has been very clear lately in announcing a radical policy shift from multiculturalism to integration. The establishment of the Commission for Integration and Cohesion; Jack Straw's veil comments (Straw 2006, online) and Blair's (2006, online) request for the Muslim community to integrate confirmed the death of multiculturalism as far as the government is concerned.

What exactly does integration mean? Is it a masqueraded process of assimilation? Has the clock been turned back 50 years? Does it depart from the existence of two or more parallel cultures, as earlier described in the Cantle Report, whose lives hardly ever intersect? Is it the postulation of a 'universal' culture that is insensitive to all the other existing cultures in Britain? This is important because it determines whether the services that are delivered to Black people take note of their cultural needs or practices, and for our purposes, services for young Black people. It determines whether respect of other cultures and the recognition of Black people as a permanent feature in the British socio-political scene is complete.

Tension, contradiction, struggle and impact on practice and services

From the earlier discourse, we can deduce that Black children are disproportionately represented in all ills. Whilst the causes for this are many, the fundamental focus of the chapter is the symbiotic relationship between the historical evolution of social policy responses to the Black presence and service provision for Black young people in relation to practice. Social welfare practitioners are at the cutting edge of the interpretation and implementation of policy, procedures and legislation. When practitioners do not understand their clients' concept of social reality, even when legislation is sensitive to this, then the engagement with or the intervention into clients' lives becomes distorted to their detriment. There are many documented instances where practitioners' interventions have resulted in more harm than good on the basis of racial bias, whether intentionally or unconsciously:

> Reports into the deaths of Black children provide evidence of a lack of intervention in situations where Black children were at obvious risk of suffering significant harm from their parents . . . reports identify that stereotyping of Black families and a reluctance on the part of white professionals to intervene for fear of being accused of racism influenced practice.

> (Dutt and Phillips, 2000: 40)

This fear of intervention by practitioners, mostly but not exclusively white, can be juxtaposed with the findings of Sallah (2005), which from a sample of Black parents and children found that:

- A Eurocentric model of parenting is not the best according to the sample of Black children and parents.
- Black childrearing practices are not respected.
- There exists a deep suspicion of Social Services.

These are very strong statements but genuinely reflect the depth of feelings encountered by the author during the interviews; to compound it:

> This view has been consistently expressed by 60 per cent of parents throughout the research; that practitioners like teachers and social workers, who deal with their children on a face-to-face basis do not sometimes know enough about the cultural background of a child, especially childrearing, to make a fair judgement in the best interest of the child.

> (Sallah, 2005: 264)

These two positions, one of practitioners not being competent enough to deal with an ethnically diverse population and on the other hand the deep suspicion and mistrust of state agencies by a significant number of Black people presents an urgent dilemma with sometimes fatal consequences.

Relativism, dogmatism and cultural competency

In our practice, do we assume a culturally dogmatic or relativist stance? Does the fear of being called racist scare white social workers from challenging accepted or perceived cultural practices that have detrimental effects on the child? As an experienced white social worker told me, he feels 'disabled' by the atmosphere of political correctness we operate in, as the stigma of being branded a racist can be very uncomfortable. In his exposé on political correctness, Owusu-Bempah (2003) argues that some white workers avoid involvement with Black clients even where they will better serve the interest of the child for this reason. This means that sometimes it is easier to turn a blind eye on Black colleagues or clients with the justification that 'it is their culture and they know best' to the detriment of the child. In other cases, some professionals are not even sure and hence the relativist approach. In this light, we need to be asking ourselves, how do we ameliorate this situation? How do we promote a safe environment for white professionals to be able to challenge established or perceived cultural practices that militate against the best interest of the child? At the other extreme of the continuum, there is cultural dogmatism, where the concept of 'the family' is postulated from a Eurocentric angle and this approach negates any other model of constructing social reality. A Eurocentric approach can prove insensitive to the needs of different cultures and is often met with resistance and even hostility sometimes by those at the receiving end. This dogmatic approach is not only adopted by white social workers but sometimes Black social workers as well. This approach to the construction of social reality, which determines the interpretation of statutory intervention, is not an issue of colour or pigmentation but sometimes a matter of training of workers, which is mainly given from a Eurocentric perspective. As a result professionals can sometimes be fixated with the ethics of the profession, which adopts a dogmatic approach practiced by both Black and white social workers. The extremes of these two approaches, dogmatic and relativist, are widespread yet very dangerous.

Social and childcare workers are by the very nature of their jobs entrusted with making life and death decisions and therefore the need to train them to a minimum acceptable standard of cultural awareness is a sin qua non, it is non negotiable as those in places of responsibility have no right to commit irresponsible acts. Social Work, Youth Offending, Probation and Youth Work must urgently and adequately address this imbalance between cultural relativism and dogmatism. What we should hope to achieve is cultural competency, as articulated by Owusu Bempah:

> *Recognising similarities and differences in the values, norms, customs, history and institutions of groups of people who vary by ethnicity, gender, religion . . . culturally competent practitioners understand the impact of discrimination, oppression, and stereotyping on practice. They recognise their own biases towards or against certain cultural groups; they rely on (scientific) evidence and moral reasoning to work effectively in cross cultural situations.*

(Owusu Bempah, 2002: 16)

| Dogmatism | Cultural competency | Relativism |

Figure 2.2 Cultural continuum

The above diagram shows the three different cultural stances that can be adopted by practitioners in their praxis. Cultural relativism and dogmatism represent dangerous and insensitive stances and stand at extreme ends of the cultural continuum; conversely the ideal situation is cultural competency, which is sensitive to cultural needs yet grounded in the best interest of the child. Cultural competency should not seek to assimilate or operate in two separate cultures that hardly intersect (parallel multiculturalism), but must strive for a situation in multicultural competency where culturally different approaches to childrearing would be respected, at the same time as the establishment of minimum acceptable standards of childrearing across all cultures.

Cases should not be assigned to Black people only because of the colour of their skin; instead the training should be sensitive enough to make any social worker competent enough to work in multicultural Britain, here I refer to multicultural competency, and not to practices that are tantamount to apartheid. This situation will also enable some white social workers to feel comfortable and confident in challenging practices justified on the basis of culture that militate against the holistic development of the child.

Blackification process

The death of Victoria Climbié in 2002 sent shock waves throughout Britain; not only because of the brutality of the abuse leading to her horrific death but also because of the fact that:

- The London Boroughs of Ealing, Brent, Haringey and Enfield.
- The following Health Authorities: Brent and Harrow, Enfield and Haringey, North West London Hospitals NHS Trust, and North West London Hospitals NHS Trust, and North Middlesex Hospital NHS Trust, and
- The London Metropolitan Police Force

were all involved before her gruesome death without being able to save her. Putting aside these shameful facts, I have been struck by Owusu Bempah's question when he asked: 'was it a freak, a sheer coincidence, that each of these agencies allocated Black workers to deal with Victoria's case?' A look at current practice will reveal that this is not an isolated incident and there are a plethora of examples where some Black staff are given cases, involved or even employed solely on the basis of their skin colour. I am all for visible diversity and the reflection of diverse communities within the workforce but where this is done to camouflage the situation and absolve the organisation/government from skilling a competent workforce able to operate in a multicultural and multiracial Britain, then it stinks. The process of blackification gives the illusion that issues to deal with race are being addressed when in actual fact potentially explosive and fatal issues are being swept under the carpet. This is wrongly premised on the observation that all Black people are cultural experts and gives the easy route out for some white practitioners not to learn to be culturally competent. Most of the training of Black practitioners still remains a largely Eurocentric affair and the result would be different face – same practice. The notion that if you sprinkle a bit of colour in the metropolitan police, social services and education; then 'it will be alright' is cowardly and irresponsible; every practitioner who works in a multicultural, multiethnic and multiracial society must be culturally competent and there is no excuse.

References

Allen, C. (2003) *Fair Justice, The Bradford Disturbances, the Sentencing and the Impact.* London: Forum Against Islamophobia and Racism.

Banton, M. (1988) *Racial Consciousness.* London: Longman.

Barn, R. and Harman, V. (2006) A Contested Identity: An Exploration of the Competing Social and Political Discourse Concerning the Identification and Positioning of Young People of Inter-Racial Parentage. *British Journal of Social Work.* Advance access 1–16.

Benyon, J. (1984) *Scarman and After: Essays Reflecting on Lord Scarman's Report, The Riots and their Aftermath.* Leicester: Scarman Centre.

Blair, T. (2006) *Blair's Concerns Over Face Veils.* BBC 17 Oct. http://news.bbc.co.uk/1/hi/uk_politics/6058672.stm

Bodi, F. (2002) *Bradford: Different Justice for the Muslim Community.* Available from http://www.org.uk/pdescription.asp?key=899andgrp+8. Accessed on the 30th of May 2004.

Brown, C. (1984) *Black and White Britain.* London: Heinemann.

Butt, J. and Mirza, K. (1996) *Social Care and Black Communities: A Review of Recent Research Studies.* London: HMSO.

Cabinet Office (2000) Extract from *Minority Ethnic Issues in Social Exclusion and Neighbourhood Renewal.*

Cabinet Office (2003) *Ethnic Minorities and the Labour Market: Final Report.* London: The Cabinet Office.

Cantle, T. (2001) *Community Cohesion: A Report of the Independent Review Team Chaired by Ted Cantle.* London: Home Office.

Cashmore, E. and Troyna, B. (1983) *Introduction to Race Relations.* London: Routledge and Kegan Paul.

Chouhan, K. et al. (1996) *Anti-racism and Black Empowerment in Britain: Principles and Case Studies.* In Aluffi-Pentini, A. and Lorenz, W. (Eds.) Anti-racist Work With Young People. Lyme Regis: Russell House Publishing.

Commission for Racial Equality (1998) *Education and Training in Britain.* London: CRE.

Commission for Racial Equality (1998) *Employment and Unemployment.* London: CRE.

Commission for Racial Equality (1998) *Young People in Britain.* London: CRE.

Dominelli, L. (1988) *Anti-Racist Social Work.* Macmillan: Basingstoke.

Dutt, R. and Phillips, M. (2000) Assessing Black Children in Need and Their Families. In DoH *Assessing Children in Need and their Families.* DoH.

Garrett, P.M. (2002) 'No Irish Need Apply' Social Work in Britain and the History and Politics of Exclusionary Paradigms and Practices. *British Journal of Social Work,* 32, 477–94.

Harrison, M. and Phillips, D. (2003) *Housing and Black and Minority Ethnic Communities.* London: ODPM.

Home Office (1999) *Statistics on Race and The Criminal Justice System,* A Home Office publication under section 95 of the Criminal Justice Act 1991.

Home Office (2005) Race and the Criminal Justice System: An Overview to the Complete Statistics 2003–2004. Available from http://www.homeoffice.gov.uk/rds/pdfs05/s95overview.pdf Accessed 4/03/07

Hooks, B. (1990) *Yearning: Race, Gender and Cultural Politics.* South End Press.

Howitt, D. and Owusu-Bempah, K. (1994) *The Racism of Psychology: Time for Change.* Hemel Hempstead: Havester Wheatsheaf.

Jacobs, B.D. (1986) *Black Politics and Urban Crisis in Britain.* Great Britain: Cambridge University Press.

Jordan, W.D. (1974) *The White Man's Burden.* Oxford: Oxford University Press.

Kloss, R.J. (1979) Psychodynamic Speculations on Derogatory Names For Blacks. *The Journal of Black Psychology,* 5: 2, 85–97.

Kundnani, A. (2001) *From Oldham to Bradford: The Violence of The Violated.* Available from: http://www.irr.org.uk/arun-kundnani/index.html. Accessed on the 30th May 2004.

Lakey, J. (1997) Neighbourhoods and Housing. In Modood, T. et al. *Ethnic Minorities in Britain, Diversity and Disadvantage, Fourth National Survey of Ethnic Minorities.* London: PSI.

Lewis, G. (2000) *Race, Gender, Social Welfare, Encounters in a Postcolonial Society.* Cambridge: Polity Press.

Macpherson, W. (1999) *The Stephen Lawrence Inquiry.* London: HMSO.

Miles, R. and Phizacklea, A. (1984) *White Man's Country: Racism in British Politics.* London: Pluto Press.

Modood, T. (1988) 'Black', Racial Equality and Black Identity. *New Community,* XIV: 3, 397–404.

Modood, T. (1990) Catching up with Jesse Jackson: Being Oppressed and Being Somebody. *New Community,* 17: 1; 85–96.

Modood, T. (1992) *Not Easy Being British: Colour, Culture and Citizenship*. London: Runnymede Trust and Trentham Books.

National Statistics (2004) *Ethnicity, Labour Market*. www.statistics.gov.uk

ODPM (2003) *Survey of English Housing Provisional Results: 2002–2003*. Number 18.

Okitikpi, T. (2005) Identity and Identification: How Mixed Parentage Children Adapt to a Binary World. In Okitikpi, T. (Ed.) *Working with Children of Mixed Parentage*. Lyme Regis: Russell House Publishing.

Owusu-Bempah, K. (1998) Race, Culture, and the Child. In Tunstill, J. (Ed.) *Children and the State: Whose Problem?* London: Cassell.

Owusu-Bempah, K. (2003) Political Correctness: In The Interest of The Child? *Educational and Child Psychology*, 20: 1, 53–63.

Patel P. and Chauhan, V. (1998) Guidelines for Developing Work with Black Young People. *Shabaab*, May.

Phillips, D. (1987) Searching for a Decent Home, Ethnic Minority Progress in The Post-War Housing Market. *New Community*, 14: 1–2, 105–17.

Phillips, M. (2002) Issues of Ethnicity and Culture. In Wilson, K. and James, A. (Eds.) *The Child Protection Handbook*. Edinburgh: Harcourt Publishers.

Phillips, M. and Dutt, R. (1990) *Towards a Black Perspective in Child Protection*. REU.

Prevatt Goldstein, B. (2002) Black Children With a White Parent. *Social Work Education*, 21: 5, 551–63.

PSI (1997) *The Fourth National Survey of Ethnic Minorities in Britain, Diversity and Disadvantage*. London: PSI.

Robinson, L. (1998) *'Race', Communication and the Caring Professions*. Buckingham: Open University Press.

Saggar, S. (1992) *Race and Politics in Britain*. London: Harvester Wheatsheaf.

Sallah, M. (2005) *Black Children and Discipline: Where Does Child Discipline Start and Child Abuse Stop?* Submitted PhD Thesis; University of Leicester.

Scarman (1981) *The Scarman Report, The Brixton Disorders 10–12 April 1981*. London: Penguin Books.

Sivanandan, A. (1982) *A Different Hunger: Writings on Black Resistance*. London: Pluto Press.

Sivanandan, A. (1990) *Communities of Resistance, Writing on Black Struggles for Socialism*. London: Verso.

Skellington, R. and Morris, P. (1992) *Race in Britain Today*. London: Sage Publications.

Smith, A.M. (1994) *New Right Discourse on Race and Sexuality*. Cambridge: Cambridge University Press.

Straw, J. (2006) *Straw's Veil Comments Spark Anger*. BBC http://news.bbc.co.uk/1/hi/uk_politics/5410472.stm 5/10/06

Tizard, B. and Phoenix, A. (2002) *Black, White or Mixed Race? Race and Racism in the Lives of Young People of Mixed Parentage*: London: Routledge.

Williams, F. (1964) *Capitalism and Slavery*. London: Andre Deutsch.

CHAPTER 3

Identity and Black Young People: Theoretical and Practice Considerations

Alice Sawyerr

The interrelatedness of Black Identity and ethnicity adds to the complex nature of the process of identity development in Black young people in Britain. The term 'Black' is used in this chapter to specifically refer to people of African and Caribbean ancestry. Although Black Africans and Black Caribbeans are generally perceived by non-Black people to be the 'same', the distinctions that Black people make in their Black ethnic identity is recognised by the government and reflected in the 2001 census in the United Kingdom. However, declaration of race, ethnicity and religion on completed ethnic monitoring forms does not automatically guarantee or result in ethnically sensitive service provision from child welfare, education or mental health services to meet the racial, ethnic, spiritual and religious needs of Black young people being looked after. The fact that Black people in Britain do not perceive themselves as a homogenous group adds to the complex process of Black and ethnic identity development for looked after Black young people especially in their placement matching, and placement needs. This whole process takes place at a time of heightened sensitivity and vulnerability for young Black people when they are faced with and undergoing separation and loss from their families, kin and ethnic communities. These are important policy implementation and practice issues needing attention, especially if the welfare of looked after Black young people are to be safeguarded effectively and if they are to be prepared for life in a multiracial society (DoH, LAC (98) 20:13). These are also timely issues needing consideration and debate by academics, social commentators, and health and social care practitioners.

Background

Over the last 20 years, a major focus in the British literature has been on the identity, development and placement matching needs of young people of interracial parentage (Small, 1986; Banks, 1992, 1995; Maxime, 1993; Tizard and Phoenix, 1993; Katz, 1996; Prevatt-Goldstein, 1999; Barn, 1999; Fatimilehin, 1999; Owusu-Bempah, 2000; Banks, 2002; Olumide, 2002; Song, 2003; Harman and Barn, 2005). The new debate in British academic literature in the field of social work, according to Barn and Harman (2005) is about the identity and correct labelling of children of interracial parentage. They also identify two competing perspectives vying for position in an ideological and political battle. This is mostly from the literature which has primarily centred on children of interracial parentage 'racial identity', i.e. are they Black or Mixed-race? The literature on the latter seems to be on the increase (Okitikpi, 2005; Goodyer, 2005; Thoburn, 2005; Owusu-Bempah, 2005; Robinson, 2005; Owen, 2005).

There is, however, a dearth of information on Black young people's Black ethnic identity development in Britain. As stated earlier nowhere is this more relevant than in the placements and placement matching needs of looked after children.

Ince (1999: 158) in her study of young Black care leavers reported:

It is striking that over a period of two decades of research little or no recognition has been given to the particular needs and experiences of young Black people and that their position within the care system has been grossly neglected.

She also commented on Biehal et al.'s (1995) research, which had investigated leaving care schemes in three local authorities and were only able to identify nine young people identified as Black, Asian or of mixed heritage. The study investigated 'race', 'culture' and 'identity' and found that it was important for young Black people in care to be given opportunities for exchange with people of 'similar origins' (Ince, 1999).

On the occasions when ethnic distinctions are acknowledged between Black African and Black Caribbean young people in the media or in the literature, it has mainly focused on Black Caribbean children's underachievement in the educational system, their troublesome behaviour or both. Examples in the literature includes reports on Black Caribbean looked after children being at greater risk of permanent exclusion from schools (Stone, 1981; Milner, 1983; Troyna, 1986; Troyna and Carrington, 1990; Gill, Mayor and Blair, 1991; Firth, 1995; Mason, 1995; Fletcher, 1997; CRE, 1997; Okitikpi, 1999). Conversely, these Black Caribbean children and young people's self-identity and distinctive Black ethnic identity needs are seldom acknowledged as pivotal to their social, emotional and psychological development and functioning or considered as worthy of attention.

This chapter looks at how Black Caribbeans and Black Africans define their Black and ethnic identities in Britain. It also looks at the distinctions they make in their Black ethnic identities and the importance of their distinct cultures, language, religion, belief systems, and values in their healthy identity development in a multiracial and multicultural society in Britain.

The chapter is organised into four main sections. An introduction, which briefly looks at: the histories of Black people in Britain, migration patterns, how Black ethnic identities have evolved for Black Caribbeans and Black Africans, how Black identities are generally perceived and socially constructed in Britain, the situation for Black looked after children and young people, Black people in the 2001 census in Britain, and the importance of spirituality and religion as an aspect of Black people's ethnic identity in Western society. This is followed by brief definitions of some of the key constructs. The third section on theoretical considerations is a selective review of empirical literature on identity development as a universal construct, theories on Black identity and theories on ethnic identity development. The fourth section on practice considerations utilises case vignettes to highlight:

- The cumulative effect of racial and ethnic hostilities and mistreatments on Black young people in their identity development in a secondary school setting.
- Effects on looked after Black young people when their Black ethnic identity needs are overlooked and neglected.

Introduction

Historical Context

Before considering the identities of Black young people, it is necessary to first look briefly at the histories of Black people in Britain and how their Black ethnic identities have evolved as this has implications for Black young people's ethnic identity development and sense of cultural belonging.

Historically, Black Caribbeans in the United Kingdom are predominantly the descendants of West Africans captured or obtained in trade from African procurers. They were then shipped by European slave traders to the West Indies to English, French, Dutch, Spanish and Portuguese colonies founded from the 16th century. On arrival, the majority of Africans were set to work on the vast Caribbean sugar plantations for the benefit of the colonial power (Black Britons find their African roots, 2003).

Migration patterns

Since World War II, many Black Caribbeans have migrated to North America, especially the USA and Canada, Europe, the Netherlands and the UK. As a result of the losses incurred during World War II, the British government began to encourage immigration from the countries of the British Empire and Commonwealth to fill shortages in the labour market (Short history of immigration, 2002). The 1948 British Nationality Act gave British citizenship to all people living in Commonwealth countries and full rights of entry and settlement in Britain (History of British Nationality law n.d.). Many West Indians were attracted by better prospects in what was often referred to as the 'mother country'. There was plenty of work in post-war Britain and industrial centres, British Rail, the National Health Service and Public transport which recruited almost exclusively from Jamaica and Barbados. (The Windrush generation n.d.).

The situation was however markedly different for a majority of, Black Africans who migrated to Britain during that same period. They came to further their education and on completion most returned home to their respective African countries e.g. Ghana, Nigeria and Sierra Leone for example where they subsequently took up prominent positions following their countries' independence from the colonial powers.

Since the 1980s, the majority of Black immigrants coming to the United Kingdom have come directly from Africa, in particular, Nigeria and Ghana in West Africa, Somalia and Kenya in East Africa and Zimbabwe and South Africa in Southern Africa (Black British: History n.d.).

The Wikipedia, Free Encyclopaedia (2006) suggests that:

> . . . *the African experience in Britain is not a homogeneous one. For example, Nigerians and Ghanaians have been especially quick to accustom themselves to British life with young Nigerians and Ghanaians achieving some of the best results at GCSE and A-level. It has not been so easy for the growing Somali community, who suffer relatively high levels of social isolation.*

These migration and adaptation patterns for Black Caribbeans and now Black Africans particularly newly arrived and first generation immigrants to Britain are worthy of attention and research. This is essential for planning purposes and for the effective and sensitive provision of services in the areas of education, mental health, housing, employment, training and other areas of personal social services in Britain.

When looking nationally and internationally, the terminology used to describe Black people in the 2001 Census in the UK and the terminology used in the 2000 Census in the USA, are marked different and worth noting. While Britain has three categories namely *Black Caribbean, Black African, and Black Other* (*also referred to as Black British*) the USA has only one category for Black people namely, '*African, or African American*'.

In the USA, African American families perceive of themselves and are perceived by the dominant culture as a homogeneous group (Smith, 1997). African Americans share a common history, language, and culture. Unlike their counterparts in the UK, i.e. Black Caribbeans (also of African ancestry and who were also enslaved) African Americans assert a shared African identity. They proudly acknowledge their African roots (as Africans forcibly uprooted from Africa as slaves and relocated in America). Although the terminology used in Britain to describe or refer to Black people of African ancestry has traditionally followed that of African Americans, Black ethnic identities in Britain owing to the displacements of some Black people from their territories and the influence of the multiplicity of their colonising powers, have resulted in continued non-homogeneity in Black ethnic identity in Britain.

In the USA, the term 'Black' seems to be used to differentiate between races, while establishing a common base that everyone is American. The use of the term 'Black' in Britain in relation to ethnic identity appears to be more complex.

Non-Black perspectives on Black Caribbean and Black African identities

The identities of Black Africans and Black Caribbeans are generally assumed, perceived and socially constructed by non-Black people as 'the same' based on genetic and physical features, as well as their similar mannerisms. These assumptions and perceptions result in conclusions that they must be a homogeneous group. While these beliefs may seem inconsequential as both ethnic groups are classified as belonging to the same 'race', the distinctions in their histories, cultures, language and ethnic identities as outlined in the previous section are significant and form the basis for their self identities. This is crucial given that culture, language, beliefs and historical origins are fundamental to healthy and positive identity development for all people, and importantly for Black looked after children and young people growing up in a multiracial and multi-ethnic society in Britain.

The situation for Black looked after children and young people

As Barn (1999:7) confirms, in British society, identity as an issue only enters the world of academic and political debate in relation to concerns about Black children:

> *Nowhere is this more hotly contested than in the area of substitute family placements of Black children . . . For Black children growing up in an extremely race conscious society, where their cultural and religious origins are given little positive significance by wider society, the concept of positive identity is paramount. It is only through*

appropriate integration into the child's experience that positive and healthy identity can be formed.

Small (1984) also argues that if a healthy personality is to be formed, the psychic image of the child must merge with the reality of what the child actually is. In addition, Chestang, (1972) advocates that Black children must also be enabled to 'transcend reality' if they are not to be engulfed and rendered impotent by such negative social images and possible feelings of personal impotence.

Although these observations and recommendations have not been challenged and corrective steps have been taken to address some of these issues through legislation (Children Act 1989, Adoption and Children Act 2002) and Local Authority guidelines, (DoH Circular LAC, 1998) it is the interpretation and implementation in practice by some local authority placement team managers and social work practitioners, which seems to be problematic.

Given the long history of transracial placements and adoption, and the coming to light of the highly disturbing experiences of Black children in transracial settings in the early 1980s (Gill and Jackson, 1983; Divine, 1983; BIC, 1984), there has been a major change in local authorities' placement policy in Britain. A 'same-race placement' policy by local authority social services departments from the 1980's to the end of the twentieth century has meant that looked after mixed-parentage children have to be placed with Black or mixed couples only (Tizard and Phoenix, 2002: 13). While this may have led to the recruitment of more Black foster carers and adopters for the placement of children of mixed-parentage and Black children, no specific emphasis seems to have been placed on matching Black African children with Black African carers only, or Black Caribbean children with Black Caribbean carers only. Although in principle social care managers and practitioners acknowledge a responsibility to comply with the relevant legislation i.e. the Children Act 1989, the Adoption Act 1976 and the new Adoption and Children Act 2002, they do not in practice prioritise ethnic distinctions made by Black African and Black Caribbean young people in their self-identities during placement into local authority care. Generally, placement with a 'Black carer' irrespective of the ethnic background is often assumed to meet the Black young person's racial and ethnic identity needs as well as their spiritual and religious needs. However, in doing so, practitioners and their managers ignore Local Authority Circular (DoH LAC (98) 20: 13) which clearly states:

> . . . *placement with a family of similar ethnic origin and religion is very often most likely to meet the child's needs as fully as possible, safeguarding his welfare most effectively and preparing him for life in a multiracial society.*

Tizard and Phoenix (2002: 13) also argue that finding the right 'terms to refer to groups of people is important', and that 'what we call people affects the way in which we construct them'.

It is therefore crucial to get the 'terms right' when referring to Black young people's Black ethnic identity. This is of particular importance when selecting appropriate placement matches for young individuals who define their ethnic identities as Black African as distinct from those who define their ethnic identities as Black Caribbean. Although young Black people born in the UK often define their ethnic identity as Black British, they continue to make distinctions between their ethnic origins through the ethnic identities of their parents i.e. Black Africans or Black Caribbeans.

Black people in the 2001 census in Britain

As previously noted, within Black communities in Britain, a majority of Black Caribbeans and Black Africans do not define their ethnic identities as being the same and do not perceive of themselves as a homogeneous group even though they have a common African genesis. This is most evident in the ways in which Black families in Britain describe their ethnic identities. The distinctions made in the process of self-identification on forms completed in education settings, social services departments and in NHS Mental Health Trusts i.e. Child and Adolescent Mental Health Services and in Adult Mental Health Services often include the following: Black African, West Indian, Black Caribbean, Afro-Caribbean, African-Caribbean and Black British.

These distinctions in Black ethnic self-identity are acknowledged and reflected in the 2001 Census in UK where three categories are designated to Black people, namely: _Black Caribbean, Black African and Black Other (or Black British)._

In the United Kingdom, Black Caribbean is the largest group for Black people with a total population of 585, 876. It accounted for 1 per cent of the total population and 12.2 per cent of the Non-White population in the UK. Black African was the second largest group for Black people in the 2001 Census accounting for 485,277, which was 0.8 per cent of the total population and 10.5 per cent of the Non-White population in the UK. The Black other population which accounted for the smallest group for Black people, 87,585, was 0.2 per cent of the total population and 2.1 per cent of the Non-White population in the United Kingdom (National Statistics, ONS, 2001).

Spirituality and religion as aspects of Black identity

An important aspect of Black identity relevant to this discourse is spirituality and religion, with its deep roots in African and Western history. Spirituality according to Smith (1997) is an admixture of non-Western and Western influences. It has its origins in traditional African beliefs and practices on the one hand, and in Western Christianity on the other.

A key question therefore is what role if any does African religion and spirituality play in Black identity development?

African religion and spirituality

Mbuti (1991: 11) addresses the question of the role of African religion in Black identity development by describing African religion as the African way of life. Having five parts, i.e. beliefs, practices, ceremonies and festivals, and religious objects and places. As such, African religion cannot be defined only by one or two of its parts. The parts have to be considered together given that religion is complex, and involves values. African religion is therefore well integrated into an African heritage which is very rich, historical, and cultural. It goes back hundreds and thousands of years and is the product of the thinking and experiences of the African forefathers and mothers, which is the men, women, and children of earlier generations. Therefore, religion has been for Africans, the normal way of looking at the world and experiencing life itself. Consequently, it is found wherever African people are found and is integrated into different areas of life.

Mbuti (1991: 14) suggests that:

. . . Since African Religion belongs to the people, when Africans migrate in large numbers from one part of the continent to another or from Africa to other continents, they take religion with them. They can only know how to live within their religious context. Even if they are converted to another religion like Christianity or Islam, they do not completely abandon their traditional religion immediately. It remains with them for several generations and sometimes centuries. A good example of this is the case of Afro-Americans and Afro-Caribbeans in the Americas and the West Indies. In spite of being suppressed, brainwashed and bombarded with another (and foreign) culture since the days of slavery which lasted up to the nineteenth century, they have retained many elements of their African religiosity to this day. It is African Religion that gives its followers a sense of security in life. Within that religious way of life, they know who they are, how to act in different situations, and how to solve their problems. This does not mean that African Religion has no weaknesses and no false ideas. But as far as it goes, it has supplied the answers to many of the problems of this life even if these may not have been the right answers in every case. Because it provides for them answers and directions in life, people are not willing to abandon it quickly, otherwise they will feel insecure afterwards unless something else gave them an additional or greater sense of security. When Africans are converted to other religions, they often mix their traditional religion with the one to which they are converted. In this way they think and feel that they are not losing something valuable, but are gaining something from both religious systems.

Smith (1997) confirms Mbuti's conceptualisation of African religion and suggests that central to most African spiritual and religious beliefs is the idea of a Supreme Being and the interrelatedness of all things. This includes a belief in the spirit world, and the idea that the Divine Spirit works in and through and beyond human activity. This belief holds true for many African American families in the USA, as well as many Black Caribbean and Black African families in the UK. He argues that for Christians, the bedrock of Black spirituality is a shared conviction of a supreme being and a belief that God sees the oppression of people, hears their cry and promises to deliver them.

Patterns of religious adaptation by African Americans, Black Caribbeans and Black Africans

In America, many African American families have traditionally been Baptist or Methodist although there are now since the 1990s increasing numbers of African Muslims from North Africa who have migrated to the USA. In addition, there are African Americans who have converted to the Nation of Islam and other religions (African-Caribbean community: religion n.d). However, the African American church is acknowledged and considered by the dominant culture and most African Americans as the single most important therapeutic and mental health resource for Black people outside the Black family. Some Black churches provide fostering and adoption services for their communities (Smith, 1997).

Black families from the Caribbean and in Britain are predominantly Christians due to their long history of European colonisation and religious indoctrination. Chevannes (1998) describes three categories of religions in the Caribbean which are well established. The first comprises those of European origins which established themselves as late as the 19th century, and includes denominations such as the Anglican, Baptist, Methodist, United Presbyterian Congregational, Roman Catholic and Moravian churches. Their middle and upper-class membership gives them much influence and power in Society. This is partly through the education system which they played a major role in establishing. The second category comprises those of new American origins, which have been establishing themselves throughout the 20th-century. Some of the leading denominations are Pentecostal, Church of God, Seventh day Adventism and African Methodist Episcopalian (AME) and Zion, which together have been growing at a fast pace. The third category includes African derived religion, an example is the Rastafari which developed in Jamaica in 1930s.

Generally, the majority of African-Caribbeans have continued their religious traditions in Britain with some following the new American style of worship in Evangelical churches.

Similarly, many Black African families in Britain are Christians as a result of European colonisation and also follow Anglican, Methodist, Presbyterian, Roman Catholic, Jehovah Witness, Seventh Day Adventist and more recently Evangelical Protestant traditions. However a significant number of Black African families in Britain from West Africa and North Africa e.g. Northern Nigeria, Northern Ghana, parts of Sierra Leone, The Gambia, Senegal, Mali and Somalia follow Islamic religious traditions (African-Caribbean Community: Religion n.d.).

From a clinical perspective (over twenty years experience with service users of all ages in statutory NHS mental health and voluntary clinical settings), significant numbers of Black families referred for assessment and psychotherapy acknowledge following Pentecostal, Evangelical, and Spiritual church traditions as these churches provide them with the necessary emotional, spiritual, practical support and guidance during 'trying times' e.g. with family relationship and behavioural difficulties, racial mistreatments and employment difficulties.

Some Muslim families have also reported receiving similar supportive services from their mosques.

However, unlike the African American churches in the USA, in Britain, in neither churches nor mosques, are supportive personal and community services or interventions acknowledged or considered by the dominant culture as therapeutic or mental health resources for Black families in need.

Importance of religion to young people's way of life

In the DfES (2006) Research Topic Paper, the Longitudinal Study of Young People in Education (LSYPE) face-to-face interviews were carried out with around 15,700 households. Ethnic minority pupils and their families and households from the six major minority ethnic groups (Bangladeshi, Pakistani, Indian, Black African, Black Caribbean and mixed heritage) were interviewed. In 15,450 of these the young person was interviewed. In 13,800 cases the young person and all resident parents (or those in loco parentis) were interviewed, and in 15,580 cases the main parent was interviewed. The young people in the sample who were all in year 9 at school in 2004, were asked what their religion was and how important religion was to their way of life.

1. Over half of the White British young people in the sample said they were Christian (55 per cent) but a large proportion (42 per cent) said they had no religion.

2. Two-thirds of White British pupils said that religion was not important at all or not very important to their way of life.
3. The vast majority of Black Caribbean and Black African pupils also identified themselves as Christian (83 per cent and 70 per cent respectively).
4. Over a quarter of Black African pupils said they were Muslim (27 per cent).
5. Religion appears to be important to the majority of young people within these ethnic groups.
6. Nearly half of Black Caribbean pupils said religion was fairly important (47 per cent) and over a third said it was very important (38 per cent).
7. A quarter of Black African pupils felt that religion was fairly important to their way of life and 71 per cent said it was very important.
8. Nearly half of mixed heritage pupils said they were Christian (45 per cent) and a large proportion said they do not know or had no religion (38 per cent) with just over one in ten (13 per cent) said they were Muslim.
9. A quarter of mixed heritage pupils felt that religion was very important to them and a third said it was fairly important. Just over a third felt that it was not important at all or not very important.

Although the data did not differentiate between young people living at home and those being looked after, it was quite evident that the majority of year 9 Black Caribbean and Black African young people as recent as 2004 belonged to a religion and the majority said that religion was important to their way of life.

Okitikpi (1999: 121) also confirms that:

> ... *although in the general population, there is a higher percentage of Black people actively involved with their religious communities; however there is little evidence to suggest that Black children being looked after enjoy the same opportunity for this as adults in the community ... For some children, their involvement with a religious community could provide the stability, continuity, and boundaries they need.*

Therefore the distinctions in Black ethnic self-identity, coupled with the importance of religion and spirituality in Black adults and young people's way of life and the non-recognition of service provision by Black churches and mosques in Britain as mental health resources are likely to have major implications especially for Black people involved in child welfare and mental health cases. Essentially in how their needs are assessed and in the services that they are provided.

Definition of key constructs

Use of terminology

It is important to define the following key constructs as terminology used in the British context in relation to race and ethnic identity issues are ever evolving. The meaning attributed to key constructs become important because of their differential usage in sociological, psychological and social work literature and practice. Resilience as an example is an important construct worth defining as it is not usually acknowledged by the dominant culture as a major strength in Black families even though it is a key factor in Black people's survival in extremely race conscious societies in the Western world.

Black

The term 'Black' has been used in this context to refer to people of African and Caribbean ancestry and parentage. Inherent in this definition is recognition that this group of people and their ancestors have a shared experience of racism and discrimination, in which a history of subjugation to European colonialism would have been an important factor (Valuing Diversity, n.d.).

Ethnicity and Ethnic Minority

Ethnicity refers to a number of shared characteristics including a shared background, origin, culture, tradition, and language. All human beings, Black or White, have an ethnicity. However, to distinguish groups whose values, beliefs and practices are not shared to a significant degree with the majority group the word Minority is either placed before or after the word ethnic. The term *Black and Minority Ethnic* is used in this chapter in an inclusive way to reflect both the common elements as well as the diversity of those who experience racism (Valuing Diversity, n.d.).

Identity

Identity is defined here as 'A growing awareness of the ''self'' as a separate and valued person, having a positive sense of one's own individuality' (Gross, 2001: 480). It includes such factors as gender, sexuality, ability, disability, race, culture, religion, spirituality, class and language. Identity is however never static. It changes over time throughout the life cycle, i.e. during childhood, adolescence, adulthood, and old age. In spite of this, some aspects of one's identity such as genetic background never change.

Looked After Children

The term *looked after children* was introduced following the implementation of the Children Act 1989 to describe all children placed in the care of local authorities with parental or child consent in England and Wales. The term *looked after* is used in preference to *in the care of* which implies a temporary provisional state. It is in line with the emphasis in the Children Act 1989 of preserving the concept of parental responsibility even when parents are not physically caring for their children. The term *children in care* is however still in use, and refers to looked after children placed with local authorities as a result of care proceedings, emergency protection orders and remands pending further court hearings. The other category of Looked After Children are referred to as accommodated, previously known as in voluntary care (Corby, 2000: 199).

Prejudice

Prejudice can be defined as using a unipolar (negative) component as in 'thinking ill of others without sufficient warrant', or incorporating a bipolar (negative and positive) component, as in 'a feeling, favourable or unfavourable, towards a person or thing, prior to, or not based on, actual experience'. Both of these definitions include an 'attitude' component and a 'belief' component. The attitude is neither negative nor positive, and the attitude is tied to an over-generalised or erroneous 'belief' (Ponterrotto, 1993).

Although prejudice can hold either a positive or a negative tone, racial and ethnic prejudice in Britain has taken on primarily negative connotations.

Racism

The term is used to describe prejudice and discrimination toward Black and Minority Ethnic people based on their skin colour, culture, language, or religion. Racism is any behaviour or pattern of behaviour that systematically tends to deny access to opportunities, or privilege to one social group while perpetuating privilege to members of another group. Behaviour refers to human action that is observable and measurable. Systematic implies that the consequences of racist behaviour are predictable and occur repeatedly (Ponterrotto, 1993).

Resilience

Being resilient means being able to withstand pressures and adversity and where possible, using a situation as the basis for developing new strengths and growing as a result of the experience. The notion of resilience as part of empowerment helps individuals to appreciate that people problem solving is not about doing things to or for people, but rather doing what one can, to help individuals resolve their own difficulties, by drawing on their strengths and using their experience to develop new strengths where possible (Thompson, 2006). Resilience is also a key factor in protecting and promoting good mental health. It is the quality of being able to deal with the difficulties in life, and is predicated on self-esteem. This in turn is generated by secure early attachments and the confidence of being loved and valued by family and friends.

Young people

'Young people' has been used in this context to refer to Black African, Black Caribbean, Black British males, and females aged 11–18 years of age.

Theoretical considerations

It is important to establish a clear understanding of the relevant constructs and how Black young people develop their Black and ethnic identity. Therefore, definitions of the key constructs and their theoretical underpinnings need to be explored and presented succinctly. As the chapter and book is aimed at a wide readership, a simple clear and succinct style of writing has been adopted for both undergraduates and postgraduates, as well as for experienced social care and mental health professionals, teachers, consultants and managers.

Identity as a universal construct

Identity is a universal and fundamental construct. Human beings in all cultures in society have the potential to develop healthy and positive identity as they go through the life span developmental stages i.e. from birth to childhood to adolescence, through adulthood and old age with the right social, emotional and psychological support. Individuals as members of families or groups (biological, fostered, or adopted) form the cornerstone of their communities. Within all societies, there are variations in cultural norms and expectations. Therefore, the ways in which children and young people's positive and healthy identities are nurtured and marked will inevitably vary from society to society around the world. Some African, Native Australian, Native American, and Native Canadian societies for example, have clearly defined rites of passage or traditional rituals for marking the passage of individual members through key developmental stages. These societies emphasise and place importance on the family, extended family and kin, clan or some other association as the most pivotal social unit. Children and young people in these societies, through socialisation within their dominant cultural settings and traditions undergo the required training to develop positive and healthy self-identities, together with pride in their ethnic identity (Rites of passage, 2000).

Although the process is culturally less defined for Europeans and North Americans there are religious and other rite of passage ceremonies, that are observed in Christianity globally e.g. baptism as an initiation rite. Some Christian churches offer a traditional sacrament of confirmation as an initiation rite recognising full membership status, and as a remembrance of infant baptism. In Judaism, a Bar Mitzvah or a Bat Mitzvah ceremony performs a similar religious coming-of-age function. These ceremonies and rituals promote a sense of group and community membership and in some cultures it forms the cornerstone for ethnic identity development (Rites of passage, 2000).

In European and North American societies, many school and training systems feature graduation ceremonies as rites of passage, marking the end of at least a stage of learning, which is usually festive and public. In adulthood, the celebration of the 18th and 21st birthdays mark the coming of age. Courtship, engagements, stag nights, hen nights, weddings, pregnancy, becoming a parent, motherhood, and fatherhood are all life span rites of passage. Retirement at age 60 and 65, being issued a senior citizen bus pass and receiving a 100th birthday telegram from the Queen (in Britain) are also lifespan rites of passage for old age (Christianity graduation, n.d.). These traditions, rituals and ceremonies serve to promote and enable group membership and healthy identity development through the life span.

Key factors that influence identity development

A key factor that influences identity development is Self-concept which is a term that normally refers to three major components: *Self-image, Self-esteem, and the Ideal-self* (Gross, 2001: 480).

Self-image: refers to the way we describe ourselves and what we think we are like. It is essentially descriptive. One way of investigating self-image is to ask people the question 'Who are you?' 20 times (Kuhn and McPartland, 1954 in Gross, 2001). This typically produces two main categories of answers – *Social Roles and Personality Traits. Social roles* are usually objective aspects of the self-image (e.g. being a son, daughter, brother, sister, mother or and student). These are 'facts' that can be verified by others. *Personality traits* are more a matter of opinion and judgment, and what we think we are like, which may be different from how others see us. However, how others behave towards us has an important influence on our self-perception (Gross, 2001).

As well as social roles and personality traits, our answers to the 'Who are you?' question often refers to *Physical Characteristics*. Examples of physical characteristics are:

tall, short, fat, thin, brown- eyed and black-haired. These are part of our body image or bodily self (Gross, 2001). Throughout our lives, as part of the normal process of maturation and ageing, we all experience growth spurts, changes in height, weight and the general appearance and 'feel' of our body. Each change requires an adjustment on our part to our body image (Gross, 2001). It is therefore ongoing. While self-image is essentially descriptive, the next major component that influences identity development is self- esteem (or self-regard) which is essentially evaluative.

Self-esteem: refers to how much we like and approve of ourselves, and how worthy a person we think we are. Coopersmith (1967) defined self-esteem as 'a personal judgement of worthiness that is expressed in the attitudes the individual holds towards himself'. Our self-esteem can therefore be regarded as how we evaluate our self-image, that is how much we like the kind of person we think we are. The value attached to particular characteristics will also depend on our culture, gender, age and social background (Gross, 2001). Self-esteem is also partly determined by how much the self-image differs from the ideal self. The final major key component of identity development is the construction of an ideal-self.

Ideal-self: If our self-image is the kind of person we think we are, then our ideal self (idealised self-image) is the kind of person we would *like to be*. This can vary in extent and degree. We may want to be different in certain aspects, or we may want to be a totally different person (e.g. the difference between cosmetic surgery to enhance or minimise facial and bodily features and major reconstructive facial cosmetic surgery). Generally, the greater the gap between our self-image and our ideal self, the lower our self-esteem (Rogers in Gross, 2001).

Black identity development theories

Black identity development like 'identity' development is not rigid, fixed or one-dimensional. It is a lifetime process and takes place within specific social and political contexts (Robinson, 1995). One of the best-known and widely researched models for understanding the potential dynamics of identity negotiation is the nigrescence model by Cross (1991). Nigrescence is a French word that describes the process of 'becoming Black'. The psychology of nigrescence is defined as the developmental process by which a person becomes Black. Black is defined in terms of one's manner of thinking about and evaluating oneself and one's reference groups rather than skin colour per se (Robinson, 1995).Other models of ethnic identity development includes; Parnham's elaboration on Cross's model, Atkinson and colleagues 'Minority identity development model' and Helm's 'People of colour racial identity development model'. (Cross, Parham, and Helms, 1991; Tatum, 1992, 1993).

In Cross's (1991) model, the individual is described as going through five stages: Pre-encounter, Encounter, Immersion/Emersion, Internalisation, and finally Internalisation-commitment. Parnham (1991) adds the lifespan perspective to Cross's model recognising that identity development is perceived as ongoing throughout the person's life. Similarly, Atkinson and colleagues (1991) proposed a five-stage model. In their model, the individual is seen as progressing from Conformity, through Dissonance, Resistance and Immersion, to Introspection and finally, Synergistic Articulation and Awareness. Helm's (1991) model also has five stages, Conformity, Dissonance, Immersion/Emersion,

Internalisation, and Integrative awareness. In addition, Helm's model also emphasises racism as a theme.

Within all these models and Parnham's (1991), lifespan perspective, identity development becomes influenced by personal experiences during the lifespan. Notably encounters in childhood are thought to influence and shape the kind of views that are constructed about one's ethnic identity at an early stage. However, as the individual develops through the lifespan and becomes exposed to several other encounters, these views begin to change as the individual adapts their values, beliefs and attitudes. The qualitative differences generated through these encounters are thought to reshape the cognitive, emotional, and attitudinal aspects of identity formation. Some aspects of early identity perception are thought to become reinforced and result in being an integral part of the individual's ethnic and cultural identity. It is assumed that other aspects may change over time and through acculturation. Therefore, the development of an individual through the lifespan provides scope for the exploration of how personal, ethnic and cultural identity can be shaped.

Black identity development theories therefore examine the psychological implications of membership in a racial group and the resultant ideologies. William Cross's Black Racial Identity Development model is often assumed to represent the racial identity formation experience of people of colour in general (Tatum, 1992, 1993).

In Cross's Psychological nigrescence model, individuals move through a predictable series of stages:

1. In the Pre-encounter stage, which is described in the model as the initial point, an individual is unaware or denies that race plays any part in the definition of who they are.
2. This is followed by the Encounter stage, in which a sequence of events forces the individual to realise that racism does affect their life.
3. In the Immersion/Emmersion stage, the individual responds by immersing themselves in their culture, and rejects with anger the values of the dominant culture.
4. The next step is the Internalisation stage, during which the individual develops security in their identity as a person of colour.
5. They then progress to the Internalisation/Commitment stage, in which the individual acquires a positive sense of their racial identity. (Cross, Parham, and Helms, 1991; Tatum, 1992, 1993).

Critique of the nigrescence and identity development models

According to Wilson (1996) (an indigenous American) Cross's model, which is the best known and most researched, represents the Black racial identity formation experience of people of colour in general, but does not hold true for Indigenous Americans or for other minority groups in society e.g. gay men and lesbians.

Wilson (1996) in her critique speculates that the Black racial identity development model and the Minority identity development models were constructed in an attempt to fill some gaps in developmental psychology. She also asserts that the models attempt to recognise the diversity of human experience by describing the developmental sequences that occur in response to the experience and context of racism. However, they do not describe the effects of the simultaneous experience of racism. Further criticisms include each of the models claiming to be nonlinear and non-hierarchical, yet each having a final stage that represents the developmental peak of mental health. She refers to this as a 'self actualised stage' where a person's identity is no longer problematic. Their bicultural adaptation within the dominant culture becomes a source of empowerment. Wilson therefore posits that, the underlying assumption is that supportive bicultural experience is available to all.

While the Black identity development theories may not be applicable in their entirety to indigenous Americans and to gay men and lesbians as Wilson suggests, her complete rejection of these theories appear to be rather unreasonable. For example the first three stages in all the models seem to be applicable, namely the: *Pre-encounter, Encounter and Immersion/Emmersion stages* or the *Conformity, Dissonance and Resistance and Immersion stages*. In real life for example, when individuals, minority groups or Minority ethnic groups encounter hostilities, exclusions, avoidance, rejections and mistreatments from majority groups, they inevitably react to these inequities. It is therefore inconceivable to imagine individual human beings not reacting emotionally, behaviourally or cognitively to prejudice, discrimination or racism in the ways that these theoretical models describe.

Wilson's critique of the final stages of each of the theoretical models appear to be partially justified but exaggerated with regard to their implicit presentation as reaching a developmental peak of mental health and a 'self actualised stage'. In this, Wilson (1996) appears to ignore both the developmental and lifespan aspects of these theoretical models. Similar criticisms are often made of theories that attempt to explain human behaviours and processes. For example 'the stages of grief' in loss and bereavement which are also considered to be applicable in most cultures (Lindemann, 1944; Kubler-Ross, 1969; Parkes, 1996). These stages are not rigid but fluid in their manifestations.

From a clinical perspective, the Black identity development stages can be considered as conceptual models rather than absolute facts, and the processes involved can be viewed in terms of reactions instead of stages. From this standpoint, Black identity development reactions do not have to be rigidly sequential, and individuals may move back and forth during the normal process of development, while experiencing a variety of emotions as they encounter recurring racial and ethnic hostilities, exclusions, avoidance, rejections and mistreatments during their lifespan. Consequently, their emotions and reactions to these, may likely appear, reappear, and at times overlap.

It can also be argued that the emotional and psychological processes involved in Black identity development (similar to the grieving processes) are not pathological states in themselves, but normal reactionary response to life cycle events which do not automatically require supportive therapeutic services for progression from one stage to the next.

In Britain, Robinson (2002) argues in support of Cross's model of Black identity development and makes reference to the fact that although the model has been developed with African-American samples in the USA, it is argued by various authors such as Maxime (1986) and Sue and Sue (1990) that other minority groups share similar processes of development. She also suggests that an understanding of Cross's model should sensitise social workers to the role that oppression plays in an individual's development. She cites Maxime (1993) in Britain, who has successfully and effectively used Cross's model in the understanding of identity confusion in Black children and adolescents in residential, transracially fostered and adopted care settings. She also cites her study (Robinson, 2000) on racial identity development and self-esteem among African Caribbean Adolescents in residential care in a city in the West Midlands, in which residential care staff found Cross's model extremely useful in therapeutic work with African Caribbean youngsters. Robinson (2002) advocates for the use of the nigrescence model because:

> *Cross's model serves as a useful assessment tool for social workers to gain a greater understanding of Black youth. Pre-encounter attitudes have been linked to high levels of anxiety, psychological dysfunction and depression (Parmham and Helms, 1985; Carter, 1991) and low self-regard and self-esteem (Parmham and Helms, 1985). Young people's perceptions of social worker are likely to be influenced by their racial identity development. Thus, young people at the pre-encounter stage are more likely to show a preference for a white social worker over a Black worker.*

Ethnic identity development

Trimble and Dickson (2005) maintain that the definition of ethnic identity varies according to the underlying theory embraced by researchers and scholars intent on resolving its conceptual meanings. The fact that there is no widely agreed upon definition of ethnic identity is believed to be indicative of the confusion surrounding the topic. For Trimble and Dickson (2005), ethnic identity is an affiliative construct, where an individual is viewed by themselves and by others as belonging to a particular ethnic or cultural group. Individuals can choose to associate with a group especially if other choices are available (i.e. where a person is of mixed ethnic or racial heritage). Cheung (1993. in Trimble and Dickson) maintains that affiliation can be influenced by racial, natal, symbolic, and cultural factors. Racial factors involve the use of physiognomic and physical characteristics, natal factors refer to 'homeland' (ancestral home) or origins of individuals, their parents and kin, and symbolic factors include those factors that typify or exemplify an ethnic group (e.g., holidays, foods, clothing, artefacts, etc.). Symbolic ethnic identity they argue usually implies that individuals choose their identity.

Jean Phinney (1990, cited in Trimble and Dickson, 2005) views subjective identity as a starting point that eventually leads to the development of a social identity based on ethnic group membership. Similarly, Peter Weinreich a cross-cultural psychologist (1986: 317 in Rex and Mason) also views identity as:

> *The totality of one's self-construal, in which how one construes oneself in the present expresses the continuity between how one construes oneself as one was in the past and how one construes oneself as one aspires to be in the future.*

Phinney also believes that identity formation and development refers to different identity states where different social contexts influence the identity state and one's actions. However, Weinreich (1986) maintains that ethnic self-identity is not a static process but one that changes and varies according to particular social contexts. Individuals, for example, may avoid situations where their identity is challenged, threatened, humiliated, and castigated; and seek out and sustain whenever possible settings that favour their identity state.

The main difference between Black identity and ethnic identity development from both sociological and psychological theorists perspectives, seems to be in individuals' having the option in the case of their ethnicity to choose whether or not to develop or declare their ethnicity and to perhaps only do so when it is favourable (as ethnicity is not necessarily obvious). While such choices and flexibility are not optional when it comes to racial distinctions such as Black identity.

Theoretical perspective on the effects of racism

Ausdale and Feagin (2001: 9) in their study with nursery age children on how children learn about the 'first R' race, discovered that recurring encounters with racial or ethnic hostility generally accumulate to a greater effect on an individual than a simple sum of the interactive incidents might suggest. They also found that when the 'wounded child' hears negative language, experience exclusion or avoidance, and has to remain alert in order to combat rejection and negative stereotypes for long periods, and eventually a lifetime, the damage assumes critical significance. The damage and critical significance they postulate is not only for the child as an individual or for her or his family and community, but also for the larger society.

They emphasised that racial or ethnic mistreatment is more than a personal matter when considering the impact of such mistreatment on children. They suggested that a child who is a victim of such mistreatment might well share the incident with their family, thereby lightening the burden, but passing on the pain to family members. The family members may in turn share the mistreatment and their pain with other members of the extended family or community. Over time, they suggested and concluded that this sharing contributes to the collective knowledge about racial or ethnic mistreatment that is often important for individual and community survival.

Practice considerations

The cumulative effect of racial and ethnic hostilities and mistreatments on Black young people in their identity development in a secondary school setting

I assessed and provided individual anger management therapeutic sessions to 10 young people in a yearlong research project. It was onsite at a troubled secondary school, where there had been serious incidents of physical violence towards teachers and between students. A uniformed police officer was present at the main reception hall daily. The deputy head teacher in consultation with the heads of year 9 and the year 10 teachers, made the referrals from a waiting list. All three teachers were White and female. Almost all the teachers at the school were White. All the administrative staff were White and female. There was a higher ratio of White students to Black and Minority ethnic students at the school.

The criterion for referral for assessment and anger management sessions was a history of physical aggression. The referred students had either been previously excluded from school for short periods following physical fights on school premises with peers or had verbally threatened staff with physical harm. Some students were on the margin of being permanently excluded from school at the point of referral.

It is important to clarify here that the explorations of the Black young people's narratives on their reported retaliatory or instigating aggressive behaviours are not intended to condone or justify their actions. The focus of this case vignette is two fold:

1. To demonstrate the cumulative effect of recurring encounters with racial and ethnic hostilities and mistreatments on Black young people, which substantiates Ausdale and Feagin's (2001) research findings.
2. To highlight aspects of the students' reactions and behaviours which demonstrated and substantiated the first three stages of the Black identity development models.

The Black young people and their parents' ethnic backgrounds

A total of 10 referred students from the waiting list were seen individually for assessment and anger management sessions on-site at the school. The sessions were weekly, each lasted for 50 minutes. All 10 students said they were born in the UK. Three male students defined their ethnic identity as White British. The remaining seven students defined their ethnic identity as Black British. 6 of the Black students were male and only one was female. Five of the seven Black students defined their parent's ethnicity as Black Caribbean and the remaining two students defined their parent's ethnicity as Black African. Their ethnic descriptions were consistent with that of the ONS (March 2005: 4) which found that:

> . . . Black young people born in Britain tend to define their ethnic identities as 'Black Other' (Black British) even though their parents may be Black Africans or Black Caribbean.

Prior experiences in primary school and in local communities

All the referred students were from years 9 and 10 and were therefore not new to the school. The Black students reported they lived in predominantly multicultural and multiethnic communities where the primary schools they had attended reflected the community population. Their primary schools also had high ratio of Black and Minority ethnic teachers and support staff. There were no known incidents of racial or ethnic hostilities or mistreatments inside or outside the schools. Most families knew each other and Black and White parents collected and delivered each other's children to and from school when they were running late or were unwell.

Experiences at secondary school

As stated earlier each student was seen weekly for 50 minutes during term time on their own on-site at the school in a room discreetly away from the view of other students. It was however necessary to offer additional family sessions to two students with their parents at the NHS mental health clinic to address family relationship issues.

In the individual sessions, the Black students described experiences in which repeated derogatory racial and ethnic name-calling, hostilities, and mistreatments were perpetrated by a particular group of White year 11 students. They initially ignored these behaviours but these intensified and escalated to levels where their mothers were being called derogatory names, described as fat, ugly and promiscuous. Their fathers were said to be absent, drug dealers, jailbirds, or 'Jamaican yardies' even though the White students had never met their parents. Some of the personal comments reported included '. . . we don't need you here any more . . . "Blackie" because the slave trade has long been over

... the jobs on the trains and buses are now taken ... go home to Africa with your HIV/AIDS jungle boy and stop sleeping with our girls'.

These comments reportedly aroused very angry feelings in them, and culminated into heated verbal exchanges during which the year 11 White students asked them to defend their honour by fighting White peers selected and organised by the year 11 White students. They reportedly accepted these fights, believing these would end the recurring racial hostilities and mistreatments at school. The organised physical fights took place away from the school premises immediately after school, with only White peers in observation. They described these physical fights as 'no-win situations'. Those who won their fights became targets for further racial hostilities and physical bullying by other White peers in class, on the playground and outside school seeking revenge. Those who lost their fights also endured further verbal racial hostilities and mistreatments by their White peers who saw them as 'weak'.

The effects of racial and ethnic hostilities and mistreatments on Black young people

The Black students reported not initially perceiving themselves as being different in status from their White peers given their British nationalities, until successive incidents of racial and ethnic hostilities and mistreatments. Each Black student admitted to not ever thinking that they would be perceived by their peers as inferior to 'White people' or seen as 'foreigners' in Britain where they were born and raised, until their first experience of racism.

From the parents and Black students' account in the individual and family sessions, the incidents were at first misconstrued by them as personal dislike. However over time, they noticed the systematic and recurring derogatory racialised language that was being used during the hostilities and mistreatments which 'shocked and horrified' them.

A parent who attended family sessions with her son said it was only on hearing persistent racial and ethnic abusive comments in her son's narrative of the incidents which led to his temporary exclusion from school, that she began to ask pertinent questions about the identities of the perpetrators to determine whether the incidents were racially motivated or not. Her son had been reluctant to share the details of his negative experiences at school with her, as he did not wish to upset her. He also did not want her to report the incidents to the school for fear of being labelled 'mummy's boy' and targeted further.

From the Black students' perspective, their complaints about the incidents to their White teachers at school were either ignored completely or dismissed as 'overly sensitive' reactions. The experience and effect of racism was described as emotionally devastating. The feelings expressed were a mixture of humiliation, deep anger, intimidation, isolation, rejection, feeling worthless as human beings, lacking in confidence, feeling fearful, being irritable, unable to concentrate in class, unable to sleep at night, and being burden with having to keep these feelings and experiences from their parents and families. Two Black students said they retaliated physically to provocations from their White peers in class, in the playground and in the gymnasium without thinking of the possible consequences if caught. The others admitted to starting physical fights at the slightest indication of disagreement even with 'White none aggressive peers' because they felt constantly on edge and distrustful and needed to be vigilant and self protective. The teachers' interventions in response to their observed physical aggression only served to further fuel their anger and feelings of injustice. The resulting behaviour was to distance themselves completely from their White peers, becoming very distrustful of their White teachers, viewing them as biased, unfair, prejudiced, incapable of understanding White racists' manipulative behaviours. They were convinced in their belief that the White teachers could not understand or imagine what it was like to be Black British and young in an extremely race conscious school and society in Britain.

Five of the seven students said they joined Black clubs, visited only Black centres, listened to only Black music and radio stations, and only associated with other Black peers in and outside of school. The remaining two Black students (which included the only female student) admitted to joining a Black neighbourhood 'gang' for security and protection at the school and in the community.

The Black students' reactions to racial and ethnic hostilities and mistreatments were remarkably consistent with the reactions described in the first three stages of the Black identity development models. Although each Black student said they were aware of racial differences in their multi-ethnic and multicultural communities, they admitted they had not thought of themselves as being different from their White peers. The emphasis for them rested on their self-identity as British nationals. Britain was their 'home' and birthplace; therefore they never considered themselves to be foreigners and had believed that their different skin colour was not an issue. Emotionally, cognitively and behaviourally, they each consciously distanced themselves from their White peers, adults and significant others at school and in their communities. They reacted to their negative experiences including rejections, hostilities and mistreatments by acknowledging that prejudice and racism does affect their lives in the education environment and surrounding community (the Encounter stage) and were rejecting with anger the values of the dominant British culture while immersing themselves in their Black culture (Immersion/Emmersion stage).

No further contacts were made with the students at the end of the academic year. It is therefore not possible to know the full continued effect of the above negative experiences on their Black and ethnic identity development at this stage of their developmental life span. The fact that they were all still living at home with their parents and families in what they described as multiethnic and multicultural communities would likely enable them to share their pain,

Effects on looked after Black young people when their Black ethnic identity needs are overlooked and neglected

This case vignette will illustrate the importance of prioritising Black young people's ethnic identity needs in their placement and placement matching.

Parenting assessment referral

Dana Zodiac aged 14 years and her younger sister Kristin Zodiac aged 12 years were referred with their mother Mrs Paula Zodiac for parenting, psychological and child psychiatric assessments by the local authority on the directions of the Family Court. The assessment was to determine whether Dana and Kristin were at significant risk of harm, the nature of their attachment to each parent and whether either parent could adequately care for them with or without supportive services.

The family's background history

Mrs Zodiac became mentally unwell, following several years of non-compliance with her medication, and not keeping outpatient psychiatric appointments. She developed a belief that she was 'God' and referred to her daughters as 'the Christ'. The family's situation came to the attention of the local authority social services department following a failed trip to Lourdes in France, during which Mrs Zodiac had written 'the Christ' with a marker over the surnames in both of her daughters' passports. The Immigration officials halted all three family members' departure from the UK due to their concern about Mrs Zodiac's bizarre presentation, and the girls' lack of plausible explanation for being out of school during term time. Their secondary school had been informed by Mrs Zodiac months earlier that they had returned to Africa permanently.

Mr and Mrs Zodiac had been divorced for seven years. Although they had shared parental responsibility for their daughters, Mrs Zodiac had denied Mr Zodiac contact with both daughters for five years and had accused him of being the devil. He had reportedly ended his contacts with Dana and Kristin for fear of reprisals from Mrs Zodiac, due to her volatile and unpredictable aggressive behaviour.

Both parents defined their ethnic identities as Black Africans. Dana and Kristin were born in the UK and defined their ethnic identities as Black Africans. Mrs Zodiac was a non practising Muslim, her estranged husband was a practising Catholic. Dana and Kristin had been brought up as Catholics attending Catholic schools.

Mr Zodiac worked full-time and lived on his own in a one bedroom privately rented accommodation. Mrs Zodiac had reportedly lost her executive job in a financial company, was unemployed and lived with her two daughters in a housing association two bedroom rented flat. She was receiving housing benefits and income support from the Department of Social Security.

Concerns about Dana and Kristin's physical safety were further heightened during the assessment process when Mrs Zodiac attacked a neighbour's child with a cleaver for spying. She also accused Dana of being possessed by the devil and communicating telepathically with her 'evil father'. Mrs Zodiac secluded herself and her daughters in the flat with the curtains drawn, refused telephone and face-to-face contact with all the professionals involved in the case as well as the police. It was necessary to section Mrs Zodiac as her mental state and behaviour was placing both Diana and Kristin at risk of significant harm. Mr Zodiac was at the time unable to physically care for his daughters therefore an Interim Care Order was granted to the local authority by the family court. This was to enable temporary placement of both girls in a place of safety while the comprehensive parenting, psychological, child psychiatric and adult psychiatric assessments were being carried out.

In the event, Dana and Kristin were placed with three consecutive Black Caribbean foster carers within a six-month period due to placement relationship difficulties. Dana and Kristin continuously requested placement with African carers and not Caribbean carers. The specific distinctions that they were making in their Black ethnic identities through their requests where not perceived as high-priority because they were in a 'same race' matched placement.

Marked physical changes were noted in Dana and Kristin's attitude, behaviour and functioning by my colleague and I and were reflected in our feedback to the social workers and the foster carers. Dana was losing a lot of weight and had become increasingly withdrawn, spending a lot of time on her own in her bedroom in the third placement. Kristin was gaining a lot of weight and was spending a lot of time in the community with her friends from school. Mr Zodiac had expressed concerns about the placements not meeting the ethnic identity needs of his daughters based on his observations and interactions with his daughters during his weekly contacts. The local authority social workers argued that Dana and Kristin had been appropriately placed with experienced 'Black carers' who could adequately meet their identified Black identity needs. The placement relationship difficulties and placement breakdowns were attributed to normal transitional difficulties and not specifically to the carers' inability to address Dana and Kristin's specific 'Black ethnic identity needs'.

Dana's behaviour deteriorated rapidly and resulted in her taking of an overdose of analgesics. She was admitted and treated in hospital. On her return to the placement, my colleague and I were instructed by the court to provide individual therapeutic sessions to Dana and Kristin and to ascertain their wishes and feelings.

During Dana's individual therapeutic sessions with me, she was able over time, to outline the following concerns and feelings:

- She was generally feeling sad and at a loss and was grieving for her mother.
- She had difficulty adjusting to the West Indian dishes that were being provided in all three placements. This was her explanation for her weight loss. Her sister was eating 'junk food' provided by her friends at school and in the community as she had been able to confide to them about being in foster care. She could not however confide in any one at school about being in foster care.
- The first two foster carers had each met her mother. They had also seen her mother when she was very upset at the end of contacts sessions and refusing to leave. Her mother had also arrived at both placements unannounced wearing a long blonde wig, inappropriately dressed and had presented as very confused and agitated. This had resulted in the police being called and her mother being charged with damage to the foster carer's property and vehicle.
- Both foster carers had subsequently asked her questions about whether or not her mother smoked cigarettes, drugs or chewed herbs. She was also asked about African rituals, curses, witchcraft, and spirituality.
- The foster carers frequently referred to her and her sister in conversation with their families and friends as 'the African girls'.
- She was of the view that the foster carers had stereotypical ideas about Black Africans which were negative.
- She believed that the foster carers could not help her make sense of her mother's mental illness because in their culture, mental illness was strongly linked to evil and is therefore a taboo subject not open for discussion.
- The foster carer in the third placement was a Seventh Day Adventist who also had fixed negative views about Africans, African spiritual beliefs in ancestors, Catholic rituals, Muslim traditions and practices, as well as the causes of mental illness.

Dana's overall feelings were that although she was seemingly placed with carers from her own race, there were major gaps in their understanding of her culture and ethnicity. She strongly believed a Black African carer would better understand her even if they were not from the same country as her parents. She also believed a Black African foster carer would have been culturally better able to understand her values beliefs and emotional needs. She said she would have been more able to risk opening up about her fears (e.g. of becoming mentally ill like her mother) to a Black African foster carer and not a Black Caribbean foster carer. In the absence of a Black African foster carer, she insisted on continued individual and family psychotherapeutic sessions with her African systemic psychotherapist following conclusion of the case in the family court.

Conclusion

This chapter has considered the distinctions made in Black ethnic identity in Britain. It has also looked at how Black identities are generally perceived and socially constructed in Britain and America. Definitions of key constructs have been reviewed. Theoretical considerations of empirical literature on identity development have been examined. These have included universal theories of identity development as well as theories on Black identity and ethnic identity development. Two case vignettes have been used to highlight the cumulative effect of racism and ethnic mistreatments on Black young people in their identity development in a secondary school setting as well as serious emotional, cognitive, psychological and behavioural effect on two looked after Black young people when their Black ethnic identity needs were overlooked and neglected.

The chapter has argued that whilst much attention has been given to the racial identity of young people of interracial parentage in their placements matching needs, very little attention has been given to the distinctions made by Black young people in their Black ethnic identity needs. The chapter also evidences (through the case vignettes) the need for recognition of such distinctions and for their incorporation in appropriate care service assessments and provisions. The fact that Black people in Britain do not perceive of themselves as a homogenous group should not be seen as pathological or divisive and must be seen in the same light as the distinctions made in White Scottish, Irish and Welsh ethnicities in Britain. The distinctions that they make in their ethnicities are not questioned or pathologised. They are perceived as healthy and positive due to their distinctive histories, cultures, language and religion.

There is therefore a need for health and social care professionals to be clearer and accepting of Black People's distinctive ethnic identities during assessments. That is their distinctive cultures, language, religion, belief systems and values, if they are serious about meeting the social, emotional, spiritual and religious needs which are fundamental to healthy and positive psychological and social development of looked after Black young people, as stipulated in the Children Act 1989.

The distinctive care needs of Black Caribbean and Black African looked after young people must therefore be prioritised as important developmental needs by social care practitioners and managers when assessing these young people's initial and ongoing placement needs.

Although it would be unrealistic and impossible to find perfect placement matches to meet the identified ethnic identity needs of each Black young person being looked after, careful assessments and appropriate training and support, needs to be especially given to placements in which Black African young people are placed with Black Caribbean carers and where Black Caribbean young people are placed with Black African carers. The importance of spirituality and religion, to these young people's way of life must be recognised as paramount to their psychological and spiritual well-being during these critical periods in their development. Especially when their feelings of separation, loss, anger or the lack of these expressed emotions may seem to be more apparent or prominent.

Health and social care professions and educators need to recognise that looked after Black young people may not always be able to verbally articulate their ethnic identity needs at the time of placement, at the placement, at school or even in counselling sessions.

Greater emphasis needs to be placed on contact sessions between looked after Black young people and their families as it is a major resource for their healthy ethnic identity development. Where this is not possible, contacts with the extended family, kinship ties and links to their ethnic communities including their churches and mosques will need to be forged and strengthened.

There is a need for higher education institutions which offer undergraduate and postgraduate degrees in social work to incorporate Cross and colleagues' models of Black identity development in their core programmes e.g. human development and social work theory curriculum for all social workers in training. This should also be incorporated into all the Post qualifying (PQ) courses.

Cross and colleagues' model should also be used in social services department training courses as well as in child and adolescent mental health services (CAMHS) training courses as part of their mandatory continuous professional development training (CPD) for all professionals. This would aid the professionals' understanding of identity confusion in Black children and adolescents in residential, fostered and adoptive care settings.

These important distinctions in Black Caribbean and Black African ethnic identities and their implications for looked after Black young people need to be acknowledged, respected and addressed (in the same way as those of children of interracial parentage in Britain) if the welfare of Black young people is to be safeguarded effectively and if they are to be prepared for life in a multi-racial and multi-ethnic society in Britain.

Looked after Black young people need to be supported to develop resilience, use and employ community resources, observe and model appropriate role models who they can identify with to develop positive self-images for themselves and envisage their presence as important, valued and cherished members of the community. Black young people need to be proud of who they are, where they come from, and the future citizens that they will become.

References

Ausdale, D. and Feagan, J. (2002) *The First R: How Children Learn Race and Racism*. Oxford: Rowman and Littlefield.

Banks, N. (1992) Techniques for Direct Identity Work With Black Children. *Adoption and Fostering*, 16: 3, 19–25.

Banks, N. (1995) Children of Black Mixed Parentage and Their Placements Needs. *Adoption and Fostering*, 19: 2, 19–24.

Banks, N. (2002) Mixed Race Children and Families. In Dwivedi, K.N. *Meeting The Needs of Ethnic Minority Children*. London: Jessica Kingsley.

Barn, R. (1999) (Ed.) *Working With Black Children and Adolescents in Need*. London: BAAF.

Barn, R. and Harman, V. (2005) A Contested Identity: an Exploration of The Competing Social and Political Discourse Concerning The Identification and Positioning of Young People of Inter-Racial Parentage. *British Journal of Social Work*, 1–16.

BBC (2006) *Black Britons Find Their African Roots*. 14th Feb. [cited 20th Oct. 2006].

BBC (2006) *Short History of Immigration*. [cited 20th Oct. 2006].

Biehal, N. et al. (1995) *Moving On*. London: HMSO.

Birmingham Council (2006) *Birmingham's Post War Black Immigrants*. [cited 20th October 2006] Birmingham.gov.uk.

Black and in Care (1984) *Black and in Care Conference Report*, Blackrose Press.

Chestang, L. (1972) The Dilemma of Biracial Adoption. *Social Work*, 17: 100–15.

Chevannes, B. (1998) *Rastafari and Other African-Caribbean Worldviews*. New Jersey: Rutgers University Press.

Coopersmith, S. (1967) *The Antecedents of Self-Esteem*. San Francisco: Freeman.

Corby, B. (2000) Looked After Children. In Davies, M. (Ed.) *The Blackwell Encyclopaedia of Social Work*. Oxford: Blackwell Publishing.

Cross, W.E. (1991) *Shades of Black: Diversity in African American Identity*. Philadelphia: Temple University Press.

Cross, W.E., Parham, T. and Helms, J. (1991) The Stages of Black Identity Development: Negriscense Models. In Jones, R. (Ed.) *Black Psychology* (4th edn.). Hampton, VA: Cobb and Henry.

DfES (2006) *Ethnicity and Education: The Evidence on Minority Ethnic Pupils Aged 5–16*. DfES.

Divine, D. (1983) Defective, Hypocritical and Patronising Research. *Caribbean Times*, 4 March.

DoH (1976) *Adoption Act 1976*. London: HMSO.

DoH (1989) *The Children Act 1989*. London: HMSO.

DoH (1998) *Adoption: Achieving The Right Balance*. Local Authority Circular LAC (98) 20.

DoH (2002) *Adoption and Children Act 2002*. London: HMSO.

Fatimilehin, I. (1999) Of Jewel Heritage: Racial Socialisation and Racial Identity Attitudes Amongst Adolescents of Mixed African-Caribbean/White Parentage. *Journal of Adolescence*, 22: 303–18.

Firth, H. (1995) *Children First: A Framework for Action*. Hampshire County Council.

Fletcher, B. (1993) *Not Just A Name: The Views of Young People in Foster and Residential Care*. London: Who Cares About Education, National Consumer Council and Who Cares Trust.

Gill, D., Mayor, B. and Blair, M. (1992) *Racism and Education Structure and Strategies*. Sage.

Gill, O. and Jackson, B. (1983) *Adoption and Race*. London: Batsford/BAAF.

Goodyer, A. (2005) Direct Work With Children of Mixed Parentage. In Okitikpi, T. (Ed.) *Working With Children of Mixed Parentage*. Lyme Regis: Russell House Publishing.

Gross, R. (2001) *Psychology The Science of Mind and Behaviour*. 4th edn. Kent: Hodder and Sloughton.

Hall, S. (1995) Negotiating Caribbean Identities. *New Left Review*, 1: 209, Jan–Feb.

Harman, V. and Barn, R. (2005) Exploring The Discourse Concerning White Mothers of Mixed Parentage Children. In Okitikpi, T. (Ed,) *Working With Children of Mixed Parentage*. Lyme Regis: Russell House Publishing.

Ince, L. (1999) Preparing Young Black People From Leaving Care. In Barn, R. (Ed.) *Working With Black Children and Adolescents in Need*. London: BAAF.

Katz, I. (1996) *The Construction of Racial Identity in Children of Mixed Parentage: Mixed Metaphors*. London: Jessica Kingsley.

Kuhn, H. and Mcpartland, T. (1954) An Empirical Investigation of Self Attitudes. *American Sociological Review*, 47: 647–52.

Mason, D. (1995) *Race and Ethnicity in Modern Britain*. Oxford: Oxford University Press.

Maxime, J. (1993) The Importance of Racial Identity for Psychological Well Being of Black Children. *Association of Child Psychology and Psychiatry Newsletter,* 15: 4, 173–9.

Mbuti, J. (1991) *Introduction to African Religion.* Harcourt Heinemann.

Milner, D. (1983) *Children and Race: Ten Years On.* London: Ward Lock Educational.

National Archives (2006) *Citizenship 1906–2003.* [cited 20th Oct. 2006].

Office for National Statistics (2005) *Census 2001.*

Okitikpi, T. (1999) Educational Needs of Black Children in The Care System. In Barn, R. (Ed.) *Working With Black Children and Adolescents in Need.* London: BAAF.

Okitikpi, T. (2005) Identity and Identification: How Mixed Parentage Children Adapt to A Binary World. In Okitikpi, T. (Ed.) *Working With Children of Mixed Parentage.* Lyme Regis: Russell House Publishing.

Olumide, G. (2002) *Raiding The Gene Pool: The Social Construction of Mixed Race.* London: Pluto.

Osler, A. (1997) *Exclusion From School and Racial Equality.* London: CRE.

Owen, C. (2005) Looking at Numbers and Projections: Making Sense of The Census and Emerging Trends. In Okitikpi, T. (Ed.) *Working With Children of Mixed Parentage.* Lyme Regis: Russell House Publishing.

Owusu-Bempah, J. and Howitt, D. (2000) *Psychology Beyond Western Perspectives.* Oxford: BPS Blackwell.

Owusu-Bempah, K. (2005) Mulatto, Marginal Man, Half-Caste, Mixed Race: The One Drop Rule in Professional Practice. In Okitikpi, T. (Ed.) *Working With Children of Mixed Parentage.* Lyme Regis: Russell House Publishing.

Patel, N., Naik, D. and Humphries, B. (1997) (Eds.) *Visions of Reality: Religion and Ethnicity in Social Work,* Sage.

Patel, T., Williams, C. and Mash, P. (2004) Identity, Race, Religion and Adoption: The Public and Legal View. *Adoption and Fostering,* 28: 1, 6–15.

Ponterrotto, J. and Pedersen, P. (1993) *Preventing Prejudice: A Guide for Counsellors and Educators.* Sage Publications.

Prevatt-Goldstein, B. (1999) Direct Work With Black Children With A White Mother. In Barn, R. (Ed.) *Working With Black Children and Adolescents in Need.* London: BAAF.

Robinson, L. (2002) Social Work Through The Life Course. In Adams, R., Dominelli, L. and Payne, M. *Social Work: Themes, Issues and Critical Debates.* 2nd edn. Open University Press.

Robinson, L. (2005) Working With Children of Mixed Parentage. In Okitikpi, T. (Ed.) *Working With Children of Mixed Parentage.* Lyme Regis: Russell House Publishing.

Small, J. (1984) The Crisis in Adoption. *International Journal of Psychiatry,* 30, Spring.129–42.

Smith, A. (1997) *Navigating The Deep River: Spirituality in African American Families.* Cleveland Ohio: United Church Press.

Song, M. (2003) *Choosing Ethnic Identity.* Cambridge: Polity Press.

Stone, M. (1981) *The Education of The Black Child in Britain: Myth of Multiracial School.* Fontana.

Tatum, B. (1992) Talking About Race, Learning About Racism: The Application of Racial Identity Development Theory in The Classroom. *Harvard Educational Review,* 62: 1–24.

Thoburn, J. (2005) Permanent Family Placement for Children of Dual Heritage: Issues Arising From A Longitudinal Study. In Okitikpi, T. (Ed.) *Working With Children of Mixed Parentage.* Lyme Regis: Russell House Publishing.

Thompson, N. (2006) *People Problems.* Basingstoke, Palgrave Macmillan.

Tizard, B. and Phoenix, A. (2002) *Black White or Mixed-Race? Race and Racism in The Lives of Young People of Mixed Parentage.* (Revised Edition) London: Routledge.

Trimble, J. and Dickson, R. (2005) Ethnic Identity. In Fisher, C.B. and Lerner, R.M. (Eds.) *Applied Developmental Science: an Encyclopaedia of Research, Policies and Programs.* Thousand Oaks: Sage.

Troyna, B. (1986) *Racism, Education and The State.* Croom Helm.

Troyna, B. and Carrington, (1990) *Education, Racism and Reform.* London: Routledge.

Weinreich, P. (1986) The Operationalisation of Identity Theory in Racial and Ethnic Relations. In Rex. J. and Mason, D. (Eds.) *Theories of Race and Ethnic Relations.* Cambridge: Cambridge University Press.

Wilson, A. (1996) How We Find Ourselves: Identity Development and Two-Spirit People. *Harvard Educational Review.* 66: 2. 1–13.

News (BBC) Sources

Black Britons find their African roots (2003) BBC news, 14th February, www.news.bbc.co.uk.

Short history of immigration (n.d.) BBC news – Race UK: Background, www.news.bbc.co.uk.

Birmingham's Post War Black Immigrants (n.d.) Birmingham Council, www.news.bbc.co.uk.

Brave New world: citizenship 1906–2003 (n.d.) The National Archives Website, www.nationalar-chives.gov.uk

Internet Sources

Christianity graduation (n.d.) www.answers.com

Rites of passage (2000) www.webpages.uidaho.edu.

Valuing Diversity (n.d.) www.scotland.gov.uk/library/documents.

Black British: History (n.d.) www.en.wikipedia.org/wiki/Black_British.

Black British (2007, January 9) In *Wikipedia, The Free Encyclopedia.* www.en.wikipedia.org/w/index.php?title=Black_Britishandoldid=99555657

The 'Windrush' generation (n.d.) www.reference.com/browse/wiki/British_African-Caribbean.community .

British African-Caribbean Community: Religion (n.d.) www.reference.com/browse/wiki/British_African-Caribbean_community

CHAPTER 4

Challenging the Stereotypes: Reaching the Hard to Reach, Young Black Men

Jennifer Izekor

Introduction

Often described as the 'hard to reach, the disengaged and disaffected; young, black, men are a constantly shifting group aged between the ages of 15–19. I use the term 'black', here narrowly, to refer to young people of African and Caribbean descent whether they are from Africa or the Caribbean. The term is also used to refer to people of dual heritage where one parent is either of African or Caribbean descent. The descriptors vary but not much; 'low-achievers, socially excluded, hard to reach, at risk of offending, not participating, difficult to engage'. As a professional working initially alongside policy makers and now as a contributor to government policy, I have spent countless meetings, conferences and events discussing the same rhetorical questions, dogged by the same themes, and what often seems the same issues – how do we reach the unreachable, engage the disaffected, include the excluded and identify what works?

From 2001 to 2005, I led one of the largest Connexions Partnerships in England covering ten inner and outer London Boroughs. My role brought me into contact directly and indirectly with many of the young men whose issues challenged policy makers and practitioners alike. There were many solutions, some which worked better than others but above all, the challenging questions remained – who are these young black men, what are their stories and how are their lives dogged and influenced by the stereotypes that society holds of them.

In my role, I met many young black boys, articulate and ambitious for the future and sometimes still full of the innocence of childhood, I often wondered at what stage they would become members of the 'socially excluded club' and at what stage in their young lives would the battle for their future be lost or won and who were the main protagonists? There is no doubt that deprivation and poverty play their part, these children are not alone in that particular group, yet for them, society will remain unforgiving in its categorisation and they will often move into their adult lives feeling shut out and with little hope of enjoying the best society has to offer. What goes wrong and how much do the labels and stereotypes that we 'stick' on these young men contribute to the poor outcomes they experience? In our zeal to help and solve the problems have we all become guilty of negative stereotyping that almost blinds us to the real issues and threatens to label all young black men irrespective of the progress they make or the natural skills, talents or abilities they are born with?

Recent reports would suggest that the attainment rates of black pupils are gradually beginning to improve (DfES *Ethnicity and Education*, 2006). Yet all young black men, irrespective of their status or economic successes, high or low-achievers, will deal with the challenge and impact of negative stereotyping at some point in their lives. For those who 'make it', either academically or indeed professionally, they will learn to wryly brush off the negative stereotyping that they will encounter in their everyday lives despite their success, and hopefully learn to treat each encounter with wry, cynical humour. For those who do not achieve academically or indeed are caught up in the deprivation and poor socio-economic factors that plague their communities, negative stereotyping, discrimination and their own misplaced coping strategies will combine to keep them excluded and act as proverbial millstones around their necks that keep them from ever achieving their full potential in their communities or for themselves.

In the beginning . . .

Perhaps the starting point is the school environment where it would appear young black people still seem to be excluded from school more often than their counterparts. Even in 2006, the national statistics for secondary schools still tell a rather dismal story:

- *In 2004/05 around 26 in every 10,000 pupils of mixed ethnic origin were permanently excluded from school.*
- *Almost 8 in every 100 pupils of Black and Mixed ethnic origin were excluded for a fixed period in 2004/05. This compares with almost 6 in every 100 pupils of White ethnic origin and around 2 in every 100 Asian pupils.*

National Statistics DFES (SFR24/2006)

In 2001, Ofsted commented that:

> *The reasons are rarely clear cut, but many Black pupils who find themselves subject to disciplinary procedures perceive themselves to have been unfairly treated . . . Black pupils were more likely to be excluded for what was defined by schools as 'challenging behaviour'.*

(Ofsted, 2001: 20)

According to Wright et al. (2005) a number of studies (in Gillborn and Gipps, 1996; Wright et al., 2000; Blair, 2001) have shown that these young people have not usually demonstrated disruptive behaviour prior to attending secondary school and are not uninterested in education. So how is it that many young black boys appear to become increasingly 'disruptive' as they progress from primary to secondary school?

A number of reports including that from the LDA *The Educational Experiences and Achievements of Black Boys in Schools 2002–2003* (September,2004), noted that young black boys often feel stereotyped within the school setting:

> *Pupil questionnaire comments, in response to being asked whether Black pupils had different experiences to white pupils, indicated that racism was the most significant factor. Being wrongly accused, watched with suspicion at lunchtimes, subject to negative stereotyping and simply being disliked on account of being Black were cited as different experiences for Black pupils. In the words of three students:*
> *'For instance gangs around the school, when it's white boys it's a group but when it's Black boys it's a gang and I think that's wrong.''*

'They are more likely to get in trouble for something even if a white pupil does the same.''

'If a white person did something bad and the black person did it with them, the black person will get a worse punishment than the other and all teachers will know about it.'

LDA (2004)

Prejudice, discrimination and negative stereotypes all work together to limit the potential of many young black boys from a very early age. It is fair to say that they are often ably aided and abetted by negative and bullish attitudes of the young men themselves, who respond to their perceived socio-enemies by seemingly fulfilling the stereotypes and finding new ways of hitting back at society that seems determined to see them as problems that need to be solved. The child and their teacher often find themselves caught in a vicious circle with the child becoming increasingly resentful of what they see as being 'unfairly picked on' and the teacher having to deal with increasingly resentful, angry behaviour. As the young men grow older, this childish resentment turns into adolescent angst that displays itself in an attitude of angry indifference often mistaken by educators as a lack of motivation or aspiration. I have met many young black boys whose eyes have betrayed their cool devil-may-care exterior; it is not that they lack aspiration or ambition but rather that they work hard to keep it concealed as this in itself is protection from a world that they perceive may make mockery of those ambitions by telling them that they are unrealistic and unachievable:

This phenomenon was recognised as the 'cool pose' approach by Majors and Billson (1992) and highlighted by Osborne and Majors (2001). They argue that Black males adopt a 'cool pose', or a ritualised form of masculinity that allows that boy or man to cope and survive in an environment of social oppression and racism. According to Majors and Billson, cool pose allows the black male to survive by projecting a front of emotionlessness, fearlessness, and aloofness that counters inner pain from damaged pride, poor self-confidence, and fragile social competence that comes from existing as a member of a subjugated group. Unfortunately, as with Steele's notion, cool pose depicts black males as victims of their coping strategies. In terms of education, cool pose often leads to behaviors, such as flamboyant and non-conformist behavior, that often elicit punishment in school settings. Equally unfortunately, the development of a cool self-concept appears to be incompatible with a hard-driving, motivated, identified student. Thus, black boys, according to this perspective, adopt a strategy for coping with group membership that appears to be incompatible with identification with academics.

(Osborne, 2004 online 48)

If this phenomenon is to be taken into consideration then it stands to reason that from a very early age, for many young black boys, the rules of engagement have been defined and it is only a matter of time before they completely lock horns with authority in a bid to either challenge or fulfil the negative stereotypes they encounter. It is often a one sided battle that can end with a permanent exclusion from the school system, leaving school with little or no qualifications or even worse becoming involved in anti-social behaviour.

For parents who try to get involved, the experience can be equally dire – Debra a 27 year old single mother of two mixed origin boys, remembers her painful encounters:

The teachers looked down on you, you could tell what they were thinking – here we go, a single mom, no dad, no control, I felt patronised and angry. They had nothing good to say about K, it was as if everything he did was bad and while I wanted to work with them, I felt someone had to stand up for my child and I wasn't going to let them treat him like that.

Hane, D.

Like many parents, Debra got into several arguments with her son's teachers and began to feel she had to protect her son from his teachers. Any chances of the school and Debra working together to address what was obviously in some cases challenging behaviour by K was lost by both sides taking opposing stances. Mindful of her own negative experiences in school, Debra lost all trust for the school and what it represented and it was perhaps unsurprising that K did not achieve his full potential in that setting.

Many schools are now forming successful partnerships with parents from all sections of the community, yet it is fair to say that Debra's experiences are more commonplace than not and this tussle between parent and teachers often leaves the young person a casualty of a senseless battle. Parents like Debra confess to getting angry and responding in a less than positive manner; the schools confronted with an angry black parent will often adopt a siege mentality, setting up each meeting with ample representation from the school, ensuring the setting is overtly formal and all precautions are taken to ensure accurate records are kept with a view to future appeals or litigation. The procedure becomes less of an opportunity to create a partnership to meet the child's needs and more of a point scoring exercise on both sides with the parent at an obvious disadvantage. For the parent this formality becomes even more intimidating and their natural defence mechanisms set in.

If we are to address this issue then we must tackle the challenge of negative stereotyping in the educational system and while there is much to do to raise aspirations and motivation among young black men and to encourage parents to work *with* the school, the real challenge is to teach the teachers and form real learning partnerships between parents from the black communities. Together, they can and will challenge the effects of negative stereotyping and ensure that they do not create barriers to the lives of pupils.

I believe negative and positive stereotypes will always exist in the minds of all adults and teachers are no exception. The media play a great role in shaping our view of society and particularly young black men and boys. Unfortunately, as Debra's example shows, it is not just the negative stereotypes of young black boys that come into play in their early years. Often their parents are equally victims of negative stereotyping, particularly single mothers, and in turn they too can be guilty of stereotyping even the teachers who genuinely wish to engage with their children and deal with poor behaviour. For such a teacher confronted with a hostile, suspicious parent, the experience can be demotivating and stop them from future interventions that could pull many other young black boys from the brink of exclusion.

Schools can work harder to address this issue by listening to the black children in the school and providing opportunities for them to discuss how negative stereotyping influences their lives within the school setting. This approach needs to start from the presumption that negative stereotyping of black children particularly boys does exist within society and indeed in each educational institution. Even the most enlightened and liberal minded school cannot smother its existence but they can rob it of its potency by exposing it and providing a range of opportunities for it to be confronted, dissected and challenged. These opportunities must involve children and their parents working with all staff not just the teaching staff. Dinner ladies, nurses and other school staff should be given safe spaces in which to explore the fears, concerns and media influences that shape their perceptions and are likely to influence their interactions with black children. Work can also be done with black boys to challenge their perceptions of themselves and how their behaviour can be perceived by others who are challenged by media stereotypes.

Organisations like *Black Boys Can* and *Black Male Forum* have developed tools to teach young black men to challenge discrimination in a more positive way, to hold onto their aspirations and to excel in education. The government's programme for Extended School services is providing more opportunities for parents to engage in the school environment which in itself breaks down many of the communication walls between parents and teaching staff. A continued shared sense of ownership between parents and the school will lead to better outcomes for young black boys and minimise the effects that stereotyping will have on them in later life.

Making them hard to reach

For youth workers, Connexions advisers and a range of other professionals engaging with young people outside the school setting, the challenge of negative stereotyping is of a different nature. Unlike the school setting, the young black men they are most concerned about are not a 'captive audience'. They are often described as 'hard to reach, difficult to engage, the marginalised, socially excluded or simply young men from BME communities'. Personally, I have always found the last category the most difficult to deal with. It is an incredibly wide grouping that means all things and nothing all at once. Five words that attempt to wrap up the needs, desires and challenges of young men from north, south, west, east and central Africa, the many islands of the Caribbean, most of eastern Europe, Asia, Muslim, Christian, Sikh, gypsy, Irish and every other minority community in England at any given time. It denotes in many ways a lack of understanding and effort by all of us who use the phrase to understand the needs of each group and to recognise that the solutions and methodology for meeting the needs of each group will and must be different. It is perhaps the most powerful negative stereotype of them all. So who are the young black men who are hard to reach and what role have negative stereotypes played in pushing them to the margins of society. In 2004, in London East Connexions Partnership we consulted a number of young black fathers as part of Black History month about their perceptions of how society viewed them. The young men from a range of black communities and aged between 18–21 had mixed views:

> It's like they expect you to be bad, expect that you are going to give them grief so you do it anyway.
>
> David 18

> Just because you dress or talk a certain way they think they know all about you, where you are coming from, what you need.
>
> Shaun

It was never quite clear who 'they' were, but for those of us who were practitioners and service deliverers, the young men's body language pointed at us in silent accusation. By the end of the evening, I was left wondering who were the 'hard to reach', was it the young men who by all accounts (including the media) prowled the streets, skulked in street corners or dominated the poverty ridden estates or was it us, the service providers, the helpers and do-gooders who had somehow created a world where we were too far removed from the young black men who tried to reach us? Were we listening or so busy debating and discussing their needs that we had forgotten to ask the one set of experts there were – the young men themselves. When we did ask them, how much did we really listen to what they had to say and what changed as a result?

There is no shortage of experts or expert opinion; the youth work annual calendar is full of courses, programmes and seminars aimed at enlightening practitioners on how best to 'reach the hard to reach'. Noted authors and scholars from both sides of the Atlantic have written numerous articles on the very issue, yet it seems that for all this technical knowledge, the truth is still evasive and the solutions to the problem of engaging and improving the outcomes for many young black men remain elusive and beyond our grasp.

Perhaps the real challenge lies not in reaching these young people, who by all media accounts are very accessible either on the said street corners or indeed in the criminal justice system, but in service providers convincing these young black men that they are genuinely interested in working with them. Working to change the patterns and lifestyle circumstances that have pushed them to the margins of society and more importantly that they can and will have a real *lasting* impact on their lives and circumstances.

This is not to suggest that there are not organisations and practitioners who are not capable of getting this message across very clearly. As a practitioner and later service provider, I came across many black male and female workers who were committed to supporting young black men to overcome barriers, yet there was a part of me that wondered how effective we all were in supporting these young men past the 'survival mode' and onto the platform from which they could really achieve.

In the late 1990s, I worked in Centrepoint Vauxhall Hostel, a 26 bed hostel for young, single homeless people aged 16–25 in South London. As a project worker and later project manager, I worked alongside many talented and skilled youth workers/project workers. Many of those colleagues, particularly the black men, were themselves victims of an unjust system at a time when society did not accept the existence of institutional racism as defined in the Macpherson Report (1999). How much had this influenced their approach to working with young black men and did it in itself create barriers to engaging the hard to reach for other non-black staff who felt threatened not just by the black young men but often by the black male staff who seemed to so easily identify with them and in some cases almost speak a common language.

Over the years I have spoken to many black male colleagues who have felt caught in this particular quandary. They have felt trapped between supporting and advocating on behalf of young black men, who they see being stereotyped and discriminated against by the very systems set up to protect them, and colleagues who have questioned their 'loyalty' to the system because they are seen to be 'too close' to the young men and not in keeping with professional boundaries.

Another side to this coin is the desire to 'can or bottle' what it is in these relationships between these black male staff and the young black men that make the difference and to define it in academic terms that will fit into a youth or social work course and can be taught to others.

My experience would suggest that neither of these approaches is productive; for the black male staff, the pressure can often prove their undoing and I have seen many colleagues' crash and burn as they have tried to switch between the demands of their clients and fellow staff. The challenges young black boys face in school settings are often replicated in hostels, youth centres and community projects across the board. Negative stereotyping, labelling and discrimination are often even more difficult to challenge in these settings and lead to young black men disengaging from these services as well as demotivation among black staff.

Yet if we are to reach the young black men who today appear to be disengaged and marginalised, then some of the vital clues to successful engagement lie with the black men who are today in their early thirties and have failed to achieve their full potential in their chosen field. The challenge is not to find and 'bottle' the secret of their engagement with these young black men but rather to develop them professionally and personally to positions where they can positively influence the nature and shape of services developed to meet the needs of young black men who are disengaged.

I have found it continuously surprising that despite the proliferation of black social workers, youth and care workers at a practitioner level, the numbers of black staff lessen considerably as you look at the top levels of any of the major professional groupings that engage most with young black men on the margins.

As a Chief Executive of one of the 47 Connexions Partnerships, I was one of only two black CEOs and I have got used to being the only black person on many of the national working groups I have attended in the past. What is it that keeps black practitioners from climbing the ladder within these professions and what bearing does this phenomenon have on the outcomes for many of the young black men they work with? Are negative stereotypes at play here too and if so, how do we combat them and reduce their ability to blight the lives of young black men and staff alike.

This writer does not propose to hold the answers to these questions but recognises that they are questions that need to be asked. Can workers who are themselves disillusioned by a system that closes its doors to their professional progression inspire young black men to aspire? Engagement is perhaps the easy bit, but these young men need more than workers who will teach them to survive or indeed empathise with their situations; they need role models who will inspire, professional achievers not just survivors and people who have a different set of experiences and tales to share of success and achievement and not discrimination and frustration. If we are to turn the tide, we must begin to create those young men now, to provide the opportunities in the teaching profession, in youth work, in social care, in education and the civil service, opportunities at management level and at policy decision making levels that allow for a meaningful engagement, but most importantly, realistically challenge the perceptions of these young men that aspiring to achieve is in itself a pointless exercise in futility.

Working with young black men to challenge stereotypes

Negative stereotypes are a fact of life and for young black men, the media is a potent and deadly enemy taking great pains to re-enforce the stereotypical characters that feed the fears of the community particularly around criminality and anti-social behaviour. It would be easy to suggest that these stereotypes of young black men are held solely within the non-black communities, yet as the controversial Channel 4 programme 'Shoot the Messenger' dared to suggest, the 'black community' is no innocent bystander when it comes to the issue of negative stereotyping of black young men and if we are to challenge its impact then we need to start from within and ask what part we, the community including some young black men play in reinforcing the stereotypes and proving fodder for the gaping jaws of the press.

As black parents, we have the power to shape the attitudes of our children and this is where we can arm them with the right tools to challenge the stereotypes. Many successful men and women set out to reach the top of their chosen field because they were told they couldn't. It is not enough to say that young black men fail because the school expects them to, as parents we have the power to counter those messages, to teach our sons to strive for success, to beat the odds and to believe in themselves. This calls for a new approach to parenting, an approach that differs from that of the parental generations of the 1960s and late 1950s when our parents believed in strict parenting that kept children in check but often at the expense of damaged self-belief and low self-esteem. A new approach that creates confident but not arrogant young black boys with an infallible belief in their ability to succeed and an unshakeable belief in their self worth and value in their community and in their homes. There are no quick and easy solutions but as more emphasis is placed on parenting skills by the government, there is an opportunity to develop the specialist field of parenting black boys drawing on the skills and expertise of child psychologists, educators and the community to develop an approach that can be shared with parents of young children as part of the foundation stage learning.

This approach to parenting needs to continue as young black boys grow into men. Much is made in the media of the absence of black fathers and its impact on the development of young black men. It is true to say that for many young black men, the closest thing they may have to a role model is the gangster rapper or a male figure in the world of sport. We do need more black male role models in professional fields and where they exist we must challenge the perception among young black boys that they are 'coconuts' or indeed 'oddities' for having made it that far. Here too parents can help. Single mothers with teenage sons should be encouraged to tap into community mentoring schemes to seek mentors for their sons and black professional men could be offered incentives to become mentors.

Raising a son in modern times alone is no easy task. For every positive message a single parent tries to give, there are a swathe of media images saying different things. I have been saddened by the number of single mothers of teenage sons I have met who have watched helplessly as their sons have slid off the rails. Often they have been isolated from their families and with no-one to help they have floundered against the professionals who have treated them as part of the problem and not the solution. National Parent line provides some support but perhaps in the future there is a role for local parenting centres with specialist staff to meet the needs of single parents who need to find a way to pull their sons back from the brink.

Support groups, training sessions and one to one sessions may equip these parents with coping strategies that may in themselves lead to more young black boys being raised to stay engaged with the educational system and to more effective and equal partnerships between the school and parents. For young mothers who have found themselves pregnant at an early age and with a teenage son and no dad, schools can be intimidating judgmental places, and the onus is on schools who wish to engage with such parents to find a way of doing this in a non-threatening environment that does not belittle the parent and child. This is an issue not just for single parents but also for those who have not experienced the British educational system who can be equally intimidated and belittled. There is an increasing role for outreach work from schools that leads to more meaningful engagement with parents in non-threatening environments and builds real relationships with the communities their children come from.

For young black boys within the school system, traditional youth work has much to offer in building self-esteem and self-worth. Schemes like the Duke of Edinburgh award and a host of others that offer children from deprived communities the ability to shine and excel at informal activities as part of the school curriculum. As aforementioned, schools need to create opportunities for open dialogue with black boys about their experiences within the school system and through that dialogue address the impact of negative stereotyping on both sides. I would go so far as to suggest that where possible schools invite previous pupils back and ask about their experiences and determine particularly if they have become disengaged and socially excluded what role their experiences in the school played in the paths they had since taken. Some of the messages may be hard to hear but they would form the basis on which to build new practices, policies and procedures that would meet the needs of a new generation.

For those working with young black men in the social care field the issues are similar; training courses, qualifications and practical experience are no substitute for honest dialogue about the experiences of black staff and clients of the service and the relationship between the two. This is a dialogue that must happen if services are to meet the needs of young black people particularly young black men. I am not suggesting that black managers are promoted at the expense of their white counterparts to respond to this challenge but there is an issue that needs exploring if black staff are constantly pipped at the post for management positions in the very fields that purport to wish to engage with disaffected black boys or if the majority of disciplinary actions are being taken out against black male staff.

In turn black male workers must appreciate that in order to meet the needs of these young men they can only be part of a whole system that works together to re-engage these young men effectively and move them onto successful outcomes in education, employment or training. It is not enough to empathise with their experiences or to teach them the skills they need to survive each day, the challenge is to teach them to challenge the stereotypes not with anger or their fists but with success and the achievement of their full potential even in the face of the greatest odds. The challenge is not to get them into the first job that comes along but to get them to see beyond that job or training course, to begin to picture and draw a future that sees them as a positive role model for their sons and sees them as well-adjusted members of society enjoying the best that life has to offer – an unrealistic dream or a potential reality.

Challenging the Media Stereotypes

In the search for images and stories that will attract audiences, the media tend to focus on issues of crime, violence, tragedy and disaster. (Check the local TV news to see how much coverage they give to what the police and fire departments did today!) While car crashes and shootings are sure-fire attention grabbers, a steady diet of these images can give us a distorted view of what goes on in the world. The negative slant of the news means that when young people (and members of other minority groups) do appear in the headlines, it is most often in the context of crime, drugs, violence, death, or some other alarming issue'.

(www.media-awareness.ca 2006)

Media stereotypes will always play a major part in shaping our view of the world and when it comes to young black boys, it is no different. Gangsters, hoodies, yobs etc are part of a staple diet fed through the mainstream media, yet it could be argued that they are reporting the news and that our distaste for the sensationalism does not detract from the fact that the images they project are based on real crimes and real issues.

Is there room to challenge the negative portrayal of black young men in the press? This is a question that remains to be answered, to change this approach we would need to change the slant of news itself and this may be a bridge too far. We can, however, in our relationships with young black men as clients or children, challenge their perception of the media's motives and demonstrate that they are not alone in the onslaught of negative stereotyping in the press. We can work together to highlight the positive images and to treat hysterical reporting with the disdain it deserves.

Conclusion

There is no doubt that negative stereotypes have a damaging impact on the lives of young black men, yet I believe the impact is more powerful because we are guilty of not taking the right steps to challenge its domain and the ability of those who use it to marginalise these young men and prevent them from achieving their full potential. To challenge it effectively, we must all work in partnership, a partnership that consists of schools, parents, policy makers, practitioners, young black men and black men generally.

We must listen to the voices of those young men who find themselves victims; their words may not be spoken across meeting room tables or indeed in seminars but rather in the hard-hitting lyrics of rap, in poetry or other artistic forms. As policy makers and practitioners we must listen.

Parents can and will play a key role in raising the aspirations of young black boys but this is not a skill that will come easily particularly to those who themselves are victims of the system. They need help and support and if we are serious about raising the achievement and aspirations of young black boys then we must recognise the vital role that parents can play in shaping the ability of these children to deal with the stereotyping they will experience in their lifetimes and to develop the tools that will see them overcome and excel.

Practitioners also have a role to play. I have seen first hand the effect that positive black men as youth workers, Connexions advisers, project workers, social workers and others can have on young black boys but that interaction can only lead to consistently positive outcomes if the professional environment in itself has tackled discrimination and attitudes that limit the potential of those workers despite their skills and expertise.

Finally, we may not be able to challenge the media stereotypes but we can point young men towards the stories that the media ignore. History books are full of positive black role models who defied the odds and succeeded despite the barriers they faced. As parents and black practitioners it is our job to raise their profile and tell their story and indeed to create our own stories by striving to succeed and by challenging the stereotypes in our personal and professional lives

I am one of two black female senior civil servants, it has been hard and like the young men I have written about I too have had to deal with the burden of negative stereotyping but as a single mother of a 10 year old black child, I unashamedly push my daughter academically with the mantra – 'you can be anything you want to be if you work hard enough and don't let anybody tell you anything different' – just in case someone tries!

References

BBC2 (2006) *Shoot the Messenger.* BBC2, 30 August, 9p.m.

DfES (2006) *Ethnicity and Education: The Evidence on Minority Ethnic Pupils aged 5–16.* Nottingham: DfES.

DfES (2006) *Permanent and Fixed Period Exclusions From Schools and Exclusion Appeals in England 2004/05.* DfES.

Hane, D. (2006) Dealing With My Son's Schools. Interviewed by Izekor, J., London, 4 July.

London Development Agency (2004) *The Educational Experiences and Achievements of Black Boys in London Schools 2000–2003.* The Education Commission.

Media Awareness Network, Professional Development Resources for Educators. [cited 8th August 2006] <http://www.media-awareness.ca>

Ofsted (2001) *Improving Attendance and Behaviour in Secondary Schools.* London: Ofsted.

Osborne, J.W. (2001) Academic Disidentification: Unravelling Underachievement Among Black Boys. In Majors, R. (Ed.) *Educating Our Black Children: New Directions and Radical Approaches.* London: RoutledgeFalmer.

Wright, C. et al. (2005) *School Exclusion and Transition Into Adulthood in African-Caribbean Communities.* York: Joseph Rowntree Foundation.

CHAPTER 5

The Voluntary Sector and Young Black People

Rod Dacombe, Manuel Souto Otero and Adam Whitworth

Introduction

The election of the New Labour government in May 1997 was heralded as a significant opportunity for Black and minority ethnic (BME) organisations to develop a voice in the machinery of government, and to become involved in the provision of public services. But how does this fit with the facts presented by the wealth of literature and empirical work on the subject? Perhaps more importantly, is the growing visibility of the BME voluntary sector in government policy and rhetoric reflected in the experiences of young Black volunteers and activists at a grassroots level.

Understanding young Black volunteering in the UK involves unravelling a complex set of factors that affect its level and impact. This chapter provides an outline of the relevant historical, social and political factors, and discusses the literature and research evidence in the area. We hope it will be of particular use to practitioners working with young Black volunteers, and to volunteers themselves.

In undertaking its analysis, the chapter draws on a wide range of resources including official data, a review of current literature, and an original analysis of relevant empirical work. This chapter also makes use of the 'real life' experiences of volunteers, and includes the results of a workshop session at the Working with Young Black People Conference run at De Montfort University on Friday, 30 June 2006.

Shifting tides: BME voluntary organisations and the state

The growing profile of the BME voluntary sector has been driven by a number of factors, collected here under two themes. First, the continuing social problems faced by young Black people in the UK have been highlighted in the government's social agenda in recent years. In particular, the recommendations of the Macpherson Report, and New Labour's adoption of a 'social exclusion' discourse have ensured that issues relating to young Black people remain active on the policy agenda. Second, New Labour has transformed the voluntary sector's role within the welfare state. Consequently, the government has frequently made clear its intentions to engage with young Black people via voluntary groups drawn from the voluntary and community sector. The role of these groups has been cemented through their specific inclusion in the compact between the state and voluntary organisations. At the same time, the voluntary sector is increasingly involved in New Labour's social agenda, its place reinforced by specific measures taken by the government. The following section critically examines each of these issues in turn.

Social problems: public discourse

Since the beginning of its tenure of government in 1997, the issues of 'race' and 'racism' have appeared with increasing frequency in the discourse and the actions of government. The ideas and concepts underpinning this rise are dealt with in detail elsewhere in this book, but we felt it was important to briefly place our discussion of the BME voluntary sector in this context.

Macpherson and institutional racism

Public policy approaches to dealing with issues of race and racism in the UK have been altered fundamentally by the recommendations of the inquiry into the racist murder of Stephen Lawrence in 1993 (Macpherson, 1999). This was set up in the wake of the scandal resulting from the investigation of the murder, which initially failed to find sufficient evidence to charge the suspects, resulting with a groundswell of public opinion criticising the methods employed by the Metropolitan Police.

Macpherson found that the Metropolitan Police (despite their denials) had demonstrated clear deficiency in both its actions and its concern around the nature of the crime and the feelings of the Lawrence family. It attributed these shortcomings to the existence of 'institutional racism' within the force.

In doing so, the inquiry adopted a definition of racism that reached into the broadest institutions of society, touching in particular the criminal justice system and education. It suggested that racist practices were deeply embedded within the culture of government institutions so that, sometimes unwittingly, public sector employees discriminated against ethnic minorities. The use of the term 'institutional racism' is not new, with its origins in the Black Power movement of the 1960s (Bhavnani et al., 2005), but Macpherson popularised the use of the concept within public life in the UK.

Macpherson's definition of institutional racism held that it:

> . . . consists of the collective failure of an organisation to provide an appropriate and professional service to people because of their colour, culture or ethnic origin. It can be seen or detected in processes, attitudes or behaviour which amount to discrimination through unwitting prejudice, ignorance, thoughtlessness, and racist stereotyping which disadvantage minority ethnic people.

> (Macpherson, 1999, Ch 6.34)

Macpherson's recommendations and approach have had a significant impact on UK public discourse around race and racism. On its publication, the inquiry was lauded by the government. In a statement to the House of Commons soon after the Report's publication in 1999, Jack Straw, then the Home Secretary, acclaimed its findings:

> I want this report to serve as a watershed in our attitudes to racism. I want it to act as a catalyst for permanent and irrevocable change, not just across our public services but across the whole of our society.

> (Straw, 1999, HC (series 5) vol. 325, col. 393)

Straw continued to outline an action plan detailing the government's plans for implementing the recommendations of the inquiry. This is indicative of the fact that institutional racism, as defined by the Macpherson Inquiry, has been adopted as the *de facto* position of the government in the UK, strongly influencing policy, perhaps most significantly, the Race Relations (Amendment) Act, 1999. This act placed a statutory duty on all public sector bodies (including schools) to promote racial equality, reforming workforce and employment policies as well as the implementation of public policy. This has clear implications for the BME voluntary sector.

The position taken by the government on institutional racism is, however, not without its discontents. Bhavnani (2001) for example, has criticised the definition of institutional racism adopted by Macpherson for its exclusion of racism based along gendered and class lines.

New Labour and social exclusion

Alongside this, it is contextually important to frame New Labour's approach to relations with the BME voluntary sector (within the frequent positioning of its interventions and policies) in a discourse focussed on social exclusion. Indeed, one of the first acts under the new Labour government in 1997 was the creation of the Social Exclusion Unit (SEU) which was to provide 'joined-up policies' to the 'joined-up problems' of social exclusion (Clarke, 2002). This supports the government's commitment to tackling social exclusion and the claim in its first National Action Plan on Social Inclusion that 'The UK Government's commitment to overcoming social exclusion lies at the core of its political programme' (Labour Party, 2001).

New Labour's adoption of the term 'social exclusion' was met with initial uncertainty in the UK, with considerable discussion as to what the concept referred to and what it added to analysis over and above terms such as 'poverty' (Room, 1995; Silver, 1995; Atkinson, 1998; Cousins, 1998; Levitas, 1998; Byrne, 1999; Room, 1999; Bradshaw, Williams et al., 2000; Levitas, 2000; Vleminckx and Bergham, 2001; Burchardt, Le Grand et al., 2002; Lister, 2004). Room maintains that the language of exclusion is real as opposed to merely rhetorical, and there does seem to be broad agreement within the literature as to the core components to a social exclusion agenda (though less agreement as to whether these are new) to include: multi-dimensionality, dynamics, agency, community-level analyses, relational, and catastrophic rupture (Room, 1995, 1999).

Despite being able to draw out these broad characteristics, it would be wrong to say that there is only one 'version' of the concept. In fact, social exclusion is a relative concept, particular distinctions are made between different paradigms of social exclusion across European nations, based in significant part upon differing notions of citizenship and differing notions of what it means to be 'excluded' (Silver, 1994; Room, 1995; Silver, 1995; Cousins, 1998). Whilst, therefore, New Labour has wholeheartedly adopted the more continental European language of social exclusion, it has been argued that the UK presents a distinctly Anglo-Saxon version of the concept based on the historical dominance of poverty (as a lack of material resources) within its study of social policy, in contrast to the continental European emphasis on relational issues such as lack of power, social participation and integration to the *lien social* (Room, 1995).

Sitting in this broader context the SEU provide the following definition of the concept:

Social exclusion is about more than income poverty. It is a shorthand term for what can happen when people or areas face a combination of linked problems such as unemployment, discrimination, poor skills, low incomes, poor housing, high crime, bad health and family breakdown. These policies are linked and mutually reinforcing so that they create a vicious cycle in people's lives.

(SEU, 2004: 3)

Whilst any of these dimensions can become causal factors to exclusion – arguably at least one 'addition' over typical notions of poverty (Lister, 2004) – paid work is the factor most central to New Labour's construction of social exclusion. Levitas sets out three 'stories' of social exclusion: a redistributionist discourse (RED) stressing a lack of money, a social integrationist discourse (SID) seeing paid work as the key to social integration and inclusion, and a moral underclass discourse (MUD) emphasising the individual's own moral failings (Levitas, 1998; Levitas, 2000). She states that whilst the government at different times use each of these three explanatory accounts of social exclusion that it is the work-focused SID version which is most strongly and most consistently used by the government, and this reflects the priorities at a European level (EC, 2000). The way in which New Labour constructs 'social exclusion' is infused with moral values and is, in particular, far from gender neutral. This has caused much feminist criticism and has led some to reject New Labour's use of the debate wholeheartedly (Daly and Saraceno, 2002).

Within its work the SEU has frequently highlighted some or all BME groups as particular 'problem groups', in terms of the various dimensions of social exclusion which it emphasises. The government writes that BME groups face additional barriers to 'inclusion' relating to their ethnicity and are disproportionately likely to perform poorly and suffer exclusion across a range of dimensions of exclusion, including; employment, educational outcomes, truancy and school exclusions, participation in post-compulsory education, poverty, homelessness, drug use, teenage pregnancy and access to public services (SEU, 2000; HM Treasury, 2003; SEU, 2004).

This is particularly true, across differing dimensions of exclusion, for Pakistani, Bangladeshi, Black-Caribbean and Black-African populations (SEU, 2004; 2005). Looking at financial poverty, 18 per cent of the white population are in the bottom quintile of the income distribution whilst 30 per cent of Indian, 25 per cent of Black Caribbean, 45 per cent of Black non-Caribbean, 36 per cent of Chinese and 52 per cent of Pakistani/Bangladeshi individuals find themselves in the bottom 20 per cent of the income distribution (DWP, 2006). Focusing on unemployment, 2004 data shows that the unemployment rates of non-white groups were all higher than the 4 per cent rate for the white population, and for most minority ethnic groups rates were between 2–3 times higher than those for the white population (ONS, 2006). Research suggests, however, that these ME unemployment figures are not driven wholly by weaker BME educational performance, given for instance that although the educational performance of Black-Caribbean, Black-African, Pakistani, Bangladeshi and Gypsy/Roma populations is worse than that of the white population, Indian and Chinese populations are the highest educationally performing groups (SEU, 2004). Nevertheless, like-for-like comparisons of educational qualifications and labour market position show that to a greater or lesser degree all BME groups are disadvantaged in the labour market relative to the white population (SEU, 2004).

Under New Labour, improvements in some areas for BME groups have been recognised – for instance in relation to the absolute educational performance of Black-African,

Black-Caribbean, Indian and Pakistani children – however, BME groups continue to be disadvantaged relative to the white population across the various dimensions of social exclusion. As a consequence, ME groups continue to be constructed as a 'problem group' within government documents relating to social exclusion. A main finding of the *Breaking the Cycle* report was that policies seem to persistently be less effective in helping some BME groups and this was highlighted as a priority area for future policies (SEU, 2004).

New Labour and the voluntary sector

Within this broad context of a social programme increasingly concerned with the problems of race and exclusion, the New Labour government elected in 1997 immediately began to look to the voluntary sector as a key social partner in dealing with their effects.

Rediscovering community: New Labour's reforms

Even before winning power in 1997, New Labour was committed to reframing its relationship with the voluntary sector.[1] The pre-election consultation document *Building the Future Together* was heavily influenced by the Deakin Commission's findings. It outlined the importance of the voluntary sector several months before the election, while New Labour was effectively government-in-waiting (Labour Party, 1997a).

Subsequently, the government has pursued a number of policies that rely on the involvement of voluntary groups for their effective delivery. This section suggests that this approach is a significant break in relations between the state and the voluntary sector, outlining a number of recent policies that place the voluntary sector at the heart of public policy.

Kendall (2001, 2003) suggests that New Labour has attempted to 'mainstream' the voluntary sector into public policy in the UK through a series of structural and programmatic reforms. This is evident in a series of policy manoeuvres aimed at placing the voluntary sector in the forefront of public service design and provision. This section focuses on three of these moves, the emergence of the voluntary sector within the machinery and policy aspirations of central government; a new tier of policy-making fora operating alongside the state at local and regional levels dependent on the involvement of the voluntary sector; and the adoption of a 'compact' governing relations between the state and the voluntary sector.

The higher profile of the voluntary sector in government is evident with the creation of the Active Communities Unit (ACU) based within the Home Office.[2] This represents an unprecedented structural change at the heart of government. The unit has received significant investment, and is charged with promoting the virtues of the voluntary sector throughout government. The ACU's influence is evident in a number of high profile government policy reviews into its relationship with the voluntary sector (HM Treasury, 2002; Performance and Innovation Unit, 2001).

---

[1] Before New Labour's 1997 victory, the influential MP Alun Michael held a series of regional seminars with voluntary organisations on future working arrangements as part of the party's 'preparations for government'.

[2] The Home Office is responsible for a number of different functions, including communities and volunteering, crime and disorder, and race relations.

These reviews have tried to set the relationship with the voluntary sector in a new and broader context rather than simply as an alternative to direct state provision. According to the Treasury Review, working in partnership with voluntary organisations could enable the state to 'enhance and deepen . . . understanding of the community, its citizens and its sense of place', while the Performance and Innovation Unit Review provides a number of embryonic policy proposals based on the promotion of social capital.

Recent years have also seen a 'horizontal' agenda in the government's dealings with voluntary organisations, enhancing the sector's capacity to co-operate with various arms of the public sector in shaping services. This is in contrast to its continued participation in established hierarchical ('vertical') relationships based on state funding and contracts (Kendall, 2003; Rao, 2000). The creation of multi-agency partnerships dealing with particular areas of public policy involving representatives from central and local government, voluntary organisations, faith groups and local businesses make this evident. Examples might include Drug Prevention Advisory Groups, and Crime and Disorder Reduction Partnerships.

Commentators have discussed the idea of 'partnership' as a theme distinguishing New Labour's approach from that of previous administrations. This indicates a search for solutions to complex and persistent social problems, rather than a blunt ideological move to reduce the state's welfare role (Newman, 2001; Powell, 1999). It is closely linked with the debate around the broad policy framework that makes up New Labour's Third Way (Anheier, 2004). However, questions persist over the appropriateness of partnership arrangements (Lewis, 1995) and the voluntary sector's capacity for meaningful participation. There are also concerns about tokenism (Thompson and Hoggett, 2001; Williams, 2004).

Perhaps the most celebrated aspect of New Labour's approach to voluntary/state relations is the adoption of a national 'Compact'.[3] Adopted in 1998 with several high profile representatives from the voluntary sector, this sets out a number of underlying principles as the basis for voluntary/state relations:

- That an independent and diverse voluntary sector is fundamental to the well-being of society.
- That the government and the voluntary sector have distinct but complementary roles in shaping and delivering public services.
- That there is an added value in working together towards common aims and objectives.
- That government and the voluntary sector have different forms of accountability but common values of commitment to integrity, objectivity, openness, honesty and leadership.

The Compact, although not legally binding, is intended as a framework for resolving disputes and a blueprint for an effective working relationship. The main principles are supplemented by 'codes of practice' covering a number of contentious areas such as funding and consultation. An example of the mutual undertakings in these codes is given in the box below:

---

[3] The national Compact has been widely replicated throughout local government.

Box 1: Mutual undertakings in the Compact Code of Practice for Volunteering

- Work together to expand the public perception of volunteering by improving the profile, status and range of volunteer activity.
- Work to effectively tackle discrimination to ensure that volunteering is open to all.
- Adopt clear policies regarding the payment of volunteer expenses.
- Make visible the value of volunteers' contributions, for example in publications.
- Ensure that arrangements made for volunteers do not unfairly exclude particular groups from volunteering.
- Recognise that voluntary activity should not be seen as a substitute for paid work.
- Work together to create and maintain a modern and dynamic volunteering infrastructure.

However, there are concerns around the implementation of the Compact. Many argue that it lacks the 'teeth' of a legally binding agreement (6, P. and Leat, 1997). There is also ambiguity over the balance of power between partners under the Compact, and a number of potential problems exist around its implementation across multiple tiers of local administration (Craig and Taylor, 1999).

This reframing of the relationship between the state and the voluntary sector has a number of specific implications for young BME volunteers. Perhaps the most significant of these are the Compact code of practice for BME organisations, and a number of specific policies and undertakings on the part of the government to increase the engagement of young Black people with voluntary activity, which are considered here in turn.

The BME Compact Code of Practice

This code aims to deal with a number of the specific problems around engaging with BME volunteers by such measures as developing capacity, funding BME groups and dealing with issues of racism and exclusion. It was subject to intense consultation during its development – the draft document has been circulated to 5,000 voluntary and community groups after initial consultation with 850 Black and ethnic minority voluntary organisations. It is based on a number of central principles, including:

- A joint commitment to taking forward the government's race equality agenda at all levels.
- Better consultation and participation in policy and implementation.
- A recognition of the role, contribution and needs of BME voluntary organisations.
- Encouraging funding, capacity-building, infrastructure development and sustainability.
- Ensuring that state/voluntary relations improve outcomes for BME communities.

Public Service Agreements

In addition to this undertaking, the government has signed up to two Public Service Agreements[4] (PSAs) that touch on volunteering and civic participation. PSA 6 seeks to increase participation in voluntary and community activities, particularly amongst those at risk of social exclusion. PSA 8 is more specific, referring to the government's commitment to increasing voluntary and community sector activity. It includes a target to increase community participation by 5 per cent over five years (2001–2006). The Home Office also has a broader aim, Strategic Objective 5. Although not a firm commitment, this is intended to provide an overall guide to policy and working practices, including the aim that 'citizens, communities and the voluntary sector are more fully engaged in tackling social problems'.

This last commitment reveals that, for the government, volunteering and civic participation are perceived as essential to dealing with complex social problems. The Home Office's Community Policy spells out the benefits of civic participation, with the intention of:

- Ensuring that all groups within society are able to become involved in shaping social policy.
- Promoting partnership between community groups and government to solve social problems.
- Enabling active communities to contribute towards democracy and civil society.

Millennium Volunteers

This project aims to recruit younger volunteers, aged between 16 and 24, to work in their local communities. It is based on nine principles: sustained personal commitment, community benefit, voluntary participation, inclusiveness, ownership by young people, diversity of opportunity, partnership working, quality and recognition of the value of volunteering. Despite the local nature of the work, Millennium Volunteers (MV) is a national movement, with 130 projects established around England, mostly based in local volunteering centres, schools or colleges.

MV is meant to be a vocational programme. After 100 hours of volunteering, the participants receive an award intended to reflect the experience they have gained. After 200 hours, they receive an Award of Excellence, signed by the Secretary of State. Initiatives that have involved marginalised young people, particularly those with a disability, have had positive effects on participants. Their status is thereby transformed from users of services to contributors. However, while a significant proportion of new volunteers have been recruited, problems have been identified around engaging hard-to-reach groups, including ethnic minorities (Doherty, 2002).

So we can see that the thrust of New Labour's social programme has not only been concerned with the social problems of race and racism, but is also inexorably tied up with the reframing of relations with the voluntary sector. The next section moves on to discuss

---

[4] PSAs are undertakings by the government to reach specific targets in the nature and provision of public services. Each PSA target is underpinned by a *technical note*, which sets out how the target is measured, how success is defined, the sources of the relevant data, and any other relevant information such as geographic or demographic coverage.

the dynamics of young Black volunteering, examining the literature and research evidence, and highlighting examples of good practice.

Young Black people and volunteering

There are two sides to our analysis of the state of young Black volunteering. First, this section profiles the participation of young Black people in voluntary activity, it then moves on to discuss some of the motivations and views of young Black volunteers (and those of non-volunteers). We do not believe that these two issues are distinct. Our analysis suggests that the motivations and perceptions of volunteers are intimately connected to the level of participation.

However, when looking at these issues, it is important to ensure that any analysis reflects the complexity of the data. When we first examined the data on young Black volunteering, we immediately found that the results are often unclear, and at times conflicting. Different studies tend to come to different conclusions, and it is difficult to point to any definite trends in participation.

There may be a number of reasons for this. The differing methods taken throughout the range of empirical work play a part. There are clear points of demarcation in the empirical data between large and small scale quantitative work, and a different emphasis in the aims and approach of the many studies attempting in depth qualitative analysis.

Some studies suffer from the small *n*, big conclusions problem. A number of quantitative studies tend to make grand claims based upon rather shaky statistical validity. Quite simply, it is difficult to make any great claims based upon this work. Some studies even include an underrepresentation of Black people in their samples. A number of writers discuss the survey undertaken for the National Coalition on Black Volunteering in 1991, which had a sample of 2.5 per cent drawn from ethnic minority groups, compared with (conservative) estimated of 5.5 per cent across the population as a whole (Bhasin, 1997). Equally, it is important to note that there is considerable difficulty in separating out *young* Black people in the data. Many studies focus their findings on either young people, *or* Black people. In our analysis we explicitly state where this occurs.

Moving on to the data, it is immediately obvious that the picture is extremely complex. However, we can say two things with some certainty, given the broad agreement of a number of studies. First, it is clear that Black volunteers are seriously underrepresented in 'mainstream' voluntary organisations. That is to say, organisations that are a mixture of paid staff and volunteers, where the client group, and/or the volunteers working in an organisation are dominantly white. This is closely tied up with a number of factors, including the legacy of the 'colour bar' of the 1950s, which applied not only to the labour market, but was also present in the spheres of civil society, including volunteering (Obaze, 1992) and the tradition of 'self help' within Black communities (Bhasin, 1997; Hedley and Rampersad, 1992).

There are also a couple of points to make about young people. Within the literature there is a general agreement that young people are far less likely to participate in any form of voluntary activity. In fact, volunteering seems most prevalent in middle age and declines soon after. There is some evidence to suggest a sharp decline in volunteering between the ages of 16 and 24, and that regular volunteering (once a month) is in particular decline amongst young people (IVR, 1998). There is also a very strong correlation between volunteering and employment identified throughout the literature and empirical work that has persisted over a number of years (Obaze, 1992; IVR, 1998; Zimmeck, 2003, 2005).

The UK Citizenship Survey (Zimmeck, 2003; 2005) breaks down voluntary and civic activity into three categories; civic participation, informal volunteering, and formally-organised volunteering. An examination of these categories serves to highlight just how complex Black volunteering in the UK actually is.

When examining engagement in *civic activity* we see a proportionally higher level of participation amongst people of mixed race, and of Bangladeshi origin. People of Chinese origin are ranked lowest, and are roughly half as likely to volunteer as those of mixed race.

Of these differences, *some* can be explained by examining the age of the respective samples. As we have seen, the literature and empirical work strongly agrees that young people are far less likely to volunteer, *regardless of race*. We can therefore go some way towards explaining the place of the Bangladeshi sample as an outlier by the simple fact that the sample was older. Amongst people aged 16–24, people of (broadly conceived) Asian origin were more likely to participate in civic activity than their white or Black peers – not the case across the samples regardless of age. However, even considering the age bias of the overall sample, there is an especially high rate of civic participation among people of Bangladeshi origin.

Conversely, there are higher rates of *informal volunteering* amongst people of white and Black African origin. There are also distinctions between informal volunteering and civic participation within the 'Asian' strata, with people of Bangladeshi origin far less likely to take part in informal voluntary activity. Similar results can be identified for *formal volunteering*. Broadly, the ethnic patterns for this kind of volunteering are the same for informal activity, *but* there are significant differences between ethnicity and age.

Other significant factors seem to be the country of birth (people born outside the UK seem less likely to undertake any kind of voluntary activity). As we have already suggested, age is a significant factor in determining the likelihood of participation in voluntary activity.

Images, motivations and experiences of volunteering

So how do all these data fit with the different understandings of volunteering held by young Black people? Most of the literature agrees that the images and meanings attached to voluntary action by young Black people are central to their participation (Bhasin, 1997; Gaskin, 1998; Niyazi, 1996a, 1996b). It is therefore important that the empirical work, described above, matches the experiences and expectations of young Black people. Are we even talking about the same thing?

This section explores the perception of volunteering held by young Black people, establishing a link between their motivations and empirical work on their experiences of working in and with voluntary organisations. The chapter will conclude with a discussion of good practice, suggesting practical steps that can be taken by voluntary organisations, infrastructure bodies and central and local government agencies to promote the engagement of young Black volunteers.

Importantly, various studies may adopt different definitions of volunteering, with clear knock-on effects in the research findings (the measurement of its size, scope and impact).

Let us begin by considering the mainstream understandings of voluntary action in the UK. Two useful approaches to understanding voluntarism in the UK can be drawn from applied research. For its National Survey of Volunteering, the Institute for Volunteering Research (IVR) takes a broad approach, defining volunteering as 'any activity which involves spending time, unpaid, doing something which aims to benefit someone (individuals or groups) other than or in addition to, close relatives, or to benefit the environment' (Davis Smith, 1998). Alternatively, Kendall and Knapp (1996) choose to focus on the organisation, rather than the activity, in an attempt to reach a definition appropriate to the UK case. They adapt the structural/operational definition (see Box 2, below), aiming to reach a 'typical, de facto understanding of what it [voluntary action] is, or should be, in this country', and so exclude organisations with close ties to the state and those who do not 'sufficiently' demonstrate an altruistic ethos, such as universities and sports clubs.

Box 2: The Structural/Operational definition (Salamon and Anheier, 1997)

Refers to voluntary organisations as being:
- formally organised
- nonprofit distributing
- constitutionally independent from the state
- self-governing
- containing some element of volunteering

In truth, working understandings of volunteering in Britain may be more intuitive than either of these approaches. Knight (1993) considers voluntary action to be 'a form of energy, stemming from free will, having a moral purpose and undertaken in a spirit of free independence'. Similarly, Frank Prochaska (1988) regards volunteering to be the expression of a voluntary 'impulse', which is 'the antithesis of collective or statutory authority'. Perhaps conversely, the government has recently tended to take a broader understanding of volunteering, promoting a programme of active community participation, based on the benefits of the involvement of the public in all aspects of civic life, but particularly political participation.

However, these understandings are not necessarily reflected in the images held by young Black volunteers. Some young people seem to have a broad problem with the term 'volunteering' (Bhasin, 1997; Niyazi, 1996a, 1996b). It is seen as boring, irrelevant, and more generally 'alien' – there can be a broad feeling of distance from 'mainstream' voluntary organisations. Indeed, the idea of 'volunteering' can be seen as middle-class and affluent, with excessive, off-putting, bureaucracy (Gaskin, 1998).

Coupled with this are a number of assumptions held by the sector about young Black volunteers. Many organisations believe that young Black people do not want to volunteer (Obaze, 1992; Niyazi, 1996a, 1996b). When they are allowed to participate, there is often a feeling that young people can only do certain basic tasks due to a lack of 'experience' and formal qualification (Gaskin, 1998). There are also some barriers of racism – seldom intentional, but often related to tokenism. This might include appointing a Black volunteer as an organisation's 'expert' on BME issues.

It is also important to understand the motivations of young Black volunteers. Most commentators suggest that these are wide-ranging and varied, and this was borne out during our conversations with practitioners. Many are motivated to 'meet needs' (Obaze, 1992). Work is often community-focussed, with a strong emphasis on advice and advocacy work. Similarly, there is a strong emphasis on informal approaches to volunteering, and the identification of this work as 'self help', jarring with the mainstream understandings of voluntary action that we outlined earlier in the chapter. Motivations are often very personal – they are questions of identity.

Conclusion: the road to good practice

Despite some of the tensions and concerns outlined above, we don't want to end the chapter on a depressing note. The research evidence, and our contact with practitioners, has highlighted a number of simple, practical steps that can help the recruitment, active involvement and retention of young Black volunteers. Given the enthusiasm and commitment of the volunteers we have encountered during the writing of this chapter, we thought it appropriate to leave these as our last word.

- *Be flexible*: Young people are not always comfortable volunteering by themselves. Try to include social groups, and perhaps families in the volunteering experience. Above all, try and relate to young Black volunteers – it is essential to understand the barriers most important to them. Equally, where you can cut through red tape to better engage with young volunteers, do it!
- *Be innovative*: Think about how you can best support young Black volunteers. Perhaps financially – by reimbursing travel costs. Shape the experience of volunteering to equip young Black people with skills that will help improve their future life chances. A positive experience of volunteering can have a knock-on effect on the future prospects of any young volunteer.
- *Be committed*: If you find that you are unable to recruit young Black people to volunteer, don't give up – this doesn't mean that they aren't interested! Contact organisations that you know are successful. Ask them what worked. Advertise widely, and not just through mainstream methods. It can also help to draw up policies supporting the role of young Black volunteers. If you do this, publicise the results.
- *Be empathetic*: Think about your own assumptions around young Black people as volunteers. Challenge yourself. As we have seen, volunteering can be an intensely personal thing for young Black people. Understand this and make the work relevant to them.

References

6, P. and Leat, D. (1997) Inventing the British Voluntary Sector by Committee: from Wolfenden to Deakin. *Non-Profit Studies*, 1: 2, 33–46.

Anheier, H. (2004) Third way – Third sector. In Lewis, J. and Surender, R. (Eds.) *Welfare State Change: Towards a Third Way?* Oxford: Oxford University Press.

Apeki, T. (1995) *Black on Board*. Conference held at NCVO on 30 November 1994. London: NCVO.

Atkinson, A. (1998) Social Exclusion, Poverty and Unemployment. In Atkinson, A.B. and Hills, J. *Exclusion, Employment and Opportunity*. LSE, Centre for the Analysis of Social Exclusion.

Bhasin, S. (1997) *My Community, My Time, Myself: Experiences of Volunteering Within the Black Community.* London: National Centre for Volunteering.

Bhavnani, R. (2001) *Rethinking Interventions in Racism.* Oakhill, Trentham Books.

Bhavnani, R. et al. (2005) *Tackling the Roots of Racism.* Bristol: Policy Press.

Bradshaw, J., Williams, J. et al. (2000) *The Relationship Between Poverty and Social Exclusion in Britain.* General Conference of the International Association for Research in Income and Wealth, Cracow, Poland.

Burchardt, T. et al. (2002) Degrees of Exclusion: Developing a Dynamic, Multidimensional Measure. In Hills, J., Le Grand, J. and Piachaud, D. *Understanding Social Exclusion.* Oxford: Oxford University Press.

Byrne, D. (1999) *Social Exclusion.* Buckingham: Open University Press.

Clarke, T. (2002) New Labour's Big Idea: Joined-Up Government. *Social Policy and Society* 1: 2, 107–17.

Cousins, C. (1998) Social Exclusion in Europe: Paradigms of Disadvantage in Germany, Spain, Sweden and the United Kingdom. *Policy and Politics*, 26: 2.

Daly, M. and Saraceno, C. (2002) Social Exclusion and Gender Relations. In Hobson, B., Lewis, J. and Siim, B. *Contested Concepts in Gender and Social Politics.* Cheltenham: Edward Elgar.

Doherty, J. (2002) *UK-wide Evaluation of the Millennium Volunteers Programme.* Nottingham: DfES.

DWP (2006) *Households Below Average Income (HBAI)* 1994/95–2004/05. [cited 3rd June 2006] http://www.dwp.gov.uk/asd/hbai/hbai2005/pdf_files/chapters/chapter_3_hbai06.pdf.

EC (2000) *Fight Against Poverty and Social Exclusion: Definition of Appropriate Objectives.* Brussels: EC.

Gaskin, K. (1998) *What Young People Want From Volunteering.* London: National Centre for Volunteering.

Hedley, R. and Rampersad, G. (1992) *Making it Happen! Involving Black Volunteers: Issues and Practical Advice on Working With Black Communities and Involving Black Volunteers.* London: Resource Unit for Black Volunteering.

HM Treasury (2002) *Cross Cutting Review of the Voluntary Sector in Public Service Delivery.* London: HM Treasury.

HM Treasury (2003) *Every Child Matters.* Cm 5860. London: HMSO.

Home Office (1998) *Compact on Relations Between Government and the Voluntary and Community Sector in England.* London: HMSO.

Home Office (2001a) *Black and Minority Ethnic Voluntary and Community Organisations: A Code of Good Practice.* London: HMSO.

Home Office (2001b) *Volunteering: A Code of Good Practice.* London: HMSO.

Institute for Volunteering Research (1998) *The 1997 National Survey of Volunteering.* London: National Centre for Volunteering.

Kendall, J. (2001) *The Third Sector and Social Care For Older People in England: Towards an Explanation of its Contrasting Contributions in Residential Care, Domiciliary Care and Day Care.* London: Centre for Civil Society.

Kendall, J. (2003) *The Voluntary Sector.* London: Routledge.

Labour Party (1997a) *Building the Future Together: Labour's Policies For Partnership Between Government and the Voluntary Sector.* London: Labour Party.

Labour Party (1997b) *New Labour Because Britain Deserves Better. The 1997 General Election Manifesto.* London: Labour Party.

Labour Party (2001) *UK National Action Plan on Social Inclusion 2001–2003.* London: Labour Party.

Levitas, R. (1998) *The Inclusive Society? Social Exclusion and New Labour.* Basingstoke: Macmillan.

Levitas, R. (2000) What is Social Exclusion? In Gordon, D. and Townsend, P. *Breadline Europe: The Measurement of Poverty.* Bristol: Polity Press.

Lewis, J. (1995) *The Voluntary Sector, the State and Social Work in Britain.* London: Edward Elgar.

Lister, R. (2004) *Poverty*. Cambridge: Polity Press.

Lukka, P. and Ellis, A. (2001) *An Exclusive Construct? Exploring Different Cultural Concepts of Volunteering*. London: Institute for Volunteering Research.

Macpherson, W. (1999) *The Stephen Lawrence Inquiry*. London: The Stationery Office.

Niyazi, F. (1996a) *Volunteering by Black People: A Route to Opportunity*. London: The National Centre for Volunteering.

Niyazi, F. (1996b) *Volunteering by Young People: A Route to Opportunity*. London: The National Centre for Volunteering.

ONS (2006) *Labour Market: Non-White Unemployment Highest*. [cited 3rd June 2006] http://www.statistics.gov.uk/cci/nugget.asp?id=462.

Performance and Innovation Unit (2001) *Social Capital: A Discussion Paper*. London: HMSO.

Rao, N. (2000) *Reviving Local Democracy*. London: The Policy Press.

Room, G. (1995) Poverty and Social Exclusion: The New European Agenda for Policy and Research. In Room, G. *Beyond the Threshold: The Measurement and Analysis of Social Exclusion*. Bristol: The Policy Press.

Room, G. (1999) Social Exclusion, Solidarity and the Challenge of Globalization. *International Journal of Social Welfare*. 8: 166–74.

Room, G. (Ed.) (1995) *Beyond the Threshold: The Measurement and Analysis of Social Exclusion*. Bristol: The Policy Press.

SEU (2000) *Report of the Policy Action Team 12: Young People*. [cited 3rd June 2006] http://www.socialexclusionunit.gov.uk/downloaddoc.asp?id=125.

SEU (2004) *Breaking the Cycle: Taking Stock of Progress and Priorities for the Future*. London: ODPM.

SEU (2005) *Transitions: Young Adults with Complex Needs*. London: ODPM.

Silver, H. (1994) Social Exclusion and Social Solidarity: Three Paradigms. *International Labour Review*, 133: 5–6, 531–78.

Silver, H. (1995) Reconceptualising Social Disadvantage: Three Paradigms of Social Exclusion. In Rodgers, G., Gore, C. and Figueiredo, J. *Social Exclusion: Rhetoric, Reality, Responses*. Geneva: International Labour Organisation.

Straw, J. (1999) *House of Commons Debate*. Hansard, HC (series 5) vol. 325, col. 393 (24th Feb.).

Thompson, S. and Hoggett, P. (2001) The Emotional Dynamics of Deliberative Democracy. *Policy and Politics*, 29: 3, 351–64.

Vleminckx, K. and J. Bergham (2001) Social Exclusion and the Welfare State: An Overview of Conceptual Issues and Policy Implications. In Mayes, D. Bergham, J. and Salais, R. *Social Exclusion and European Policy*. Cheltenham: Edward Elgar.

Williams, M. (2004) Discursive Democracy and New Labour: Five Ways in Which Decision-Makers Manage Citizen Agendas in Public Participation Initiatives. *Social Research Online*, 9: 3.

Zimmeck, M. et al. (2003) *2001 Home Office Citizenship Survey: People, Families and Communities*. London: HMSO.

Zimmeck, M. et al. (2005) *2003 Home Office Citizenship Survey: People, Families and Communities*. London: HMSO.

CHAPTER 6

Racial Harassment, Black Young People and Schools

Mandeep Rupra

I shall remember this for eternity and will never forget.
Monday: my money was taken.
Tuesday: names called.
Wednesday: my uniform torn.
Thursday: my body pouring with blood.
Friday: it's ended.
Saturday: freedom

(Jaffrey, 1997: 2)

This poem was written by 13-year-old Vijay Singh in October 1996. Vijay had been subjected to sustained racial harassment and it is believed that the Saturday he refers to is the day he committed suicide by hanging himself (Jaffrey, 1997).

Introduction

Racial harassment constitutes an endemic, persistent and widespread problem in contemporary Britain (Chouhan and Jasper, 2001; Francis and Matthews, 1993). Every year thousands of people in Britain, both young and old, are terrorised, have to live with their freedom curtailed and their life chances impaired as a result of racial harassment (Virdee, 1997, 1995). Moreover, racial harassment is not only highly injurious to those who suffer it, but it is also pernicious to the wider society itself. This was identified by the Home Office Select Committee, which described all forms of racial harassment as 'the most shameful and dispiriting aspect of race relations in Britain' (Holdaway in Mason, 2000: 117).

Although experiencing racial harassment is not confined to a particular age group, young people constitute a significant proportion of the victims and perpetrators of such abuse. This was acknowledged by the Macpherson report (1999) on the racist attack and murder of Black teenager Stephen Lawrence in 1993, which revealed young people as being 'central to the issue of racial attacks – as perpetrators, victims and activists' (Chouhan and Jasper, 2001: 157). Although a small number of studies have illustrated the reality of racial harassment in the lives of young people there is still very little known about the extent, nature and impact of the phenomenon. However, what is known from those studies is that although young people experience racial harassment in a variety of settings, the school setting is the most common (Rupra, 2004; MacLeod, 1998; Troyna and Hatcher, 1992a; Ahmad et al., 1991). This is extremely worrying considering that school is a major focus of a young person's life. What is even more worrying is that whilst many Black young people have experienced, and continue to experience, racial harassment within the school setting the education system has been slow to respond to the issue. This is a concern that cannot be ignored, as it has serious implications for the educational performance, achievement and well being of many Black young people. Within this chapter the term Black will be used in its inclusive political sense and refer to all non-white communities and individuals who suffer from racism. Moreover, it should be noted that the examples in this chapter are in reference to African, African Caribbean and Asian young people.

Despite the reality of racial harassment in schools it is only comparatively recently that the problem has become a recognised and researched phenomenon and there is consequently still a great deal to know about the way in which schools deal with the issue. Based on this it is believed that the current analysis will provide a valuable insight into an area, which still requires much attention. In addition to examining available research on the area the analysis will be based on my own observations as a practitioner within the education system and race equality field. The chapter will begin with a consideration of the definition of racial harassment. This will be followed by an examination of the extent, nature and impact of racial harassment in the lives of young people at school. The approaches adopted by schools in dealing with racial harassment will then be considered, where I will draw upon my experiences as a researcher and racial harassment youth officer. The chapter will conclude by exploring the implications of the analysis and considering, based on the evidence presented, whether racial harassment is an issue for young people and schools. The wider issues of dealing with racial harassment in schools will also be commented on.

What is racial harassment

Racial harassment is not a new phenomenon and has existed within Britain for many centuries (Virdee, 1997; Francis and Matthews, 1993; Fryer, 1984). However, despite its history, racial harassment in Britain was only formally acknowledged in 1981 in the Home Office report *Racial Attacks* (Mason, 2000). This marked a turning point for racial harassment and public policy and placed the issue as a matter of urgent priority. Concern over the problem continued into the 1990s, during which time several key developments, one of the most famous being the Stephen Lawrence Inquiry, signalled a formal change in official attitudes to racial harassment and placed it on the agenda of many public and community agencies (Lemos, 2000).

For many academics and practitioners racial harassment can only be understood as an expression of racism. However, racism and racial harassment are contentious terms that have generated a great deal of debate amongst theorists and practitioners. In order to successfully analyse the interrelationship between the two, the definition of racism adopted in this analysis will be similar to that used by various contemporary theorists. In this paper racism will be defined as an ideology, which seeks to obscure, internalise and naturalise relations of racial domination, exploitation and privilege (van Dijk, 1993). Racism is an ideological, structural and historic stratification process, which is based on the belief that races are distinct and can be regarded as 'superior' or 'inferior' (Yeboah, 1997). As an ideology racism operates through discourses and practices through which dominant representations of difference function to provide subject positions as fixed and unchangeable for those who are exploited (Belsey in Young, 2000). It is within this context of racism in which racial harassment occurs. Racism provides the rationale and motivation to discriminate against others, on the basis of an individual's putatively different racial membership, through a variety of actions (Solomos and Black, 1996). Thus racial harassment is a variety of acts constituted by 'a power relation of domination between a majority (superordinate) group and a minority (subordinate) group. It is a doctrine and action of superiority' (Chahal, 1999, online).

To some extent racial harassment can be 'typologised'. It can be understood as a variety of acts, the most serious being murder, but also including verbal abuse, threats, insults, physical assaults, criminal damage and the distribution of racist material (Sibbitt, 1997). Clearly this description of racial harassment is not exhaustive and does not include what might be described as 'hidden' or 'indirect' forms of abuse such as mimicry, tone of voice, exclusion and body language. These forms of more 'trivial' incidents can be experienced in routine everyday social situations, which can be cumulative in their effects and contribute to a general atmosphere of harassment and intimidation. Moreover, racist victimisation is not solely about being attacked either physically or verbally, it is also about the denial of movement, the loss of family relationships 'the accumulation of negative experiences which impact on people's day-to-day decision making' (Chahal and Julienne, 1999: 37). For Virdee (1997) all these forms of racial harassment represent 'the most extreme component and expression of the racism faced by Britain's ethnic minorities' (Virdee, 1997: 276). A distinguishing feature of racial harassment, in comparison to other forms of harassment, is that racist abuse is committed against individuals because of their real or alleged membership to an ethnic minority community. Thus racial harassment is far more than an attack on a person purely as an individual: it can be understood as an attack on the victim's family and their ethnic community as a whole (Virdee, 1995; Oakley, 1992).

In defining racial harassment it is equally important not to obscure the fact that the overwhelming majority of victims of racist abuse and harassment in Britain today are the 'visible minorities'. This is supported by Chahal (1999) who believes that 'the routine nature of racist abuse, insults and threats is the key to British society accepting that the Black experience is fantastically different from the white experience' (Chahal, 1999, online). However, it is important to note, that for some theorists racial harassment can only be experienced by Black communities (Gillborn, 1995; van Dijk, 1993). For many theorists racial harassment is an outcome of white racism and subsequently makes a clear statement about Black people's position in British society (Oakley, 1992; Gordon, 1990). For Troyna and Hatcher (1992b) the fundamental significance of racial harassment is 'the asymmetrical power relations between Black and white citizens in Britain' (Troyna and Hatcher, 1992b: 16). Consequently, current definitions of racial harassment and incidents are inadequate as they do not illustrate the true nature of racial harassment as being expressive of an ideology of white racism. The debate over the nature of racial harassment and who can and cannot be the victim of such abuse has led to a lack of consensus and uncertainty in defining the phenomenon. However, whenever employed in this chapter racial harassment should be understood as being motivated by, reflecting and reinforcing an ideology of white racism present in wider society through a range of behaviours.

Racial harassment in the lives of young people at school

The claim that young children are 'colour-blind' and free from the malign influences of individual racism has been refuted by various studies (Lemos, 2005; Troyna, 1993; Short and Carrington, 1992; Carrington and Short, 1989; Aboud, 1988). There is an abundance of evidence that demonstrates children are not only 'able to understand and articulate racist sentiments, but they do not have to live in a multicultural environment to hold racist beliefs' (Gill et al., 1992: 251).

From an early age 'race' and racism emerge as plausible, significant and appealing modes of reasoning in the cultural and social lives of young people. Milner (1983) asserts that between seven and nine years children begin to internalise societal ideologies of racism and learn 'complex information about racial groups, stereotypes about their characteristics, and notions of social status' (Milner, 1983: 110). Furthermore, it is primarily interactional ideologies, within children's cultures that animate these racist ideologies and translate them into social practice. However, racial harassment in the lives of young people should not be viewed as consistent or unified. Young people's participation in such behaviour is complex and often contradictory. For example, studies have shown how young people are able to hold anti-racist beliefs and condemn discrimination, whilst still perpetrating racist behaviour (Barter, 1999).

Based on this understanding it is no surprise that racial harassment is a part of the everyday experience of many young people, as either victims, bystanders or perpetrators. It is the everyday experience of many Black young people who are subjected to this form of abuse in a variety of different settings. What is even more interesting is that, although Black young people constitute approximately 10 per cent of the total child population of Britain, they are more likely to experience bullying than their white counterparts and this bullying will invariably consist of racist abuse and harassment (Barn, 2001; Barter, 1999; MacLeod, 1998).

Although there is little research on the issue of racial harassment and young people what is evident from the available research is that a significant proportion of the racial harassment experienced by young people occurs within the school setting. In 1985 the Commission for Racial Equality (CRE) conducted a survey of the incidence of racial harassment in educational settings in England, Scotland and Wales and concluded that 'young people in schools and colleges suffer no less than men and women on the streets and in their homes on housing estates' (CRE, 1988: 5). Akhtar and Stronach's (1986) study further reveals the endemic nature of racist abuse within schools. The data obtained in this study clearly illustrates that from as early as four years of age Black children experienced considerable and sustained racist abuse from their white peers. Akhtar and Stronach (1986) also concluded that this form of abuse got worse for children as they grew older and moved through the different stages of school life. Similarly, studies by Rupra (2004), Cline et al. (2002), Odedra (1997), Wason-Ellam (1996), and Swann (1985) also provide clear evidence of the existence and pervasive nature of racial harassment in schools. These studies also highlight that for many Black young people racial harassment is a common and daily experience.

While the forms of racial harassment in schools vary, the most salient form is name-calling. This was highlighted in Troyna and Hatcher's (1992b) perceptive study of three mainly white primary schools. The study highlighted racist name-calling being used by white young people as an assertion of dominance and a part of the school lives of almost all the Black young people that they talked to:

> *For some it may be almost an everyday happening. For others it is less frequent, with occurrences remembered as significant events whose recurrence remains a possibility in every new social situation. For all, it is in general the most hurtful form of verbal aggression from other children.*

(Troyna and Hatcher, 1992b: 195)

Studies by Kelly (1990) and Cohn (1989) exploring name-calling also confirm that not only is racist name-calling an important strategy within many white young people's interactional repertoire, but that it is also the most prevalent and powerful form of name-calling within schools.

It is evident that racist name-calling constitutes a significant proportion of the racial harassment experienced within schools. Nevertheless, it would be incorrect to assume that racial harassment experienced by young people does not involve violence (Cline et al., 2002; Bhate and Bhate, 1997). Although research evidence is minimal it does seem to imply that a significant minority of young people will experience racist violence in school. For instance, Wright's (1992) study of four schools concluded that being subjected to racist name-calling and physical abuse from white peers was almost a daily experience for Black young people. Similarly, MacLeod's (1998) examination of calls from young people to Childline between 1994 and 1995 illustrated that racial harassment experienced by Black young people in schools involved, not only verbal abuse but also being punched, kicked, spat at or beaten.

One of the most tragic incidents of racist violence in a school was the racist attack and murder of 13-year-old Ahmed Ullah in 1986. Ahmed was stabbed by his white peer Darren Coulbourn, in the playground of Burnage High School in Manchester, after which he exclaimed 'I've killed a Paki' (Macdonald et al., 1989). The inquiry into the killing identified that all forms of racial harassment were widespread within the school and that for Black pupils schooling took 'place in an atmosphere of constant intimidation, and amidst the ever-present threat to life and limb' (Hill, 1990: 99). However, the Runnymede Trust (1989) contends that the levels of racial harassment present in Burnage High School are unfortunately nothing new and can be seen wherever a Black population is present in Britain.

The impact of racial harassment on young people

The impact of racial harassment on young people is profound and complex. However, it is an aspect of the problem, which is often neglected or underestimated, and thus little is known about how young people are affected by it (Gordon, 1989). Any discussion on the impact of racial harassment must begin by acknowledging that the impact of any form of racist abuse will always be greater than other forms of harassment because of the racist motivation behind the act (Fitzgerald and Hale, 1996). Racist motivation can transform seemingly trivial incidents into ones that are distressing and frightening for both the victim and other members of the ethnic group. Furthermore:

> *the impact of racial violence on ethnic minority children and young people may be compounded by the fact that it serves to reinforce their unequal position within a racist*

society, adding to a cumulative body of experiences which inform them that their identity is not valued by white culture.

(Barter, 1999: 30)

Whether it is verbal or physical, research suggests that racial harassment has an insidious effect on a child's emotional, physical and psychological development and can significantly damage a young person's chances of fulfilling their potential (Barn, 2001; Barter, 1999; Bodalbhai, 1993). One of the greatest effects of racial harassment is on a young person's emotional well-being and sense of identity. This is understandable given the fact that a young person's sense of self is interrelated with an understanding of their ethnic identity and of how it might impact on others. Therefore, experiencing racial harassment will invariably affect a young person's self-image and self-esteem. As Akhtar and Stronach (1986) state, racial harassment causes 'a quiet erosion of identity and self-esteem, brought about by nice white children on nice brown children' (Akhtar and Stronach, 1986: 23).

Lack of self-esteem and poor self-image can also be caused by a young person internalising the value judgments conveyed by racial harassment (MacLeod, 1998; Fanon, 1993). As a result of internalising their oppression a young person will begin to feel self-doubt, self-invalidation and deserving of mistreatment. Ultimately a young person will develop an inferiority complex and begin to hate and despise themselves (Memmi, 2003; Fanon, 1993). This is highlighted by the following example from a young victim of racial harassment 'I hate myself. I hate my father, he made me Black' (MacLeod, 1998: 5). A further disturbing outcome of the reality or threat of racial harassment is that many Black young people accept it as a part of life. Consequently racist abuse becomes normalised as highlighted by the following examples from two Black young people, 'you learn to live with it, you have to it's a way of life' and 'it happens so much, it's natural, the norm' (Rupra, 2004: 24–9). This is highly concerning and raises a fundamental point of the importance of empowering Black young people to understand that they have rights and should not accept racist abuse as a lifelong burden.

Evidently racial harassment is deeply hurtful, destructive and can cause an increased level of vulnerability in the lives of young people (Barn, 2001). In addition to damaging a young person's self-concept it can leave a young person feeling isolated, angry, inadequate, scared, confused, ugly and insecure. However, getting a young person to talk about their experiences will be extremely difficult because of their feelings of despair and shame, which MacLeod (1998) asserts are similar to those who suffer from sexual abuse. However, it should be noted that for many young people being given the opportunity to talk about their experiences in a safe, sympathetic and sensitive environment is fundamental to the process of recovery and will contradict their feelings of isolation and hopelessness. Nonetheless, the reality is that many Black young people are not given the opportunity to discuss their feelings and feel that their schools will be unsympathetic. As highlighted by the following example from a Black male 'when we want to say something, our part of the story, they don't let you speak. They don't wanna hear it' (Rupra, 2004: 28).

The emotional impact of racial harassment can also cause various physical symptoms that can have an intense effect on a young person's health. For instance young people may experience depression, a loss of confidence, sleeping difficulties such as nightmares, insomnia or bed-wetting, anorexia, self-injury, headaches, stress and stomach aches. In extreme cases, sustained racial harassment will render some young people so despondent that they will attempt or commit suicide. As Jaffrey (1997) states racial harassment often leads 'quite simply, to the loss of childhood' (Jaffrey, 1997: 2).

The physical and emotional impact of racist victimisation will also seriously damage a young person's quality of life. For instance, 'taken-for-granted, everyday activities can become major tasks involving avoidance of the perpetrators, changes in routines or habit' (Chahal and Julienne, 1999: 27). Depending on the level and impact of racial harassment a young person's education will also be disrupted. For example, a young person may be unable to concentrate in class, be referred to a special educational unit or psychological service, truant or choose to transfer to a different school, all of which will constrain their educational potential and achievement. Academic achievement can also be inhibited by the fact that some victims of racial harassment are excluded from school as a result of retaliating or acting in self-defence from racist abuse (John, 2003; Bourne, 1994). This was noted by the Office for Standards in Education (Ofsted) which found that unequal treatment within schools 'was noticeable in the disproportionately high number of Afro-Caribbean boys excluded for incidents where boys had retaliated against racial harassment' (Ofsted in Barter, 1999: 14). This raises an important point in that, until schools tackle racial harassment effectively the educational performance and achievement of many Black young people is unlikely to improve. Lemos (2000) further contends that the impact on educational attainment has lasting consequences as it can also impact on economic opportunity in adulthood. It can also inform adulthood in the way that individuals raise their children and become a part of the anti-racist movement (Virdee, 1995). Finally, it is important to emphasise that young people are not just passive victims to racial harassment. Rather it is a problem they actively resist on a day-to-day basis by employing a variety of different coping strategies.

Dealing with racial harassment in schools

Schools are one of the key agencies of socialisation and cultural transmission and consequently play an important role in the transmission of a racist culture. This is evident, in the range of evidence already presented demonstrating the tenacity and pervasiveness of racial harassment in schools. Consequently, concerns about how to tackle racial harassment in schools have been dogging education providers ever since the late 1970s and despite the best efforts of those who have tried to find ways of addressing the issue it remains as high a priority as it ever was (Dadzie, 2000; Troyna and Hatcher, 1992a).

Although there have been various attempts to address racial harassment within the education system, one of the most significant and influential has been the Macpherson Report (1999). This report clearly demonstrated the important role schools can play in tackling racist abuse and the need for a committed response from educational institutions. Once the report was published central government responded in a variety of ways. For example a Department for Education and Skills (DfES) circular was produced stating that the government regarded issues around racial harassment as fundamental to its social inclusion policies and that all staff and pupils should know how to deal with it. The Race Relations Act 1976 was also amended in 2000 placing an enforceable duty on all public bodies, including LEAs and schools to eliminate racial discrimination and promote racial equality and good relations between different racial groups. In order to meet these duties schools had to begin by developing a race equality policy and action plan, both of which had to incorporate how the school intended to deal with and prevent racial harassment (DfES, 2004). Schools are also required when completing self-evaluations to consider whether pupils feel safe from racist abuse, and the extent to which they feel able to talk to staff and others when at risk.

Moreover, based on one of the three recommendations for schools in the Macpherson report, schools now have a duty to report information on racist incidents to their LEAs and tackle the issue of underreporting. This is to ensure the levels of racist incidents locally and nationally are monitored, to look for any patterns in their occurrence and to plan strategies to address such behaviour. The Children's Act 2004, Education Act 2005, School Standards and Framework Act 1998 and *Every Child Matters* document also all make reference to the importance of young people feeling safe from bullying, which includes racial harassment. A further significant development came in March 2006 when the DfES launched a substantial web-based piece of guidance. This guidance is grounded in an in depth consultation process, which has taken place over the last two and a half years. This is a hopeful and promising development as it is the first time national guidance for schools has explored the issue of racial harassment in such depth and clarity.

Although the developments over the last seven years are extremely encouraging there remains a need for more in-depth research to highlight if and how schools are dealing with the issue. Unfortunately, the information that is currently available does not present a positive picture. For instance, while developing a whole-school policy to deal with race equality has been identified as an important step for any school, the CRE states that of all the public institutions, schools have been the slowest to comply to their statutory duties under the Race Relations Amendment Act (2000). Cline et al.'s (2002) study of 35 LEA areas and 14 schools also found that although all schools had written policies on bullying and established procedures for handling complaints about it, only a minority of these policies explicitly covered racial harassment. Many of the schools treated racial harassment as an aspect of the bullying to be expected in any school environment, consequently, Cline et al. found only one school with a formal procedure in place for recording racist incidents separately.

The notion of dealing with racial harassment as a bullying issue is not something new and far more palatable for many within the school system. For some teachers race is not a significant characteristic and simply one amongst others such as weight or wearing glasses that can be chosen by a bully to target an individual. As a result, rather than developing a specific policy to deal with racial harassment, schools deal with the problem under a bullying or behavioural policy. However, to do this illustrates a lack of understanding of the issue of racial harassment. As already highlighted the impact of racial harassment differs from other forms of harassment and it informs a young person's wider experience of racism within society. Therefore, if we are to meet the needs of Black pupils, schools must have a distinct policy on dealing with racist abuse. Furthermore, to conflate these forms of discrimination and victimisation is to misunderstand the nature and degree of racial harassment experienced by Black young people and invariably means that it will be dealt with inappropriately and marginalised.

This lack of commitment to dealing with racial harassment through the development of a specific policy is extremely disappointing and can be partly attributed to a culture of denial in regards to the seriousness and importance of racial harassment. This culture of denial has lead to a deeply entrenched legacy of ignoring racist abuse, causing many schools to either underestimate the true extent of the problem or to pretend the problem does not exist at all (Gaine, 1995; Willey, 1984). For example when speaking to schools, many will present a 'no problem here' attitude yet, when working in the schools and speaking to the pupils, it is evident that racist abuse and harassment is a reality for some or many of the Black young people. What is even more disturbing is that, in some instances, when the Black pupil's experiences are presented to the school they are often dismissed or excused in some way. This was also highlighted in a study by Jones (1999) which highlighted Black students being continually subjected to racial harassment whilst their respective schools denied any existence of the problem. As Jones states 'the most conspicuous spectre that haunted my data was "silence" ' (Jones, 1999: 138).

Despite this culture of denial, LEAs and many schools have produced policy statements stressing the need to be vigilant over matters relating to racial harassment (Ofsted, 2005). Developing a race equality policy serves as a public declaration to everyone involved in the school community that the school takes racism seriously (Dadzie, 2000). Even though such prescriptions are produced for the purpose of action and can be effective in reducing racial harassment as highlighted within an Ofsted report (2005), they are not always put into practice and the link between policy and practice can often be patchy or even non-existent (Troyna and Hatcher, 1992b). Research has also shown that having a school policy is not in itself indicative of whole school commitment to tackling racist abuse (Dadzie, 2000; Scott, 1990; Pumfrey and Verma, 1990; Willey, 1984). For example, in some schools, although a racist incidents policy may exist some members of the school community such as learning support assistants, lunchtime supervisors and even some teachers are unaware of the policy and the procedures to deal with racist abuse. Because of this careful consideration must be given to how such policies are disseminated to the school community.

The disparity between policy and classroom realities can be further highlighted in relation to the reporting and recording of racist incidents, a statutory requirement for all schools. For instance, the Inquiry team into the murder of Ahmed Ullah at Burnage High School found that the level of incidents reported by young people during interviews was far in excess of the number reported under the City Council's procedure for notification of incidents of racist abuse (Macdonald et al., 1989). These findings were echoed in Cline et al.'s (2002) study, which found that only half of the young people who had reported incidents of racist abuse to the researcher had reported them to teachers.

The underreporting of racial harassment is a general problem in dealing with the phenomenon. However, in schools, strategies to deal with incidents of racist abuse rely on teachers being informed of their occurrence therefore the rate of non-reporting is of crucial significance. Underreporting in schools can be accounted to various factors. For instance, an Ofsted report (2005) found that racial harassment was being underreported 'because of the perceived lack of confidence in defining and reporting incidents or a lack of clear LEA guidance' (Ofsted, 2005: 15). This lack of confidence will invariably lead to inappropriate responses. Research has also shown that for those Black pupils who have tried to take grievances of racial harassment to teachers, their victimisation is not only questioned but also often disputed, which has resulted in many pupils no longer reporting such incidents (Cline et al., 2002; MacLeod, 1998; Odedra, 1997; Macdonald et al.,

1989). This is highlighted in a study by Rupra (2004) on the experiences of young people and youth workers in Leicester City, which found that the young people consulted with, had a lack of trust in their respective school's ability to be supportive and effective in dealing with racial harassment. 'Although there was a small minority of young people who felt better as a result of telling teachers the majority of young people were critical of the failure of class teachers to take effective action' (Rupra, 2004: 27).

Rupra's study highlights examples of inaction, inappropriate responses and nothing identifiable happening as a result of young people reporting racial harassment to their teachers. As highlighted by the following 'teachers don't know how to deal with it' and 'I wouldn't go to a teacher coz they don't do anything' (Rupra, 2004: 54). Despite DfES guidance outlining the importance of pupils knowing how to deal with racist abuse the study further revealed that the young people were not only unaware of their respective school's procedures to deal with racial harassment but that they were also extremely reluctant to go to a teacher for support and had a lack of confidence in the effectiveness of reporting. 'Young people reported that they felt teachers did not take racism seriously or were racist themselves, reinforcing feelings of powerlessness' (Rupra, 2004: 27). The young people also felt that their experiences would be dismissed or that they would be seen as an inconvenience for the teacher. This is all highlighted by a variety of examples all of which provide a damning example of schools and teachers, in their ability to deal with racial harassment appropriately. For example, one male explained, 'in class lots of times I'd be called Paki and the teacher would tell me to get out of the class', whilst a female stated 'I wouldn't tell a teacher it's not as if anyone's gonna believe you' (Rupra, 2004: 28).

This evidence is very concerning and questions the representativeness of the statistics presented by the Leicester LEA. It also challenges MacLeod's (1998) view that young people in multicultural environments are less likely to experience racial harassment and that the adults within these environments are more responsive to the issue of racial harassment. Additionally, the study highlights the importance of talking to young people. It is clear when speaking to Black young people that they welcome being given the opportunity to discuss the issue of racism in a safe environment, where their contributions will be valued. Therefore, if Black young people are to be afforded a positive schooling experience, schools must genuinely deal with the issue of racial harassment by firstly listening to and involving their pupils. By genuinely listening to young people schools will be able to assess what is actually happening within their school gates and take effective action. Moreover, if such initiatives are to work, schools must be sincere and accept what they are being told, all of which will assist in establishing trust between the school and its pupils.

The issue of underreporting is not only due to the culture of denial present in some schools, but can be attributed to a variety of other reasons. For example, studies have suggested that schools are ineffective in dealing with racial harassment because many teachers feel great discomfort when discussing any form of racism as it is viewed as a particularly controversial and threatening issue (Gaine, 1995; Troyna, 1988). Accordingly, many teachers are reluctant to tackle the issue at all because they fear talking about it will make things worse, as they may say the wrong thing and leave themselves open to accusations of racism (Jones, 1999; Nieto, 1997). Some teachers also feel that by drawing attention to the issue they will create problems in the school that might never have surfaced. This rationale invariably allows some teachers to deny the importance of dealing with it. Ultimately this has an adverse effect on Black young people as they are often left to deal with racist abuse without appropriate support and in isolation.

To some extent this reluctance can be attributed to a lack of understanding and uncertainty experienced by some teachers, in regards to the practicalities of dealing with the problem. For instance, when speaking to teachers in several Manchester schools Kelly (1990) found that 'teachers readily acknowledged that they felt less assurance on this aspect of their work than in other areas of pupil behaviour' (Kelly, 1990: 88). Although guidance produced by LEAs and the DfES attempt to address this issue there is still the issue of how staff conceptualise the issue of racism and consequently interpret the guidance. Guidance alone does not ensure school staff have the appropriate understanding and skills to deal with racial harassment in an appropriate way. Because of this staff training should be understood as an integral part of a school being effective. However, sending key members of staff on racial harassment training is not enough, as the whole school community needs to be aware of how to deal with the issue. Often schools send mentors or the race equality co-ordinator to training sessions however, this will only ensure that these individuals are fully equipped to deal with the issue. Thus if schools are to be effective in their responses to racist abuse every member of the school community must receive regular training and guidance as a part of their professional development. Until effective training packages, that demonstrate the relevance and consequences of dealing with racial harassment are created, the issue will continue to be marginalised and Black young people will continue to be let down. Teacher training also has a fundamental role in determining the way racial harassment is responded to and understood. In a recent survey the Teacher Training Agency revealed that only 34 per cent of Newly Qualified Teachers (NQTs) felt that they were adequately prepared to work with Black young people, which clearly puts into question the way NQTs will deal with racist abuse.

This lack of understanding and uncertainty leads some teachers to either feel hostile to dealing with the problem or causes them to ignore incidents of racist abuse that are not only reported to them, but are also witnessed by them (Odedra, 1997; Epstein, 1993; Macdonald et al., 1989). For many Black pupils this is translated as teachers condoning the abuse and highlights their lack of commitment to dealing with the problem (Troyna and Hatcher, 1992b). However, it should be noted that the absence of intervention by some teachers is also because they are unsympathetic to the issue. There is a range of evidence suggesting that the personal racism of some teachers is a fundamental obstacle in dealing with racial harassment effectively, as they not only condone racist abuse but can at times be the perpetrators of the abuse themselves (Rupra, 2004; Jones, 1999; Odedra, 1997; Epstein, 1993; Troyna and Carrington, 1990).

Although the majority of studies exploring how schools deal with racial harassment highlight the difficulties faced by schools, it would be wrong to think there are no examples of good practice. For instance a report by Ofsted (2005) identified numerous examples of good practice from LEAs and schools. Furthermore, those schools that deal with racial harassment successfully do so firstly because they have a strong leadership team which makes a clear stance against racist abuse and is open to exploring the topic. There is also recognition that a school community reflects wider society thus racial harassment is inevitable and not indicative of a failing school. Schools that adopt this stance generally deal with racial harassment in a multifaceted and meaningful way.

Developing a school policy is only the starting point. Other strategies involve regular staff trainings and meetings, involving the pupils in discussions and preventative work and providing appropriate support to victims. For example in Cline et al.'s (2002) study the schools that dealt effectively with racial harassment were those that identified strategies that made it easier for pupils to report racist abuse through anonymous 'Bullying Boxes', which received staff attention within 24 hours. Certain schools also demonstrated strategies, such as 'thinking sheets' and 'circle time', aimed at encouraging pupils to reflect on racist incidents. Gillborn's study (1995) also illustrates the benefits of actively engaging pupils in the process of challenging racial harassment through anti-racist work. For Gillborn (1995) the two secondary schools in his study were successful in their attempts to deal with racial harassment because they dealt consistently with accusations of such abuse and took the perspectives of both Black and white pupils seriously.

Conclusion

Racial harassment experienced by young people at school is little documented and receives little attention. However, what is clear from the current analysis is that racial harassment is a highly contingent aspect of school life for many Black young people and is much more extensive than is commonly realised. This analysis has provided a disturbing picture of the reality of racial harassment within schools and has shown that a number of our children are learning in fear. It has shown that incidents occur in all aspects of school life and range from verbal abuse to violence, leading to injury and even death. In addition to showing the extent of racial harassment in schools, the analysis has highlighted that racial harassment has a profound impact on young people. It not only hinders a young person's chances of fulfilling their educational potential, it can have a profound impact on their social, emotional and psychological development. Ultimately, racial harassment can affect a young person's life chances (Akhtar and Stronach, 1986).

Although racial harassment impacts on the educational careers, security and welfare of young people, it has been shown that there remains a number of important gaps and limitations in dealing with the issue in schools. For instance, despite being a pervasive feature of many schools, the seriousness of racial harassment is not matched by a corresponding awareness and sense of urgency on the part of some schools (Jones, 1999). For Chouhan and Jasper (2001) this can be attributed to the nature of institutionalised racism within education. Many schools also underestimate the true extent of the problem or are unable or unwilling to do anything about it (Cline et al., 2002; Bagley, 1992).

It has also been shown that for some of those schools that have developed a policy to deal with racial harassment, there is a problematic relationship between the policy and the reality of implementation and practice, as some teachers, for various reasons, do not follow the approved procedures. For instance, some teachers are themselves racist and have a lack of value and willingness to address the issue (Jones, 1999; Epstein, 1993). However, to simply write off teachers as racist is to obscure the complex issue of why racial harassment is not being addressed effectively in schools. It also obscures the fact that there are many teachers who are committed to an anti-racist education system. Gillborn (1995) further attributes the failure of school policies to the fact that 'some school policies serve a primarily cosmetic function; existing only because they are required (by central and/or local government) or as a politically expedient symbol of the school's awareness of particular issues' (Gillborn, 1995: 119). Consequently, such policies are not always an affirmation of practice but act as mere paper exercises, which do not imply whole school commitment to tackling racial harassment.

In addition to the various reasons already highlighted as to why schools are unable to deal with racial harassment appropriately, lack of clarity on the dynamics of racism and racial harassment is another important factor. Corson (1998) contends that lack of understanding in regards to dealing with racial harassment influences the effectiveness of policies as 'teachers are being asked to make policies about complex matters for which they have little training or expertise' (Corson, 1998: 39). Therefore, if schools are to respond constructively to racial harassment, policies and practices must be based on a more comprehensive understanding of the issue.

In order to fully understand why schools have difficulty in dealing with racial harassment the larger pedagogical issues must also be addressed. It is important to look at the wider issues of the debate, as this will provide a context to explain why schools are unable to deal with racial harassment effectively. In order to do this the political climate of the last 20 years must be considered as it has led to a new plateau of professional indifference when it comes to issues related to social justice, especially anti-racist education (Jones, 1999; Deem et al., 1992). In the late 1980s the unified education system originally established under the 1944 Education Reform Act (ERA) began to be dismantled under the 1988 ERA. The 1988 ERA introduced sweeping educational reforms that reconstructed the education system primarily by shifting educational and financial control away from LEAs and giving it to individual schools (Bridges, 1994; Jones, 1989). Most significantly of all, delegated budgets were to be determined strictly in line with a 'per capita' formula fixed on the number of pupils on each school's roll. The government's educational ideology represented a free market philosophy, extolling the virtues of competition, privatisation and efficiency (Jones, 1999; Hargreaves and Reynolds, 1989). The education system became firmly set within capitalist social relations.

As a result of the changes in education, schools have become privatised institutions, which LEAs have little control over. Therefore even when a LEA or the DfES produces guidance on dealing with racial harassment they are unable to enforce the document as they have little control over what schools do or do not decide to implement. It is at the discretion of the school whether they take the guidance on board. Furthermore, schools have greater freedom to manage their own affairs including the content of their policies and 'deciding whether racial harassment is an issue for the school, whether particular incidents are defined as racial harassment and serious enough to warrant intervention' (Odedra, 1997: 17). The consequences of this, is that there is less direction from LEAs and the ways in which schools deal with racial harassment can be limited.

The 1988 ERA also intensified central intervention in the curriculum and in the early 1990s the National Curriculum was implemented to 'ensure the conformity of teaching objectives to centrally-established criteria' (Jones, 1989: 21). With the advent of the National Curriculum and the drive towards literacy and numeracy, anti-racist teaching has been marginalised almost out of existence (Ball and Troyna, 1989). This was initially received with hostility from those committed to the ideals of anti-racism, as they felt compelled to de-prioritise the issue. Consequently, anti-racist education has become conceptually, practically and ideologically adrift of classroom practice (Dadzie, 2000; Deem et al., 1992). Schools have been overtaken in the classroom by issues of assessment and locked in a systemic arrangement of schooling which puts pressure on teachers to meet the targets set out in the National Curriculum (Blair and Arnot, 1993). As Jones (1999) states, teachers find 'themselves buried beneath the weight of educational legislation and parental pressure to achieve within the stated guidelines' (Jones, 1999: 12).

The National Curriculum also made education 'qualification-focused' as it stipulated the levels of attainment that students were expected to reach, which were also to be presented in league tables. League tables have become increasingly significant as they provide the narrow means through which a school's success is measured, illustrating the quantifying culture of schools (Bridges, 1994). League tables not only provide school consumers (parents) with market information, they also provide a way in which schools can advertise themselves and consequently ensure an advantageous market position (Hargreaves and Reynolds, 1989). Moreover, because racial harassment is not a marketable or consumable concept for schools they do not want to draw attention to the issue, thus the notion of 'no problem here' present in many schools is tightly bound with the fear of adversely affecting the school's position within a competitive market place.

Jones (1999) describes this system of education as having created a 'typology of disappearance' in regards to dealing with racism and racial harassment. For Jones not only has racial harassment in schools been systematically ignored, but also:

Institutional practices have effectively managed to spawn an entire generation of teachers who have no understanding of the situation or needs of ethnic minority children, who have no strategies to deal with racist behaviour in the classroom and playground.

(Jones, 1999: 142)

and who can

. . . only conceptualise the issue by convincing themselves of its irrelevance. Consequently, the absence of any educational input on issues of race has meant that many teachers are unable to recognise the importance of acknowledging and understanding ethnic status in the classroom, nor do they have professional strategies to combat the racism present in the education system.

The implications of this analysis are far-reaching and clearly illustrate that the changes in the education system have meant that racial harassment has until recently not been given the attention it deserves. By ignoring or dismissing what is in fact an ever present and all pervasive shadow over the everyday lives of many Black young people, schools are failing to uphold their responsibility to give every young person an equal chance to learn in an environment conducive to mutual respect and co-operation; an environment free from racial harassment (Swann, 1985). For the Runnymede Trust the failure of schools to guarantee the safety of Black young people 'as they compulsorily attend those corridors of terror is one of the biggest indictments of the English schooling system' (Runnymede Trust, 1989: 27). If we are to open opportunities for ways of dealing with racial harassment and young people are to learn in an environment, which is free from racist abuse and conducive to learning, all schools and LEAs need to address the issue openly and with commitment (Troyna and Williams, 1986). For example it should not be deemed sufficient for one or two representatives of a school to receive racist incidents training as there is no indication of how the information provided during the training will be disseminated to the whole school community or implemented within the school. It is vital everyone within a school receives training and is given the opportunity to explore the issue. If changes are not made racial harassment will continue to be a feature of Britain's schools. Change will only occur if schools begin by bringing the issue of racial harassment into the open, accept that it exists and are able to talk about it. The culture of silence must be broken.

Although there has been significant pressure because of the Macpherson Report for schools to make the goal of challenging racism and valuing diversity central to their practice 'current evidence suggests that the education system has failed to learn from the tragedy of Stephen's murder and the resultant inquiry. Schools have been slow to respond to their new duties and most appear content to take no further action' (Gillborn, 2004: 24). For Dadzie (2000) a change will only occur if there are significant changes in the mindset of many teachers, as well as time and resources to develop new ways of working. This is not to say the new guidance produced by the DfES is not a welcomed development. However, it should be considered how this web-based guidance is going to be disseminated to all those working within a school community and who will ensure it is implemented?

Dealing with racial harassment should not be an option as it has implications not just for the whole of the education system but also for the society within which it operates. Although education alone cannot remove racial harassment from society it can make a powerful difference assisting to create an anti-racist Britain of the future (Richards, 2003, online). MacLeod (1998) recognises that this places a great responsibility on schools. However, she also recognises that there is nowhere else which offers the same opportunities to tackle racial harassment. Teachers are in an invaluable position to bring about change in the lives of all young people. Therefore, if we are to meet the needs of Black young people schools must acknowledge and respond to racial harassment sincerely. Until this happens Black young people will continue to be disadvantaged.

References

Aboud, F.E. (1988) *Children and Prejudice.* Oxford: Basil Blackwell.

Ahmad, Y., Whitney, I. and Smith, P. (1991) A Survey Service For Schools on Bully/Victim Problems. In Smith, P. and Thompson, D. (Eds.) *Practical Approaches to Bullying.* London: David Fulton Publishers.

Akhtar, S. and Stronach, I. (1986) They Call Me Blacky. *Times Educational Supplement,* 19th Sep. 23.

Bagley, C.A. (1992) In-service Provision and Teacher Resistance to Whole-School Change. In Gill, D., Mayor, B. and Blair, M. (Eds.) *Racism and Education Structures And Strategies.* London: Sage.

Ball, W. and Troyna, B. (1989) The Dawn of a New ERA? The Education Reform Act, Race and LEAs. *Educational Administration and Management,* 17: 1, 23–31.

Barn, R. (2001) *Black Youth on The Margins. A Research Review.* York: York Publishing Services.

Barter, C. (1999) *Protecting Children From Racism and Racial Abuse. A Research Review.* London: NSPCC.

Bhate, S. and Bhate, S. (1997) Racial Violence and Young People. In Varma, V. (Ed.) *Violence in Children and Adolescents.* London: Jessica Kingsley.

Blair, M. and Arnot, M. (1993) Black and Anti-Racist Perspectives on The National Curriculum and Government Educational Policy. In King, A.S. and Reiss, M.J. (Eds.) *The Multicultural Dimension of The National Curriculum*. London: The Falmer Press.

Bodalbhai, E. (1993) Responding to Racial Harassment: Practical Strategies in Education. In Francis, P. and Matthews, R. (Eds.) *Tackling Racial Attacks*. Leicester: University of Leicester.

Bourne, J. (1994) Stories of Exclusion. In Bourne, J., Bridges, L. and Searle, C. (Eds.) *Outcast England How Schools Exclude Black Children*. London: Institute of Race Relations.

Bridges, L. (1994) Exclusions, How Did We Get Here? In Bourne, J., Bridges, L. and Searle, C. (Eds.) *Outcast England How Schools Exclude Black Children*. London: Institute of Race Relations.

Carrington, B. and Short, G. (1989) *Race and The Primary School Theory Into Practice*. Berkshire: NFER-Nelson.

Chahal, K. (1999) The Stephen Lawrence Inquiry Report, Racist Harassment and Racist Incidents: Changing Definitions, Clarifying Meaning? *Sociological Research*, [Cited 1st August 2006]. http:/www.socresonline.org.uk/socresonline/4/lawrence/chahl.html.

Chahal, K. and Julienne, L. (1999) *'We Can't All Be White!' Racist Victimisation in The UK*. York: York Publishing Services.

Chouhan, K. and Jasper, L. (2001) *A Culture of Denial The 1990 Trust Report on The Racist Murder of Stephen Lawrence*. London: The 1990 Trust.

Cline, T. et al. (2002) *Minority Ethnic Pupils in Mainly White Schools*. Norwich: DfES.

Cohn, T. (1989) Sambo: A Study in Name Calling. In Kelly, E. and Cohn, T. (Eds.) *Racism in Schools New Research Evidence*. Stoke-on-Trent: Trentham Books.

CRE (1988) *Learning in Terror: A Survey of Racial Harassment in Schools and Colleges*. London: CRE.

Corson, D. (1998) *Changing Education for Diversity*. Buckingham: Open University Press.

Dadzie, S. (2000) *Toolkit for Tackling Racism in Schools*. Staffordshire: Trentham Books.

Deem, R., Brehony, K. J. and Hemmings, S. (1992) Social Justice, Social Divisions and The Governing of Schools. In Gill, D., Mayor, B. and Blair, M. (Eds.) *Racism and Education Structures and Strategies*. London: Sage Publications.

DfES (2004) *Schools' Race Equality Policies: From Issues to Outcomes*. London: DfES.

Epstein, D. (1993) *Changing Classrooms Cultures and Anti-Racism, Politics and Schools*. Stoke-on-Trent: Trentham Books.

Fanon, F. (1993) *Black Skin White Masks*. London: Pluto Press.

Fitzgerald, M. and Hale, C. (1996) *Ethnic Minorities, Victimisation and Racial Harassment*. Research Findings No. 39, London: Home Office Research and Statistics Department.

Francis, P. and Matthews, R. (1993) *Tackling Racial Attacks*. Leicester: University of Leicester.

Fryer, P. (1984) *Staying Power: The History of Black People in Britain*. London: Pluto Press.

Gaine, C. (1995) *Still No Problem Here*. Staffordshire: Trentham Books.

Gill, D., Mayor, B. and Blair, M. (1992) *Racism and Education Structures and Strategies*. London: Sage.

Gillborn, D. (2004) Are Your Children Being Set up to Fail? In Stephen Lawrence Charitable Trust (Eds.) *The Stephen Lawrence Charitable Trust 2004–2005*. London: Stephen Lawrence Charitable Trust.

Gillborn, D. (1995) *Racism and Antiracism in Real Schools Theory Policy Practice*. Buckingham: Open University Press.

Gordon, P. (1990) *Racial Violence and Harassment*. London: Runnymede Trust.

Gordon, P. (1989) Hidden Injuries of Racism. *New Statesman and Society*, 49: 2, 24–5.

Hargreaves, A. and Reynolds, D. (1989) *Education Policies: Controversies and Critiques*. Sussex: Falmer Press.

Hill, D. (1990) The Macdonald Report: A Report and Commentary. In Pumfrey P.D. and Verma, G.K. (Eds.) *Race Relations and Urban Education: Contexts and Promising Practices*. Hampshire: Falmer Press.

Jaffrey, M. (1997) Children, Young People and Racism: Comment by The CRE. *Childright,* 134, 2–3.

John, G. (2003) *The Crisis Facing Black Children in The British Schooling System A Call to Independent Action by Black Students and Black Parents.* Lancashire: The Gus John Partnership.

Jones, R. (1999) *Teaching Racism or Tackling It? Multicultural Stories From White Beginning Teachers.* Staffordshire: Trentham Books.

Jones, K. (1989) *Right Turn The Conservative Revolution in Education.* London: Hutchinson Radius.

Kelly, E. (1990) Use and Abuse of Racial Language in Secondary Schools. In Pumfrey P.D. and Verma, G.K. (Eds.) *Race Relations and Urban Education: Contexts and Promising Practices.* Hampshire: Falmer Press.

Lemos, G. (2000) *Racial Harassment: Action on The Ground.* London: Lemos and Crane.

Lemos, G. (2005) *The Search for Tolerance.* York: Joseph Rowntree Foundation.

Macdonald, I. Et al. (1989) *Murder in The Playground The Report of The Macdonald Inquiry Into Racism and Racial Violence in Manchester Schools.* London: Longsight Press.

Macleod, M. (1998) *Children and Racism: A Childline Study.* London: Childline.

Macpherson, W. (1999) *The Stephen Lawrence Inquiry.* [Cited 16th August 2006]. http://www.archive.official-documents.co.uk/document/cm42/4262.html

Mason, D. (2000) *Race and Ethnicity in Modern Britain.* Oxford: Oxford University Press.

Memmi, A. (2003) *The Coloniser and The Colonised.* London: Earthscan Publications.

Milner, D. (1983) *Children and Race: Ten Years On.* London: Ward Lock Educational.

Nieto, S. (1997) School Reform and Student Achievement: A Multicultural Perspective. In Banks J.A. and Mcgee, C.A. (Eds.) *Multicultural Education Issues and Perspectives.* London: Allyn and Bacon.

Oakley, R. (1992) *Racial Violence and Harassment in Europe.* Strasbourg: Council of Europe.

Odedra, S. (1997) *Racial Harassment in Schools, A Report of Research Commissioned by Community Against Racism Multi-Agency Project in Warwick District.* Coventry: Coventry University.

Ofsted (2005) *Race Equality in Education Good Practice in Schools and Local Education Authorities.* London: Ofsted.

Pumfrey, P.D. and Verma, G.K. (1990) *Race Relations and Urban Education: Contexts and Promising Practices.* Hampshire: Falmer Press.

Richards, J. (2003) *Saris and Samosas Won't Beat Bigot*ry. [Cited 20th July 2006]. http://www.tes.co.uk/search/story/?story_id=385461.

Runnymede Trust (1989) *Racism, Anti-Racism and Schools: A Summary of The Burnage Report.* London: Runnymede Trust.

Rupra, M. (2004) *Responding to Racist Incidents A Project Report on The Views, Experiences and Needs of Youth Workers and Young People in Leicester City.* Leicester: Leicester and Leicestershire Racial Equality Council.

Scott, J. (1990) *A Matter of Record.* Cambridge: Polity Press.

Short, G. and Carrington, B. (1992) Towards an Antiracist Initiative in The All-White Primary School: A Case Study. In Gill, D., Mayor, B. and Blair, M. (Eds.) *Racism and Education Structures and Strategies.* London: Sage.

Sibbitt, R. (1997) *The Perpetrators of Racial Harassment and Racial Violence.* London: Home Office.

Solomos, J. and Black, L. (1996) *Racism and Society.* Basingstoke: Macmillan.

Swann, M.L. (1985) *Education for All. The Report of The Committee of Inquiry Into The Education of Children From Ethnic Minority Groups.* London: HMSO.

Troyna, B. (1993) *Racism and Education.* Buckingham: Open University Press.

Troyna, B. (1988) The Career of an Anti-Racist School Policy: Some Observations on The Mismanagement of Change. In Green, A.G. and Ball, S.J. (Eds.) *Progress and Inequality in Comprehensive Education.* London: Routledge.

Troyna, B. and Carrington, B. (1990) *Education, Racism and Reform.* London: Routledge.

Troyna, B. and Hatcher, R. (1992a) Racist Incidents in Schools A Framework for Analysis. In Gill, D., Mayor, B. and Blair, M. (Eds.) *Racism and Education Structures and Strategies.* London: Sage.

Troyna, B. and Hatcher, R. (1992b) *Racism in Children's Lives A Study of Mainly White Primary Schools*. London: Routledge.

Troyna, B. and Williams, J. (1986) *Racism, Education and The State*. Kent: Croom Helm.

Van Dijk, T. A. (1993) *Elite Discourse and Racism*. Newbury Park, CA: Sage.

Virdee, S. (1997) Racial Harassment. In Modood, T. et al. (Eds.) *Ethnic Minorities in Britain: Diversity and Disadvantage*. London: Policy Studies Institute.

Virdee, S. (1995) *Racial Violence and Harassment*. London: Policy Studies Institute.

Wason-Ellam, L. (1996) Voices From The Shadows. In Epp, J.R. and Watkinson, M.A. (Eds.) *Systematic Violence: How Schools Hurt Children*. London: Farmer Press.

Willey, R. (1984) *Race, Equality and Schools*. London: Methuen and Co.

Wright, C. (1992) Early Education: Multiracial Primary School Classrooms. In Gill, D., Mayor, B. and Blair, M. (Eds.) *Racism and Education Structures and Strategies*. London: Sage.

Yeboah, S.K. (1997) *The Ideology of Racism*. London: Hansib Publishing.

Young, L. (2000) Imperial Culture, The Primitive, The Savage and White Civilisation. In Black, L. and Solomos J. (Eds.) *Theories of Race and Racism A Reader*. London: Routledge.

CHAPTER 7

Anti-oppressive Work in an Oppressive State

Dawn Summers

Introduction

Analysing the discourse of governments enables readers to glimpse the underlying philosophies that drive policy. In the case of immigration policy, an analysis of the language used in the white paper *Secure Borders, Safe Haven* (Home Office, 2002) would have forewarned those of us working with young people seeking asylum and refugees of the deteriorating circumstances that have come to pass. Subsequent acts, amendments and regulations would not have come as a surprise and forewarned would have left us fore-armed. Instead we missed the finer details and became so subsumed in the growing number of acts and amendments that effective opposition became incredibly difficult and policy change unlikely.

The language used in the white paper was not complicated, it made no attempt to hide its objectives in the language of academia, it did not use long, unfamiliar words nor did it bury its intent in jargon. As such its real power lay in the ability to use familiar, every day and apparently harmless language in the oppression of vulnerable people that have sought protection on British soil.

Thirty years ago racist language was easy to identify and anti-racist youth and community work had a readily accessible canvas on which to work the magic of anti-oppressive practice. But times have changed and the 21st century brings new challenges to those of us committed to ending oppression because we must face up to our own complacency.

We have learnt, as have others, the language of political correctness, we know which words to avoid and we can, at will, spout the philosophy of equal opportunities. In the 3rd millennium blatant racism is neither fashionable nor popular and accusations of such are virulently denied. We believe we have made progress. The truth however, is that we have not kept up with the changing face of racism. It has become more subtle, more covert than overt, more implicit than explicit, more devious and therefore much more dangerous.

The task now before us creates a dilemma that threatens the very fabric upon which youth and community work has traditionally been built because before us lies the task of working with young people who are subjected to an array of policy, practice and protestations about their legitimacy that have found a place in British law. Young people subjected to institutional racism at all levels including our own.

Youth and community work is founded on four principles, participation, empowerment, equality and education. The research discussed in this chapter seeks to uncover the oppressive nature of the state in discriminating against those seeking protection in Britain and thus poses the question of how do we apply these principles when working with young people subjected to that oppression. How do we ensure the participation of young people seeking asylum in democratic processes when they are excluded from them? How do we empower young people and encourage them to find a voice when policy effectively silences them and our ignorance silences us? What do we tell them about equality when their ability to access even the most basic of human rights is at best conditional and at worst non-existent? How do we educate them about the world in a way that fosters understanding and acceptance whilst we stand idly by and do nothing to alleviate their suffering, knowing that they have already experienced some of the worst this world has to offer? How do we explain that, how do we justify our own position?

There have been two occasions in my life when the foundation of my understanding of the way the world works has been challenged and found wanting. The first was my experience of working with some of the most exciting, challenging and humane young people I have ever met, young people who were seeking asylum in Britain. The second was more recent and involved meeting young people in Palestine who were living under an occupation and who suffered oppressive practice on a daily basis. I have no idea where the latter will lead me but the first has brought me here, to writing this chapter and sharing my thoughts with you the reader. If my writing causes you to analyse your own practice then this is good. If it causes you to analyse the politicians under whose gaze we live our daily lives, then this is better. However, if it creates within you a challenge, a need to reconsider your understanding of racism and the way this can be perpetuated on a daily basis with the open handed freedom of invisibility, then I shall be content. Buddha asked of his followers that they accept nothing as the truth until they had critically appraised its validity. I humbly ask that you do the same.

Imagine

Imagine living in a country where the government labels you as undesirable, subversive and criminal.[1]

Imagine living in a country where the powerful insist you speak their language and not your own,[2] a country that dismisses your hard won academic qualifications and employment history; a country that denies you the right to work and support yourself and your family.[3]

Imagine living in a country where you are segregated from the general population, placed in camps and denied the right to freedom.[4] Imagine a country that reserves the right to discriminate against you because of your ethnic origin.[5]

Imagine a government which openly declares its intention to rid the country of your kind,[6] a country where the press demonise you and the fascists beat you and the police are unable to protect you.

---

[1] Home Office, White Paper, Secure Borders, Safe Haven, 2002.

[2] Home Office, White Paper, Secure Borders, Safe Haven, 2002, (2.13:32).

[3] Home Office, Nationality, Immigration and Asylum Act, 2002.

[4] Home Office, White Paper, Secure Borders, Safe Haven, 2002, (4.15:52).

[5] Explanatory Notes to Race Relations (Amendment) Act 2000 Chapter 34 (paragraph 16).

[6] Home Office, White Paper, Secure Borders, Safe Haven, 2002, (4.73:65).

Imagine a country that refuses to accept you are entitled to be treated as a human being with rights: a country that puts its name to the Universal Declaration of Human Rights, and then refuses to apply its basic tenets, in your case: a country that declares itself able to deny your children their rights as defined by the Convention on the Rights of the Child.[7]

Imagine a country that is prepared to leave you to starve on its streets, without access to food or water, clothing or shelter for an administrative error that claims you failed to contact the relevant authorities fast enough.[8] And having left you destitute, imagine a regime that will remove your children from your care whilst forcibly returning you to the horror of further persecution, possibly torture and death.[9]

Imagine a country that would deny to the new born their basic right to adequate nutrition and good health. A country content to expose a baby to the risk of HIV infection or inadequate nutrition because the government creates regulations that exclude you from schemes designed to ensure adequate infant nutrition.[10]

A country ruled by a government who have removed your right to legal redress where their decisions have breached the law.[11] Where your need for protection is dismissed and obligations under Article 31 of the Refugee Convention are ignored.[12]

Imagine a country therefore that has a history of abusing human rights and openly declares its intention to continue, a country committed to increasing its persecution of your kind. Would you flee? Would you seek refuge in a 'safe' country?

And if you didn't need to seek refuge elsewhere because you weren't one of those targeted for this particular kind of treatment, is this the kind of country you want to live in, is it a place to raise your children? Are you prepared to stand by and do nothing?

This country is real, this country is Britain and I find myself ashamed to be part of it.

The personal context

I have been a full time youth and community worker for some 15 years and in 2002 I became involved in working with young people seeking asylum and refugees.

The group consisted of young people who were at varying stages of the immigration process and, as workers, we found ourselves on a steep learning curve as we struggled to understand the raft of immigration policy affecting these young people in order to support them adequately. What we discovered shocked and dismayed us as informal educators and for the first time in many years we found ourselves fighting both outright racism and covert discrimination from both local and national organisations, statutory and voluntary agencies, workers and funders. What shocked us most was the almost totally open way in which this form of racism was expressed. It was almost as if issues concerning immigration allowed racist sentiment and action as an acceptable approach

---

[7] Review of the UK's Reservations to International Human Rights Treaty Obligations. http://www.liberty-human-rights.org.uk. Accessed 15/02/04.

[8] Section 55, Nationality, Immigration and Asylum Act 2002.

[9] The Asylum and Immigration (Treatment of Claimants) Bill 2003, Clause 7.

[10] Regulation 4, Welfare Food Regulations 1996.

[11] The Asylum and Immigration (Treatment of Claimants) Bill 2003. Clause 10. http://www.refugeecouncil.org.uk/downloads/bi112003/2003bi11_jan04.pdf.

[12] The Asylum and Immigration (Treatment of Claimants) Bill 2003, Clause 2.

to managing young people subject to immigration control on a day to day basis. As professional youth and community workers we were stunned, as human beings we were incredibly angry.

The emotional cost of working with young people who had been subjected to torture, who had witnessed the rape of their mothers and the murder of their families was incredible and we were ill prepared for such but the constant need to explain and justify our work with this group of young people to others within the community only added to the cost.

The question we repeatedly asked ourselves was why? Why did it appear to be socially acceptable to behave in a racist manner towards people subject to immigration control?

I came to believe the answer lay in the attitude of government and I believed the evidence existed within government policy to demonstrate this clearly. My intention in studying the discourses used in the document *Secure Borders, Safe Haven*, David Blunkett's white paper on immigration and the basis on which present day immigration law stands, was to show that permission to behave in a racist way towards those seeking asylum is given in the discourses of negativity and criminality inherent in texts concerning immigration control. As Teresa Hayter argues I intended to demonstrate that 'immigration controls embody, legitimate and institutionalise racism' (Hayter, 2000: 21).

The research

The research on which this chapter is based was undertaken over the course of 2003. The main tenets of *Secure Borders, Safe Haven* were being put into practice and it was becoming clear just how harsh these practices were going to be.

The context within which this white paper was produced cannot be underestimated. Historically, it was the fore runner to the 2002 Nationality, Immigration and Asylum Act which was itself the latest in a long line of parliamentary acts that successively applied increasingly restrictive laws and regulations that affect the rights of immigrants in general and those seeking asylum in particular. Ideologically and politically New Labour have repeatedly made clear that they wish to control the number of people seeking entrance to the UK and in particular, to reduce the numbers of people seeking asylum. New Labour's white paper *Secure Borders, Safe Haven* sets out their plans for achieving this. Presented to government by the Home Secretary, David Blunkett MP in February 2002, it begins with a foreword by the same, followed by an executive summary of the main features of the paper chapter by chapter. The summary is followed by an invitation to readers to comment on the 'proposals' contained in the white paper. Although inviting people to comment on the white paper, the discourse used by New Labour is repeatedly produced from a position of power, comment may be invited but there was no indication that it would be heard.

Use of rhetoric – 'us' and 'them'

The language used is that of information giving and of educating, of preparing the ground for what is to come and of power and control. It does not appear to be based on consultation or collaboration and is not therefore an example of democracy in action. The paper is not just informative it is also promotional, it seeks to sell its ethos to the reader built on assumptions about what the problems are and therefore what solutions should be put in place. Dialogue between reader and writer is therefore unlikely (Fairclough, 2001). Thus the white paper represents New Labour in action and it stands not only as a descriptive account of proposed legislation but as government in action and policy in the making.

Although consent may not be seen as necessary there is evidence that it is seen as desirable and the document makes use of a number of rhetorical strategies in order to achieve this. Such strategies are evident throughout the white paper and we begin to see this as we examine the use of the term 'we'.

Although the paper's authors are repeatedly referred to as the 'government' and more often as 'we', there are times, especially in David Blunkett's introduction and in the executive summary, when the word 'we' is used in a much broader sense insofar as it connects with the 'we' of the British people. For example, in 'we need to be secure in our sense of belonging' (Foreword 1.13) and 'we should be proud that this is the view of the UK' (Foreword 2.6.) Using 'we' in this kind of inclusive manner draws the reader in, building alliances and attempting to create identification with the emotions, values and norms of the writer. 'We' are part of the same group, 'we' are alike and in this case, 'we' are British; and if we are alike and are perceived to share the same values and norms of the writer, 'we' should share/understand the policies and procedures being suggested.

This is even more apparent when examining the use made of the word 'our' where, with a few exceptions, it is used in an inclusive sense as far as people with British nationality are concerned and exclusively as far those who are not. Examples include 'our social well being and economic prosperity' (Foreword 1. 10), 'those coming into our country' (Foreword 5.19), 'our cultural vitality, the strength of our economy and our strong international links' (10.5.7). Other references include 'our communities', 'our values', 'our society', 'our democracy' and 'our laws' amongst many others.

There is one sentence where the word *'our'* is used seven times:

> . . . *our standards of service, our welcome to those who need our protection and who can contribute to our society and our unequivocal messages of deterrence to those who break our laws and abuse our hospitality will remain under close scrutiny.*
>
> (106.(8.1) 1–5)

The inclusive use of the word 'our' in this instance does more than create an implicit alliance between writer and reader since it brings the reader into an assumed agreement with the action proposed in the white paper, in this case the act of deterrence. This opens the way for the government to introduce measures designed to act as such whilst the language used to describe the people we need to deter, 'those who break our laws and abuse our hospitality' (106.(8.1) 4) serves to legitimise those measures being harsh.

This particular sentence demonstrates the use of repetition as a rhetorical strategy whilst at the same time providing an example of how positive self-presentation, coupled with negative 'other' presentation, plays into descriptions of 'us' and 'them' because as well as using the inclusive language of 'we' and 'our' to identify those of British nationality as 'us', the paper uses exclusive language to identify those without British nationality as 'them'. Examples include 'procedures that will apply to **them**' (14.18.10) 'legal routes open for **them**' (16.25.3/4) and 'around 191,000 of **them** came here primarily to work' (40.(3.11) 4). There is an assumption here, however, that those with

British nationality all feel the same and would agree that they are part of 'us' and this raises questions about how the discursive use of the terms 'us' and 'them' affects the security of those migrants who are already settled in the UK. This muddies the water somewhat for understanding who exactly is included in the 'we' and the 'us' of New Labour discourse; it is much clearer, however, to identify those referred to as 'them'.

There are other examples where 'us' and 'them' meet as in 'helping **them** to contribute to **our** economy (38.(3.6) 5/6) and 'what will happen to **them** is an essential part of **our** reforms' (54.(4.22) 1/2). It is worthy of note that the inclusive and general nature of the term 'our' changes to a specific use to refer to the government in the latter example since the language changes from that of promotion to that of power as it moves to the purpose of the document, that of immigration reforms. Power is very much apparent in the use of 'they' and 'those' as in '**those** coming into **our** country have duties that **they** need to understand' (Foreword 4.19/20).

The use of such exclusive language distances the paper's authors, and consequently the readers, from the people concerned, creating division and emphasising difference. It also serves to dehumanise since it uses anonymous labels to describe people rather than terms with which we could identify: families, men, women and children. Repetition ensures that we remember and may well repeat those labels reproducing the language of exclusion thereby discriminating between those we see as 'us' and those we see as 'them'.

Repetition of the words like 'our' serves to emphasise the ownership of nationality, 'this is our country', and it implicitly makes it clear that it is not 'theirs'. This also suggests a threat to ownership since declarations of ownership are usually only necessary when this is in dispute. This threat is compounded further by the description of 'them' as abusing our hospitality and breaking our laws so that not only may we need to protect some of the 'others', we also implicitly need to protect what is 'ours' from 'others'. Thus repetition can help build climatic expectation, giving rise to emotion; in this case that emotion may be one of fear, fear that what is ours may be taken from 'us' by 'them'. Again, this legitimises the government application of harsh measures, especially if those measures are seen to protect what is 'ours' from 'others'; that which we consider home.

Positive self-presentation is part of a rhetorical strategy that is used in the document to identify the writers, British government, British people and the British way of life with positive qualities whilst attaching negative qualities to those seeking to enter and settle in Britain. In the sentence above this can be understood as 'we are welcoming in our provision of services and protection' whilst the 'other' is described as someone who commits crimes and abuses our hospitality. Positive 'us', negative 'them'.

Defining 'genuine' refugees and asylum seekers

Positive self-presentation is often accompanied by disclaimers which have the effect of presenting 'us' in a very positive light and presenting 'them' in a negative light whilst justifying action taken by 'us' to deal with 'them'. On page 48 we have an example of this whereby the government combines positive 'us' and negative 'them', with a calculated disclaimer that makes several presuppositions:

> *We will continue to honour our obligations not to return refugees who have arrived in the UK and to integrate fully those we recognise as refugees. But there is a world of*

difference between offering sanctuary to those in genuine fear of persecution and allowing asylum seekers to stay simply because the UK is their country of preference.

(48.(4.2) 1–4)

The positive 'us' is fairly self-explanatory although there is a presupposition that the UK has honoured its obligations in the past for it to be able to continue to do so. The negative qualities of 'them', is more complex. First we have a commitment not to return refugees who come to the UK but this is followed by a power statement that promises to integrate only those the government recognises as refugees. The 'we' in this instance being government specific since the general public do not have the power to return or integrate. Here we have a clear indication that the government will only aid those refugees it recognises as refugees, it suggests that some refugees won't be recognised as such and although it promises not to return them, it does not offer to integrate them fully. An explanation for this is offered below.

Secondly, there is a presupposition that there are 'genuine' refugees and implicitly therefore some that aren't genuine; it raises questions around a perceived difference between someone 'genuinely' in need of sanctuary and someone who has chosen the UK as a place to acquire that sanctuary? Are you one and not the other; or can you be both?

There is also confusion here in terminology. Asylum seeking is effectively excluded from a definition based on 'genuine *fear of persecution*' since the sentence splits these to create two differing referents: those fleeing persecution (refugees) and those seeking asylum. This is despite the fact that any and all people subsequently accepted as refugees, have, without exception, sought asylum first. This is reminiscent of the difficulty created in the depiction of refugees and those seeking asylum throughout the document since the paper tries to extol the virtue of protecting refugees (positive us) whilst condemning those seeking asylum (negative them) as bogus, cheats and criminals: it tries to depict and discuss them as separate beings when in fact they are, by definition, one and the same.

The reason for this becomes clear when examining paragraph 21 of the executive summary which states that:

In reforming the asylum system the government intends to establish a resettlement programme with the UNHCR, which will effectively mean that only those accepted as refugees will come to Britain; there will be no one to seek asylum. Those that do get to Britain by other means will be dealt with by the government introducing a managed system of induction, accommodation, reporting and removal centres to secure a seamless asylum process.

(15.21.4/5)

It is interesting to note that they don't include the possibility of resettlement or integration here and in the light of recent legislation this is not surprising. Such measures include introducing sanctions for those who arrive without documents and criminal offences for those suspected of having destroyed them: making claims extremely difficult for those who do not make an application immediately on arrival and expressing plans to deport those who have travelled through a safe third country. The main difficulty with the latter is that as there are no legal routes into the country to seek asylum and as Britain is an island, it would be almost impossible to actually reach Britain without having travelled through a so called 'safe country' since most refugees lack the necessary paperwork, permits and passports necessary to use formal routes that may avoid this. Seeking protection on British soil is being phased out.

Use of discourse to criminalise asylum seekers

The association of asylum seeking with criminality is made very clear in paragraph 4.73 where those seeking asylum who have had their claim rejected are initially called 'failed asylum seekers'. (65.(4.73)1). However this is followed by:

> *The protocol establishes a mechanism whereby the police will assist and support the Immigration Service in the removal of immigration offenders. It also aims to develop Immigration Service expertise in the arrest of immigration offenders without the support of the police whilst ensuring the safety of immigration officers.*

(65.(4.73) 3–7)

Thus those who fail to secure asylum become 'immigration offenders' in need of 'arrest' and then dangerous offenders from whom immigration officers need protection. This illustrates one of the assumptions mentioned earlier, namely that anyone who has their application turned down, is implicitly assumed to be and is described as being bogus and/or not genuine refugees. This is one of several assumptions within the paper. It is assumed that the performance of immigration officials is adequate and accurate (this is never questioned nor raised as an issue), despite the fact that 22 per cent of all initial decisions to reject claims are found to be incorrect on appeal.

Of those that are rejected, it is assumed that the claimants have made 'unfounded' (64.(4.69) 4) or 'fraudulent' (14.16.6) claims, despite the fact that 24 per cent are rejected because, although there is an acceptance that they would be at risk if returned, they do not meet the specific criteria of the 1951 Convention. As such they are given leave to remain temporarily. Of the remaining rejections, 15 per cent are turned down because the paperwork, which consists of a 19 page document that has to be completed in English and returned within ten days, is incorrectly completed (Kundnani, 2003). This administrative error is called 'non-compliance'. Despite this there are a number of strategies being used to underline the idea that those who have applications turned down are criminal.

The use of metaphor as a rhetorical strategy in this sense makes use of what is known as an enthymeme. Enthymemes are similar to syllogisms in so far as they make links between categories, but in this case one of the premises is missing. Thus we have:

- Illegal immigrants are criminals
- Asylum seekers are illegal immigrants

But instead of completing the syllogism with 'asylum seekers are criminals', the reader is left to complete the enthymeme themselves by creating coherence from within their own belief system, whether this is done consciously or not (Van Dijk, 2003: 171). In this instance, that belief system has already been fed repeated visions of those seeking asylum as criminals and as such questions must be asked about how far such belief systems can be described as one's 'own'.

This insistence on the criminality of those seeking asylum serves to introduce the reasoning for the treatment of those seeking protection, since in this case they portray 'us' as having done the best we can, whilst portraying 'them' as having undermined this; i.e. we are meeting our obligations as humanitarians but they are often bogus. This is a powerful strategy that lays the blame for any subsequent ill treatment at the door of those identified as 'other' whilst it justifies and legitimises harsh treatment meted out in order to correct this; 'they' have brought it on themselves.

Discrimination

Not content, however, with labelling groups of people as criminals, the discourse used goes on to discredit them further in a way that clearly differentiates 'those', 'them' and 'they' as 'other' which implicitly leads the way for discrimination. Not only does such discourse align asylum seeking with criminal behaviour, it also associates immigrants with unacceptable cultural practices. For example, on the issue of marriage it is felt necessary to point out that 'there are certain norms in relation to marriage in this country which we recognise as acceptable' (99.(7.2) 1/2), which implicitly means there must be norms in other countries that we do not regard as acceptable. The following, which appears in the section of citizenship and British values, is more specific:

> *The laws, rules and practices which govern our democracy uphold our commitment to the equal worth and dignity of all our citizens. It will sometimes be necessary to confront some cultural practices which conflict with these basic values.*

> (30.(2.3) 2–4)

This is a complex pair of sentences that manage to achieve positive self-presentation and negative 'other' presentation mixed up with issues around equality. 'We' are committed to ideas of equal worth and dignity; others hold values that conflict with this. However, the latter sentence describes these values as 'basic' which infers that those who do not hold these values are operating on a much lower, below basic, level of understanding around humanitarian principles. We are portrayed as enlightened; others are inferred to be otherwise. 'They' are culturally inferior. Echoes of colonialism loom very large.

The presentation of 'us' as anti-oppressive, open and accepting of cultural difference (and yes, they do contradict themselves here) is found in a further example of positive self-presentation in paragraph 5 of the executive summary:

> *The UK has responded successfully to diversity. Unlike many other countries, British nationality has never been associated with membership of a particular ethnic group. For centuries we have been a multi-ethnic nation. We do not exclude people from citizenship on the basis of their race or ethnicity. Similarly, our society is based on cultural difference, rather than assimilation to a prevailing monoculture. This diversity is a source of pride, and it helps to explain our cultural vitality, the strength of our economy and our strong international links.*

> (10.5.1–7)

Whilst there are a number of factual points with which one could take issue in this paragraph, it is overwhelmingly positive in its representation of the UK and, more importantly, it paints a picture of race equality that is extremely rosy and precludes any argument or accusation that people in the UK (note the use of 'we' and 'our') could in any way be considered racist if racism is defined as a matter of, or belief in, white supremacy or cultural dominance. Not only is this not the case, it is actually portrayed as 'never' having been the case. Perhaps someone should read the Macpherson Report into the death of Stephen Lawrence.

Here the government appear to be defending their position as law makers by answering any accusations of racism before they are made. Why would they do this? If they are as sure that their policies are not racist, why try to defend the position taken? The answer is not hard to find.

Discussion

Attention to the linguistic strategies used by governments for the purpose of persuasion enables readers to become more aware of the underlying approaches to the issues being discussed. In this instance it allows us to build a picture of power and oppression within political text and talk. It allows us to look for evidence of racism.

Van Dijk defines racism as being:

> . . . *implemented by generalised everyday negative practices and informed by shared social cognitions about socially constructed and usually negatively valued racial or ethnic differences of the out-group.*

> (Van Dijk, 1993: 25)

Thus positive self-presentation and negative 'other' constructions are an expression of underlying practices informed by 'prejudiced attitudes or ideologies' (Van Dijk, 1993: 24)

Chapter 47, Item 12, of the Macpherson Report into the death of Stephen Lawrence defines a racist incident as: 'any incident which is perceived to be racist by the victim or any other person' and they recommend that 'this definition should be universally adopted by the Police, local Government and other relevant agencies' (Macpherson, 1999). Van Dijk likewise states that social practices are 'interpreted as racist practices when minority group members, on the basis of their generalised knowledge about racism, interpret them as such' (Van Dijk, 1993: 25)

In other words the decision about whether or not something or someone is racist, is determined by the person/victim concerned. This shifting of power to decide whether or not something is racist from the oppressor to the oppressed has not met with the approval of several people. The Institute for the Study of Civil Society published their views on this saying that 'the notion that the perception of a fact makes it a fact is a legal and philosophical monstrosity' (Green, 2000: online) but they do not acknowledge the reverse. If they have trouble accepting that simply saying something is racist makes it so, they must also recognise the difficulty that simply saying something or someone is not racist, does not make it so either.

As demonstrated earlier, the government make several statements within the white paper that declare themselves anti-racist and determined to stamp out racism wherever it is found. And yet they hold a reservation on the Race Relations Act that specifically gives them permission to behave in a racist manner where issues of immigration are concerned. Placing the reservation implies that not only are immigration laws racist but that the government knows they are racist. This is not the unwitting or unintentional racism of the Macpherson report, this is deliberate institutional racism, implemented to achieve certain governmental aims and objectives. Could immigration laws be anything else? There are many that would argue not since they inevitably involve decisions based on someone's nationality. But the discussion around the need for immigration control is never considered in this document.

The reservation on the Race Relations Act does make discrimination on the basis of colour illegal, even within immigration control, but, they would argue, discrimination is based on nationality not colour. However, by its own definition of indirect racism, colour is still an issue since the majority (84 per cent according to Home Office Statistics) of immigrants are not white.

Leaving aside the so called need to discriminate on the grounds of nationality inherent in immigration control, the discourse of criminality, of unacceptable cultural practices, the depiction of immigrants as lacking understanding of basic human rights, are all expressions of racist thought and talk and as such, they are unacceptable in an enlightened society committed to humanitarian objectives. They are particularly unacceptable in the actions of a democratically elected government.

Various sections of the press have picked up on the discourse used by government and they have been particularly vindictive in their approach to those seeking asylum and although:

> . . . the government cannot be held responsible for what the newspapers write – one must ask whether press officers do not strategically anticipate it and in that sense use the media to convey implicit messages.

> (Fairclough, 2001: 132)

We can, however, hold governments responsible for the discourses they use in official documents, in their speeches and in their press releases and we can hold them accountable for the consequences of such discourse:

> . . . namely that discourse of the political elites – may claim popular support while at the same time preformulating the terms that help create the state of mind that gives rise to such support.

> (Van Dijk, 1993: 100)

In other words, government discourse helps create public discourse and if government policy:

> . . . excludes or discriminates against a particular group, it implies that they are undesirable, encouraging the majority to believe that they're not acting wrongly if they treat them badly.

> (Bourne in *Race and Class*, 2001: 9)

As such, the public criminalisation of people seeking asylum by New Labour, filters down to the general public implicitly permitting racist behaviour thereby explaining (but not excusing) the actions and statements I encountered in some of my colleagues.

Such government productions as the white paper, represent the carefully thought out, planned and managed application of language to achieve certain objectives. The content is not accidental, there is no unguarded slip of the tongue. Fairclough argues that all such products are the result of New Labour's ability to 'calculatively manipulate language' (Fairclough, 2001: vii) and he suggests that they see language use as 'part of the process of policy formation' (Fairclough, 2001: 5) which is 'tightly monitored to make sure that it sends the 'right' message' (Fairclough, 2001: 3). Which, if he is correct, leaves us with only one conclusion: if there is racism in the discourse of New Labour, it is deliberate racism.

Why would New Labour do this? Why would a government that vocally expresses its commitment to challenge racism at every level, indulge itself in the vilification of a people to the extent that accusations of racism can be made and justified? The simple answer would be that they were responding to the views of the electorate, therefore securing the votes of the general public. But it is more complicated than this because as has already been argued the government can be seen to be partly responsible for the views that the electorate hold. Thus we have a diminishing circle of cause and effect. The government believe the public want a reduction in the number of people seeking asylum, they therefore put in place certain laws that make it harder and harder for people seeking asylum to apply successfully for protection. In so doing, they abuse the human rights of these people and in order to get unjust and inhumane laws past the objections of the public, they promote a view of people seeking asylum that is based on a racist ideology that devalues and discredits them, thus increasing calls for a reduction in numbers. As the number of unsuccessful applications for asylum rises, the government claims justification for its view that most of those seeking asylum are bogus, thus warranting even harsher laws and further human rights abuses. Unfortunately such justification also serves as a condemnation of government action since the rise in numbers also shows that government policy in reducing numbers is failing. This is a circle that cannot be squared, because no one can win.

The persecution of immigrants in general and of people seeking asylum in particular has continued apace since the publication of the white paper. Some of the harsher laws that have followed, whilst having a basis in the white paper, were significantly under played and minimised, 'in order to mitigate our responsibility and to keep – others – from seriously objecting to them' (Van Dijk, 1993: 81).

That the Nationality, Immigration and Asylum Act 2002, was subjected to 'something in the order of 342 amendments and 25 new clauses – between Second Reading and its final stages' (Malins MP, 2004, Column 4, Parliamentary Publications) also served to overwhelm those attempting to keep up with such changes: further reducing their ability to object. We have subsequently been drip fed a series of increasingly 'tough' legislation that has progressively denied people seeking asylum their basic human rights.

The determination to stamp out asylum seeking in Britain borders on ethnic cleansing but despite those campaigns that condemn such practices; despite the outcry from asylum and refugee support groups; despite the individuals that have made it their business to get involved, there is no sign to date that the government has any intention of changing their plans. In fact, they have gone several steps towards a situation where there is no longer any legal challenge to their decision making from the High Court or the Court of Human Rights which Tony Blair has described as '*judicial interference*' (Blair, 2003, online) Where the government cannot change such interference, as in the European Convention on Human Rights, it proposes to opt out which:

> . . . *demonstrates that the UK Government is increasingly viewing its commitment to human rights as an expendable obligation rather than a necessary responsibility.*
>
> (Islamic Human Rights Commission, 2004: 1. www.ihrc.org)

New Labour is becoming a law unto itself and as Cherie Booth (Blair) points out:

A political regime – even one supported or elected by a majority of the population – which sought to deny basic rights to those falling within its care would be in danger of forfeiting the right to call itself democratic.

(Booth, 2003, online)

That danger has found a foothold in reality.

So why haven't youth and community workers taken to the streets in protest? Why isn't the racism of government the talk of every youth worker meeting, the basis of collective action, the subject of training? Why has a profession committed to principles of equality and justice not made it their business to get involved?

Some of us are employed by the government and we have to face, head on, the ethical dilemma that comes from working for a government whose aims and objectives may not match our own. We (meaning youth and community workers) have sat on the fence long enough on this issue and the time is coming when we will have to answer the ultimate question: can we truly lay claim to challenging oppressive practices whilst doing nothing to challenge an oppressive government? Have we bought into the rhetoric of government? New Labour is not alone here, all major political parties are committed to reducing the number of people seeking refuge in Britain. The only difference is that some parties are more open about their intent.

Perhaps we could claim ignorance, perhaps until you read this chapter you had not realised that such an argument could be made about government policy. Before conducting the research I only suspected, I didn't **know** just how manipulative the discourse of government could be. But I know now and so do you. The question then is what are you going to do about it?

As stated in the introduction we have become complacent. We have bought into the rhetoric of equal opportunity and we believe the fight is won. Hopefully we can now agree that it is not won, in some ways the fight has not even begun. All is not lost however. It is possible to understand the changing face of racism and to work against it. If we examine closely the discourses that people use to talk of others and if we learn the ways in which oppression is implicit in the talk and text of people at all levels in society, we can begin to challenge this through our own discursive practices, we can develop 'oppositional, anti-racist practices and ideologies' (Van Dijk, 1993: 17) We can, as Foucault foresaw, challenge dominant discourses and 'dislodge them from their position as "truth"' (Burr, 2000: 70).

The message is simple, racism is alive and well and we must learn new skills to fight it.

Glossary

1951 Convention Relating to the Status of Refugees

The 1951 Convention was signed on the 28 July 1951 after the Second World War created large numbers of refugees in Europe. Originally it only applied to European nationals but in 1967 a United Nations protocol extended the convention to include any person, anywhere in the world. The convention and the protocol form the basis of all refugee law and are a fundamental part of international human rights legislation. Signing the Convention commits the signatories to offering protection to people who would be in danger should they return to their country of origin and not to return them.

Significantly, signatories are expected to extend to refugees the same rights as every one else in their country:

> It also stipulates that states should not impose penalties on refugees when they have entered the country illegally or return a refugee to a country 'where his life or freedom would be threatened on account of his race, religion, nationality, membership of a political social group or political opinion'.

(Scottish Refugee Council, 2001: 1)

Refugee

A refugee is defined by the 1951 Convention Relating to the Status of Refugees as someone who:

> ... owing to well-founded fear of being persecuted for reasons of race, religion, nationality, membership of a particular social group of political opinion, is outside the country of his nationality and is unable or, owing to such fear, is unwilling to avail himself of the protection of that country; or who, not having a nationality and being outside the country of his former habitual residence as a result of such events, is unable or, owing to such fear, is unwilling to return to it.

(Scottish Refugee Council, 2001: 1)

Asylum Seeker

An asylum seeker is a refugee who has applied for protection in a safe country and is awaiting a decision.

References

Amnesty International (2003) *AI Criticises Government Plans to Prosecute Asylum Seekers Over Travel Documents.* [cited 18th December 2003] http://www.amnesty.org.uk/news/refugees/271003.shtml.

BBC News (2003) *Blair's Asylum Stance Chilling*, [cited 18th December 2003] http://news-vote.bbc.co.uk/go/pr/fr/-/1/hi/uk_politics/3152982.stm.

BBC News (2003) *Blair Attacks Asylum 'Myths'*. [cited 18th December 2003] http://news.bbc.co.uk/go/pr/fr/-/1/hi/uk_politics/3290353.stm

Booth, C. (2003) *Over Attack on Refugees.* [cited 19th January 2004] www.asylum.info.

Bourne, J. (2001) The Life and Times of Institutional Racism. *Race and Class*, 43: 2.

Brown, A. (2002) *Britain is Losing Britain.* [cited 27th October 2003] www.migrationwatchuk.com.

Browne, A. (2003) Age Bar to Curb Forced Marriage. *Times*, [cited 2nd January 2004] www.timesonline.co.uk/newspaper/0,,172-679732,00.html.

Burman, E. and Parker, I. (1993) *Discourse Analytic Research.* London: Routledge.

Burr, V. (2000) *An Introduction to Social Constructionism.* London: Routledge.

Cohen, L., Manion, L. and Morrison, K. (2000) *Research Methods in Education.* 5th edn. London: Routledge Falmer.

Cohen, S. (2001) *Immigration Controls, The Family and The Welfare State.* London: Jessica Kingsley.

Cohen, S. (2003) *No One is Illegal: Asylum and Immigration Control Past and Present.* Staffordshire: Trentham Books.

Connexions (2002) *The Youth Service Overview: Working Together Connexions and Statutory Youth Services.* Nottingham: DFES.

Denscombe, M. (2000) *The Good Research Guide: for Small Scale Social Research Projects.* Buckingham: Open University Press.

Dwyer, D. (2004) *Second Change: Service Level Agreement.* Loughborough: Charnwood BC.

European Committee Against Racism and Intolerance (2000) *Second Report on The United Kingdom.* [cited] http//www.hri.ca/fortherecord2001/euro2001/vol2/ukecri.htm

European Economic and Social Committee (2002) *Communication From The Commission to The Council and The European Parliament on A Common Policy on Illegal Immigration.* [cited 18th December 2003] www.ecre.org/seville/index.shtml.

Fairclough, N. (2001) *New Labour, New Language.* London: Routledge.

Folwell, S. (2001) *Homelessness.* Loughborough: Charnwood BC.

Freire, P. (1993) *Pedagogy of The Oppressed.* London: The Penguin Group.

Green, D.G. (2000) *Institutional Racism and The Police: Fact or Fiction?* [cited 10th October 2004] http://www.civitas.org.uk/pdf/cs06.pdf.

Hague, W. (2001) *A Safe Haven, Not A Soft Touch.* [cited 10th October 2003] www.conservatives.com.

Harris, M. (2003) *Tomorrow is Another Country: What is Wrong With The UK's Asylum Policy.* London: Civitas.

Harris, N. (2002) *Thinking The Unthinkable: The Immigration Myth Exposed.* Cornwall: MPG Books.

Hayter, T. (2000) *Open Borders: The Case Against Immigration Controls.* London: Pluto.

Home Office (1996) *Welfare Food Regulations 1996.* London: HMSO.

Home Office (1998) *Fairer, Faster and Firmer: A Modern Approach To Immigration and Asylum.* London: HMSO.

Home Office (2000) *Explanatory Notes to Race Relations (Amendment) Act 2000.* London: HMSO.

Home Office (2002) *Nationality, Immigration and Asylum Act 2002.* London: HMSO.

Home Office (2002) *Secure Borders, Safe Haven, Integration With Diversity.* London: HMSO.

Home Office (2003) *Race Relations Act 1976 (Amendment) Regulations 2003 Guidance.* [cited 8th January 2004] www.homeoffice.gov.uk/docs2/rragidnce.html.

Home Office (2003) *The Asylum and Immigration (Treatment of Claimants) Bill 2003.* London: HMSO.

House of Lords (1999) *Hansard,* Text 18.10.99.(191018-26). [cited 21st November 2003] http://www.parliament.the-stationery-office.co.uk/pa/ld199899/ldhansrd/vo991018/text/91018-26.htm.

House of Lords (2002) *A Common Policy on Illegal Immigration, With Evidence: Session 2001–2002, 37th Report.* London: HMSO.

Islamic Human Rights Commission (2004) *Briefing: Derogation From A Non-Derogable Right? Article 3 of The European Convention on Human Rights, Immigration and the British Government.* [cited 12th June 2004] http//www.ihrc.org

Kundnani, A. (2003) *Immigration Statistics.* Institute of Race Relations. [cited 7th January 2004] http://www.irr.org.uk/cgi-bin/news/printable.pl.

Liberty (2004) *Review of the UK's Reservations to International Human Rights Treaty Obligations.* [cited 15th February 2004] http://www.liberty-human-rights.org.uk.

Malins, H. (2004) *Standing Committee B, Column 4.* Hansard Directories. [cited 13th January 2004] http://www.publications.parliament.uk/ pa/cm200304/ cmstand/b/cmasylum.

May, T. (2001) *Social Research: Issues, Methods and Process.* Buckingham: Open University.

Mayall, B., Hood, S. and Oliver, S. (1999) *Critical Issues in Social Research.* Buckingham: Open University Press.

Potter, J. and Wetherell, M. (2001) *Discourse and Social Psychology: Beyond Attitudes and Behaviour.* London: Sage.

Sarantakos, S. (2000) *Social Research.* 2nd edn. South Yarra: Macmillan Education.

Schiffrin, D., Tanne, D. and Hamilton, H. (2001) *The Handbook of Discourse Analysis.* Oxford: Blackwell.

Scottish Refugee Council (2001) *Briefing UN Convention.* [cited 19th December 2003] http://www.scottishrefugeecouncil.org.uk.

Sivanandan, S. (Ed.) (2001) Three Faces of Racism. *Race and Class,* 43: 2.

Spencer, S. (Ed.) (1994) *Strangers and Citizens: A Positive Approach to Migrants and Refugees.* London: IPPR/Rivers Oram Press.

Thompson, N. (2001) *Anti-Discriminatory Practice.* 3rd edn. Basingstoke: Palgrave.

United Nations (1954) *1951 UN Convention of The Status of Refugees.* [cited 10th October 2003] http://www.unhchr.ch/html/menu3/b/o_c_ref.htm.

United Nations (1990) *Convention on The Rights of The Child 1989.* [cited 14th july 2003] www.uncrc.info.

United Nations (2003) *International Convention on The Elimination of All Forms of Racial Discrimination, Sixty-Third Session.* [cited 18th December 2003] http://www.justice.org.uk/images/pdfs/cerdconob.pdf.

Van Dijk, T.A. (1993) *Elite Discourse and Racism.* London: Sage.

Van Dijk, T.A. (2003a) *Discourse as Structure and Process.* Vol. 1, London: Sage.

Van Dijk, T.A. (2003b) *Discourse as Social Interaction.* Vol. 2, London: Sage.

Waterson, J. (2001) Britain in Decline. *Socialist Review,* 248. [cited 10th January 2004] http://pubs.socialistreviewindex.org.uk/sr248 /waterson.htm.

Wetherell, M., Taylor, S. and Yates, S.J. (2001) *Discourse Theory and Practice: A Reader.* London: Sage.

Willig, C. (2001) *Introducing Qualitative Research in Psychology: Adventures in Theory and Method.* Buckingham, Open University Press.

Wodak, R. and Meyer, M. (2001) *Methods of Critical Discourse Analysis,* London: Sage.

General Web Sites

www.asylum.info
www.ind.homeoffice.gov.uk

Working with Young Refugees and Asylum Seekers through Participatory Action Research in Health Promotion

Raksha Pandya

In order for the oppressed to be able to wage the struggle for their liberation they must perceive the reality of oppression, not as a closed world from which there is no exit, but as a limited situation which they can transform.

(Freire, 1996: 34)

This chapter draws on lessons learnt from a piece of work called the Routz Project. In Freirian terminology, an 'oppressed' group of young Refugees and Asylum Seekers (RAS) were empowered to work with a local drug treatment service to learn about and meet their needs.

The chapter explains why refugee and asylum seeker communities have different needs to those of 'established BME communities', along with issues to consider in the broader political context and reasons why it is paramount for anti-oppressive practice to develop through engagement via Participatory Action Research (PAR) (Whyte, 1991) with RAS to better equip health and social care related mainstream service delivery.

Immigration and migration to the UK

Conflicts around the world have led to an estimated 21 million refugees becoming exiled from their homelands. Nearly half of all refugees are children (UNHCR, 2003). United Kingdom's (UK) government statistics guesstimate 103,080 individuals applied for asylum in the UK in 2002 and this figure includes dependant children. 6,200 were unaccompanied children and young people aged 17 and under (Ehntholt et al., 2005). As a signatory to the 1951 Geneva Refugee Convention (Refugee Action and EMCARS 2006) Britain has provided a 'safe haven' for those in search of escape from war (Bloch, 1999; Holmes, 1991).

Throughout the history of immigration and asylum in Britain, attitudes and reception towards these individuals have varied. Burr (1995) in Lynn and Lea (2003: 425) argues a social constructionist view which recognises that every day life consists of social processes and that social processes are determined through ideologies, opinions and attitudes. Lynn and Lea (2003: 426) also believe that social constructionist perspectives recognise that this understanding is both culturally and historically specific. They argue that negative media depictions have represented refugees and asylum seekers (RAS) as a danger to society and a challenge to 'British cultural distinctiveness', with this, the media encourages the view that a host of migrants were and still are, 'laying siege to British coastal ports'. Additionally, assigning the status of 'refugee', 'asylum seeker' or 'illegal', locks a stereotypical image as '. . . all subsequent interpretation of their actions is in terms of the status to which they have been assigned' (Jary and Jary, 1995: 236). Therefore this generates a powerful vehicle to 'facilitate and maintain' oppression and discrimination.

BME and RAS – the difference

In Britain the experiences of refugees and people seeking asylum (RAS) must be set in the context of those of other black and minority ethnic (BME) communities which they become part of once their immigration has been resolved. Although the exile experience remains an important one in differentiating this group from other BME migrants and British born BME populations (GLADA, 2004: 39).

Digging deeper in differentiating BME groups, policy needs to be explored. Wehlbeck (1999) argued that in Britain there have been very few policies designed to help the settlement process of refugees. In its place, policies developed for economic migrants have been used towards refugees. Furthermore theories of multiculturalism grew to be popular in Britain from the 1960s. These became the adopted governing models for the merging of immigrants into British culture (Abercrombie et al., 1988; Anthias and Yuval-Davis, 1992; Rex and Tomlinson, 1979). These theories argued, 'that individuals can maintain their individual identity and their membership of a minority group whilst at the same time become part of the wider society' (Kelly, 2003). However Werbner (1991) believes that divisions can happen within minority groups and the preoccupation with community can obscure the diversity within them.

Moreover, multiculturalist approaches and policies have typically focused on self help and the role of communities and their recognised networks in providing services tailored to meet their own needs (Candappa and Joly, 1994; ECRE, 1998). More recently Refugee Community Organisations (RCO) have also adopted multiculturalism as their dominant model.

Kelly (2003: 38) believes that the role of refugee associations or what I refer to as RCOs have had a positive impact on resettlement. She refers to Rex et al., (1987) who found that community associations have four primary functions:

- Overcoming isolation.
- Providing material help.
- Defending the community's interest.
- Promoting the community's culture.

Indeed, it is suggested that through networking and information sharing, RCOs provide a vital role in supporting the adaptation of the community members to the host society (Joly, 1996). However, it has also been argued that this type of integration process is a reflection of the 'British way', i.e. recognition of *groups* rather than *individuals* (Joly, 1996) and is therefore not a natural tendency.

Key differences between RAS communities and BME communities are the factors prompting their exile arrival in the UK. Economic migration often means chain migration i.e. new arrivals following the steps of earlier migrants and seeking support and advice from them. For those who come to Britain as refugees for political reasons, they often arrive not having any kinship and therefore building self help and support is even more difficult (Gold, 1992).

In contrast to the multiculturalist approach and isolated work of RCOs the aim of the Routz Project was to influence non-culturally defined organisations and equip them to meet the unmet needs of RAS. Specifically, to inform workers within mainstream, general health promotion agencies, specialist sexual health and drug treatment services. I contend that RAS needs and issues fall within the duty of care and responsibility of all service providers. All services should deliver an equitable service; RAS needs are not just a RCO responsibility.

A united responsibility

Over the last 20 years strong evidence has been given defining inequalities in health and the clear link between health status and social class, geographic location, gender and ethnic origin (Naidoo and Wills, 2004: 41).

Four points of crucial action were identified in the Ottawa Charter (WHO, 1986) by Benzeval et al. (1995) (in Naidoo and Wills, 2004: 46). These were of planned policy proposals:

- Strengthening individuals.
- Strengthening communities.
- Improving access to facilities and services.
- Encouraging a healthy public policy.

In 1998 the UK Department of Health released a paper called *Our Healthier Nation* (1998: 12). In this document the government recognised that 'Tackling inequalities generally is the best means of tackling health inequalities . . .'

Keeping the above in mind, Naidoo and Wills (2004) state that the World Health Organisation defined health promotion as 'enabling people to gain control over their lives' (WHO, 1986). They further argue that the enabling people approach:

> . . . *helps people to identify their own concerns and gain the skills and confidence to act upon them. It is unique in being based on a 'bottom up' strategy and calls for different skills from the health promoter.*

(Kendall, 1998 in Naidoo and Wills, 2004)

To help minimise the risk of RAS becoming more vulnerable and increasing the level of cultural competence, health and social care workers can adopt participatory and developmental approaches to improve service delivery and policy. Working with RAS communities whose first language isn't English, to promote health or reduce uptake of illicit or harmful substance misuse (See McCormack and Walker, 2005) or promote safer sex messages (Naidoo and Wills, 2004: 80), community education workers need to engage creatively (See Norton and Cohen, 2000: 79) with RAS.

Feldman et al. (2002) articulate that many mainstream voluntary and statutory establishments in health are now finding it difficult to expand their remits to include anti-racist and intercultural schemes or expand their capacity to respond to the needs of 'new minorities'. Community development and established support groups have been struggling to build bridges to make up for often unplanned, under-resourced, poorly implemented government policy and service provision. Subsequently, community workers are responsible for extending the focus of their work to address needs, and provide a culturally competent, RAS friendly service.

However, government funding for local research in and around issues relating to racism, integration, anti-discriminatory practice and service provision has increased in recent years (Feldman et al., 2002). In addition, internationally, (Feldman et al.) argue that the World Conference Against Racism recognised that research methodologies needed participation from victims of racial abuse themselves.

Hence, the RAS movement and migration demographics, together with the information for action from the World Conference Against Racism leads to the conclusion that in order for mainstream services to be competent, RAS need to be involved in all research linking their needs to services. It also encourages and acknowledges that RAS bring with them experience, knowledge and expertise necessary to help mainstream voluntary and statutory services to define the link.

Academics and practitioners have argued that Participatory Action Research (PAR) helps to balance out the unequal power relationships that are formed in conventional research strategies between the elite professional researcher and the respondent (see Whyte et al., 1994). PAR shares the ethos that research is only necessary when it generates practical outcomes, produces functional knowledge, contributes to the capacity building of individuals and groups about whom the research is conducted (Reason and Bradbury, 2001). Thus PAR is about information gathering and implementing social change.

Whyte (1991) in Sarantakos (1998: 115) explains that this model of research design adds, '. . . political character, strengthening the degree of commitment to the study and puts pressure upon the government to implement the findings'.

The idea of PAR is for the researcher and researched to enter into a mutually participatory process designed to develop a shared understanding of the subjective–objective experience of both parties. Despite its flexibility and empowering dynamics, PAR has been criticised by some as being oppressive and disempowering . . .

> *In this process all unilateral design decisions of the social researcher places personal preferences and values on those being studied and is thus oppressive and disempowering, however this enlightens the values.*

(Heron, 1996)

Heron's critique is important, although it can be argued that other research techniques are much more oppressive in nature. The PAR model looks directly into the political scope of the researcher's presence (Khan, 1994) and the inherent hierarchical relationship is research where the researcher has control. Reasons (1994) suggests that because of the intra and interpersonal dynamics of the participation; 'the participation should be undertaken only by researchers willing and able to participate in the lives of others in both a self aware and self reflective manner'.

Routz Project – Case study

At a refugee and asylum seekers (RAS) forum, it was anecdotally identified to the author (at the time who worked as Black and Minority Ethnic (BME) Community Development Drug worker) by a youth group leader that some newly arrived young (16–24 year old) RAS from Iraq, Iran, Afghanistan and Albania were drinking large quantities of alcohol and smoking cannabis and that they did not know the difference in potency between a pint of beer and a pint of vodka or the effects of smoking cannabis and other harder drugs.

Around the same time, the University of Central Lancashire was running the Department of Health's BME substance needs assessment project called the 'Community Engagement Programme'. The CEP was undertaking its third year investigating nationally the drug and alcohol related needs of marginalised groups.

Through this scheme Turning Point Loughborough and Northwest Leicestershire decided to carry out some research into this group of RAS to:

- Explore the current and perceived alcohol and drug use issues amongst RAS.
- Clarify the issues surrounding problem drinking/ drug use amongst this group of individuals.
- Identity current levels of understanding around substance misuse.
- Identify potential gaps in service provision.

Like any other BME community member, not born in the UK, RAS were likely to experience language barriers and differences in cultures when speaking with other people from a different background. Additionally further anecdotal evidence suggested that some RAS had not heard of what a substance misuse service was or what one did (sic). Therefore it was clear that the research needed to be carried out by RAS themselves. Turning Point approached existing 'Refugee Community Organisations' (RCO) to locate RAS who may have wished to be involved in this research study, the criteria for selection was the following:

- Aged 16 to 24 years old.
- Is a RAS.
- Lived within a 15 mile radius of the local area the study was to cover.
- Spoke English and two other languages that were spoken within the RAS communities.
- The persons to be recruited were also to be genuinely interested and willing to take part in the project.
- The RAS recruited were to be paid and therefore needed a work permit.
- Had access to other RAS within their own networks of friends/family and acquaintances.

Eventually Turning Point recruited two people to drive the actual work through the technique of Participatory Action Research (PAR). The researchers were trained by University of Central Lancashire (UCLAN) through six days of intensive training on drugs and alcohol and research methods.

Two research methods used by the researchers were focus groups and structured interviews. In total 46 participants took part.

It appeared from the research that RAS have a particular vulnerability to substance misuse. Furthermore, accommodation for those seeking asylum can sometimes be shared with drug users and exposure to substances more generally seemed to happen both in transit and in the early stages of arrival. Many of the participants were aware of where to get drugs and had been offered substances. The vulnerability of young unaccompanied *asylum seekers and refugees was compounded with increased isolation, insecurity and anxiety, as well as a lack of knowledge and understanding of substance misuse.*

As an outcome from this work, local commissioners, policy makers and strategists made positive adjustments in ways of working with this group of young people, i.e. the local Drug and Alcohol Action Team documented future resources to be allocated to this group. The Routz Project also fed into a local communication strategy for working with young people. Finally the work was referred to in other research on RAS communities and substance use needs carried out by a local university.

Considerations when working with young RAS in PAR

Ehntholt et al. (2005) argue that despite the variations of hardship experienced by these young RAS, they are exceptionally resilient. Unfortunately, notwithstanding this, many RAS young people risk developing mental health problems due to the multiple traumatic occurrences and losses they have dealt with in their country of origin (Hodes, 1998; Rousseau, 1995). Ehntholt et al. (2005) carried out a psychiatric experiment with traumatised refugee children in British secondary schools who received Cognitive Behaviour Therapy (CBT) to help them come to terms with their negative experiences and losses in relation to war and trauma. Their experiment showed children who had regular psycho-social therapy made significant improvements in their mental health and well-being. Some may have experienced torture, rape, or other physical and emotional violence. Others may have had to deal with separation from family or even in some cases death of family (Livingston, 2004: xiii). For many young RAS, fleeing to the UK is a relief; however, for some, the reasons that I mentioned earlier increase vulnerability and could reduce the impact and effectiveness of messages mainstream services may promote.

It is paramount to note that the incidence of single or multiple stress factors in a young person's life, does not itself forecast problematic behaviours such as drug and alcohol misuse, practicing unsafe sex or being involved in anti-social behaviour. However, it is fair to note, the higher the stress and risk present in their lives the greater the likelihood of engaging in some type of risk taking or problematic behaviour (GLADA, 2004: 2).

Practical issues

Lessons from the Routz Project provide direction and advice for working with RAS in PAR and suggest considerations for the community worker depending on the aims of their research.

Figure 8.1 explains the process in which the PAR model can be implemented; the worker needs to show an understanding of this.

Furthermore, it is crucial for the community worker to consider other practical issues in relation to RAS they may need to consider during the process of PAR:

- The community worker to help the RAS understand the agenda under investigation.
- If a criminal record check on RAS is carried out ensure to allocate extra time for this to go through, as tracing previous address histories etc. can take time.
- Ensure a training budget is allocated for the researchers to learn the skills of research.
- Set a realistic timescale and stress the importance of keeping to it; bear in mind that the importance of time and concept of urgency can vary from culture to culture.

Demographics/anecdotal evidence suggests a local trend/need for a special service in a community.

▼

As a community worker/practicing professional ask questions of the local community of concern and other professionals at local meetings about the issue.

▼

If there is a need, enquire about locally available funds to carry out a research project, ideally speak with the local community and services to help with this.

▼

Explain to the community involved how you can help with the work and how it is important that they drive the research design, delivery and findings. Set up an appropriate research team.

▼

Provide training and/or allocate from the funding received a small amount of money for training and expenses for the community members to learn how to carry out research.

▼

As the community development worker to engage as the facilitator for this work ensuring the core of the work is delivered through empowering the research team.

▼

Ensure that the community being studied is the community that is researching the issue of concern.

▼

Upon completion of the research and the report continue to empower the community to disseminate the findings. These findings are to be presented at a launch of the research report. At the launch invite key service providers and commissioners that the issue concerns.

▼

Ask at launch, how the recommendations from the work can be followed up in policy and practice. Stress the importance of multi-agency work. Suggest further research and 'bottom up' policy work.

Figure 8.1 Implementation process in the PAR model

Young RAS Country of Origin	Young RAS Host Country
Traditional clothes	Western clothes
Regular maintenance of religion	Irregular maintenance of religion
Family and friends	Alone
Alcohol may have been prohibited	24 hour drinking culture
Sex after marriage	Sex before marriage
Social activity: eating together	Social activity: clubbing

Figure 8.2   Torn cultural shock

- Try to minimise words lost in translation. Provide researchers with a language converting dictionary.
- A 'torn cultural identity' or 'cross cultural shock' as in Figure 8.2 needs to be present in the community worker's mind throughout the research process.

Conclusion

Taylor (2003) questions community empowerment, is it myth or reality. Arnstein's (1969) ladder of participation can be used to suggest using PAR as a form of citizen power; it addresses issues of empowerment and anti-oppressive practice. Only with time on researching the effectiveness of PAR itself will we understand who the actual beneficiaries of the research are. Is it the RAS or the professionals? Nair and White (1994) argue that research on participation itself is necessary in order to:

> . . . *understand how such participatory development is to happen . . . [for] the rhetoric about participation is meaningless unless its methodologies can be operationalised, validated and applied. It must become an integral part of the community and its processes in order to become a strong motivating force for self-reliance.*

This echo's Foucault (1972) argument of exercise of power by professionals. Foucault suggests that there is a strong relationship between the systems of knowledge that codify methods and practices for the exercise of social control and domination, consequently oppressing the value of equality. Feldman et al. (2002) pointed out that 'RAS are suffering the consequence of being over researched'.

A challenge for PAR is to ensure that all voices are heard; the less confident or assertive participants may not raise their concerns. They may also be inhibited by fear of deportation, especially giving accounts of their experiences on the taboo nature of drug use or sexual practice.

Turning Point caption – *We turn lives around everyday by putting the individual at the heart of what we do, inspired by those we work with, together we help build a better life. Turning Point is the UK's leading social care organisation. Providing services for people with complex needs, including those affected by drug and alcohol misuse, mental health problems and those with a learning disability.*

University of Central Lancashire (Uclan) *one of the largest universities in the UK, The centre for Ethnicity and Health is a specialist department within the Faculty of Health. The centre's main activities lie in the fields of drug and alcohol use, mental health community engagement, criminal justice, regeneration and health, equality and diversity strategy development. The centre has a significant national and international reputation, involving work with central government departments, regional government, local authorities and a range of local and regional partners and agencies*

Definitions

Asylum seeker

'An asylum seeker is someone who has fled persecution in their country of origin, has arrived in another country, made themselves known to the authorities and exercised their rights for Asylum' (EMCARS 2006a).

Black and Minority Ethnic (BME)

'Many terms are used to refer to the many diverse communities in England. Black is a political term denoting those who identify around a basis of skin colour distinction or who may face discrimination because of this or their culture. BME also acknowledges the diversity that exists within these communities, and includes a wider range of those who may not consider their identity to be "Black" but who nonetheless constitute a distinct ethnic group' (GLADA, 2004: 16).

Economic migrant

'An economic migrant is someone who has moved to another country to work' (EMCARS 2006b).

Failed asylum seeker

'A failed asylum seeker is someone whose asylum application has been turned down and is awaiting return to their country of origin. If it is not safe for the refused asylum seeker to return, they may have to stay for the time being' (EMCARS, 2006c).

Illegal Immigrant

'An illegal immigrant is someone who has arrived in another country and has no legal basis for being there' (EMCARS, 2006d).

Illegal asylum seeker

There is no such thing as 'Illegal Asylum Seeker'; an illegal immigrant upon entry into another country has the legal rights to apply for asylum under the 1951 Geneva Refugee

Convention. Even if an asylum seeker enters the country illegally e.g. without a passport or with forged documents, as soon as they claim asylum they have legal status. (See EMCARS, 2006e.)

Participatory Action Research (PAR)

'. . . some of the people in the organisation or community under study participate actively with the professional researcher throughout the research process from the initial design to the final presentation of results and discussion of their action implications' (Whyte, 1991: 20).

Refugee

'A refugee is someone whose asylum application has been made successful and who is allowed to stay in another country' (EMCARS, 2006f).

Unaccompanied minor

'A child as being under 18 years old outside of their country of origin and separated from both parents or their previous legal or usual primary carer' (UNHCR, 1994 in GLADA, 2004: 17).

References

Abercrombie et al. (1988) cited in Kelly, L. (2003) Bosnian Refugees in Britain: Questioning Community. *Journal Sociology*, 37: 1, 35–49.

Anthias and Yuval-Davis (1992) cited in Kelly, L. (2003) Bosnian Refugees in Britain: Questioning Community. *Journal Sociology*, 37: 1, 35–49.

Arnstein (1969) cited in Taylor, M. (2003) *Public Policy in the Community*. Basingstoke: Palgrave Macmillan.

Benzevel (1995) cited in Naidoo, J. and Wills, J. (2000) *Health Promotion: Foundations for Practice*. London: Bailliere Tindall.

Bloch (1999) cited in Lynn, N. and Lea, S. (2003) A Phantom Menace and The New Apartheid: The Social Construction of Asylum Seekers in the United Kingdom. *Discourse and Society*, 14: 4, 425–52.

Burr (1995) cited in Lynn, N. and Lea, S. (2003) A Phantom Menace and The New Apartheid: The Social Construction of Asylum Seekers in the United Kingdom. *Discourse and Society*, 14: 4, 425–52.

Candappa and Joly (1994) cited in Kelly, L. (2003) Bosnian Refugees in Britain: Questioning Community, *Journal Sociology*, 37: 1, 35–49.

ECRE (1998) cited in Kelly, L. (2003) Bosnian Refugees in Britain: Questioning Community, *Journal Sociology*, 37: 1, 35–49.

Ehntholt, K.A., Smith, P.A. and Yule, W. (2005) School-based Cognitive Behaviour Therapy Group Intervention for Refugee Children who Have Experienced War-related Trauma, *Clinical Child Psychology and Psychiatry*. 10: 2, 235–50.

Feldman, et al., (2002) *Research, Development and Critical Interculturalism: A Study on the Participation Of Refugees And Asylum Seekers in Research and Development Based Initiatives*, Social Science Research Centre.

Foucault (1972) cited in Chevannes, M. (2002) Social Construction of the Managerialism of Needs Assessment by Health and Social Care Professionals. *Health and Social Care in The Community*, 10: 3, 168–78.

Freire, P. (1996) *Pedagogy of the Oppressed.* Harmondsworth: Penguin.

GLADA (2004) *Young Refugees and Asylum Seekers in Greater London: Vulnerability to Problematic Drug Use Final Report.* University of Central Lancashire, Greater London Authority.

Gold (1992) cited in Kelly, L. (2003) Bosnian Refugees in Britain: Questioning Community, *Journal Sociology,* 37: 1, 35–49.

Heron (1996) cited in Coughlan, F.J. and Collins, K.J. (Date Unknown*)* Participatory Developmental Research: A Working Model. *International Social Work,* 44: 4, 505–18.

Hodes (1998) cited in Ehntholt, K.A., Smith, P.A. and Yule, W. (2005) School-based Cognitive Behaviour Therapy Group Intervention for Refugee Children who Have Experienced War-related Trauma, *Clinical Child Psychology and Psychiatry.* 10: 2, 235–50.

Holmes (1991) cited in Lynn, N. and Lea, S. (2003) A Phantom Menace and the New Apartheid: The Social Construction of Asylum Seekers in the United Kingdom. *Discourse and Society,* 14: 4, 425–52.

Jary and Jary (1995) cited in Lynn, N. and Lea, S. (2003) A Phantom Menace and The New Apartheid: the Social Construction of Asylum Seekers in the United Kingdom. *Discourse and Society,* 14: 4, 425–52.

Joly (1996) cited in Kelly, L. (2003) Bosnian Refugees in Britain: Questioning Community.*Journal Sociology,* 37: 1, 35–49.

Kelly, L. (2003) Bosnian Refugees in Britain: Questioning Community. *Journal Sociology,* 37: 1, 35–49.

Kendell (1998) cited in Naidoo, J. and Wills, J. (2000) *Health Promotion: Foundations for Practice,* London: Baillière Tindall.

Khan (1994) cited in Coughlan, F.J. and Collins, K.J. (Date Unknown) Participatory Developmental Research: A Working Model. *International Social Work,* 44: 4, 505–18.

Livingston (2004) cited in GLADA (2004) *Young Refugees and Asylum Seekers in Greater London: Vulnerability to Problematic Drug Use, Final Report.* University of Central Lancashire, Greater London Authority.

Lynn, N. and Lea, S. (2003) A Phantom Menace and The New Apartheid: The Social Construction of Asylum Seekers in the United Kingdom. *Discourse and Society,* 14: 4, 425–52.

Naidoo, J. and Wills, J. (2000) *Health Promotion: Foundations for Practice.* London: Baillière Tindall.

Nair and White (1994) cited in Feldman, et al. (2002) *Research, Development and Critical Interculturalism: A Study on The Participation of Refugees and Asylum Seekers in Research and Development Based Initiatives.* Social Science Research Centre.

Norton, R. and Cohen, B. (2000) Elements for Effective, Relevant and Appropriate Youth Work Provision in Refugee Communities. In NYA. *Out of Exile.* Youth Work Press.

Ottawa Charter (1986) WHO cited in Naidoo, J. and Wills, J. (2000) *Health Promotion: Foundations for Practice.* London: Baillière Tindall.

Reason, P. and Bradbury, H. (2001) *Handbook of Action Research.* London: Sage.

Reason (1994) cited in Coughlan, F.J. and Collins, K.J. (Date Unknown) Participatory Developmental Research: A Working Model. *International Social Work,* 44: 4, 505–18.

Refugee Action and EMCARS (2006) *Refugee Rights are Human Rights.* Melton Mowbray: Refugee Action and EMCARS.

Rex, et al. (1987) cited in Kelly, L. (2003) Bosnian Refugees in Britain: Questioning Community. *Journal Sociology,* 37: 1, 35–49.

Rex and Tomlinson (1979) cited in Kelly, L. (2003) Bosnian Refugees in Britain: Questioning Community. *Journal Sociology,* 37: 1, 35–49.

Rousseau (1995) cited in Ehntholt, K.A., Smith, P.A. and Yule, W. (2005) School-based Cognitive Behaviour Therapy Group Intervention for Refugee Children who have Experienced War-related Trauma. *Clinical Child Psychology and Psychiatry,* 10: 2, 235–50.

Taylor, M. (2003) *Public Policy in the Community.* Basingstoke: Palgrave Macmillan.

UNHCR (1994) cited in GLADA (2004) *Young Refugees and Asylum Seekers in Greater London: Vulnerability to Problematic Drug Use. Final Report,* University of Central Lancashire, Greater London Authority.

UNHCR (2003) cited in Ehntholt, K.A., Smith, P.A. and Yule, W. (2005) School-based Cognitive Behaviour Therapy Group Intervention for Refugee Children who have Experienced War-related Trauma. *Clinical Child Psychology and Psychiatry,* 10: 2, 235–50.

Wehlbeck (1999) cited in Kelly, L. (2003) Bosnian Refugees in Britain: Questioning Community. *Journal Sociology,* 37: 1, 35–49.

Whyte (1991) cited in Sarantakos, S. (1998) *Social Research.* 3rd edn., Hampshire: Palgrave Macmillan.

Whyte et al. cited in Feldman et al. (2002) *Research, Development and Critical Interculturalism: A study on the Participation of Refugees and Asylum Seekers in Research and Development Based Initiatives.* Social Science Research Centre.

World Conference Against Racism cited in Feldman, et al. (2002) *Research, Development and Critical Interculturalism: A study on the Participation of Refugees and Asylum Seekers in Research and Development Based Initiatives.* Social Science Research Centre.

Werbner (1991) cited in Kelly, L. (2003) Bosnian Refugees in Britain: Questioning Community *Journal Sociology,* 37: 1, 35–49.

CHAPTER 9

Uprisings, Community Cohesion and Muslim Youth

Shahid Ashrif

The Prophet Muhammad said:

Acquire knowledge. It enableth its possessor to distinguish right from wrong; it lighteth the way to heaven; it is our friend in the desert, our society in solitude, our companion when friendless; it guideth us to happiness; it sustaineth in misery; it is an ornament among friends, and an armour against enemies.

(Ahmad Ibn-Hanbal)

In this chapter, I intend setting out some of the experiences and the condition of South Asians,[1] particularly Muslim youth in Britain. The development of anti-terrorism legislation and its attendant practices, including curtailing of certain civil liberties has combined with a major policy shift characterised by community cohesion (gone mostly unremarked by most Britons) to result in the targeting of Muslim communities by the state and its institutions. In addition Muslim communities have been undergoing an unprecedented politicisation, due to their material deprivation and Islamophobia. The chapter ends with some specific and practical steps to bolster the identity of African Caribbean and South Asian youths and thereby to empower them to challenge racism and the rise of Islamophobia.

Context

Socio-economic background

British Asians are among some of the most deprived communities within Britain. Of the various ethnic groups within this broad category, Pakistanis and Bangladeshis fare particularly badly in indices of poverty (Chahal, 2000) especially overcrowding and unemployment. Alongside the material deprivation particularly Pakistanis and Bangladeshis are also some of the poorest attainers in schools (Gillborn and Mirza, 2000). Despite the entrenched racism of many teachers (Muir and Smithers, 2004) and the Eurocentric curriculum, some British Asians, notably Indians, have succeeded, while Pakistanis and Bangladeshis have lagged behind (Gillborn and Mirza, 2000). At least one (if not two) generations of these young people have completed their education with little or no qualifications. The unemployment rate for Asian and African Caribbean communities has stubbornly remained at roughly twice the rate for White people. The

---

[1] The term 'South Asian' is a recognised nomenclature used in the sociology literature. It refers to people from the Indian subcontinent, and includes Indians, Pakistanis, Bangladeshis, Sri Lankans etc.

unemployment rates for young Asian and African Caribbean people have generally been even higher. Even though minority ethnic students are proportionately more likely to be in higher education than their White peers, minority ethnic people are less likely to gain entry into red-brick institutions, are likely to be awarded a lower grade in their degree and experience greater difficulty in entering the jobs market (Connor et al., 2004).

Islam in Britain is primarily South Asian in character. Most Muslims in Britain originate from Pakistan (687,592), Bangladesh (261,833) and India (133,783). All together Muslims of South Asian origin constitute almost three-quarters of the Muslim adherents in Britain (Samad, 2004). In addition, Muslim groups have faced additional discrimination within the job market due to Islamophobia. Candidates with English-sounding names are nearly three times more likely to get an interview as those with names suggestive of being Muslim (Muir, 2004).

Pakistanis show *lower* levels of upward mobility than their white British counterparts, even when taking account of their educational levels (Platt, 2005). Bangladeshis also show some of this disproportionate disadvantage (Platt, 2005). Exploring differences between religious groups reveals that, controlling for their backgrounds and other characteristics, Muslims have lower chances than other religious groups of ending up in a higher social class. Platt found that this is not just down to ethnicity. Differences within the Indian ethnic group show that Hindus are much more successful than both Sikhs and Muslims.

The social and economic disadvantage of British Muslims emerged in an analysis by the Office for National Statistics highlighted in the *Guardian* (Carvel, 2004). It found Muslims had the highest rate of unemployment, the poorest health, the most disability and fewest educational qualifications. Compared with people from other religious groups, Muslims lived in the biggest households and were the least likely to own their own homes. In 2003/4 Muslims had the highest unemployment rate. Among men it was 14 per cent, compared with 4 per cent among Christians. Muslims aged 16 to 24 had the highest unemployment rates of all at 22 per cent, compared with an average for Christians of 11 per cent. Muslim men and women were more likely than other groups to be economically inactive. Muslims had the youngest age profile of all religious groups, with 34 per cent under 16 compared with 25 per cent of Sikhs, 21 per cent of Hindus and 18 per cent of Christians. Muslims had the lowest level of educational qualifications, with 31 per cent of men of working age having none, compared with 23 per cent of Sikhs and 15 per cent of Christians.

The rise of Islamophobia

The position of Muslim communities has worsened dramatically due to the rise of Islamophobia, which was never far below the surface. This Islamophobia manifested itself in a very public manner particularly during the Salman Rushdie affair. The Gulf War, the September 11 terrorist attacks in the US and the more recent American and British military interventions in Afghanistan and Iraq have all contributed to the Islamophobia in Britain. Many commentators single out September 11, 2001 as a watershed in the treatment of British Muslims at the hands of the government and the British public at large. The European Monitoring Centre on Racism and Xenophobia (EUMC) implicated the British government and the media in the rise in Islamophobia warning British politicians and the media to avoid demonising immigrants and asylum seekers in the wake of mounting anti-Muslim prejudice across the continent (Black, 2002). The EUMC reported that Britain had seen a significant increase in violent assault, abuse and attacks on Muslim property, some considered very serious. Both the Prime Minister and the Foreign Office were accused of giving mixed messages. Moderate Muslim voices were largely overlooked, with Islamophobic stereotypes shaping the popular image of young British Muslim men. It therefore came as no surprise that a survey of nearly 2,000 respondents, conducted by YouGov for the Islamic Society of Great Britain, revealed that more than 8 in 10 Britons believed suspicion of Muslims had increased since September 11 (Dodd, 2002). Equally important was the admission by the vast majority of respondents that they knew little or nothing about Islam.

The government and media continue to mislead the public with their take on terrorism focussing on Muslim communities, when of those convicted under the anti-terrorist laws, many are not Muslim but White Loyalists and/or racists (Athwal, 2004). This aids the government and media in demonising the Muslim population.

Fekete (2005) in her article on the rise of anti-Muslim racism makes the important point:

What appears to have happened post-September 11, though, is that the parameters of that institutionalised xeno-racism – anti-foreignness – have been expanded to include minority ethnic communities that have been settled in Europe for decades – simply because they are Muslim. Since Islam now represents 'threat' to Europe, its Muslim residents, even though they are citizens, even though they may be European born, are caught up in the ever-expanding loop of xeno-racism. They do not merely threaten Europe as the 'enemy within' in the war on terror, their adherence to Islamic norms and values threatens the notion of Europeanness itself. Under the guise of patriotism, a wholesale anti-Islamic racism has been unleashed which itself threatens to destroy the fabric of the multicultural society.

(Fekete, 2005: 4)

Prior to the London bombings of July 2005, the draconian measures taken by the Blair government were resulting in the abrogation of human rights and the criminalisation of Muslim communities (Vasagar, 2002). The stop and search practices of the police have drawn criticism from Muslim communities, civil liberty groups and antiracist groups (Kundnani, 2004). A report published by the Home Office showing that Black people continue to be eight times – and Asian people three times – more likely to be stopped and searched than their White counterparts led the CRE to warn the police to end discriminatory stop and searches (CRE, 2003).

The use of counter-terrorism stop and search powers have increased sevenfold since the July 7 attacks on Britain, with Asian people bearing the brunt of the increase (Dodd, 2005). People of Asian appearance are five times more likely to be stopped and searched than a White person, according to the latest figures compiled by British Transport police. Yet none of the stops have resulted in a terrorism charge, according to the force. Such has been the concern of Muslim communities that days before the London bombings the Muslim Council of Britain complained of the criminalisation of Muslim youths (Cowan, 2004).

The doubled standards of the government in response to terrorism, the redundancy of some of the new legislation proposed after the tube bombings and its potential for worsening the situation were highlighted by Toynbee's piece in the *Guardian*:

. . . why is it only when confronting the Islamist threat in the 2000 Terrorism Act that it became a legal duty to inform on possible terrorists? . . . But the law never forced the Irish to inform . . . But why are we putting a higher expectation on Muslim families, equally in fear? It seems as if we fear these new terrorists as more alarmingly alien, less one of us, though Catholic and Islamist bombs have the same effect.

(Toynbee, 2005)

Leaving aside for the moment insulting pronouncements from a variety of politicians, this Islamophobia has manifested itself in the form of attacks on Muslims and their properties including places of worship. More than one in three Muslims (38 per cent) said they or their family had personally experienced hostility or abuse from non-Muslims because of their religion (Travis, 2004).

The surge in Islamophobia since the terrorist attacks on the underground has been tracked and catalogued on the Institute for Race Relations website. The Metropolitan Police recorded a sharp rise in attacks on mosques, physical attacks and verbal abuse following the London attacks. In the three days after the bombings, police in London recorded 180 racial incidents. A total of 58 faith-related crimes were recorded, compared with one in the same period the previous year (Dodd and Muir, 2005).

Such has been the concern about the harassment following the London bombings that some Muslim websites have set up third party reporting of racist harassment. The terrorism issue colours the interpretation of all inequalities and potential trouble spots in society in much the same way as the cold war made it possible to suspect trade union activists of being Soviet agents (Hornqvist, 2004).

Since the uprisings of 2001 in northern England a new racialisation has been brought into play to pathologise South Asian communities. Issues of gang-culture, forced marriages, drug abuse, inter-generational conflict, being Muslim, resistance to integrating and speaking English have all routinely being mobilised to explain away racism and justify dubious policies. Post September 11 these communities have increasingly been constructed as the new 'enemy within' (Bagguley and Hussain, 2003).

Community cohesion: the new ideology

The concept of community cohesion has become incorporated within a political circle of exclusion, segregation and control (Burnett, 2004). Instead of asking how society excludes Muslims and how this exclusion contributes to a process of ghettoisation, the questions asked are about Muslims refusing to integrate (Kundnani, 2005).

There is the expectation that integration or even community cohesion is somehow the responsibility of minority communities. The media and government never discuss what measures White communities might adopt to promote social cohesion or integration and yet there is the constant whine that somehow the presence of minority communities has been/is denying people the right to be English. The reality is that the majority community is the one that demonstrates a reluctance to reach out. According to a YouGov poll which asked 2,065 White and 808 ethnic minority people aged over 18 for details of their closest 10 to 20 friends in an internet survey, more than nine out of 10 White Britons have no or hardly any ethnic minority friends (Dodd, 2004). It has been my experience (and that of many of my colleagues working in the equalities field) that White people believe they are more open minded than minority communities about whom they form relationships with. The facts contradict this. While people from South Asian backgrounds are the least likely of the minority ethnic groups to marry outside their own group with figures for Indians at 6 per cent, Pakistanis at 4 per cent and Bangladeshis at 3 per cent, it is considerably rarer for White people to marry outside their own group. Only 1 per cent of White men and women married someone outside the category White (Carvel, 2005).

A special *Guardian*/ICM poll showed that British Muslims live less segregated lives than imagined, with more than 60 per cent saying they count 'a lot' or 'quite a few' non-Muslim people among their closest friends (Travis, 2004). Furthermore, researchers investigating housing in Leeds and Bradford have challenged the idea that Asians *self-segregate*. This is important to draw attention to because what began as a racial myth – 'Asians don't mix' – has became established as the main explanation for the disturbances in northern English towns. This supposed self-imposed segregation by Asians is also blamed for the ignorance among many White people which, in turn, leads to a collapse of social cohesion! However, research by the universities of Leeds, Warwick and the South Bank reverses this explanation (Kundnani, 2002).

It appears that under the guise of community cohesion, the assimilation/integration door has been re-opened and failed approaches of the late 1960s and 1970s have been dusted off for re-use. Gary Younge in the *Guardian* indicates some of the concerns around the issue of integration:

> . . . the value of integration is contingent on whom you are asking to integrate, what you are asking them to integrate into and on what basis you are asking them to do so. The framing of the current debate is flawed on all three fronts. It treats integration as a one-way street – not a subtle process of cultural negotiation but full-scale assimilation of a religious group that is regarded, by many liberals and conservatives, as backward and reactionary. It is hardly surprising that many Muslims would not want to sign up to that.
>
> (Younge, 2005)

Youth dimension and the uprisings

Black youths have been problematised in a variety of ways. African Caribbeans were associated with mugging (Hall et al.,1978) and then came the uprisings of 1981 and 1985 – portrayed by the popular press as mostly criminality rather than a response to policing, unemployment and assertions of identity. While Asian youth were well represented in these major disturbances (Bagguley and Hussain, 2003) it was not until the 2001 uprisings in Oldham, Burnley and Bradford that the rebelliousness of Asian youths came to government and public attention. Their old image of passivity has given way to one of aggression and criminality, an image apparently confirmed by the street disturbances, and then heightened by the government's war on terrorism (Kundnani, 2002).

As pointed out by Bagguley and Hussain (2003), the Denham (Home Office) Report attempted to incorporate all the other official findings into the disturbances of 2001, into the dominant Home Office discourse of social cohesion, versus segregation. The various official reports constructed segregation as pathological and contrasted it with the ideas of an integrated community. Besides hearsay, the reports presented no evidence about segregation nor did they examine its causes and consequences in any worthwhile detail.

They instead re-racialised British South Asians – specifically South Asian Muslims. Although the reports were careful to avoid explicit references to Islam, terms like Pakistani and Bangladeshi were coded terms meaning Muslim. Furthermore, while the reports may have claimed there is no single dominant culture within Britain, they make clear that everyone is expected to speak English. When English in this way is made the defining feature of a new national identity it also acts as a mechanism of cultural exclusion. Despite token reference in the reports to multiculturalism, non-English cultures were excluded from British identity (Bagguley and Hussain, 2003) in a stance more reminiscent of the days of Enoch Powell.

According to Bagguley and Hussain (2003), older men and younger men displayed sharply contrasting views of the 2001 'riots'. The older men were strongly critical of the actions of the younger men, who when protecting their own community could not comprehend why they faced such hostility from their elders. The older generation although keen to discuss the attacks, compared them to their own experiences. In the face of attacks by White people in the 1960s and 1970s, their generation had refused to engage in any form of conflict or riots. However, by only focusing on the age or cultural differences within South Asian communities, and how the disturbances of 2001 exposed rifts between generations, this inadvertently supports attempts to criminalise Asian youth by suggesting that the violence that occurred was an Asian problem (Burnett, 2004).

This is not to deny that there are differences between the generations, with younger people having more expectations of equality, greater expectations of education and the jobs market, despite disillusionment with the continuing and prevalent racism, as well as the older generation's compromises with the white power structure (Bagguley and Hussain, 2003). Some analysts see this as Asian leaders being permitted a cultural *laissez-faire*, largely free from state intervention (Kundnani, 2002). Interestingly, during the Manningham (Bradford) disturbances in 1995, community leaders were heckled when they attempted to mediate between the police and the Muslim youth involved (Singh, 2001). Singh argues that South Asian youngsters do not feel any traditional obligation to or reverence for leaders who neither understand youth problems nor have a track record of taking action to address such concerns. According to Singh it is wrong to assume that community leaders are losing control over their youths. The existence of any such control is seen as illusionary (Singh, 2001). The young people present at the Manningham disturbances of 1995 seriously questioned the leadership position of the Asian elected officials. Young people even accused the elected officials of using their position only for self-advancement while ignoring young people's particular problems. Singh concludes that there is little evidence to support the view that South Asian politicians have successfully acted as opinion-makers on general issues or in leading their communities (Singh, 2001).

As already mentioned, the uprisings were viewed as a cultural problem, with certain Asian groups perceived as insular and inward looking. The state sought to deal with this by focusing curiously on issues of citizenship, nationality and belonging. This focus simultaneously targeted the beliefs and identities of particular communities while disregarding those communities' realities and experiences (Burnett, 2004). The Cantle Report overlooked the wealth of research documenting the discriminatory imposition of formal police powers upon certain Asian communities, the rising levels of unemployment and residential segregation within certain Asian communities and the inexorable rise of an insistent far-Right ideology (Burnett, 2004). Despite the government's anti-racism legislation racism is now to be understood as an *outcome* of cultural segregation – not its cause. According to government, segregation is self-imposed (and implicitly, South Asians have only themselves to blame!). The real problem faced by these communities is identified as alleged cultural barriers, rather than institutional racism or deprivation (Kundnani, 2002).

While Bagguley and Hussain contrast the different views of the earlier 1981 and 1985 uprisings to those of 2001, they fail to take account of the fact that despite the community cohesion perspective the disturbances in northern England still resulted in Britain's largest criminal investigation (Bodi, 2002). Incommensurate sentencing resulted in large numbers of South Asians with no criminal history being imprisoned (Bodi, 2002). Furthermore, Bodi sees these prosecutions as a demonstration of the government's intention to treat the Muslim community as a law and order problem instead of a community relations challenge, despite the alleged community cohesion approach. Quite rightly, Bodi (2002) draws attention to the fact that in contrast to a senior judge like Lord Scarman, an unknown civil servant like Ted Cantle headed up the investigation into the disturbances of 2001. Further contrasts with the approaches to the earlier uprisings in relation to the more recent disturbances are made – namely that Scarman located the riots in the social, economic and political complex of acute deprivation and discrimination, while Cantle only acknowledged in passing that unemployment and Islamophobia contributed to the riots (Bodi, 2002). While Scarman's Report supported the reform of legislation, Cantle proposed repressive legislation including quotas for Muslim schools and oaths of allegiance (Bodi, 2002). Scarman had no reluctance in talking about a Black community but Cantle had difficulty in even mentioning a Muslim community – preferring instead the term 'Asian community' (Bodi, 2002).

New Labour has no understanding of what communities (Black or White) are, and this accounts for some of the risible suggestions it has proposed to tackle antisocial behaviour and lack of social responsibility. Feelings of community develop out of different people living and sharing together. That includes sharing joy, pain and sorrow. Feelings of community develop out of shared experiences and struggle. Only a naïve government would believe it can be imposed (Kundnani, 2005). Social cohesion cannot exist hand in hand with large-scale economic inequality. Without addressing institutional racism there can be no social cohesion worthy of the name. Certainly we cannot have any degree of social cohesion while the government's approach to terrorism stigmatises an entire group of citizens as the 'enemy within' (Kundnani, 2005).

Muslim identity and young people

Even before the disturbances of 2001, many young Muslims (and some from the older generation) were stressing their Muslim identity over that of being South Asian despite their shared heritage with others from the Indian subcontinent (Ashrif, 2001). For those living within Muslim communities or interacting with them regularly, it could not have passed unnoticed that for the last 10 to 15 years, certain changes have been developing within those communities. Young women who were not particularly radical or even deeply religious began to wear the hijab even when there had been no family tradition of wearing the headscarf. It is common today to hear South Asian Muslims use the greeting *Allah Hafiz*[2] instead of the traditional *Khuda Hafiz*. These actions can be interpreted as assertions of Muslim identity.

A growing number of Muslims in Britain are identifying themselves by their faith over ethnicity. This has been one of the consequences of the increased politicisation of Islam post-September 11, leading to a greater political consciousness amongst Muslims, as some Muslim analysts argue, but this trend had been developing before the terrorist attacks. It is, however, worth drawing attention to the fact that Muslim faith identity is often nothing to do with religious practice (Fulat, 2005). It is also noteworthy that while the path for most immigrant communities have been that parents are traditional and conservative, while their children attempt to introduce secularism, the opposite is also happening in many Muslim households (Fatah, 2005). There are two very distinct and opposing trends at work here and neither can be ignored.

The first evidence of Muslim youth becoming involved in mass Islamic politics was with the Rushdie controversy and later with the protest against the two Gulf Wars. Up to this point Muslim youths' active engagement with Islamic organisations was minimal (Samad, 2004). Kabbani explains the attraction of young Muslims to their communities' religious institutions as due to the mainstream's failure to admit them, secular institutions to interest them, lack of money spent on their localities and a lack of either training opportunities or jobs. This, according to Kabbani resulted in many young Muslims flocking to the mosques, often to the alarm of their self-effacing parents. Not surprisingly, given the importance of religion to those communities, the doors were opened to them, first to receive these young Muslims, and then to claim them (Kabbani, 2002). However, the older generation neither listened to nor remedied their problems as already indicated. Furthermore, traditional methods of conducting affairs even within these community organisations, and the various taboos about certain social and religious issues – all contributed to some alienation and considerable disillusionment with their elders. Some argue that the slide from ethnic identity where Islam is implicit to Muslim identity where ethnicity becomes implicit is linked to a loss of proficiency in ethnic languages and the assertion that they (Muslim youth) are primarily British (Samad, 2004). It is likely that the British identity results in part due to the lack of proficiency in community languages and the adaptation of Muslim beliefs/values to life in secular Britain.

Many young people from Pakistani and Bangladeshi backgrounds feel no connection with their parents' countries of origin and may have never visited there and not unexpectedly reject the labels associated with them. Not being from Pakistan (or Bangladesh), they reject the identity of Pakistani (or Bangladeshi). They however cannot easily swap *Pakistani* for *British* when so many of them feel rejected by Britain. The identity of *Muslim* helps to fill the gap (Freedland, 2005). The majority of these young people were born here and either reject or cannot relate to the politics of 'back home'. They have fashioned a form of British identity that suits their needs and experiences. While first-generation Muslims in Britain may have focused their sights on politics 'back

---

[2] The term Kuda Hafiz has been the traditional 'goodbye' in India among Muslims for generations. All Indians understand it as it uses the Indian word 'Khuda' for God. The use of the Arabic word for God, 'Allah', emphasises the paramount importance of Muslim identity over Indian identity. It can also be interpreted as a denial of one's Indian cultural identity and roots.

home' the younger generations are more engaged by social issues here in Britain (*Guardian*, 2004).

Johnson's research into London teenagers' ideas about identity and cultural belonging supports the points about religious and cultural identity. Her findings confirm what others have said about religion playing a part in determining how people describe themselves in terms of cultural identity. For some young people, religion was found to be a more important factor in identity than ethnicity. Young people from Pakistani and Bangladeshi backgrounds were more likely than any other group to use religion to describe their identity (Johnson, 2004). Insecurity, low self-confidence, experiences of failure, deprivation, racism and since September 11, oppressive anti-terrorist measures along with increasing Islamophobia have all contributed towards young people forging a common Muslim identity. The present younger generation asserts with increasing confidence being Muslim, as a *political* identity (Bunting, 2004).

White participants in the CRE's attitude surveys resented Asian, and especially Muslim people, whom they saw as importing a foreign culture into their country (CRE, 1998). The surveys also confirmed that both Pakistani and Bangladeshi young people felt that Islam is central to their identity, providing a moral and social framework for their lives and behaviour, and that everything else comes second. While younger Muslims in the group were also acutely aware of the stereotypes of Islam that prevail in British society, they were at pains to emphasise the positive aspects of their religion (CRE, 1998). South Asians' cultures and religions were subject to racial hostility. South Asian children at school were bullied by White children because of a particular religious garment or practice. Young Muslim women in the group said they received routine abuse for wearing headscarves (CRE, 1998). A more recent study confirmed that a significant minority of White young people admitted to not liking Muslims and Asians. Perceptions persisted among some White young people that minority ethnic communities are not entitled to live in Britain and should be in their own country. Some also saw minority ethnic communities as the *source*, not the victim of hostility (Lemos, 2005).

The out-casting of Muslims from notions of British identity, as something alien as well as threatening is comprehensible in terms of Brah's analysis:

> ... *cultural differences is also the site of identificatory processes figuring narratives of belonging and community* ... *Cultural specificities do not in and of themselves constitute social division. It is the meaning attributed to them, and how this meaning is played out in the economic, cultural and political domains, that marks whether or not specificity emerges as a basis of social division.*

(Brah, 1996: 235)

The Black Families Talking project spoke to Asian and African-Caribbean parents about how they coped with exclusion and other difficulties in British society. The study found that those who held on to or developed cultural identities and values, which opposed the perceived materialism and individualism of the majority UK community, felt they coped better with most problems. This often involved reliance on community spirit and spirituality, with regular group meetings and discussions. It was found that support was also gained from family, friends, religious and cultural networks and prayer (Social Policy Research Paper, 1997). This research is also consistent with the earlier explanation of why some South Asians emphasise their religious identity.

Having already mentioned the initial interest of South Asian Muslims in their religious institutions and practices, and their subsequent alienation, it is worth noting Dr. Siddiqui, the leader of the Muslim Parliament's frank admissions in a press release after the 7/7 bombings:

> *Most mosques are not equipped to deal with young people . . . They do not have the staff equipped with Islamic knowledge, experience and professionalism. Young people have drifted away either because they were banned to discuss controversial issues in the mosque or found nothing inspiring on offer there. Our mosques are largely tribal and controlled by old men on-the-dole with no understanding of the changing world around them. Expansion of mosque activities could have provided the opportunity to many young men and women to become involved in youth projects. The unwelcoming and suffocating atmosphere within mosques did not allow this to happen. Many radical and active young people began drifting away organising themselves outside the influence of the mosque structure . . . Muslim youth have nowhere to go to learn, discuss or get professional advice on issues relating to growing up.*

(Press release 2005)

Comments like those above only gave ammunition to those sniping at Asian communities for not listening to their young and supports the older White view of culture conflict between Asian youngsters and their elders. However, Muslim leaders have no more connection with troubled Muslim youth than government ministers or local politicians do with troublesome White youths (Appleton, 2005) and hence the government's consultations with so called Muslim leaders is doomed to failure. Interestingly, Hazel Blears[3] was accused of listening to the wrong people as she began a tour of English towns and cities in a government effort to improve community relations and root out extremists in the wake of the London bombings (Stokes, 2005). That aside, the limited ability of community structures to address their troublesome youths lies in the fact that today's mainstream Muslim organisations have their origins in the late 1990s, and developed under the influence or patronage of a New Labour regime. Some Muslim groups work closely with government, and even receive government project funding. Such organisations cannot deal with the so-called fundamentalist problem because they themselves are products of Blairite times. Their brand of Islam, intimately tied to officialdom may not prove particularly attractive to young Muslims (Appleton, 2005). According to Appleton, a bland, consensual brand of Islam that shies away from firm beliefs and shoves disagreements under the carpet is partly responsible for the current alienation of Muslim youth. New Labour refuses to acknowledge that very alienation from mainstream British society and its institutions is the source of the problem for young Muslims.

Supporting young Black people

Through my experiences of working as a teacher, then Education Adviser and subsequently as a lecturer at De Montfort University I have noticed that both Asian and African Caribbean young people have little knowledge or understanding of battles fought, or difficulties endured, to reach where we are today as a multi-ethnic nation

---

[3] Hazel Blears was the Minister of State for Crime, Security and Communities and was involved in the consultations with Muslim communities following the 7 July bombings.

(Ashrif, 2001). Even when 'anti-oppressive practice' is a core module for degree courses its effectiveness is blunted. Such modules assume schools and colleges have given students an understanding of slavery, colonialism and the history of black immigration to Britain. In my experience of working with schools and young adults in other settings, including Glen Parva Young Offenders Institution, significant numbers of black people do not posses such knowledge, and this has been confirmed by research (Johnson, 2004). There is a need for a compulsory core module on Black History for *all* young people in schools and it needs also to be a vital element in youth and community work.

The committee set up in the late 1980s to advise on the multicultural dimension to the National Curriculum was abolished. Antiracist approaches were squeezed out of the National Curriculum and most teachers (and the DfES) forgot the rationale and practices that had been developing prior to the advent of the National Curriculum (Ashrif, 2002). The QCA developed an interest in multicultural education in the wake of the Macpherson Report. Despite the remit from the Education Secretary issued in 1999 the QCA only began this project seriously in Autumn 2001 after the civil disturbances in northern England. However, the QCA guidance was non-statutory and most teachers ignored it. This, and the fierce battles over the contents of the National Curriculum history syllabus can be understood in the context of Apple's contention:

> There is, then always a **politics** of official knowledge, a politics that embodies conflict over what some regard as simply neutral descriptions of the world and what others regard as elite conceptions that empower some groups while disempowering others.

(Apple, 1996: 23). (Original emphasis)

It is clear that young people of minority background feel that there should be more emphasis on Black History in school as part of the National Curriculum although White youngsters do not (Johnson, 2004). Black History would bolster the self-pride and confidence of minority ethnic young people (and adults!) as others and I teaching in this field have learned. This was certainly the case when Wolde Selassie and I (on behalf of the Leicester Black Prisoners Support Group) delivered Black History to South Asian and African Caribbean inmates at Glen Parva prison. Surprisingly, we were one of the first groups of trainers to deliver Black History to an ethnically mixed audience. The evaluations of the training by the inmates were overwhelmingly positive. The training rapidly generated respect from the young adults towards the trainers and each other. (Prison officers regularly exploited perceived differences and animosities between South Asian and African Caribbean inmates.) The young people were explicit about how Black History was both a source of pride and a shield against racism. In my experience with minority ethnic young people and adults, Black History never fails to engage people and give those communities a sense of pride, self-confidence and a better insight into their situation as minorities in Britain. However, this same Black History is important for White young people because it challenges some of their racist perceptions. The continual omission of the achievements of Black individuals and communities confirms in young people the idea that Black people have contributed nothing to world knowledge.

There are growing numbers of websites devoted to Black History, and of course the established annual Black History Month, but the main focus of these is often African Caribbean history. While the curriculum in schools remains essentially Eurocentric and the racism in society also remains entrenched, Black History is a vital tool in the hands of teachers and community workers. However, this Black History approach needs to be developed further, not only to specifically include a wider range of minority ethnic people but also to address the upsurge of Islamophobia so that no one should need to question what Black or Muslim people have contributed to modern society.

The case for Islamic studies

Islam has the second largest following of any religion and its adherents are found in substantial numbers all over the world, with the Arab Muslims constituting only a small fraction of the total. It is important to investigate how a religion that emerged around 600 CE in Saudi Arabia came to be so widespread. Despite its huge following, Islam is poorly understood, if at all, in the West, and in this country, for a long time the media has consistently misrepresented the aims of Britain's 1.5–2.0 million Muslims. The distorting mirror of racism still caricatures Islam in terms of polygamy, purdah, religious zealotry – and more recently, a militant fundamentalism that threatens the economic and political domination of the western nations (Ashrif, 2001).

A study of Islam simply in terms of religious beliefs and practices is to marginalise a major cultural force and political block that has had a pronounced impact on many ideas and institutions both in Europe and the rest of the world (Semaan, 1980). The Renaissance of which Europeans are justly proud would not have been possible without the seminal cultural infusions of Moorish and Jewish scholarship (Carew, 1992).

To address the distortions and omissions concerning Islam and to give young ethnic minority people pride and self confidence I suggest that a new topic of Islamic Studies, as a component of Black History, be explored with young people. It is indefensible to make pupils aware of European influences upon culture without acknowledging the profound impact of Islamic civilisation upon world cultures, including those in Europe.

Islamic contribution to western civilisation

Muslim scholars translated the works of Aristotle, Plato, Ptolemy, Euclid, Heracleitus, Galen, Hippocrates and others, and significantly improved upon them. Muslims drew from their wide-ranging intellectual experiences and observations throughout the huge territories they ruled. These scholars not only absorbed but also attempted syntheses of the varied knowledge of the Ethiopians, the Nubians, the Egyptians, the Jews, the Phoenicians, the Greeks, the Chinese, the Persians and the Indians (Carew, 1992). The Muslim world made enormous contributions to science, technology and medicine with many Muslim scientists like Avicenna and Averroes becoming well known in Europe (Al-Hassan and Hill, 1986).

The traditional Morris Dancing, always considered a quaint English custom is actually a corruption of Moorish dancing performed with a hobby horse and bells in the manner of Arab minstrels. Arabic influences upon European languages have been substantial, particularly with reference to Spanish and Portuguese. The Arabic contribution to the Spanish language is seen in the vocabulary of commerce, travelling, weighing, measuring and keeping order in the town or markets, fruits and vegetables, houses and their furnishings etc. (Watt and Cachia, 1996). Even English is not without its Arabic influences as seen in words like zenith, algebra, monsoon, cotton, mattress, syrup, alcohol, sofa, admiral etc.

A subject like Islamic Studies could consider the crucial and far reaching Islamic influence upon the Iberian Peninsula and Southern France. For centuries during the Muslim domination of the Iberian Peninsula, Muslims, Christians and Jews lived side-by-side, and, in many instances, had so intermarried that numerous families were part Muslim, part Christian and part Jewish. Significantly, the teachings of the Prophet regarding the issues of 'race' and colour were practised not merely preached (Carew, 1992). Christians in Spain also adopted the Arabic culture in terms of language and attire (Watt and Cachia, 1996). The Moors introduced numerous new crops like oranges, pomegranates, bananas, coconuts, maize and rice. With new crops and irrigation systems Muslims brought about an agricultural revolution in Spain (Carew, 1992). The tolerance of the Spanish Moors, and their thirst for knowledge permitted Spain to become the intellectual centre of Europe. The cross fertilisation of ideas in Islamic Spain and in Sicily was crucial to the subsequent development of the European Renaissance (Carew, 1992).

The extremism of the Spanish Inquisition was partly a reaction to the occupation of Spain by the Muslims. After the *Reconquista* the Inquisition put to death large numbers of Muslims and Jews and was to harass and torture many others (Carew, 1992). Later, Spain attempted systematically to eradicate many of the signs of the Moorish presence. The Moors who remained after the *Reconquista* were involved in many uprisings in response to the harsh treatment they received. In fact, the violent rebellion of 1568 was so serious that King Philip II had to call on help from Don Juan of Austria to put it down (Read, 1975). Ironically enough, the three pilots guiding Columbus to the Americas, the Pinzon brothers, were Moors (Carew, 1985).

With the media focus on troubles in the Middle East, Europeans tend to forget (or perhaps were not aware) that Muslims are found in substantial numbers in Africa as well as Indonesia and the Indian subcontinent. There have been many African Muslim empires. At its height, the Moorish Empire stretched from the western half of Algeria through Morocco and as far south as Ghana. In Europe, this empire extended from the Atlantic coast, across the Pyrenees to the Rhone valley and parallel to the Bay of Biscay as far north as Tours in France (Carew, 1992).

Despite the Crusades cultural and scientific ideas continued to be exchanged between Muslim nations and Christendom albeit most of the traffic went *to* Europe. The Crusades, although important, are all too frequently misrepresented in textbooks, which rarely investigate either the *politics* of the conflict, or the importance of securing trade routes. There is no attempt by the majority of textbooks to suggest that with the more pressing matter of Seljuks and the Mongols, the Crusades were perhaps of minor importance to the Islamic Empire.

The Islamic conquest of the Indian subcontinent was to have profound political, cultural and social consequences in that part of the world. Indeed it could be reasonably argued that the partition of India and Pakistan in 1947, and the subsequent emergence of Bangladesh, were all a direct consequence of the former Muslim domination of India. The development of Urdu and modern Hindi and their widespread use in the Indian subcontinent derives directly from the Turkish and Persian influences. The pre-Islamic custom of purdah and veils brought to India by the Muslims was readily adopted by upper class Hindus and subsequently infiltrated the entire Indian population.

Islam has also served as a form of resistance to European colonialism (Keddie, 1968). Purdah was a useful method to conceal weapons during the Algerian fight for independence. The present politics of the Middle East cannot be separated from its legacy of struggles against European colonialism. A proper understanding of the Muslim world's relation with Europe and the US would also have a place in any Islamic Studies syllabus.

Topics for study

Below is outlined a suggested Islamic Studies syllabus, with an attempt to gauge the depth of study by ascribing topics to foundation, standard and advanced levels. This categorisation is not intended to be definitive, but the beginning of a process of debate concerning the parameters of Islamic Studies.

- Foundation Level Islamic Studies
- History of the rise and expansion of Islamic civilisations.
- Islamic art and architecture.
- Muslim traders.
- Muslim women in history.

- Standard Level Islamic Studies
- The lives of Muslims in Britain.
- Diversity of Muslim countries and cultures.
- Islamic influences on sciences and mathematics.
- Muslims' impact on Spain and Portugal.
- Islamic influences in the Indian subcontinent.
- The Crusades.

- Advanced Level Islamic Studies
- Diversity in Islamic practices and legislation throughout the Muslim world.
- Attitude of Muslims to non-Muslims: a comparative approach.
- Islam's role in the Renaissance of Europe.
- Impact of Islam on literature.
- The Muslim world's struggles against European colonialism and imperialism.
- Comparisons between Arab and Western forms of imperialism.
- The portrayal of Islam in the West.

Conclusion

Informed South Asians are perfectly aware of the colonial practices that helped keep the British in power in the subcontinent. That Raj mentality, however, is pervasive in present day city councils as well as in the organs of the state. In my experiences as a senior professional in various local councils, as a political activist and as a consultant trainer, working nationally, local governments are essentially afraid of Asian and African Caribbean communities. If these communities were further politicised and united, a great deal could be achieved in bettering the condition of the majority of black communities. However, then as now, there is an easy collusion between the powers that be and the 'elders' or self-appointed leaders of various ethnic and religious communities. Furthermore, the politics of 'back home' continue to run interference in the solidarity of various ethnic and religious groups and the effectiveness of such communities in negotiating with the governments in power. But a newer generation of South Asians is emerging upon the scene – a generation that see Britain as its home, a generation that is more politicised and is better educated and most importantly rejects the politics of 'back home'. This generation is not subject to being bought off so easily or bamboozled by local or national politicians. This internet-savvy generation is unlikely to accept formulaic solutions, and gives some grounds for hope that the Raj politics will be replaced by a genuine concern for the material condition of young black people.

The new racism and Islamophobia of the Labour government manifested in its community cohesion policy and implementation of anti-terrorism legislation needs to be examined and discussed. Young people who are often at the receiving end of these policies and practices would benefit from a better understanding of how and why they are the targets of discriminatory behaviour that denies them their rights as citizens. (Currently it is commonplace for Muslims young and old to equate the 'why' with Islamophobia although they are less clear on the details of the 'how'.) The role of education and community work is vital in facilitating this empowerment. Young black people need pride in themselves and their identities. They also need the knowledge and skills to both articulate and challenge their condition. An understanding of Black and Islamic histories can make a powerful contribution towards this.

References

Al-Hassan, A.Y. and Hill, D.R. (1986) *Islamic Technology. An Illustrated History*. Cambridge University Press.

Apple, M.W. (1996) *Cultural Politics and Education*. Open University Press.

Appleton, J. (2005) *Why the Extremism Taskforce Will Fail*. [cited 24th November 2006] http://www.spiked-online.com/Articles/0000000CACA2.htm

Ashrif, S. (1985) Blinkered Vision. *Times Educational Supplement Scotland*, Nov. 15.

Ashrif, S. (2001) Beyond Islamophobia. *Multicultural Teaching*, 19: 2.

Ashrif, S. (2001) Charting the Development of Multi-ethnic Britain. *Multicultural Teaching*, 19: 3.

Ashrif, S. (2002) QCA and The Politics of Multicultural Education. *Multicultural Teaching*, 20: 3.

Athwal, H. (2004) *Analysis: Who Are The Terrorists*. [cited 12th August 2004] https://www.irr.org.uk/2004/august/ak000007.html

Bagguley, P. and Hussain, Y. (2003) *The Bradford 'Riot' of 2001: A Preliminary Analysis*. Paper presented to the 9th Alternative Futures and Popular Protest Conference, Manchester Metropolitan University, [cited 24th April 2003]. www.leeds.ac.uk/sociology/people/pbdocs/Bradfordriot.doc

Black, I. (2002) End Growing Anti-Muslim Prejudice, EU Report Urges. *Guardian*, May 24.

Bodi, F. (2002) Muslims got Cantle. What we Needed was Scarman. *Guardian*, July 1.

Brah, A. (1996) *Cartographies of Diaspora: Contesting Identities*. Routledge.

Bunting, M. (2004) Young, Muslim and British. *Guardian*. Nov. 30.

Burnett, J. (2004) Community, Cohesion and the State. *Race and Class*. Institute of Race Relations.

Carew, J. (1992) The End of Moorish Enlightenment and The Beginning of The Columbian Era. *Race and Class*. Institute of Race Relations.

Carvel, J. (2004) Census Shows Muslims' Plight. *Guardian*, Tuesday Oct. 12.

Carvel, J. (2005) First Figures For Inter-Ethnic Marriages Published. *Guardian*, Mar. 22.

Chahal, K. (2000) *Ethnic Diversity, Neighbourhoods and Housing*. [cited 12th January 2001] http://www.jrf.org.uk/knowledge/findings/foundations/pdf/110.pdf

Chahal, K. (2004) *Foundations: Experiencing Ethnicity*. [cited 24th November 2004] www.jrf.org.uk/knowledge/findings/foundations/pdf/914.pdf

Cowan, R. (2004) Young Muslims 'Made Scapegoats' in Stop and Search. *Guardian*, July 3.

CRE (1998) *Stereotyping and Racism: Findings From Two Attitudes Surveys*. CRE.

CRE (2003) *CRE Warns Police to End Discrimination in Stop and Search*. [cited 21st December 2003] http://www.cre.gov.uk/Default.aspx.locID-0hgnew03f.htm

Chrisafis, A. (2001) Muslim Pupil Excluded Over Dress Code. *Guardian*, October 10.

Connor, H. et al. (2004) *Why the Difference? A Closer Look at Higher Education Minority Ethnic Students and Graduates*. Institute for Employment Studies.

Dodd, V. (2002) Muslims Face More Suspicion. *Guardian*, Nov. 5.

Dodd, V. (2004) 90% of Whites Have Few or no Black Friends. *Guardian*, Jul. 19.

Dodd, V. (2005) Asian Men Targeted in Stop and Search. *Guardian*, Aug. 17.

Dodd, V. and Muir, H. (2005) Police Pledge Tough Action as Race Hate Attacks Rise. *Guardian*, Jul. 12.

Fatah, N. (2005) *Muslim Youth: An Identity Dilemma*. [cited 8th January 2006] http://www.cbc.ca/news/viewpoint/vp_fatah/20050722.html

Fekete, L. (2004) Anti-Muslim Racism and the European Security State. *Race and Class*, 46: 1.

Freedland, J. In the Grip of Panic. *Guardian*, Jan. 22.

Fulat, S. (2005) Recognise Our Role in Society. *Guardian*, Jan. 21.

Gillborn, D. and Mirza, H. (2000) *Educational Inequality: Mapping Race, Class and Gender*. Ofsted.

Guardian (2004) How Would You Describe Your Identity? *Guardian*, Nov. 30. [cited 12th December 2005] http://www.guardian.co.uk/print/0,3858,5074360-115039,00.html

Hall, S. et al. (1978) *Policing the Crisis. Mugging, The State and Law and Order*. MacMillan.

Hornqvist, M. (2004) The Birth of Public Order Policy. *Race and Class*, 46: 1.

Johnson, E. (2004) *In-between Two Worlds: London Teenagers' Ideas About Identity, Cultural Belonging and Black History*. London Museums Hub Research; Front-end evaluation. [cited 12th December 2005] http://www.almlondon.org.uk/uploads/documents/HUB_BHM_5_evaluation_report.pdf .

Kabbani, R. (2002) Dislocation and Neglect in Muslim Britain's Ghettos. *Guardian*, Jun. 17.

Keddie, N.R. (1968) *An Islamic Response to Imperialism; Political and Religious Writings of Sayyid Jamal Ad-Dinal-Afghani*. Univ. California Press.

Kundnani, A. (2002) *Asians do Mix, Say Researchers*. Dec. 17; [cited 12th December 2002] irr.org.uk

Kundnani, A. (2002) The Death of Multiculturalism. *Race and Class*, 43: 4.

Kundnani, A. (2004) *'Anti-terrorism' Policing Leads to Arbitrary Use of Stop and Search*. Jan. 20. [cited 15th February 2004] irr.org.uk

Kundnani, A. (2005) The Politics of a Phoney Britishness. *Guardian*, Jan. 21.

Lemos, G. (2005) *The Search For Tolerance. Challenging and Changing Racist Attitudes and Behaviour Among Young People*. [cited 13th November 2005] http://www.jrf.org.uk/bookshop/eBooks/1859352855.pdf.

Muir, H. (2004) Muslim Names Harm Job Chances. *Guardian*, Jul. 12.

Muslim Parliament (2005) *Siddiqui Tells Muslim Conference: Confront Extremism*. [cited 8th December 2005] http://www.muslimparliament.org.uk/confrontextremism.htm

Platt, L. (2005) *Migration and Social Mobility: The Life Chances of Britain's Minority Ethnic Communities*. [cited 14th November 2005] http://www.jrf.org.uk/bookshop/eBooks/1861348223.pdf.

Read, J. (1975) *The Moors in Spain and Portugal*. Totowa, NJ: Rowman and Littlefield.

Samad, Y. (2004) *Muslim Youth In Britain: Ethnic to Religious Identity*. Paper presented at the International Conference Muslim Youth in Europe. Turin, Jun. 11 2004. [cited 6th July 2004] http://www.cestim.it/02islam_uk_sanad.pdf.

Seeman, K.I. (1980) *Islam and the Medieval West: Aspects of Intercultural Relations*. NY State University Press.

Singh, R. (2001) *Future Race Relations in Bradford: Factors that Matter*. [cited 14th November 2001] http://www.bradford2020.com/pride/docs/Section%208.doc

Social Policy Research (1997) *Black Families' Survival Strategies: Ways of Coping in UK Society.* [cited 3rd December 1997] http://www.jrf.org.uk/knowledge/findings/socialpolicy/pdf/sp135.pdf .

Stokes, P. (2005) Minister Accused of Failing to Listen to Views of Muslim Youth. *Telegraph,* Aug. 3.

Toynbee, P. (2005) Why Was The IRA Less of a Threat Than Islamist Bombers? *Guardian,* Sep. 20.

Travis, A. (2004) Optimistic, Integrated and Devout. *Guardian*, Nov. 30.

Vasagar, J. (2002) War on Terrorism 'Used to Erode Rights'. *Guardian*, May 29.

Watt, W.M. and Cachia, P. (1996) *A History of Islamic Spain.* Edinburgh University Press.

Younge, G. (2005) Please Stop Fetishing Integration. Equality is What we Really Need. *Guardian*, Sep. 19.

CHAPTER 10

Can White Youth Workers Effectively Meet the Needs of Black Young People?

Ann Marie Lawson

Introduction

It is my aim in this chapter to explore whether or not White youth workers can effectively meet the needs of Black young people. As a student I struggled personally and professionally with this question. The more my level of awareness was raised as to the concept of Black sociology and the Black perspective the more concerned I became as to the service Black young people were receiving from White youth workers like myself during some of the most difficult years of their lives in terms of identity and culture. This chapter is based on personal experiences and observations.

I am not an academic but I am a youth work practitioner and a member of society and as such I am influenced by the norms, values and commonsense beliefs of that society as are all the other youth workers who have a role to play in the lives of the young people they work with. This is a huge responsibility and one that I believe we should be accountable for by constantly analysing our work to ensure we fulfil our obligation to provide a quality service to the young people we work with; if we fail to do this we become deficient and therefore merely a tokenistic or symbolic youth worker.

It is for this reason precisely that I felt the need to examine how the Black perspective is considered in youth work practice today. Initially I believed that if I treated all people equally and fairly then I could not in any way, shape or form be linked to racism. My upbringing had taught me that racism was destructive and wrong but I recognised it only as individual acts of discrimination and oppression that people chose to be involved in, not as an unsought racial dominance located within social systems, policy and structure that is bestowed on all members of White society from birth. I now believe it to be if not invisible at least pernicious and more difficult to detect in the covert form it presents itself in Britain today.

I live and work in a predominately White community and as the realisation hit me that I had never thought much about racial identity I began to feel uncomfortable. If I subconsciously or not believed that racial identity was a process of development that Black people faced and only ever discussed racial identity as a factor pertaining to Black and ethnic minority groups how many other White people behaved in this manner? I reflected on the many conversations and shared dialogues I had been part of with colleagues and friends on racial identity and was perplexed that at no point had we considered our White identity. I question whether our ignorance is a choice as the knowledge is there to be found if only we had taken the time to explore the impact our White identity could have on the delivery of our work.

I began to ask people I worked with, both colleagues and young people what racial identity meant to them and was astounded by some of my findings. One young White person when asked to describe his ethnic background told me he didn't have one because he was White. On further exploration he said ethnicity was what Black people had when they live in Britain because they couldn't be British. As our discussion deepened he said he had never felt the need to look at his own racial identity because he just felt normal because he belonged to Britain and 'they' didn't. This young male had been accessing youth provision for more than a year. I found this alarming, yes his youth club had a cultural calendar and a kick out racism calendar but he had no real awareness or understanding of race, identity or culture.

I spoke to a youth worker who said that when she had completed her diploma in youth work she struggled with the notion of institutional racism and began to feel guilty about being White. She said that this was a common feeling amongst her fellow students. I asked her how she felt she had moved on from that and she said she didn't think she had because it was difficult as she lived in a predominately White community. These feelings of guilt and shame are an obstacle in the quest for a positive White identity that will do more to combat racism than a conscious inability to move forward due to demographic limitations. This self indulgent guilt allows White superiority to exist unchallenged as long as we have a perceived culpability that allows apathy to breed.

I believe, therefore, that in order for White youth workers to effectively meet the needs of Black young people they must first of all achieve a healthy sense of White identity by understanding the impact of the ideology of White superiority and unpick the psychological implications of this unsought racial dominance bestowed on all members of White society from birth. Like the youth worker above, if our understanding of the world comes from a predominately White community reinforced by media stereotypes and language, the message conveyed in terms of White superiority and the assumed inferiority of ethnic minorities will shape our perceptions of the reality of racial norms and influence our interactions with others.

Helm's model of racial identity

Many people whose only living experience of culture comes from White settings believe they are simply part of the racial norm as it should be in Britain today and never give a thought for the diversity of cultures in our society. They accept this racial norm and take for granted their privilege without ever giving consideration to the significance of their racial identity. I believe it is in these instances where people have no-one to compare themselves to that it is all the more important to develop a healthy White identity that will enable us to have a growing awareness of racism that can be linked to White superiority and racial dominance.

Janet Helms' (1990) model of how White people can achieve a healthy White identity is direct and instructive. She states that for White people there are two major developmental tasks in this process, the abandonment of individual racism and the recognition of and opposition to institutional and cultural racism. She believes these tasks occur over six stages: contact, disintegration, reintegration, pseudo-independent, immersion/emersion and autonomy.

Firstly, if we loosely describe the contact stage as being a time when we place little or no significance in our own racial identity, the disintegration stage as a growing awareness of racism that leads to a cognitive dissonance of inconsistent thoughts, beliefs and attitudes and the reintegration stage as a time of anger and fear where we prefer to blame Black people for any problems relating to racism to negate ourselves of all responsibility for social change, have we identified the position that the young person and youth worker I spoke of earlier are at? I believe we could easily place the young man in the contact stage. He has never considered his racial identity and believes himself to be just normal implying that not to be White and British means in his opinion that you may be described as abnormal. The youth worker may be more difficult to position. She may never have moved from the disintegration stage with personal feelings of guilt and shame at her own prejudices, or she may have moved into the reintegration stage believing that as she was not witnessing overt racism in her predominately White community, then it is obviously the Black people living in multi-cultural communities that are creating the problem. The benefits of this argument are that it alleviates her from all feelings of guilt or shame and negates her of responsibility to act as an agent for social change.

She may of course have moved into the pseudo independent stage where she has an intellectual understanding of institutional racism as a system of advantage but is unsure as to what she can do about it. If this was the case then I would suggest that her training failed both her and the young people she would be working with. Surely if we are going to raise peoples level of awareness about racism we must also ensure they have the knowledge and the tools to move toward constructive action. Failure to do this excuses people from reflecting on their own White identity development by permitting them to believe that awareness and understanding is one and the same thing. This perceived understanding based on our individual interpretation of the knowledge and awareness imparted on us allows us to bask in the glory of the political correctness of being racially aware. It does nothing to enhance the delivery of our work or encourage us to move forward in our own White identity development where we can begin to truly understand the changing but continuously destructive face of racism in Britain today.

In my work within a predominately White community I think it is perhaps more important to be pro-active in our conversations and discussions around race. It is arrogant and ignorant to suggest that children and young people living in such communities do not imbue race with consideration or meaning. They may not show any outward signs of thinking about race, they almost certainly will not have contemplated their attitudes or beliefs about race in any depth; however, they will have been influenced by the many negative images and stereotypes still evident in society today. I do not just mean the gradual and subtle subliminal messages given to us by White media today which as they attempt to show tokenistic attempts at political correctness paradoxically confuse us to the point where we try to make sense out of nonsense. The majority of Black people in the media are either portrayed as gangsters, criminals or educationally subnormal or they are upwardly mobile professionals who are deemed to be successful and a credit to their race which only serves to perpetuate the myth that they are not widely accepted as ordinary people living ordinary lives in Britain today. This explains why many of the young people in predominately White communities cannot relate to Black people on an individual level. They assume that if a Black person is not a successful music star or sports person then they must be deviant and dangerous. They cannot comprehend that there are many Black people just like themselves who are trying to get on with their ordinary lives in a society obsessed with their racial identity whilst arrogantly denying the impact of their own racial identity in terms of White identity development.

Following the pseudo independent stage of White racial identity development comes the immersion/emersion phase. This can be explained as the stage where we consent to accepting who we are and embracing the affinity we have now developed with our White cultural heritage. We understand the need to continue to work towards a more positive self-definition, although for many people this stage proves to be the most solitary part of their journey towards racial self-actualisation. We may now be more comfortable with our Whiteness and better equipped to challenge racism but this can make us unpopular with some of the people we come into contact with who by not questioning the marginalisation of those who oppose racism in our society actually condone it. If we choose to continue in our quest for racial self-actualisation the last of Helms' stages of White racial development will be reached, this last stage is known as autonomy. This self-governing freedom represents the culmination of the White racial development process. I see this stage as reaching an equilibrium which is comfortable as we feel more balanced and in tune with ourselves and others, we can naturally consider the uniqueness of each other regardless of our group membership without denying the constant effects of such group memberships for the individual. This stage is exciting because it is the point where we fully understand that all people are works in process and that racial identity development never ends; this encourages us to remain open to new information and modes of thought about racial and cultural contemporary developments.

If we consider Helms' stages of racial identity development, is there a minimum standard as to the stage a White youth worker should be at in order to effectively meet the needs of Black young people? Does this stage change if they work in predominately White communities? In my opinion it is essential for all youth workers to have at least embarked on the journey towards racial self-actualisation and a positive White identity. They should understand that it is an ongoing process and one that they should be committed to travelling. White youth workers working in predominately White settings should at the very least be in the disintegration stage; they could serve no purpose to the young people they work with if they remain in the contact stage where they have paid no significance to their racial identity. If they still believe they are part of the racial norm then all the connotations that come with the word normal will serve to perpetuate the miasma of racism within our society today.

If they have at least moved towards the disintegration stage then it may be possible to share that journey with the young White people they work with through positive intervention and shared dialogue. They should be willing to have those awkward and difficult conversations around racism with their colleagues who are further along in the process of racial identity development as this will support them in the journey and enhance their practice delivery. Some experts believe that the disintegration stage is the ideal time to show images through the media of the dehumanising or stereotyping of Black people. I once used a video which I showed to my peers before using it in a session with young White people. The video showed powerful images of Black people in many of their stereotypical roles which are still portrayed in the media today. Some of the images were of stupid but happy Black men, invisible maids, Black whores and menacing street gangs consisting solely of young Black males. I learnt a harsh lesson very quickly during that session on racial awareness. I learnt that as the young people I worked with had no living concept of Black people the media images and stereotypes were stronger than I had ever envisaged. Not one of the young people in the project had ever met a Black person. It is said in the disintegration stage that as the cycle of racism becomes more visible White people begin to experience feelings of shame and guilt and are uncomfortable in the assumed superiority of Whiteness. This was not my experience. I wrongly believed that as we had worked on racial identity on two previous sessions, both challenging but enlightening leading me to believe that I understood where the young people were at in terms of racial identity that they were ready to see this film. I now realise that I had not taken other factors into account, for example their age and the environment we were working in. During the sessions on racial awareness there was a power imbalance: as the youth worker who had planned the session and held the funding for the venue much of the power lay with me. On reflection, I believe that as I challenged them I became a victim of the halo effect, with the young people telling me what they thought I wanted to hear, so that we could move on. This gave me the false impression that the group were ready to move out of the contact stage.

As I began to show the film I realised that the group moving out of the contact stage was my idealistic notion of what had happened and not the reality of the state of things as they actually existed. Throughout the film the group reinforced the stereotypical images shown by relating them to other examples from film, television and music, whilst highlighting that they believed that not only were these images real, they were as they should be. They spoke of the hard rap of many young Black male rappers who addressed women as bitches and whores. If Black men describe women of their own culture as such then that is what they must be. It is unfortunate that by sexually dehumanising and socially denigrating Black women in this misogynist manner, young Black artists are reinforcing the stereotype of the over-sexed Black woman. This objectifying of their own Black women perpetuates the stereotype of Black women in White ideological society, encouraging White men to think all Black women are oversexed and happy to be used for sexual gratification.

I was aware that many of the young people in the group were fans of the Black female artist Beyonce Knowles and challenged them by splitting them into two groups and asking them to give me three words that would describe her. The first group used talented, fit and beautiful, and the second group used successful, beautiful and American. I asked them why they did not think that she as a Black woman was a bitch or a whore. What I heard next astonished me; they laughed and told me she was not Black. They could not equate her beauty and her Blackness, choosing to deny her colour. I found it difficult to convince them, but nevertheless this provided me with the much needed opportunity to open the dialogue in a more positive manner around perceptions and stereotypes and how they impact on our understanding of the social world.

I knew then that I could not encourage or motivate these young people to take the journey to racial identity development and in trying to do so I was in fact manipulating the situation. People of all ages will only embark on this journey when circumstances dictate it will be to their benefit, such is the power of White superiority that as part of the dominant culture with all the advantages of being White we are happy to maintain the status quo.

I knew then that the best way to work with these young White people that would challenge their perceptions and hopefully benefit any Black people they encountered throughout their lives would be to make valid contributions that would encourage them to explore their understanding of culture and diversity and the importance of the Black perspective. They needed to see Black people as fully paid up members of a society they had arrogantly claimed as their own. We could do this by looking at not only positive Black role models but also positive White role models who had been engaged in anti-racist activities. We could further explore media images and relate them to other false media images in relation to young people for instance. It is my experience that young people understand better when they can relate to personal feelings or experiences. We could celebrate Black history month and Black contribution to music and the arts in a more relevant manner than that of the cultural calendar, or the poster that says welcome in 20 different languages, has ever done. We can visit cultural places of interest and cultural projects to enable young people growing up in predominately White communities to have a living and real understanding of who Black people are, and will encourage them to challenge the discrimination and oppression of Black people on a personal and cultural level. This may lead to them questioning the structures that work to discriminate and oppress these people by perpetuating the cultural norms that are part of our society today.

White youth workers working with Black young people should examine their level of awareness in terms of race; they must be sure of where they stand on all issues and have a clear understanding of their own racial identity development. Any less would be to the detriment of the young Black people they work with.

There is a growing critique amongst Black people as to why White people are so interested in the oppression of Black people, and many groups consisting of Black people are suspicious of the motives of the White person who tries to gain access to their group. Who can blame them, when much of the access has resulted in the infiltration of such groups, with the White person surreptitiously gaining knowledge and awareness that has been used to merely tick the box of tokenistic political correctness, thus meeting their target whilst maintaining the status quo in terms of the power of White superiority.

In my profession I have been invited to work with Black groups on several occasions, yet when I requested to come in and discuss race with one of these groups my request was ignored. My e-mails were not answered and my phone calls were not returned. I believe I experienced a form of social closure due to the subject I wanted to discuss, since closure gives one group power to deny access to another and this group was exercising that power. They wanted to maintain the power balance within their own group and they did not need a White woman from the dominant culture using them to meet her own needs, nor did they need her to tell them what they wanted, needed or was best for them. This had been their experience of previous work with White people and therefore their reality. They were protective of their group seeing themselves as gatekeepers of their community and the perceived power, influence and status that came with it.

I discussed this form of social closure with a Black friend who said that she understood it; she said that even though she respected my views and knowledge of the Black perspective, I needed to remember I would only ever have an awareness because as a White person I could never truly understand. She said that even as a 36-year-old woman she was still uncomfortable when a White person used the term Black, because no matter how much they thought they knew about race issues or the Black perspective, it was still said with all the negative connotations instilled in them by White society. She said that she was sick and tired of the race debate because the more we talked about it the more she believed we could never understand.

This led me to question if understanding and awareness were the same thing. We can increase our level of awareness to give us a perceived understanding of the miasma of racism in our society today, but how can we as White people comprehend the real life tangible feelings experienced by Black young people as they encounter inequality and discrimination based simply on the colour of their skin?

My experience of youth work to date has been that the majority of work with Black young people is targeted work that may serve to further marginalise Black young people by tending to emphasise the difference between Black young people and White young people. Difference in this context is not difference in the sense of celebrating the distinctness and uniqueness of Black young people. It is more likely to suggest that this difference is linked to inferiority. We may seek to challenge the stereotypes, but in doing so we continue to highlight the differences that have been exposed for generations and paradoxically perpetuate the negative connotations linked to young Black people.

Much of the work targeted at Black young people compartmentalises them into categories related to their problematic behaviour, such as the Black young offender, the Black under-achiever and the Black drug user. This objectification of Black young people further reinforces the difference between young Black people and young White people. White youth workers do not, for example, identify drugs work with young White people as working with White drug users; therefore by defining drugs work with young Black people as working with young Black drug users, they are implying that race is somehow linked to the problem. This insensitive use of language in youth work today further reinforces the stereotype of problematic young Black people in Britain today. This in turn results in the externalisation of the Black young person by emphasising difference in a negative manner that classifies and imprisons them within their race. This conceptual connection between the problem and the race of the young person results in young Black people internalising the notion that they are somehow inferior to the young White person.

Is it then any wonder that many Black young people prefer to work with Black youth workers? If they see White youth workers as associating their problems with their colour they would be right in thinking that these workers are part of the dominant culture of White ideology that has excluded them from British society and resulted in the pathologisation of Black young people in Britain today. How can these young Black people build a relationship based on trust when they believe their problem has been inadvertently linked to their race before they have even met their worker?

I spoke to one young Black male who said: 'It didn't surprise me that they thought my drug use was so bad because I was Black, after all I am used to being treated like a criminal because I'm Black. I get stopped by the police regularly although I haven't done anything and I get followed round shops by security guards who are convinced the only thing Black people go into shops for is to shoplift, and I see women holding onto their handbags so tightly they nearly cut the circulation to their fingers off!' I asked him if he had considered that these situations may occur simply because he is a 17-year-old male and society perceives young people to be deviants. His reply was powerful and impressive, saying: 'With all due respect there you go, another White person trivialising my truth . . . the situations occurred because I am Black in the same way as you are here to speak to me today because I am Black, that is the first thing all White people see in me, my Blackness.' I felt humbled as I began to understand that he was indeed right. His Blackness is salient to him because his experiences have taught him that it is his most prominent feature in the eyes of the people he has already met, and will no doubt continue to be in the eyes of the people he has yet to meet in a White ideological society.

I continued to speak to young Black people in my quest to discover whether or not they thought that White youth workers could effectively meet the needs of Black young people. It was during these meetings that I began to fundamentally believe that, as a White person, I could have my awareness of race and racism raised, but I would never fully understand the impact of race and racism on Black people. I began to understand their suspicions as to my motives for wanting to speak to them. One group I had managed to meet with after some initial resistance were open and candid in their dialogue with me. In fact, there were times when I felt almost attacked as they tried to make sense of my interest in their views and feelings. One young woman asked my views on the oppression of Black people in British society, and as I shared my views she became quite confrontational and asked if I felt sorry for them. I said that I sympathised with their struggle and supported Black people in their fight against racism; I said that I believed that as a society we all had a part to play in challenging racism. As our conversation deepened she became warmer towards me and said that she believed I would be a person who would stand side by side with Black people in their fight for equality and not the type of person who would hold the reins to make me feel better about myself. She said her experience of working with White people was that by believing they could help you they were insinuating that they knew they had the power to do so and this, simply, for her, reinforced their superiority. I discussed with this young woman my experience of accessing the aforementioned Black youth group and asked whether or not she thought I had experienced a form of social closure. She said that I should concentrate more on how I felt when I managed to access the group to allow me to understand the reason for the probable social closure. Her explanation humbled and enlightened me with a new-found consciousness of how young Black people may feel about White people accessing their groups. She said, when you come through this door, you lose your power for a couple of hours. When we go out of this door, we lose our power for a week. She did, however, go on to say that she thought a token White person was 'handy' for advocacy as she felt that she was still taken more seriously by people in authority when accompanied by a White worker. She said she was happy to use a White worker in these instances because after all 'White people have used Black people for centuries'. I found it sad that in 2006 young Black people still experience a level of discrimination from agencies that forces them to turn to a White person in order to be treated fairly and equally in our imagined multi-cultural society that is no more a reality than Brigadoon or Utopia. I did not think it was a case of the oppressed becoming the oppressors, more an example of surviving to the best of our ability using the resources we have.

Multiculturalism – panacea or obstacle

It was during a discussion with this group that I began to question whether or not multiculturalism and assimilation were a panacea or an obstacle in the struggle for equality that young Black people face. One young Black African Caribbean male said that he believed himself to be British and as such had assimilated to the British way of life. He said that he was proud to be thought of as British and felt that this did not mean that he was not proud of his cultural heritage, just that he thought his cultural heritage was a more private 'thing' and that by bringing it in to the public arena it just accentuated the difference and made him feel like a victim when he wasn't. This young male was a high achiever who was heading for university and had no doubt he would succeed in life in Britain. He then posed a question directed at myself. 'If you are fully diverse and I am fully assimilated, why don't we get each other'? He had no intention of explaining himself so I was left to reflect on the question and analyse any meaning or connotation implied.

I related his question to the debate around multiculturalism. The assumption that pluralism and the multicultural society are the only means to ensure tolerance between the diversity of cultures within Britain today serves to intensify the notion that the government aim to find a solution to the problems of race in contemporary British society. One of the flaws with multiculturalism is that it has no universal meaning; therefore in order to understand it we must appreciate that it means many different things. It is the level at which multiculturalism operates that determines whether it is a panacea or an obstacle in the struggle for equality that young Black people face. At one end of the scale multiculturalism is merely a tokenistic attempt at tolerating the diversity within our society such as the sampling of different cultures, for example the festival of light or displaying the poster saying welcome in 20 different languages and the cultural calendar in our community centres and youth clubs. At the other end of the scale the increased awareness of other cultures encourages people to challenge structural inequalities. If we do not challenge structural inequalities we will never have cultural diversity.

Many multiculturalists believe that human beings have a fundamental, almost biological need, for cultural attachments and that in order to meet that need we must create a society that sanctions and protects different cultures. We should be seeking to treat all cultures with equal and mutual respect, but in order to do this we must be able to compare different cultures to each other. What kind of message does this give to our young people? Who are we to judge and compare others' values, ethics and beliefs? In endorsing this practice we encourage young people to compare the differences in cultures with their own beliefs and values and yet multiculturalists believe such cultural values are incommensurate. It is this dichotomous confusion that leaves many young people unsure of the principles of difference and how they should apply them to their everyday lives. It is naïve to believe that by highlighting or showcasing the difference between cultures we can demand respect for them without appealing to the universal principles of equality and justice, which can never be agreed in a multicultural society. Without having this common sense of equality and justice young people feel no affinity towards other cultures or any obligation to have a tangible respect for them. They either veer towards indifference to other cultures or believe that this difference has given them the green light to hate, abuse or openly discriminate against them.

In order to treat different cultures with equal respect we need to have an agreed measure or judgement. However, the establishment of such a measure would be impossible in a multicultural society where difference is embraced and celebrated as the answer to racism. If we as a society accept this diversity in favour of the pursuit for equality we are simply maintaining the status quo by saying its good to be different even if this means the power balance is left unchallenged.

The young male who made the earlier comment about assimilation and diversity had considered the impact of making our cultural beliefs part of the public domain. He knew that in order to be treated equally we could not afford to allow multiculturalism to subvert the value of cultural diversity. He believed that culture, faith, ethics, morals and beliefs should be an aspect of our private lives and not something to be scrutinised by authorities of the state. Diversity should allow us to compare and contrast different values and beliefs without the fear of being attacked for not being politically correct, it should encourage us to critically debate in order to create more universal language of citizenship. This would allow citizens the freedom to embrace their culture privately whilst allowing them to be treated as political equals in contemporary British society.

If we as youth workers take this diversity into account in our practice we can begin to inspire young people to expand their horizons by gaining an awareness of different cultures and religions and making informed judgements on them that fosters respect and tolerance in a way that multiculturalism fails to do. If we instil in young people an appreciation for their own culture and a vision for diversity we negate the need for them to nurture hatred for other cultures who are privately celebrating their own culture whilst collectively joining the struggle for a more equal democracy.

Another of the negative consequences of multiculturalism is the sagacious politicisation of identity in ethnic terms. In the past immigrant minorities in Britain worshipped or celebrated their racial traditions in private, or collectively with other members of their ethnic group, their ethnicity rarely entered the public arena. This newfound politicisation of ethnic identity has placed a great responsibility on many young people in Britain today. The identity of being a young Muslim, for instance, has come to define such young people to the exclusion of all other aspects of their identity. It forces young Muslim people to adopt a label placed on them by British society in a way that their parents did not need to. It encourages communities of resistance to form, as much of the resources available to ethnic minority groups are aimed at the victim as promoted by the multiculturalist. This may be the stimulus for groups to adopt the role of victim, exaggerating any signs of victimhood in order to provide them with the status and recognition that will allow them to access funding. The problem with this highlighting of victimisation is that it may be catastrophic in the long term as communities of resistance form proving that no meagre allocation of resources will ever be enough to prevent some people from seeking retribution against their oppressors, real or imagined.

Conclusion

As I come to the end of this chapter, I ask myself the same question again. 'Can White youth workers effectively meet the needs of Black young people?' I am compelled to say that I have seen nothing that will convince me that they can. When discussing the question with colleagues after my research was completed I was told on more than one occasion 'Of course you are going to say that we can,' with no valid rationale as to why they thought this should be so. This only served to convince me more that there is an arrogance that accompanies membership of the dominant culture that fails to recognise the reality of living as a Black young person in Britain today. Speaking to young Black people provided me with enough reason to believe that as they reach adolescence their awareness and experiences of living in a racist society increases to such an extent that it is extremely useful for them to share these experiences with other Black people who have a living understanding of the challenges they encounter on a daily basis. Young Black people who do not have access to the support of other Black people outside of their family circle often experience social isolation as even though White friends, youth workers, teachers etc. may be willing to listen to their issues and concerns with regard to growing up in a White ideological society they can never really share the experience. I believe, therefore, that it is important that young Black people have access to support from workers who share the same ethnic background as only they can truly understand. One young Black person I spoke to told me that White teachers or youth workers think that by telling you the story of Rosa Parks they show you that they understand. He said that whilst Rosa Parks did not give up her seat on the bus, Stephen Lawrence was killed before he could even get on the bus, but they never speak to you about that because 'it is too close to home'.

I do not propose that White youth workers do not work with Black young people. More that they work alongside Black youth workers to join in the struggle for equality that Black young people face. This allows Black youth groups to maintain their power whilst still providing opportunity for cross-racial dialogue. The problem would then be, how many youth workers would choose to work in Black youth groups? I would suggest that we would then come back to the question of positive White identity whereby a person who had gained the autonomy that racial self-actualisation provides would be comfortable to develop their skills in this area and others who were not so far along in their White identity development may not accept the challenge. This issue raises concern as I believe that it is a training issue that is often overlooked in youth work today. The young people I spoke to did not believe that our educational establishments acknowledged appropriately the reality of racism in Britain today. This is a gap that the informal education provided by Black youth groups can fill, by encouraging racial identity development which empowers these young people by allowing them to achieve an internalised sense of personal security by providing them with strategies to cope with miasma of racism in our society today.

Reference

Helms, J.E. (1990) (Ed.) *Black and White Racial Identity: Theory, Research and Practice.* Westport, CT: Greenwood.

CHAPTER 11

Forced Marriages: Is Britain Doing Enough to Protect Asian Young People?

Harjeet Chakira

Case study

Sameena was 17 years old when she was forced into a marriage against her will. She left school after the compulsory school age of 16 and was sent to work by her parents. Her father would escort her to and from work and she was not allowed out unless she was with another member of her family. Sameena's parents controlled practically every aspect of her life, including opening her mail and checking her bank statements. Despite this Sameena met somebody through work and decided to tell her parents she would like to marry him. Their initial reaction was one of outrage; they accused her of bringing shame on the family by engaging in pre-marital relations. They told her she had been influenced by the evils of the western world. They said her only salvation was to go back home to Pakistan so she could learn the true values of being an Asian woman. Sameena refused; this is when the physical abuse began. She was confined to the house and not allowed to return to work.

Within two weeks Sameena's parents had booked flights to Pakistan and made arrangements for her to marry her first cousin who she had never met. Sameena was unaware her parents had arranged her wedding and thought she would be returning home after a few weeks.

Once in Pakistan her parents took her passport away from her and after the wedding returned to the UK without her. Sameena was left completely alone, she knew nothing of the country and of where she could get help. Sameena was effectively trapped by members of her own family. She told her husband she did not want to consummate the marriage because she hardly knew him and was not ready. However, one night soon after the wedding, he came into her room and raped her. Sameena told her mother and sister in law hoping they would help her, but they told her this was ok and a good wife would never have denied her husband this right in the first place, thus excusing the violation.

Things got particularly bad for Sameena over the next few months. She was treated like a domestic slave, she was not allowed out and she had no friends. Sameena knew that her parents were eager for her husband to gain entry into the UK and so decided she would go along with their suggestion of her sponsoring him. Sameena had no intention of staying with her husband if she returned to the UK, but kept this to herself. Once back in the UK, Sameena waited for an opportunity to escape and with the assistance of the police she managed to go into hiding.

This scenario is a good example of what happens to many Asian young people living in Britain. It describes the types of issues young people face when it comes to marriage and relationships and describes how many young people feel caught between two very different cultures and lifestyles. They find it challenging to adapt to the 'western' way of life when their families have certain expectations of them, which are in line with traditional values and customs. This chapter aims to highlight the repercussions experienced by many Asian young people when they choose to challenge these expectations. The focus of this chapter is forced marriage because this particular practice is very relevant to young people and has recently received high media coverage and political discussion.

According to the Government Paper *Working Together to Safeguard Children* (2006) many children suffer from both direct and indirect forms of domestic violence. It suggests that where there is a risk of domestic violence between the parents or guardians of children often the children will also be at risk of neglect or abuse. The Domestic Violence, Crime and Victims Act 2004 define domestic violence as:

> . . . *any incident of threatening behaviour, violence or abuse (psychological, physical, sexual, financial, or emotional) between adults who are or have been intimate partners or family members, regardless of gender or sexuality.*

> (Home Office, 2006)

This recent definition has allowed for the recognition of forced marriages as a form of domestic violence by including acts perpetrated by extended family members as well as intimate partners. Forced marriages are now seen for what they really are – an abuse of human rights and a form of child abuse rather than cultural practices, which should not be interfered with. A distinction will be made later on in the chapter between forced marriages and arranged marriages. In my opinion arranged marriages are a widely accepted cultural practice and forced marriages are a distortion of that practice, which breaches a number of national and international human rights standards.

During the passing of the Domestic Violence, Crime and Victims Act 2004 it was first suggested by Labour MP for Keighley Ann Cryer, that forced marriage be criminalised and a specific offence of 'forcing someone to marry' be created. Currently there is no specific offence of this nature and forced marriage is regulated under offences such as kidnap, abduction, threats or physical assault. The impact of criminalisation will be considered in more detail during the course of this chapter. Forced marriage affects a significant number of children and young people – that is to say persons under the age of 18 years. Although they can be seen as both a form of domestic violence and child abuse, detailed knowledge of the dynamics of forced marriage cases are essential over and above the normal childcare or care proceedings criteria.

In my experience some practitioners working with young people in the statutory and voluntary sector still feel less inclined to involve themselves in cases of forced marriages. The justification for this has centred on forced marriages being 'private' or 'cultural' affairs as they predominantly take place within the family environment. This approach has been taken due to concerns of potential accusations of racism, lack of understanding and empathy and interfering with the norms and values of particular cultures. There is, however, a fundamental differentiation which needs to be highlighted, between forced marriages and the widely accepted cultural practice of arranged marriages. It is the aim of this chapter to highlight this difference and clear up some misconceptions held by practitioners working with young people who may be at risk.

Forced marriage is a marriage conducted without the valid consent of one or both parties, where duress is a factor (Eekelaar et al., 2004). Duress can include emotional pressure as well as criminal actions such as assault and abduction. It can take place both in the United Kingdom and abroad. Forced marriages breach section 12c of the Matrimonial Causes Act 1973, which states that a marriage shall be voidable if 'either party to the marriage did not validly consent to it, whether in consequence of duress, mistake, unsoundness of mind or otherwise'. Forced marriages can involve a host of associated harms, crimes and abuses. These include interruption or termination of education, damage to career opportunities potentially leading to economic dependence, emotional and physical abuse, theft (typically of passport, money or belongings) unlawful imprisonment and restrictions on freedom of movement, abduction and kidnap, rape, enforced pregnancy, childbirth and abortion and murder (*Forced Marriage: Guidance from the Law Society*, 2004).

Forced marriage can affect both men and women but it seems to affect more women in general (Home Office and Foreign Commonwealth Office, 2006). Estimates from the Forced Marriages Unit at the Foreign Commonwealth Office and other organisations that come across cases of forced marriage, suggest that every year at least 1000 women and young girls are being affected. They are abducted from the UK by their families, taken to a foreign country and forced into marriage or they are forced to marry other UK nationals. According to the Forced Marriage Unit, up to 15 per cent of cases might involve men being forced to marry against their will. These figures reflect only those cases coming to the attention of statutory and voluntary organisations and are at best conservative estimates. The sensitive nature of forced marriages means that many cases each year are going unrecognised.

The majority of cases that do surface appear to be from the Pakistani, Indian and Bangladeshi communities. For the purpose of this chapter forced marriage will be discussed in relation to women and young girls originating from these communities. This is not to say that forced marriage is a problem specific only to these communities. The Forced Marriages Unit deals with cases from all races and religions including Christians and Jews and with cases from the Middle East, Western Balkans and Africa (Home Office Minister, Rt. Hon Baroness Scotland QC in *You Have a Right to Choose* Forced Marriage Information Campaign, 2006). However, my specialism and expertise focuses on domestic violence within the Asian community. My work with young Asian women who are subject to domestic violence will provide the reader with a detailed insight into the dynamics and power relations, which are present within the culture, not only between the two sexes but also between first, second and third generation Asians.

The importance of marriage within the Asian culture

Women and young girls have been forced into marriage for many years. Having worked in the domestic violence sector myself I have seen children as young as 10 being forced into marriage. Perpetrators are usually family members often including parents. Many parents do not view their actions as being wrong and in many cases genuinely believe they are doing the best for their children. In order to understand the existence of forced marriages it is important to understand how the Asian culture views marriage as an institution and the importance it plays on family honour.

According to Warrier it is important to give some consideration to what is meant by the term culture, particularly what it means to certain members of the Asian community. Warrier's analysis of culture argues that '. . . we have come to understand cultures to be very stable patterns of beliefs, thoughts, traditions, values and the things that are handed down from one generation to the next to ensure the continuity of these systems' (Warrier, 2005). In relation to the Asian culture there is a visible difference in how families interpret these beliefs and values, which explains why some families hold onto traditions and practices of the past while others do not. When discussing family violence it would be inappropriate to assume the Asian culture per se perpetuates domestic violence, however it can be argued that there are certain traditions of the culture which do condone patriarchy (Apidv Institute, 2002).

Marriage is one such practice and ironically one of the most important institutions within the Asian culture. Especially for Asian women, traditionally they are taught from a very young age that eventually they will be marrying a man of their parent's choice and this is their sole purpose in life. They are made to believe that divorce or separation is not an acceptable option within their communities. Family members usually arrange marriages with the bride and groom getting little or no say in the process. It is therefore a contract between the two families rather than the two people. In most cases women are held back from ending a marriage unless they have 'permission' from their families (Southall Black Sisters, 1992).

The value attached to marriage and the notion that women are the upholders of the family's honour means that it is only in extreme and compelling circumstances that an Asian wife will consider leaving her husband. This usually only happens as a result of physical abuse or sexual assault. Although, in most cases, Asian women will endure extreme durations of violence in order to please the community and protect the family's reputation. The social and cultural milieu in which many Asian women in this country and abroad live, demands their total obedience and loyalty to the institution of marriage. Most women therefore marry for life (Mirza, 1997: 261). The view is that women belong to their husbands and once they are married they are no longer their father's responsibility. Pre-marital relationships are inhibited as this could reduce the chances of being accepted into a respectable household. Some parents exercise increased levels of control over their daughters to ensure they do not bring shame onto the family.

Honour based violence

Honour based violence tends to occur when customs and beliefs of the family or community are challenged (Gill, 2006). This can lead to exaggerated forms of control when young Asian women or young girls challenge the pressure to engage in arranged marriages. Exaggerated forms of control can include either physical or emotional abuse or violence and in some cases murder. Forced marriage can be used as a means to punish wrongdoing or pre-marital relations. If a young woman is found to have a boyfriend or is seen to have 'gone off the rails' parents will often feel that getting her married will act as redemption for the 'unacceptable' behaviour and in turn remove the burden of shame she has caused upon the family. The highly publicised case (*Guardian*, 1999) of Rukshana Naz, a 19-year-old Asian woman from Derby who was killed by her family for refusing to stay in a forced marriage, demonstrates the extremes to which some families are willing to go to in order to preserve their honour within their families and communities. Rukshana was strangled by her brother while her mother held her down by her feet. The family stated the reason for the killing of their daughter was because she had shamed the family by refusing to stay in a forced marriage. In such cases the families believe they have done the right thing and are not afraid at the prospect of going to prison for their actions.

BBC News Online recently documented the case of two brothers from Southall jailed for life for murdering their sister after she fell in love with an asylum seeker. Azhar Nazir 30, and his cousin Imran Mohammed just 17 years old stabbed Samaira Nazir (*Guardian*, 2006) 18 times at their family house in April 2005. This worrying example shows the importance of honour to many Asians living in this country. More worrying is the fact that second and third generation Asians as well as first generation Asians are upholding this honour. The need to educate these young people is paramount if we are to avoid these types of atrocities from continuing.

Arranged marriages and forced marriages

An arranged marriage is one where parents or other family members introduce young people to potential marriage partners and allow them the opportunity to say no if they do not wish to accept the offer. Arranged marriages have been practiced for centuries, a lot of young people accept them as an important and in some cases useful way of finding a marriage partner. If conducted without duress arranged marriages can be compared with commercialised dating agencies.

It is when the free will of one or both parties has been suppressed that an arranged marriage turns into a forced marriage. Determining consent can sometimes be problematic and there is often a fine line between an arranged marriage and a forced marriage. Many young people become forced into marriage through deception, abduction or coercion. They can often be taken abroad under the pretence that they are going on holiday or to visit a dying relative. Blackmail is often another mechanism used by some families to convince young people. For example, parents will often say that they will kill themselves if their son/daughter will not consent to an arranged marriage.

Marriage and the sense of obligation

Many young people are often caught between the values their parents have brought them up with and the influences of the western world. They may not agree with the concept of arranged marriages and want to exercise their own free will in choosing a marriage partner but feel duty bound not to let their parents down. In some cases many young people may well agree to arranged marriages out of a sense of obligation and the feeling that they owe something to their parents. Are these marriages arranged or forced?

It becomes increasingly difficult to answer this question particularly where there is no evidence of physical or emotional abuse. Young people have often said that they love their parents and do not want to lose them. Likewise many parents have said they love their children and by choosing their partners they are trying to ensure a loving and respectable family will look after them. In many cases young women give up their partners or boy friends in order to have an arranged marriage. It is very difficult to penalise parents or family members in this type of scenario. I would argue that no law could be passed which will change these beliefs and customs which have been practiced for years and which make up the very essence of the Asian community. Effort should be aimed at educating people and raising awareness through the media, which Asian communities tune into such as Zee TV, Sony TV, and BBC Asian Network. These can all be utilised to document the negative impact of forced marriage, which in turn can attempt to shape the Asian community's perspective of marriage.

Recent efforts have been made by the Forced Marriage Unit to publicise forced marriages in this way. In March 2006 a National Public Information Campaign was launched supported by famous Asian actors Meera Syal and Ameet Chana. The campaign involved a series of radio and press adverts, TV fillers and poster campaigns. It aimed to increase awareness of the issues involved for young people. It highlighted the differences between arranged marriages and forced marriages and made it clear that forced marriage is a form of domestic violence. The campaign publicised the support available to young people and encouraged them to seek help. It highlighted the damaging emotional consequences to families and the crimes involved in forcing someone into marriage. This campaign not only advocated the support networks in place for victims of forced marriages but also sent a distinct message to the older generation of Asians. The message was that although their culture and traditions are respected and arranged marriages do have a place within society, forced marriages are fundamentally wrong and the difference is the lack of freely given consent.

Another such initiative was the production of the documentary 'Loved Snatched: Forced Marriage and Multiculturallism' directed by Gita Sahgal, a respected film maker and author (to obtain a copy of this video contact: Faction Film, 26 Shacklewell Lane, London E8 2E). The documentary addressed the practice of removal and abduction of women and girls from the UK to various countries in South Asia. It set out examples of good practice by lawyers, non-governmental organisations and law enforcement agencies. The documentary is recommended to any practitioner who comes into contact with young people at risk of forced marriage (Hutchinson, 2002).

The responsibility of the state

By assuming that it would be inappropriate to intervene in cultural practices, significant harm to young people can be and has been ignored for years. What if the dominant culture defines harm in a different way from that of the child's culture? The report into the death of Victoria Climbié, a young girl from the Ivory Coast brought to the UK by relatives, observed that:

> *Cultural heritage is important to many people, but it cannot take precedence over standards of child care embodied in the law . . . A child is a child regardless of his/her colour and he or she must be kept safe. Cultural issues must be considered, but the objective is the safety of the child.*

(Eekelaar, 2004: 9)

The government has noted that the failure to tackle cases of forced marriage and the abuses involved is in turn a failure to protect and endorse the rights of all UK residents to be treated equally before the law, regardless of race, culture or religious affiliation. Viewed in this light the fear that tackling forced marriage is somehow racist or culturally insensitive is out of place. Speaking at the time, the then Home Office Minister said 'Multicultural sensitivity is no excuse for moral blindness' (O'Brien, 1999).

According to Rights of Women[1] (2005) sensational media portrayals of forced marriages and crimes of honour can succeed in alarming and outraging the British public and contribute to the feeling of attack that these communities are already under. This can in turn lead to these communities holding onto the traditionalistic elements, which perpetuate abuses against women such as forced marriage and honour crimes. Intervention by the state must seek to protect women and young girls at risk of being forced into marriage but must also have an understanding of the cultural context in which forced marriages occur. If ignored there is a real danger of Asian communities becoming stereotyped and labelled as 'traditionalistic', 'authoritarian' and 'uncivilised'.

What has the government done so far?

In 2001 the Home Office Working Group on Forced Marriage published an official report *A Choice by Rights* highlighting forced marriages as a problem affecting many young people living in the UK. Since then the government has been working on measures to protect young people here and overseas. In January 2005 The Forced Marriage Unit was launched, this was a joint venture by the Home Office and the Foreign Commonwealth Office and they are now said to deal with approximately 300 cases of forced marriage a year. The Forced Marriage Unit is the government's central unit dealing with forced marriage casework, policies and projects. It provides information and assistance to potential victims and to concerned professionals on how to tackle the problem. The official report also saw the development and implementation of guidelines to the police, social services and educational practitioners.

In 2005 a nationwide consultation was also launched called *Forced marriage: A Wrong not a Right* in order to consider the possible implications of creating a specific offence of forcing someone to marry. The proposal was made during the passing of the Domestic Violence Crime and Victims Act 2004, which was the largest overhaul of domestic violence legislation in the last 30 years. Government accepted the majority opinion that criminalisation was a bad idea as it could potentially have an adverse effect on young people. The view of various women's organisations was that it would disproportionately impact the black and minority ethnic communities and might be misinterpreted as an attack on them and could send forced marriages underground. The proposal was made on the notion that by having primary legislation to govern forced marriages a strong deterrent message will be sent out to communities who practice it and that in the long run it would change public opinion.

However, as mentioned previously, many families who force their children into marriage do not believe they are doing anything wrong. They therefore might not feel implicated by such an offence especially if they think their children willingly consented, not realising the consent was obtained under duress.

---

[1] Rights of Women – is a women's voluntary organisation committed to informing, educating and empowering women concerning their legal rights. Founded in 1975, they offer free confidential legal advice to women through their advice line. They offer specialist advice in family law, divorce and relationship breakdown, children and contact issues, domestic violence, sexual violence, discrimination and lesbian parenting.

Civil law as opposed to criminal law

Employing the use of civil law as opposed to criminal law in cases of forced marriages has proven to be more effective. Family Law solicitors across the country have often commented that young women might be reluctant to seek help if they think their parents could get punished through the Criminal Law System that could at worst send them to prison. Victims are to some extent in control of civil proceedings under Divorce and Family Law but this control would get lost in criminal proceedings. There is also an element of further risk in criminal cases where the whole community will become aware and other family members or siblings could turn on the victims for getting the parents into trouble. It could effectively 'turn family members against family members'. Ann Marie Hutchinson is a leading family lawyer in London who specialises in matters relating to children, in particular international custody disputes and child abduction. She has also represented many victims of forced marriage and in her experience nine out of ten women that she sees want the reassurance that their parents will not get into trouble and only then decide to proceed with criminal cases. Civil procedures allow for the women and young girls to be protected and move on with their lives usually away from their families in hiding, instead of the possibility that they may have to turn up again to give evidence in court (Hutchinson, 2006).

Another civil option available under the Matrimonial Causes Act 1973 is that a marriage which has been entered into under duress can be annulled (Hutchinson, 2006). Solicitors have employed the use of nullity procedures over that of divorce, which is the preferred option, as some women believe divorce will bring shame on them as well as their families. However a petition for nullity must be sought within three years of the marriage, often meaning women and young girls are unable to rely on these provisions, especially if they are unaware that this provision is available. Women and young girls who are taken abroad and left there will also lose out on this option if they return after the three-year period.

There have been several cuts in access to legal aid in the past few years particularly in the areas of Family and Immigration Law – the two areas that affect Asian women and young girls experiencing domestic violence and forced marriage issues. The official report *A Choice by Right* (2001) identified access to legal services as a problem for women and young girls experiencing forced marriage particularly in cases where victims are being held against their will. The problems highlighted were securing legal aid, giving instructions and providing evidence in courts. In cases where young women are being held against their will little can be done to protect them. It has been noted that The Legal Services Commission has pledged to fast track the application procedure for such cases. However, in my experience it has taken up to two months for some young women to be awarded legal aid. If civil proceedings are the preferred choice for young women they need to be made more accessible, and solicitors and other criminal justice agencies must be mindful that instructions are taken directly from the applicant without the presence of other family members wherever possible.

Non-legislative measures

The government has provided guidance to the police, social services and educational practitioners on how to deal with forced marriages. They are currently working on guidance for health professionals. The guidance details best practice on how to recognise and deal with cases of forced marriages to ensure a unified approach is adopted across the country. However, in a recent consultation carried out by the Newham Asian Women's Project and Roehampton University – *Joint Response to Consultation Paper on Forced Marriage in the UK*, it was found that few professionals used the guidance issued on how to deal with forced marriage. This paper consulted about 100 different representatives of various organisations as well as survivors of forced marriage. The consultation was funded by the Joint Home Office and the Foreign Commonwealth Office. Some were unaware of the existence of these guidelines and in cases where professionals were aware they may not have received the training on how to implement them.

Despite the guidance for social services on how to identify and deal with forced marriage cases social workers have been known to reunite young women, who have run away from home, back with their families through mediation and reconciliation. This action is in direct contradiction to the guidelines stated on page 10 of the Home Office issued *Practice Guidance for Social Workers*, which clearly indicates mediation, reconciliation or family counselling as a response to forced marriage can be extremely dangerous. Social workers undertaking these activities may unwittingly increase the young person's vulnerability. It is extremely worrying if social workers are encouraging mediation despite the fact the guidance states otherwise.

In my own experience of working with young women who have fled from forced marriages I have observed further difficulties particularly in accessing local authority housing. Many housing departments fail to acknowledge forced marriage as a form of domestic violence. I advocated for a client recently in this situation where the local housing department was totally unaware about the issues involved with forced marriages; they came across as unsympathetic and even patronising at times. They thought because there was no evidence of physical abuse in this case, it did not amount to domestic violence and the usual domestic violence concessions should not apply. The client was advised she could submit an application but because she was deemed as being 'adequately housed' her application could take anything up to two years.

The same is true for young women trying to access welfare benefits. Often they are faced with judgmental practitioners who lack the understanding needed to work with women subjected to forced marriage. Guidance in these areas therefore would be of benefit. It was noted that this inconsistency in the way practitioners deal with forced marriage may be due to the uncertainty of its definition. Introducing a specific offence could alleviate some of this ambiguity and people would be aware that it is illegal and so have a duty to protect potential victims.

Other refuge or specialist services can help in cases of forced marriage and provide non-legislative methods of intervention. They have proven to be useful sources of information to organisations that are unsure or unfamiliar with cases of forced marriage. Most refuges for young women, including the one I work with, sees many cases of young girls fleeing from the parental home as an attempt to escape forced marriage. Young people tend to seek assistance through the educational services including their schools or colleges first and later get referred to specialist services. Moving away from their families into safe and secure accommodation is often the preferred choice. They then build new lives away from their families with assistance from refuge support workers.

Children and the law

The courts have a range of common law and statutory civil powers that can be used to protect children at risk of being forced into marriage. The 1989 Children's Act section 31 provides for care and protection orders to be made by courts on application by a local authority. While such an order is in place, no person may remove the child from the UK without the consent of every person with parental responsibility, including the local authority. Section 44 of the act allows for the provision of Emergency Protection Orders to prevent children being removed from the UK. Likewise section 46 provides the police with powers to remove a child to suitable accommodation where there is reasonable cause to believe that the child would be likely to suffer significant harm. This existing legal framework affords children a great deal of protection above and beyond the civil and criminal measures available to protect adults from a forced marriage.

Conclusion

National and international law instruments consider marriage to be a consensual and egalitarian relationship between adults. They uphold the right to marry including the requirement of free and full consent from both parties. However, we have seen a systematic failure by law enforcement officials as well as inappropriate policies and procedures to uphold the human rights of many Asian young people.

We understand arranged marriages are an integral part of the Asian culture and it can be argued that families who fail to understand the transgression from arranged marriages to forced marriage would continue to believe they are justified in their actions. Particularly if families genuinely believe what they are doing is acceptable and justifiable. In my opinion education and preventative measures aimed at second and third generation Asians would have a more positive and effective impact. Educating second and third generation Asian young people and providing them with the knowledge that being made to marry someone under duress is unacceptable and there is protection for them will be emancipating for many.

Any organisation coming into contact with children and young people currently undergoes child protection training; forced marriage should become an integral and compulsory feature of such training so that there is no confusion about what forced marriage is and how the state can intervene to protect young people who are at risk. Awareness about voluntary organisations and culturally specific projects is essential, as is access to safe and secure alternative accommodation.

All young people in the UK attend compulsory education until the age of 16. Efforts to educate young people in schools and colleges that forced marriage is wrong and against the law should be made mandatory. As has already been suggested by other women's organisations, including Refuge (a national charity for women and children experiencing domestic violence) all forms of violence against women must become a core part of the education curriculum so that young women and young girls are made aware from a young age about abuses of this nature. Alongside this they should be educated about freedom of speech and freedom of expression and educated to challenge the different forms of control and abuse they may or may not be experiencing within the family environment.

Government has come a long way since the early Working Group in 2001 and introduced a number of key initiatives which have brought forced marriage onto the political agenda. However, without a fully funded forced marriage prevention and education campaign little can be achieved in the way of eradicating it completely in the long term and sending out the message that forced marriage is against the law and socially unacceptable.

References

Apidv Institute (2002) *Gender Violence and Cultures of Patriarchy.* Proceedings from the National Summit on Domestic Violence in Asian and Pacific Islander Communities, [cited]July 2006]. http://www.apiahf.org/apidvinstitute/CriticalIssues/culture.htm

Asian and Pacific Islander Institute on Domestic Violence (no date) California [cited 2nd August. 2006] http://www.apiahf.org/apidvinstitute/CriticalIssues/culture.htm

Asian Women's Resource Centre (2005) *Forced Marriage: Practice Development Seminar Report.* Asian Women's Resource Centre.

Eekelaar, J. (2004) Children Between Cultures. *International Journal of Law Policy and the Family.*

European Case Digest (2004) Forced Marriage: Guidance from the Law Society. *International Family Law Journal.*

Gill, A. (2006) Patriarchal Violence in the Name of Honour. *International Journal of Criminal Justice Sciences,* 1: 1.

Gill, A., (2004) Voicing the Silent Fear: South Asian Women's Experiences of Domestic Violence. *The Howard Journal.* 43: 5, 465–83.

Guardian Unlimited (1999) *A Question of Honour* [cited 11th July. 2006]. http://www.guardian.co.uk/women/story/0,3604,296033,00.html

Guardian Unlimited (2006) *'You're Not My Mother Anymore,' Shouted Samaira. Then Her Family Killed Her.* [Cited 17th August 2006.]. http://www.guardian.co.uk/crime/article/0,1821073,00.html

Home Office (2005) *Domestic Violence: A National Report.* Home Office Website [cited]June 2006]. www.homeoffice.gov.uk

Home Office (2006) *Forced Marriage: A Wrong Not a Right, Summary of Responses to The Consultation on The Criminalisation of Forced Marriage.* Foreign Commonwealth Office, Scottish Executive.

Home Office, Foreign Commonwealth Office (2005) *Dealing with Cases of Forced Marriage: Guidance for Police Officers.* 2nd edn. Home Office, Foreign Commonwealth Office.

Home Office, Foreign Commonwealth Office *Young People and Vulnerable Adults Facing Forced Marriage: Practice Guidance for Social Workers.*

Hutchinson, A.M. (2002) Forced Marriage and Multiculturalism: Recent Developments. *International Family Law Journal.*

Hutchinson, A.M., Hayward, H. and Gupta, T. (2006) *Forced Marriage Nullity Procedure in England and Wales.* Jordon Publishing.

Newham Asian Women's Project and Roehampton University (2005) *Joint Response to Consultation Paper on Forced Marriage in the UK.*

Newsline (2000) *Forced Marriage Initiatives.* Jordan Publishing.

Newsline Extra (2005) *Forced Marriage Consultation.* Jordan Publishing.

Refuge (2006) *Refuge Response to the Forced Marriage Consultation: A Wrong Not a Right.*

Rehman, Y. (2001) *Metropolitan Police Service: Forced Marriage Seminar.*

Singer, S.P. (2001) *When is an Arranged Marriage a Forced Marriage?* Jordon Publishing.

Southall Black Sisters (2004) *Old Stories New Lives: Raising Standards to Tackle Violence Against Black and Minority Women.* A National Conference QE II Conference Centre, London.

Southall Black Sisters (2006) *Domestic Violence and No Recourse to Public Funds.*

Warrier, S. (2005) Culture: What it is, Who owns it, Claims it, Changes it. [cited August 2006] http://www.apiahf.org/apidvinstitute/CriticalIssues/culture.htm

Do Black Young People Matter? Universal Differentiated Services for Black Young People

Tony Graham

Introduction

The deaths of Stephen Lawrence and Victoria Climbié have proved critical not just in terms of race relations but also the very foundation by which services to all young people irrespective of their ethnicity have been built. Nonetheless, within all those changes the question remains: do Black young people matter?

Consequently, what this chapter will offer is a critical reflection of national, regional and local strategies and policies. In doing so, it will analyse their effectiveness in terms of their impact on service delivery to Black young people.

There will also be an examination of past strategies, policies and initiatives such as the Connexions Service; the Youth Service – 'the Transforming Youth Work agenda'; Youth Offending Service; the Every Child Matters and Youth Matters agendas and regeneration initiatives e.g. Single Regeneration Budget (SRB) and Local Strategic Partnerships (LSPs) and ask what lessons, if any, have been learnt.

There will be an attempt to predict what impact the new and emerging initiatives (or religions, as I call them) such as Local Area Agreements and Children's Trusts will have on the lives of Black young people. Further, it will explore the possible reasons why these new 'religions' are being foisted upon us – 'are these new 'religions' a covert way of directing energies away from improving service delivery?'

In addition, it will seek to explore the possible reasons why schools are arguably being given more and more autonomy (a view generally held by Black parents and Black community activists) particularly in an environment where schools continue to fail Black young people, whether that be in terms of academic achievement and attainment or exclusions.

Furthermore, it will examine why OfSTED chooses not to fail schools that do not provide parity of services for Black young people, which in turn puts into question the effectiveness of Race Equality Schemes (RES).

But not least, the chapter will demonstrate that despite the invariable difficulties that practitioners from the public, voluntary and community face, both in terms of human and financial resources, there are still some exemplary pieces of work being undertaken.

NB: Most of the work that I have done as a youth work practitioner has been with African Caribbean Black young people. Consequently, the examples that I cite to illustrate my points are from those experiences.

The current position

In the Stephen Lawrence Inquiry Macpherson (1999) defined institutional racism as:

> *The collective failure of an organisation to provide an appropriate service to people because of their colour, culture or ethnic origin. It can be seen or detected in processes, attitudes and behaviour which amount to discrimination through unwitting prejudice, ignorance and racist stereotyping which disadvantage minority ethnic people.*
>
> (Section 6.34)

That 'disadvantage' was no more evident than in the death of Victoria Climbié, the young girl who was horrifically abused and tortured, and eventually killed by her great aunt and the man with whom she lived, which evoked an unmatched furore amongst the general public.

Victoria Climbié's murder provoked the government into producing a formal response to her death and a green paper, which prompted an unprecedented debate about services for children, young people and families (DfES, 2006a). As it was recognised that despite a number of previous failures to adequately safeguard young people (The Victoria Climbié Inquiry, 2003), it took the murder of Victoria Climbié to fully accept that there had been a breakdown of communication between and within the very agencies that have statutory duties to safeguard the well-being of children and young people.

Having written the green paper, there was widespread consultation with professionals working in children's services, and with parents, children and young people. The outcome was *Every Child Matters (ECM): the Next Steps*, and the Children Act 2004, providing the legislative spine for developing more effective and accessible services focused around the needs of children, young people and families (DfES, 2006a).

In July 2005, the Department for Education and Skills (DfES) produced another consultation paper – *Youth Matters*: Green Paper (2005) which focused on 'Young People and Services Today'. In this paper the DfES argued that by 'improving outcomes[1] for all young people, while narrowing the gap between those who do well and those who do not' it will meet every young person's needs. In other words, provide universal but differentiated services. The paper goes on to say:

> *That there is much that is good about services for teenagers, but there is a lot that could be better. In particular:*
> * *Services do not always meet the needs of individual young people.*
>
> (DfES, 2005)

The impact of 'services not always able to meet the individual needs' has over the years, disproportionately affected particularly groups of Black[2] young people, which is recognised in the ECM consultation paper, as it asserts: '. . . teenagers from some black and minority groups face greater challenges than others in growing up' (*Youth Matters*: Green Paper. 2005: 13).

The impact of poor service delivery to some Black young people is compounded by the fact the minority ethnic population is over represented in almost all measures of social

---

[1] The five outcomes from the *Every Child Matters* consultation are: Be Healthy; Stay Safe; Enjoy and Achieve; Make a Positive Contribution; and Achieve Economic Well-being (DfES, 2006a).

[2] Black includes young people of African, Caribbean, South Asian and South East Asian origin.

exclusion (ODPM, 2003), and their poor socio-economic position is closely associated with low educational attainment, which in turn impacts on their prospects to gain employment which in turn often times results in being drawn into a life of crime.

A canter through some of the socio-economic issues facing Black young people paints a fairly bleak picture:

- More than half of people from African Caribbean and African backgrounds and over a third of people from South Asian backgrounds live in districts with the highest rates of unemployment.
- People from African, Pakistani and Bangladeshi ethnic groups are two and a half times more likely than White people to have no earner in the family.
- The Pakistani population is twice as likely to be on housing benefit as the White population.
- Pakistani, Bangladeshi and African Caribbean people are more likely to report suffering ill health than White people.
- Minority ethnic young people are more likely to be at risk of experiencing most of the problems of deprivation and social exclusion.
- School exclusion rates for African and African Caribbean pupils are significantly higher than for others.

Furthermore, evidence suggests that Black young people with multiple barriers fare worse than White young people, as Black young people are:

- More likely to be in care. The two groups most highly represented in the public care system include, Caribbean and those of mixed Caribbean/white parentage (Barn, 2001).
- Disproportionately represented amongst the homeless. A national survey of the homeless in urban areas found that almost 20 per cent were minority ethnic (Smith, 1999).
- Less likely to turn to statutory and voluntary agencies for support.
- African Caribbean young men in particular are over represented at every stage of the criminal justice process.

With all of the above, the challenge that *ECM*, *Youth Matters* and the Children Act 2004 face is whether they will be able to dismantle, as stated at the beginning:

The collective failure to provide an appropriate service to people because of their colour, culture or ethnic origin.

(Macpherson, 1999 Section 6.34)

The providers of services to young people

The situation that preceded *Every Child Matters* was and to some greater or lesser degree still is, a variety of youth services, which come in the guise of youth services; Connexions services; youth offending teams; learning and skills councils; local authority education departments; child and adult mental health services, etc. All of these services are accountable to different government departments or sections within departments, and as a consequence have to produce business plans that adhere to their individual business planning guidelines.

Each service has different business planning criteria and targets, but have a number of common areas which they must address, which includes:

- Ensuring the young people's physical and mental well-being is improved and maintained.
- Encouraging, preparing and supporting young people, for and into employment, education and training.
- Ensuring that those young people who are deemed as being 'vulnerable' are given support appropriate to their needs.

As alluded to, there are some Black young people who suffer disproportionately in terms of the service areas outlined above and as such are deemed as being vulnerable, as the inappropriate service which they receive reduces the possibility of them fulfilling their potential and narrowing the gap between them and the rest of society.

Of the service areas outlined above, it is argued that educational attainment is the single most important factor/determinate to judge how a young person will fare, particularly economically, in adult life. However, it must be noted that educational attainment on its own is not always sufficient to predict a young person's life chances, as there are other contributing factors. I will discuss this topic in more detail later in the chapter.

David Blunkett, the former Secretary of State and indeed the ex-Prime Minister, Tony Blair have both proclaimed that New Labour's main concern was 'Education, Education, Education' (New Labour's Manifesto, 1997). Therefore it would be reasonable to assume that the then Department for Education and Employment (currently the Department for Education and Skills) is an essential ingredient in making Britain a more inclusive society. As it is legally duty bound, by the Race Relations (Amendment) Act 2000, to ensure that everyone who receives a school education is in receipt of an education that will positively promote their ethnic background, culture, spiritual belief system and belief in self. Furthermore, DfEE (1999) claimed that it aimed:

> *To give everyone the chance, through education, training and work, to realise their full potential and build an inclusive and fair society and a competitive economy.*

> (DfEE, 1999)

To examine the relationship between Black young people and educational attainment, below is a review that was undertaken on behalf of Nottingham's Local Strategic Partnership, now known as One Nottingham, which highlights how Black young people's academic school achievements are affected (Grant, 2006).

Case Study Educational Attainment – Focus On Black Boys

How are Black Boys Performing?

Nottingham reflects the national picture of negative outcomes for Black boy pupils by the time they reach Key Stage 4 (GCSEs). The most recent national GCSE figures confirm this fact, with 37.5 per cent of Black Caribbean pupils and 43.3 per cent of Black African pupils achieving 5 or more GCSEs with C grades or better, compared to the national average of 52.3 per cent. In Nottingham the figures for the most recent year, 2004, are as follows:

The table below shows that only one group of black boys, (those of African background) achieved a score higher than the city average and none of the groups achieved a score

Table 3.1　Educational attainment

Ethnic description	Number of Pupils	% Achieving 5+ A*–C
Caribbean	61	23.0
White and Black Caribbean	39	12.8
Other Black background	39	15.4
African	11	45.5
White and Black African	10	20.0
City total – all ethnic backgrounds male pupils	1,368	35.2

comparable to the national average. This low level of achievement was not reflected in the scores of boys from other ethnic minority backgrounds. For example, boys from Indian backgrounds scored 70 per cent, those from Bangladeshi backgrounds 66.7 per cent and those from Pakistani Backgrounds 53.9 per cent (Grant, 2006).

Performance Across the Range of Key Stages

Of importance to note is that the performance of Black Caribbean and Black other pupils at the first monitored key stage is higher than for all other ethnic groups. However, when monitored at the last key stage (Key Stage 4) Black Caribbean and Black other pupils are the poorest performing groups. Consequently, the decline in performance over the school career of these pupils is therefore more severe than for any other group of pupils.

The review goes on to say that both locally and nationally it would appear that Black children and some groups in particular, gain less from their schooling than white children (Gilborn, 2004).

The review concludes by suggesting ways in which Black young people's achievements might be improved, which were in four key principles of good practice:

- A culture of high expectation.
- Respect, recognition and an understanding of the multiple needs and identities of Black boys.
- Support and access to a broad, balanced and inclusive pre and post 16 curriculum.
- Partnership working with parents.

Whilst the suggestions in the case study review of how to address the 'epidemic' nature of Black young people's educational underachievement and under-attainment, are ones that have been shared with schools and Local Education Authorities, we are still faced with a situation where significant numbers of Black young people are being systematically failed by the British education system, as successive governments have continued with the rhetoric of 'equality', whilst pushing a one size fits all agenda.

With the above in mind, there is another pertinent question to be asked – is education in isolation sufficient? An observation made by a former Director of an SRB funded Partnership concluded that:

> In areas of high deprivation, it is vital that we tackle the problems of educational low attainment and under-achievement in the round. It would be facile to pretend that

poor social conditions, lack of jobs, difficult family circumstances and lack of money and therefore opportunity, do not affect a child's education. To deal in the three R's without looking behind the child to see what the major factors causing under-attainment are, is to waste money and resources.

(Learning Elements Report of the SRB 1998: 1)

However, despite the fact there is a recognition that young people must be looked at in the 'round' generally, and that particular groups of Black young people are disproportionately affected, the providers of services to young people, particularly schools, have not been held to account, for their continual failure to provide an adequate service to Black young people. In other words the government departments and the sections within departments, that are responsible for ensuring that the providers of services to young people adhere to their business planning guidance (which is oftentimes bound by legislation), will not impose sanctions, withhold funding or cancel a contract, if it is found through an inspection that there has been systematic failure to adequately address the needs of Black young people.

Inspection Regimes

It has been established that as well as having to comply with dictates of various government departments, youth service providers are also subjected to external scrutinies, which are conducted by auditors or inspectors, such as the Audit Commission, OfSTED and the Youth Justice Board etc. But, how effective are these inspections? For whilst the inspectors are duty bound by law to carry out their inspections in line with the Race Relations (Amendment) Act 2000 (Home Office, 2006), which in so doing, should ensure that the organisations have a Race Equality Scheme in place to keep up standards, the situation for Black young people remains the same.

The inadequate service provision for Black young people is probably most evident in schools. Schools are youth service providers and are listed as public bodies in the statutory Code of Practice produced by the Commission for Racial Equality (DfES, 2006b), and as such are required to meet the general duty to promote race equality by eliminating unlawful discrimination; promoting equality of opportunity and promoting good relations between people of different races. Furthermore the Race Relations (Amendment) Act 2000 states that the governing body of a school must have a race equality policy. All of which sound admirable.

However, when subjected to greater scrutiny, we discover that in 2005 OfSTED announced that it was going to change the way in which it inspected schools. They would no longer carry out-in depth inspections, which in the past happened, on average, every five years. Instead they would carry out 'lighter touch' inspections, every three years, which will be informed by the school's own self-evaluation process (DfES, 2005).

The self-evaluation provides details about the school's statutory requirements, which include issues of equality and how they must comply. The guidelines on the surface are sound and appear to leave very little room for a school that is performing poorly, in any area of equality, to slip through the 'inspection net'. However, on inspection, the essence of the guidance here is no different to what was in place before, and as alluded to, with schools being public sector bodies since May 2002, they have had to adhere to the Race Relations Act 1976 as amended by Race Relations (Amendment) Act 2000, which:

. . . gives public authorities a statutory general duty to promote race equality. The aim of the general duty is to make promoting race equality central to the way public authorities work; and this includes schools. The general duty says that the body must have 'due regard' to the need to:

- *Eliminate unlawful racial discrimination; and*
- *Promote equality of opportunity and good relations between people of different racial groups.*

HLSRef

In addition, the Act places specific duties on schools to help them meet their general duty. They are a means to an end; that is, they should result in an improved educational experience for all children, in particular those belonging to minority ethnic groups. It should not become a bureaucratic exercise. These specific duties are:

- *To prepare a written statement of the school's policy for promoting race equality, and to act upon it;*
- *To assess the impact of school policies on pupils, staff and parents of different racial groups, including, in particular, the impact of attainment levels of these pupils;*
- *To monitor the operation of all the school's policies, including, in particular their impact on the attainment levels of pupils from different racial groups; and*
- *To take reasonable steps to make available the results of its monitoring.*

(DfES, 2006b)

Furthermore, schools also have a duty to adhere to the objectives set out in the National Curriculum, namely: 'The school curriculum should contribute to the development of pupils' sense of identity through knowledge and understanding of the spiritual, moral, social and cultural heritages of Britain's diverse society' (The National Curriculum, 2006). However, despite the fact that schools have a legal and (I would argue) a moral[3] duty to provide a service that fulfils the objectives set out in their RES and in the National Curriculum, I am not aware of any school that has been put into 'Special Measures' or a similar hard-hitting sanction, where a school has failed to comply with the RRAA. In fact, I am not aware of a case where sanctions have been imposed; funding withheld or a contract cancelled and awarded to another provider, because a provider has systematically failed to adequately address the needs of Black young people. But who knows, through the new inspection regime we may be entering a new era – I think not!

Race equality Legislation

In an attempt to address race inequality the Supporting Children and Young People Group (SCYPG), which is the section within the DfES that is responsible for the 47 Connexions Partnership, sent out a Bulletin in 2003, that asked the Partnerships to establish methods of 'Securing and Improving Better Outcomes for Young People from Black and Minority Ethnic backgrounds'. SCYPG did not make this a requirement for

---

[3] The notion of a school having a moral duty to provide the best service for all of its pupils, is born out of the fact that teachers as human beings are obliged to treat other human beings (pupils) with respect. Consequently, teachers should have high expectations of all of their pupils, and in so doing enable them to realise and fulfil their potential. This is a view shared by Paul Grant, author and founder of Nottingham Black Parents in Education, who expresses his views in a case study later on in the chapter.

partnerships, they only gave examples of what was considered to be good practice, and left it up to individual partnerships to develop mechanisms of how best to turn their (SCYPG's) mission into a reality.

When challenged as to why they had not made the task of Securing and Improving Better Outcomes for Young People from Black and Minority Ethnic backgrounds mandatory, SCYPG's retort was that Connexions Partnerships are not public sector organisations and as such are not bound by law (the RRAA 2000) to produce a RES and adhere to it.

From the above it would be reasonable to conclude that the tenets necessary to deliver Race Equality are not in place, and when they are in place it requires more than good leadership to ensure that they are adhered to. The requirements include the whole gambit of policy/objectives, action/delivery, training, performance indicators, monitoring, milestones, reviews, and evaluation/reflection on the investment of human and financial resources. However, it would appear that where a government department or section within that department can avoid putting these requirements in place, they do.

What is even more worrying is the fact that race inequality is not a new phenomenon in Britain. Over the last 50 years Briton's have heard educationalists and sociologists argue and substantiate their claims of what can only be described as institutional racism (Fryer, 1984). Chauhan (1989) in his publication *Beyond Steel Bands 'n' Samosas: Black Young People in the Youth Service* lists nearly 30 years of reports which outline access or the lack of it, for groups of Black young people. From The Albemarle Report in 1960 through to the 1987 Commission for Racial Equality report: *Working with Black Youth* and concludes:

> *Amongst the various strands which surface the debate and separate versus integrated provision seems to be one which can be buried once and for all. If the Youth Service can recognise that racism exists and has to be tackled, and if it recognises that Black young people have special needs, then it has an obligation to meet them through whatever form of provision is appropriate, including separate provision. Otherwise, the needs of Black young people will continue to be undermined and their access to youth service provision will continue to be restricted.*

(Chauhan, 1989: 22)

Since Chauhan's observations 17 years ago, what has changed? I would argue very little. In fact I would argue that the situation has become worse, because, as alluded to, throughout this chapter, the social and economic position of Black young people and their families, has largely remained in a state of 'survival' (Grant, 2003, p. 34). Wright et al. (2005) quotes Osler (2006) who explains this situation in terms of the underachievement, attainment and exclusions of Black young people as follows:

> *... there is general agreement when examining those groups considered to be vulnerable to exclusion, particularly permanent exclusions, that there is a disproportionately high rate of exclusions among people from African Caribbean background (Ofsted, 2001). This is particularly true for boys with African Caribbean heritage who are 4 and 15 times more likely to be excluded than white boys, depending on locality Sewell, 1997; DfEE, 2000a). African Caribbean girls are four times more likely to be permanently excluded than white girls (Osler et al., 2002).*

(Wright et al., 2005: 3)

To compound the issue of 'race' is the one of class. The Neighbourhood Renewal Unit asserts that 70 per cent of England's Black and Minority Ethnic communities live in the 88 most deprived local authority areas. Furthermore, only 3 per cent of the pupils receiving free school meals go to the top 200 schools compared to 17 per cent nationally (Chouhan et al., 2005). Alcock (1996) argues that the attempts by the state to eradicate or minimise the disparity between the classes have failed. He informs us that some studies and research conducted by Le Grand and others supports this view:

> . . . *study of health and education reveal that these services were frequently of greater benefit to middle class users, and were not effective in promoting greater equality within British society.*

(Alcock, 1996: 224)

Consequently, it can be argued that the Race Relations Act 1976 was never fully utilised or implemented and that the Race Relations (Amendment) Act 2000, which holds so much promise is in danger of becoming a white elephant (Chouhan et al., 2005).

Chouhan et al. (2005) argue that if the above Acts are going to achieve their goals the government must implement the recommendations they set out. Here are just a few:

- Ensure that the general duty of public authorities to promote good relations, ensure equality of opportunity and elimination of unlawful discrimination is also extended to the private sector.
- Make a declaration under Article 14 of the International Convention for the Elimination of All Forms of Racial Discrimination (ICERD) to allow individuals the right to petition the Committee. This is already the case for women.
- Sign, ratify and incorporate within the Human Rights Act 1998 Protocol 12 to the European Convention on Human Rights, which provides for freestanding protection from discrimination by public authorities.
- Ensure there is no dilution of the focus on race equality via the proposals for the Commission for Equalities and Human Rights. The preferred position of Black communities is for a federated model of six equality commissions, (which ensures the retention of the CRE and an overarching Human Rights Commission (a 6 + 1 model).

Until these radical, just and moral proposals are put in place Black young people will remain socially, economically, educational and politically disproportionately disadvantaged in the UK.

But will any government, Labour or Conservative; have the foresight and courage to put these measures in place. I would argue that putting such measures in place will increase the numbers of young people who are better educated. Therefore one would anticipate that 'better educated' ought to mean more employable and greater 'demand' on employment. Will the UK be able to respond to the raised expectations in this respect? With this being the case, I argue that there is a need for significant numbers of young people to fall though the education 'net'. In other words it's important to produce young people who have been excluded from school; are uneducated; have no worldview or concept of the impact that external influences have on their lives; suffer from depression and other forms of mental health problems, which in turn ensures that they are criminalised and unemployable.

It would therefore be reasonable to assume that the adage 'idle hands make mischief' plays a role in the ongoing refusal by the government, its departments and their inspectors not to hold failing providers of services to account. Particularly, as Wright et al. (2005) demonstrate, when there is an inextricable link between school exclusions and criminal behaviour:

> *The recent Youth Survey conducted by the Youth Justice Board (2003) indicates that the attachment to school protects young people from involvement in criminal activity. This is especially the case for boys from 12 to 16 years old. Success in school is an even stronger protective aspect. Some young people in the study reported their involvement in offending activities coincided with being excluded from school. However, these young people also reported that they stopped offending when they became engaged in education or employment.*

(Wright et al., 2005: 64)

That said, the imposition of sanctions and other radical measures is only one facet of what is required to ensure that Black young people receive adequate and appropriate services.

The changing policy environment (the new religions)

Wright, Robinson and Devanney (2005) in their report *Securing and Improving Better Outcomes for Young People from Black and Minority Ethnic Backgrounds*, contend that the main barriers to accessing services are: Geographical location and proximity to services; service responsiveness to group differences; professional engagement and representation; and cultural issues. Further they argue that the parity of service to and for Black young people can only be achieved through a multi-agency approach and recommends the following to Connexions, Schools, LEAs, Youth Services, Learning Skills Councils and the voluntary sector:

- Improved development and strengthening of strategic planning and decision making.
- Improved strategic coherence to reduce service fragmentation.
- Improved collaboration between agencies.
- Improved communication with young people.
- Enhanced training and assessment of Personal Advisers.
- Improved support from schools.
- Increased involvement of Black and minority families and community groups.
- Tackling deprivation and poverty amongst Black and minority ethnic young people.

If we were to analyse the first three recommendations of Wright et al., 2005 (see above), the parallels between them and the structures which the DfES (through *Every Child Matters*) propose as being the ideal structure for achieving integrated children services would soon become apparent, namely:

- integrated governance
- integrated strategy
- integrated process
- integrated frontline staff
- clear objectives

Consequently, I could argue, that if the objectives set out in ECM are met, the needs of Black young people will also be met. In other words, through the development of a strategy, where priorities are agreed and communicated, targets set, monitoring arrangements put in place, staff trained and the most effective governance structure put in place, those young people who are in most need will have their needs addressed, in a culturally sensitive manner.

However, will this be the case in an industry where in terms of improved outcomes for Black young people little has changed over the last 20 years? I would argue it is unlikely, because the examination of recent policy documents such as ECM and the *Youth Matters* green paper, in the context of cultural sensitivity, do not inspire hope. Consequently, the terms government policies and cultural sensitivity, oftentimes do not sit well together. For whilst the authors of the policies attempt to demonstrate that they are aware of the issues that affect particular groups of Black young people, and bring these issues to the fore, the manner in which these issues are brought to the fore, raises concerns for a number of Black professionals, as they argue that negative stereotypes are over used. For example in the Green Paper: *Youth Matters* only three references were made about Black young people, all of which were negative:

> . . . *teenagers from some black and minority groups face greater challenges than others in growing up.*
>
> (*Youth Matters*: Green Paper. 2005: 13)
>
> . . . *the under performance of Black African, Black Caribbean, Pakistani, Bangladeshi.*
>
> (*Youth Matters*: Green Paper. 2005: 49)
>
> . . . *quarter of teenagers who are not participating in activities are from black or ethnic minority communities.*
>
> (*Youth Matters*: Green Paper. 2005: 98)

It is important to note that the arguments are not about having to refrain from highlighting the negatives, but that there should be a balance, with perhaps Black young people being used to cite examples of good practice, as other communities are cited on 'both sides of the coin', as illustrated in ECM.

Children's Trusts

The 2004 Children Act places a duty on local authorites to bring together (through a Children's Trust) all providers of services to children and young people (0–19) in their area, and in so doing encourage their cooperation to focus on improving outcomes for all children and young people. Children's Trusts will also support those who work every day with children, young people and their families to deliver better outcomes (DfES, 2006a).

Youth Matters: Next Steps (2006) states, amongst other things, that Children's Trusts must:

> . . . *find out what young people want and need, and arrange services that fits this. The voluntary and community sectors have good experience of working with young people living in especially difficult circumstances.*

The report goes on to say:

> *Children's Trusts have four main challenges: ensure that young people have things to do and places to go and that these facilities meet the national standards; encourage and support voluntary action by young people in their local communities; ensure that*

young people can access high quality information, advice and guidance; and ensure young people living in especially difficult circumstances get the support they are entitled to.

And that:

Children's Trusts must keep records of young people's progress, and do all they can to ensure improvements are made.

The duties placed on the Trusts are welcomed; however it will require the 'radical reshaping of provision' (*Youth Matters: Next Steps*, 2006) if the above is going to be achieved. In this context, what will be the impact for voluntary and community sector organisations that deliver services to Black young people.

The Black voluntary sector was born out of 'mainstream' schools not providing Black young people with an adequate education, and came in the shape of supplementary schools. Supplementary schools have been here in the UK for more than 40 years, and its needs are epitomised by Bernard Coard in his book *How the West Indian Child is made Educationally Sub-Normal in the British School System*. Mike Phillips and Trevor Phillips in their book *Windrush*, express the need for supplementary schools during the 1970s as being as a result of the following:

The school experience began as a trauma for the majority of black parents and went on to be a rallying point and a radicalising issue for their parents. Throughout the seventies the anxiety of Black parents expressed itself in the organisation of such bodies as the Black Parents' Movement and the 'supplementary schools', which operated at weekends and in the evenings.

(Phillips and Phillips, 1998: 257)

As alluded to throughout this chapter – 'Institutional Racism' and its impact has not waned over the last 50 years. Consequently, neither has the need for a strong, independent and responsive Black voluntary and community sector. However, whilst the Black voluntary and community sector possess the required passion, it is argued that currently, it lacks the capacity to respond to the ever changing environment (the new religions); it does not have the resources required to adequately fill the void left by schools and therefore cannot 'respond to the unmet need in the Black community' (Wright et al., 2005). This position is compounded, I argue, by the Black voluntary and community sector's dependence on 'grant aid' for its existence.

Therefore if Children's Trusts are going to 'use the experience' of the voluntary sector, it has to resolve an ongoing culture of short term funding and pilot projects for Black young people, which it could achieve through commissioning processes that are driven by need and quality assurance.

Another area where Children's Trusts have to make huge strides is: 'keeping records of young people's progress, and do all they can to ensure improvements are made'. Again, we have had decades of legislation where similar guarantees and promises have been made, and as I have contended throughout this chapter, the legislation has not produced the required and/or desired impact.

In order to 'do all they can to ensure improvements are made' Children's Trusts must, as suggested earlier, be prepared to impose sanctions; withhold funding or cancel contracts. If sanctions, etc. are not imposed, we would have gone through the restructuring of children services only to maintain the status quo. Lets hope that this is not going to be the case.

However, if the Children's Trusts do not fulfil their duties, a new arrangement that was introduced by the government department formerly known as the Office of the Deputy Prime Minster, now the Department for Communities and Local Government, which came into effect on 1 April 2006, might assist. The new arrangements give existing Local Strategic Partnerships the additional responsibility of producing and delivering Local Area Agreements, which are made of four Blocks, one of the Blocks being the Children and Young People's Block – the Children's Trust.

Local Area Agreements

Local Strategic Partnerships (LSPs) were introduced as a result of the Local Government Act 2000 and on the 1st April 2002 the government introduced what they considered would make radical changes to the way in which funds would be administered from Whitehall to local communities. The aim of the changes were to improve the devolution of power and give greater autonomy at all levels, and in so doing accelerate the government's vision of narrowing the gap between deprived neighbourhoods and the rest of the country, so that within 10 to 20 years, no one should be seriously disadvantaged by their geography.

It was envisaged that 'narrowing the gap between deprived neighbourhoods and the rest of the country', would be achieved through the development of the Neighbourhood Renewal Units (NRU) and their Local Strategic Partnerships (LSP).

The guidance for the development of LSPs, from the NRU, clearly states that they should target the 'hardest to reach' groups, of which as stated earlier the African, Caribbean and Asian Communities are disproportionately represented, as 70 per cent of all BME communities live in the 88 most deprived local authority areas in England.

More recently, the Office of the Deputy Prime Minster's consultation paper *Local Strategic Partnerships: Shaping their future* (2005) explains that a lot is expected of LSPs, in particular, the development and implementation of Local Area Agreements (LAA), which is a new responsibility that was given to LSPs in April 2004. It goes on to say that:

> This enhanced role provides new challenges to many LSPs. They need to be able to attract senior membership, taking difficult decisions and challenging members where necessary, in order to drive forward local public service improvements and manage the performance of the elements of the partnership.

(ODPM, 2005: 9)

The LAA has four themed Blocks, which are Children and Young People (the Children Trust), Health and Elderly People, Safer Stronger Communities and Economic Development and Enterprise. Through these, there is an expectation that priorities and plans are agreed, sums of monies allocated and services delivered.

Therefore, whilst the LSP does not have statutory powers over any of the Blocks, it does have a statutory responsibility (with the local authority) to 'drive forward local public service improvements'. Therefore, I would argue that it would be reasonable to conclude that the LSP must be able to 'influence' and where necessary veto the decisions of its partners, and in so doing ensure that services to Black young people are improved.

The review carried out on behalf of Nottingham's LSP (see above), did result in a citywide target being set to increase the 'achievement and attainment of Black boys', and insists that all providers of youth support services have to demonstrate how they are contributing to this target. But, we will have to wait and see if the LSP manages to ensure that this target is met.

The impact of the changing environment: the new religions

Before looking at the chosen case studies set out below, I want to consider what impact the changing policy environment (the new religions) is having on service delivery and in particular, how it affects Black young people.

Children and Young Peoples' Services are being reorganised, as are the Police, Crime and Drug Partnerships, Primary Care Trusts, and Learning and Skills Councils, to name but a few. There is a view that 'this is necessary' as improvements are required. However, whilst it is accepted that improvements are necessary, the question must be asked – why are so many services and partnerships being asked to reorganise at the same time?

It is argued that the reorganisation of services reduces frontline service delivery for about two years. So what will the cumulative affect be on the end user, whilst these simultaneous reorganisations are taking place? In the online magazine *John Kay*, the author of an article entitled 'A New Public sector' states:

> . . . *hardly a day passes without some new targets, new objectives, or new control mechanism being rolled out. These mechanisms will not work. They will not work because public services have complex and multiple objectives, because both the balance among these objectives and the best means of achieving them change constantly, and because the centre has no means of knowing what local targets are realistically achievable.*

(Kay, 2004)

The other possible sufferers of these 'simultaneous changes' are the voluntary and community sector organisations, who as stated above, 'have good experience of working with young people living in especially difficult circumstances' (DfES, 2006a), but have limited financial and human resources. Therefore, it would be reasonable to assume, that without support, the voluntary and community sector will find it difficult to keep abreast of these policy changes, which will invariably result in poorer service delivery. I say this because even when the policy environment is relatively stable, the voluntary and community sector find it difficult to keep up with the policy requirements. A position that has been evident for the last 20 years, as the voluntary and community sector has struggled to grapple with the plethora of past 'religions' which have included the following initiatives and programmes: the Task Force; Manpower Service Commission; City Challenge; Health Action Zone (HAZ); Primary Care Group (PCG); Sure Start; SRB4, 5 and 6; New Deal for Communities (ND4C); Education Action Zone (EAZ); Employment Zone (EZ); Capital Modernisation Fund (CMF); URBAN; European Social Fund (ESF); European Regional Development Fund (ERDF), the list goes on.

So why are we in the midst of continual upheaval, the likes of which, I would argue, have not been witnessed before? It is argued, by some, that the restructuring of services is the government's ploy to maintain 'central control' (Kay, 2004). Whilst others (members of the Black voluntary and community sector, which include the interviewees of the three case studies below), hold the view that this upheaval is merely a continuation of being 'force fed' new programmes and initiatives, which are designed to maintain the 'status quo'. In other words, the impact that might have been achieved through one programme is dissipated, as the sector has to become familiar with the new one.

Irrespective of the rationale, I would argue that the government and its various departments have to recognise that the current level of change has invariably resulted in those who are deemed as being most vulnerable fairing the worst.

However, despite the fact of funding difficulties, challenging school environments, poor inspection regimes, lack of sanctions and an ever changing policy environment, there are a number of Black voluntary and community sector organisations that have proved their resilience, and are providing extremely valuable, high quality services to Black young people. The section below looks at three such organisations.

Case studies

The following is an analysis of three case studies that were carried out with Take One Recording Studio, Sheifton Supplementary School and Nottingham Black Families in Education.

Take One Recording Studio has been running since 1998, and was born out of the founder member's own experiences of having difficulties in pursuing his chosen career path, due to the lack of available Studio Engineering courses, which was further compounded by the entry level qualification requirements for those courses that did exist. Sheifton Supplementary School was born out of the demands that were made by a significant number of Black young people, who regularly attended a youth club in the late 1970s and early 1980s, but felt that their cultural needs were not being met. Nottingham Black Families in Education (NBFE) was established in 1998, and came out of the need that was recognised by the then Co-ordinator of Nottingham's Divert Trust. The Co-ordinator realised that despite the fact that there was another organisation that had been funded to advocate on behalf of Black young people excluded from school, they were not providing a satisfactory service, which resulted in a growing need to advocate on behalf of those young people and support their parents during the exclusion period.

What each of the organisations had in common was the fact that they came out of the unmet needs of Black young people – 'mainstream'/public sector service providers not providing adequate services. In their endeavours to improve the service provision for Black young people, they engaged in lengthy discussions with the public sector but were each met with inflexible attitudes, and consequently, felt they had no choice but to set up their own provision.

Passion and tenacity were common traits of each of the interviewees and it would appear that these are essential ingredients for success, as their fervour regarding fairness (Black young people are entitled to the same level of provision as any other group) and their refusal to give up, in the face of unfavourably odds, has led to longstanding, well respected and effective organisations.

Each organisation expressed their frustration with past and present funding regimes and felt that successive governments knew exactly what they were doing. In other words the government is aware of the damage that a constantly changing funding environment has on the Black voluntary and community sector organisations. However, for NBFE, limited funding has had a positive and empowering effect, as they have learnt to become more self-reliant and not to be solely dependant on external funding for their survival. Consequently, they have recruited new volunteers who work as advocates for the young and their parents. This is an area of work where the founder member felt that NBFE had had most impact, as both the young people and their parents were aware that the support they receive is, by and large, provided by volunteers who are advocates from the Black community:

> *Them being volunteers has a strong psychological impact on the parents, as the parents (even the white parents) know they (the volunteers) care and trust them. They will visit parents in the evenings etc . . . for the volunteers it's not a 9–5 job.*
>
> (Founder and Former Divert Trust Coordinator, 2006)

When asked what was good about the voluntary and community sector, volunteers expressed very similar views, which were in essence that they felt a real sense of achievement as they witnessed the personal growth and development of both the young people and their parents.

Take One's Project Manager said that he enjoys working in the sector and cherishes being able to see young people who have been 'written off' by others make something of themselves.

For Sheifton the strength of the sector is found in its ability to understand and respond to the needs of its client group – Black young people. To exemplify the point the Leader in Charge (LIC) and founder member, gave the following example:

> *Sheifton's reputation of their students doing well in State schools had become well known and we began to receive referrals from schools. However, our success was questioned and a lecturer from Nottingham University was commissioned to ascertain, "what was the 'secret' behind our success?"*
>
> *The lecturer attended a class where a young boy aged 10 was being taught. The boy who had recently arrived from Jamaica was having real problems with the teachers at his State school, as the teachers could not understand what he was saying and did not invest any time to try to understand him or his needs.*
>
> *As a result the teachers at the state school could not engage the boy. But here he was at the supplementary school engrossed in work and interacting with his peers and the volunteer teachers. The lecturer from Nottingham University, asked me, 'what is your secret to success?' I replied, look around! He asked again and again I replied, look around, the answer is in front of you. But he just couldn't see it. I had to explain to him that the class was made up of Black young people and Black adults (the volunteers). The teachers understand patois and the young people's wider cultural needs. That's the secret to our success.*

Lastly, in terms of what they felt was required for the future success of the sector, there was much emphasis placed on self-reliance. Take One's Project Manager felt that although he was relatively new to the sector, the sector could overcome many of its difficulties if it overcame 'personality politics' and developed joint projects under themes e.g. health, education or crime etc. The benefits of this way of working, he claims, would be that young people would have more opportunities to work with a wider range of people, which would assist in them developing a wider view of the world.

Sheifton's LIC felt that the sector's cycle of dependence has to be broken:

We need to buy our own building, a 'Centre of Excellence' that can be used as a social enterprise, provide a sense of pride and assist with providing role models for the young people.

NBFE's founder member felt that there was a chronic need for members of the Black community to have their own schools, which included home schooling, and eloquently expressed his view as follows:

We know that we NBFE are a sticking plaster on a cut jugular vein. We need our own schools (including home schooling), which are African owned, ran and led, and then have an African centred curriculum.

From the analysis of case studies it can be concluded that if the Black voluntary and community sector is well resourced, whether through grant aid or self generated finances, it will be able to provide good quality services to Black young people. Consequently, they could provide these services on behalf of the public sector, as the organisations and their staff better understand Black young people and have the necessary passion, tenacity, flexibility and a sense of wanting to 'give something back to the community' – a sense of moral duty. All of which will go a long way to ensuring that the needs of Black young people are met.

Conclusion

This chapter has demonstrated that over the past five decades successive governments have introduced a plethora of interventions designed to address the imbalance of the quality and effectiveness of service provision between Black young people and their white counterparts. However, despite these numerous interventions, which have been reinforced by legislation (RRAA, etc.) coupled with the fact that services are held to account through inspection regimes, it is evident that the gap between Black young people and their white counterparts remains.

Therefore it would be reasonable to conclude, that the various youth support service providers, who are accountable to different government departments or sections within departments, do not take the issue of race inequality seriously, which I argue is simply because their success is not dependant on this key component. Consequently, whilst their energy is being adsorbed by those targets that will affect their success e.g. GCSE A-C grades and reducing the number of young people who are not in employment, education or training etc, significant numbers of Black young people are being systematically failed.

This systematic failure to provide adequate services to Black young people will continue, until the provision and initiatives that are put in place are those which have been developed, designed and where possible delivered by the Black voluntary and community sector, Black young people and their parents, and not by politicians and 'professionals' who think they know best, as they (the politicians and 'professionals') have become accustomed to defining the needs of, and the solutions for the Black voluntary and community sector, Black young people and their parents. A situation made worse by this government's obsession with change, reform and restructure ('new religions'), because frontline service delivery is affected as the service providers attempt to manage the imposed changes.

The voluntary sector, who are often times best placed to work with Black young people (*Youth Matters*: Green Paper, 2005) are doubly disadvantaged, as they lack the capacity to keep abreast of the changes which affects their ability to secure funding and retain staff, which in turn impacts on frontline service delivery and capacity. In other words the situation creates a continuous vicious downward spiral.

In order for the government to be viewed as though it is taking the issue of Black young people's socio-economic position seriously, and that it does indeed believe that 'Black young people matter', there are a number of radical policy and legislative changes that need to be made. These changes include:

- Ensure there is no dilution of the focus on race equality via the proposals for the Commission for Equalities and Human Rights. The preferred position of Black communities is for a federated model of six equality commissions (which ensures the retention of the CRE and an overarching Human Rights Commission (a 6 + 1 model).
- Ensure that all agencies who provide services for children and young people set ambitious targets regarding race inequality, which are in line the RRAA 2000.
- Ensure that where Inspectors find that an organisation or agency does not meet a required minimum standard or has systematically failed Black young people, that severe financial penalties are imposed.
- Ensure that the elected members responsible for children and young people in a LA area are held to account if Black young people are failed through their Children's Trust.
- Ensure that, where appropriate, Children's Trust have a group that will advise, monitor and scrutinise race equality issues as a part of its governance structure.
- Ensure that where a Children's Trust fails to provide adequate services to Black young people, that LSPs are empowered to implement sanctions.
- Reduce the number of funding streams and the frequency in which changes, restructures and reforms (new religions) are imposed.
- Have long-term dedicated financial resources for the Black voluntary sector, which includes provision for capital purchases.
- Provide a set of minimum race equality standards for all providers of services to young people, which will include:
  - Multi-agency, multi-sector training for all staff.
  - Monitor recruitment, retention and progression of BME staff.
  - Share information and data.
  - Set targets.
  - Adopt an evidence based approach.

The above approach is more than necessary, for far too many years Black young people have in real terms become 'the acceptable socio-economic causalities' – the collateral damage of race inequality.

Consequently, all policies, decisions and proposed funding allocations must be evidence based, 'equality proofed' and performance managed. In so doing, this would remove the 'colour blindness' that has for many years hindered the importance that should have been placed on equality of opportunity, which in turn has limited the contributions that should have been made to the UK's Gross Domestic Produce (GDP) and Gross Value Added (GVA) by its BME communities. Which has left the answer to the question 'do Black young people matter?' as being, well . . . it would appear not for the government, its various departments and their youth support service providers.

However, the answer to the same question for the Black voluntary and community sector is a resounding, yes. Even though their battle is being fought in an environment where both financial and human resources are becoming increasingly more difficult to secure; the numbers of Black young people who need support is on the increase and their needs are becoming more complex. Despite this, the sector is prepared to shoulder the burden of providing services to Black young people, due to the continued failure of the public sector to provide adequate services, and in so doing they (the Black voluntary and community sector) are improving Black young people's life chances – a moral duty for us all if we believe that Black young people matter.

References

Alcock, P. (1996) *Social Policy in Britain: Themes and Issues*. London: Macmillan.

Barn, R. (2001) *Black Youth on the Margins*. Joseph Rowntree Foundation Research Review.

Chauhan, V. (1989) *Beyond Steel Bands 'n' Samosas': Black Young People in the Youth Service*. NYB.

Chouhan, K. et al. (2005) *A Black Manifesto*. London: The 1990 Trust.

Coard, B. (1971) *How the West Indian Child is made Educationally Sub-Normal in the British School System*. London. Beacon Press.

CRE (1976) *The Race Relations Act 1976*. London: HMSO.

CRE (2000) *The Race Relations (Amendment) Act 2000*. London: HMSO.

DfEE (1999a) *Social Inclusion: Pupil Support Circular 10/99*. London DfEE.

DfES [cited 18th May 2006] < http://www.everychildmatters.gov.uk/aims/background/.

DfES [cited 21st May 2006] < http://www.standards.dfes.gov.

Ferguson, R.W. Jr. (2006) *The Importance of Education at the Commemoration of Black History Month*, The Johns Hopkins University Applied Physics Laboratory, Laurel, MD. [cited 1st September 06]. Available from http://www.federalreserve.gov/BoardDocs/Speeches/2006/20060224/default.htm.

Fryer, P. (1984) *Staying Power: The History of Black People in Britain*. London. Pluto Press.

Gilborn, D. (2004) *Black Young People in Education*. The University of London Institute of Education.

Grant, P. (2003) *Niggers Negroes Black People and Afrikans. The Human Dimension of Building Effective Organisations: An Afrikan Centred Perspective*. Nottingham: Navigator Press.

Grant, P.I. (2006) *Saving Our Sons: Strategies and Advice for the Parents of Afrikan Teenage Sons*. Nottingham. Navigator Press.

Kay, J. (2006) *A New Public Sector* [cited 1st September 2006]. http://www.johnkay.com/political/204.

Lamming, Lord (2003) *The Victoria Climbié Inquiry*. London: DoH/Home Office.

Learning Elements of the Single Regeneration Budget (1998) *The Report*. [cited 15 July 2000] http://www.lifelong.co.uk/srb/sect10.htm.

Macpherson, Sir, W. (1999) *The Stephen Lawrence Inquiry Report*.

New Labour (1997) *New Labour's Manifesto*.

ODPM (2003) Neighbourhood Renewal Unit: Black and Minority Ethnic [cited 20th May 2003] http://www.renewal.net

ODPM (2005) *Local Strategic Partnerships: Shaping Their Future*. ODPM Publications.

Wright, C. et al. (2005) School Exclusion and Transition into Adulthood in African Caribbean Communities. York: York Publishing Service.

Wright, C., Robinson, Y. and Devanney, C. (2005) *Securing and Improving Better Outcomes for Young People from Black and Minority Ethnic Backgrounds*. Nottingham: Nottingham Trent University.

CHAPTER 13

Youth Services and How They Work With Black Young People

Chester Morrison

Introduction

This chapter will focus attention on the situation of Black young people and the approaches used by local authorities to deal with them or not as the case may be. In this instance Black is used within a broad political understanding encompassing people from a variety of ethnic backgrounds but who are identified by colour. For some readers the term people of colour might be more appropriate but since this is equally flawed and might be interpreted by others as an attempt to avoid using the label Black, it will be kept in abeyance. This question of labelling is of the greatest importance because therein resides the process of dividing people against their interests. Time will not allow a full exploration of this process so the reader is invited to make that contribution through actively thinking about the purpose of labelling and in doing so provide their own rationale. Additionally, this chapter will examine some of the basic tenets underpinning youth work with Black young people and its centrality within a portfolio of tackling social disadvantage. A note of caution is the different context in which the term Black is used. Given its different uses and understanding when it is quoted from secondary sources there is no guarantee that it is used consistently or is being inclusive.

Background

Many in the youth service will claim that they have been to the forefront of anti-discriminatory and anti-oppressive practice in its recent history. (One could say cynically, yes, but you are no longer there.) They will go further to claim that through that association they have enabled access for young people who were then 'immigrants' in the early 1960s and 1970s. The Hunt Report (1967) *Immigrant and the Youth Service*, tried to raise the issue of the nature of the relationship between immigrant young people and the social educational arm of the state. Nearly 40 years later one could not appropriately use the same title in respect of the majority of Black young people in the UK but the same sentiments, if not the same concerns, could be expressed about new arrivals, under a range of different banners.

The anecdotal evidence suggests there have been some hostilities between British born Black young people and other Black young people, who are seen as new arrivals, whether they are refugees or asylum seekers. Given the lack of understanding that such hostilities represent, one needs to question the role of youth services in helping to manage the interface between different Black young people. One thing is clear, Black young people are as susceptible as the population as a whole to ideas and practice of territorialism. In

Wolverhampton for example, Black young men from Whitmore Reans, an area of the city that was in the 1960s and 1970s deemed to be the Black area are now in open conflict with Black young men from elsewhere across the city. They seemed to identify themselves as Black on one level but as being from Park Village, Heath Town or Blakenhall on another level. Since geographical location provides the basis for their animosity one could argue that these parochial identities are stronger than their affiliation to Blackness. A case of their commonalities being minimised and their differences accentuated and made momentous.

When the Hunt Report was published, the social engineers of the 1960s were hopeful that time-related integration through education and economic advancement would help to reduce friction between young people from different ethnic and cultural backgrounds. Recent incidents in Birmingham and Merseyside would suggest that such optimism was not wholly justified. People of African Caribbean and Asian descent living in Birmingham found themselves in open hostilities when a report on a local radio station suggested that a teenage Caribbean girl had been raped by up to 16 Asian men. Such spontaneous uprising would suggest the existence of a residual undercurrent of hostility between these communities. Communities who were once united in opposing the onslaught of racism found themselves caught up in violence severe enough to render one African Caribbean young man dead and his Asian assailant confined to prison for life. One of Greater Merseyside's proud boasts, depending on the prevailing mood, is that it has one of the longest established Black communities in the United Kingdom. Yet after more than 300 years it was still possible for a white young man to kill Anthony Walker in summer 2005 for no other reason than his black skin colour. If the death of Anthony Walker on Greater Merseyside is to have wider significance we must all be concerned. Because our hope for a better future will not be realised without concerted and sustained actions to deal with the existence of prejudice and racism among young people. In that regard, a pertinent question must be, what is the place of Black young people in that future and how will youth services contribute to its realisation.

It is ironic that the youth service's role in dealing with young immigrants seemed clearer when the social policy conditions were less conducive to change. Arguably, the social policy framework in Britain today better embraces issues of equality and inclusion than at any time in British history. At least it gives the impression that it does and there are numerous and some would say rampant advocates proclaiming the centrality of equality in all they do. However, as I travelled England inspecting youth services, a persistent area for development remained the work that was undertaken or not with Black and Minority Ethnic young people. Recent concerns about Muslim young people have given rise to the label 'Muslim Youth Work' suggesting a new departure for local authorities' youth work practice. The issue of work with Muslim young people will be dealt with elsewhere. However, this new heightened awareness begs the question, does it take violence on a grand scale or the perception of one before those responsible will provide for the basic needs of young people in Britain, whether they are Muslims or non Muslims? Within the framework of a local authority we have placed emphasis on the role of the youth service because of its role in catering for those young people who are marginalised whilst pursuing a comprehensive approach to delivery.

As indicated above, the policy framework in 21st-century Britain is far more conducive to issues of inequality but the plight of Black young people has not changed comparatively from the 1960s. With the recent enactment of anti-discrimination legislation based on age one could argue that the once narrow focus on specific groups has been widened to encompass everyone in society. This position is supported by a number of studies from a range of perspectives; some institutional and others from the concerns of African Caribbean and Asian communities. A themed report *Educational Inequality* (Gillborn and Mirza, 2000) clearly highlighted the educational achievements and under-achievements of Black children within the education system. Particular focus was placed on the situation of Black boys whose achievement as a group was at the bottom of the ladder. Brian Richardson (2006) has skilfully revisited the vexed question of how the British school system disadvantages Black pupils. Appropriately, he started with a review and a re-presentation of Bernard Coard's small but seminal book. Coard (1972) used the appropriate title, *How the West Indian child is made educationally subnormal in the British school system: the scandal of the Black child in schools in Britain.* Apart from the need to delve into the contents to ascertain the evidence for his assertion the concerns were adequately expressed in the name. If we were to compare the issues raised over the last 40 years it becomes apparent that there are many similarities with the concerns that were expressed then and now.

The situation of Black children within the contemporary social context seems to be a conundrum. So much has changed to embrace difference when previously the reluctance to do so seemed to have been at the heart of the problem initially. Once where there were spotlights we now have floodlights; multiculturalism has been replaced by anti-oppressive practice; the needs of Black young people are covered by the umbrella of diversity. Power is no longer explicitly stated as a crucial component in the definition of racism and racism within institutions has become faceless. If all of the above is to be believed we have achieved a kind of perverse equality, one in which there is no apparent hierarchy of needs so there is no imperative for a particular focus on service delivery. Perhaps more importantly, the historical and social circumstances of Black young people are damagingly forgotten, leaving a gap between their individual and collective realities, policy aspirations and everyday practice. This situation is evidence by the enforced coalition between all so-called disadvantaged groups. Racism and colour based discrimination have become part of the homogenisation of the social factors underpinning societal disadvantage. One wonders how such distinguished scholars and activists like W.E.B Dubois who said, 'The problem of the 20th century is the problem of the colour line' would have responded in the 21st century. No amount of optimism could overcome the reality that Stephen Lawrence, Anthony Walker and Zahib Mubarak, to name but a few, died because they were Black. Lawrence and Walker were subjected to unprovoked attacks and killed by white young men, whilst Mubarak died in prison at the hands of his white self-declared racist cell mate. In Mubarak's case the tragedy was made more poignant since his death occurred at the end of his sentence, just prior to him leaving prison. Disturbingly, the prison authorities knew that he was likely to be attacked, yet allowed that situation to occur.

One only has to mention the possibility of making a direct response to the specific needs of Black young people and await the reaction. Invariably that reaction starts by making comparisons with, for example, the educational under-achievement of white working class boys. Before long it widens to include every possible way in which a person or a group of people could be disadvantaged in society. In other words, the inference suggests the needs of Black young people are not unique and if their position is to improve then that of all other disadvantaged groups must also improve. This however, cannot be done sequentially but in parallel. Such many fronted approaches then become a sedative, which induces paralysis of action. Simplification of the issues and a reduction to the lowest common factors does nothing to contribute to, or improve, the lived realities of Black young people. Interestingly, most people who accept that something needs to be done are very quick to confront and challenge new proposals for action. However, their expertise seems to reside in the firm knowledge of what will not work rather than what will work. It is tantamount to seeing a person drowning whilst debating and testing the fibres of various ropes to determine which is the strongest to throw to them. Whilst we look for tried and trusted solutions, Black young people continue to experience the ravages of the society as new rationales for stop and search are produced for example. Educationally, a significant proportion of Black boys continue to be denied the education required to make them effective participants in the knowledge-based economy (Gillborn and Mirza, 2000).

Clearly this is a generalised view and as we know, to every generalisation there are exceptions, which bring us to another point. We generally accept that Black children, boys in particular, under-achieve within the British education system. This focus on under-achievement has ensured that in the majority of cases, when Black children achieve against the odds, their achievements are not recognised. Consequently, when we speak about Black boys and their educational achievements or under-performance it must be set within the context of some Black boys. This is necessary because generalisation tends to lead to collective condemnation or praise, which in turn will negatively or positively affect the group to which it refers. For Black young people it is likely to be condemnatory and that can have a de-motivating effect on the entire group. The following extract from a poem by the author highlights the need for one to acknowledge the positive, as a counter-balance for that which is negative. It suggests that the experience of Black boys exists on a continuum. This issue therefore is not a desire to ensure that all Black children are able to achieve the same levels as everyone else, irrespective of their ability. It is the need to ensure that they are able to achieve to levels which are commensurate with their abilities, as represented by normal distribution. The challenge is to ensure that all Black children have access to opportunities to realise their full potential. Were we to achieve this goal the result would be an even distribution of Black children along the achievement continuum rather than what appears to be a clustering at the bottom of the achievement ladder.

> *Black men a succeed and Black men a fail*
> *Though most of them free some languish in jail*
> *Black men in work, Black men looking for a job*
> *Some of them a prosper some of them a get robbed*
> *Some Black men a lion, some Black men a mouse*
> *Some a dem homeless, some own fancy house*

Effective practice

We have indicated that there are exceptions in practice; some of which is good while others are stereotypical. Whatever the situation, work with Black young people needs to take place within an overall context; a context which recognises their social reality and should not be done in relation to some other group. Constructive work with Black young people needs to take account of the factors affecting their educational performance and degree of social coherence. One frequent mistake is to treat them as a homogenous group, isolated from the social pressures exerted by society. When, for example, young people of African Caribbean descent are overtly hostile to Somali young people some of us within the youth service are surprised. Yet the sociological analysis from our training provides evidence to suggest that those who are lower down the social ladder are most threatened by newcomers, whom they may see as being below them but threatening their position.

The sociological situation of Black young people is quite complex. It is therefore difficult to present a full analysis of the factors affecting their achievements even if that knowledge was available. That having been said, if we are to approach our work with Black young people with purpose and understanding it seems we need to take the following factors into account:

- negative peer affiliation;
- oppositional behaviour;
- institutional and individual expectations;
- self-identity and self-esteem;
- experiences of oppression;
- fear of failure and quality of support.

For youth services to embrace the types of practice pertinent to effective work with Black young people, the above factors should be developed as a framework. Before such a framework can be developed, an understanding of the factors presented needs to be cultivated through a set of brief definitions and their likely effects on Black young people's behaviour.

Peer affiliation

Affiliations occur at every level of human maturity. In their early years children cling very closely to their parents. But as they grow and develop, a symbol of their increasing independence from their parents is their affiliation with their peers. Importantly, parents accept this as a process of development and will often try to influence whom their children form close affiliations with. Pragmatically, most parents try to direct their offspring towards those of their peers whom they consider to be possibly more positive influences. This is a type of role modelling among peers in which positive re-enforcements are desired. For Black young people where those positive peer models do not exist in sufficient numbers their influence is reduced and a number of negative peer affiliations are developed. Let us not get too alarmed about negative peer affiliations because it is a human phenomenon. Instead let us see it as a fulfilment of the need for acceptance. It is one of the cornerstones of youth gangs. Consequently, if service providers are to make meaningful interventions in that culture they have to provide alternatives that those young people can value. Negative peer affiliations as well as oppositional behaviour may develop as a reaction to previous or ongoing experiences of rejection.

If we focus on peer affiliations it makes it easier to draw parallels between the experiences of Black young people and that of their parents. Often concerns are expressed about the formation of separate communities across Britain and the likely impact on society's goal of achieving community cohesion. Disturbances in Bradford and Burnley, to name but two cities in Northern England, were attributed to the degree of separateness which existed between Asians and whites. Having spoken to some elders from both the Asian and African Caribbean communities they were clear that the enclaves they now occupy resulted from necessity. Rebuffed to find accommodation let alone become integrated, they observed white flight from neighbourhoods even when those neighbourhoods were not the most desirable. The corrosive effect of separate development was a main focus in Cantle's Report (2003) on the disturbances in Burnley, Bradford and other northern cities. Another unlikely parallel is that of the 'Alternatives', which is an aspect of contemporary youth culture in the 21st century. This group of young people have adopted a different lifestyle to that generally expected from society. They meet together in city centres like Liverpool for collective security but their very presence acts as a threat to other users. The main point here being it is not unusual for people to come together for fraternity and collective security but under the pressure of rejection the motive force is usually negative.

Oppositional behaviour

Perhaps the most potent example of oppositional behaviour is that of Black boys who regard academic studies as a white or female activity. Since by definition they cannot be white or female they then create various environments to accentuate their difference. Although they may present their resistance with pride and flamboyance a closer look reveals their strong sense of being excluded. Often to counter such feelings of rejections they create a different social system in which they can attain status and significance. Their social structures are underpinned by a set of values which gives scant regard for conventional society. Malcolm X (1963) claimed Black people in America catch hell because they were not seen as Americans; because if they were Americans they wouldn't catch hell. It means, by being at the margins Black young people are even less likely to have their needs addressed. Through this process of de facto internal exile, Black young people adopt oppositional behaviour which sometimes results in the rejection of many of the dominant values in society. Erroneously, they will on occasions present their positions as being rooted in their culture or religion. If we in the youth service are to work with some of these Black young people successfully we need to understand that this oppositional behaviour will on occasions turn in on itself. Consequently, it will chastise other Black young people who may be seen as acting white, whatever acting white represents at that time. It may, for example, be actions against intellectualism because for some, intellectualism is white and is definitely not cool.

Institutional and individual expectations

Jordan (1964) asserted that Black children failed because the system of education is designed to encourage their failure. One could argue that this encouragement has developed into expectations and is certainly applicable to the British context. Damagingly, these expectations quite often become internalised and have become barriers to Black young people realising their full potential. Milner (1976) demonstrated that Black children under-performed when they knew their results would be compared with white children.

On the other hand their performance increased when they knew that they would be compared to other Black children. There are many aspects of Black people's behaviour in society for which this is relevant, some of this will be explored by the use of examples later. Within this area of analysis expectations exist internally and externally. Where it is internally rooted that has to be the starting point of any work with Black young people where each individual will need to be engaged in a process relevant to them. In saying this it must also be remembered that individualism can be divisive to the collective good and must be seen within an overall context. To effectively challenge institutional expectations, it is often necessary to give the collective experience sovereignty over that of the individual. However, one must be careful to avoid undermining individual achievements since they might also be useful as role models. This is a really difficult balance to achieve because the pressure to apply simplistic solutions to complex issues is always present.

One of the most damaging areas to counteract in the development of individual expectation is that of internalised racism. Where society is unwilling to meaningfully intervene it uses it to justify and in some cases promote division between Black people. It seems to me that Black individualism becomes important in society when it supports the dominant viewpoint and can be used effectively to undermine the collective effort.

Self-identity and self-esteem

Within society each of us has multiple identities. However, they do not all have the same status and currency because often our dominant identity is not internally determined. Recent developments in social policy in the UK have introduced a test for British-ness for would be citizens. This suggests that one can have an objective measure to determine at least one aspect of one's identity. If we assume that the test is common to all, how does it take into account the concept of diversity? Perhaps this means, diversity is allowed in areas which are marginal to society's understanding of British-ness. This takes us back to the notion that greater institutionalisation of the processes of equality are sometimes designed to keep equality at the margins. Ethnic monitoring procedures require young people as youth service users to self-identify. Available evidence suggests this is not as easy as one might expect. In some instances obviously Black skinned young people will identify themselves as white or refuse to self-identify.

In a recent debate in Liverpool (August 2006) under the banner 'Shades of Blackness' chaired by professor Stephen Small, a 20-year-old young man questioned his identity. He was of mixed parentage (White and African) as the new census categories have determined. However, his lived reality, as he expressed it, was that of being a Black young man in Liverpool. Yet there were people who wished to deny him his right to a self-definition, based entirely on his African heritage.

Once there are Black young people who find it difficult to self-identify that becomes a problem which goes beyond notions of individual choice. In such circumstances one would have to question the levels of self-esteem of such individuals. Importantly, that should be a signal to indicate that there is something in the environment which is undermining the self-confidence of such persons. Nathan and Julia Hare (1985) argued that the development of the Black boy needs to happen in an overall social context which gives him a sense of self and a feeling of being centred. That is a situation that is not only appropriate to the development of the Black boy but also applicable to the Black child.

Identity is such an important aspect of the human condition that it's worth spending a few moments exploring its effect. Split personality or schizophrenia is as the informal title suggests a condition where the individual is not wholly secured in a single identity. Not surprisingly incidences of mental illness associated with schizophrenia are disproportionately prevalent among young people identified as being of mixed parentage.

Experiences of oppression

'What you are doing speak so loud I can't hear what you are saying.' As indicated earlier, the social policy framework embraces diversity and promotes all forms of anti-discriminatory practices. Not wishing to be cynical, it seems that more effort is expended in getting the language right than in changing practice. Despite the policy framework we are still confronted with distressing statistics about the experience of Black young people in British society. A CRE report (2002) indicated that over half the racial attacks against South Asians, and more than one in three against Black Caribbean, are committed by 16–25 year olds. In nine out of ten cases the perpetrators are white.

Youth services are required to reach at least 25 per cent of the 13–19 year olds in each local authority boundary and to work more generally with 11–25 year olds. Additionally, in Resourcing Excellent Youth Services (DfES, 2002) of the 25 per cent of those reached, 60 per cent should undergo personal and social development resulting in accredited outcomes. Within the brief of youth services, particular attention must be placed on hard to reach young people, in their attempts to create more inclusive and participatory processes.

On the question of economic well-being, Black graduates are fives times more likely to be unemployed at the end of their first year after graduation than their white contemporaries (CRE, 2002). These experiences of racism either directly or through siblings do affect Black young people's world view.

Concerns with young Muslims have sharpened attention on their movements. Consequently they have become the targets of police activities, in particular, stop and search, which now even the Association of Black Police Officers are expressing concerns about. Such experiences of oppression only serve to instil negative feelings of difference in these young people.

Fear of failure

We have pointed out as Milner (1976) did, that the fear of failure becomes an acceptance of failure very soon in Black young people's lives. Their experience suggests performance is not always the most important component in success. In a limited unpublished survey by Timiti Arts (2001) Black young people's perception of some very popular television competitions based on the performing arts were studied. Many did not expect a Black person to become the outright winner however good they were. They could over a number of years identify Black performers whom they considered being excellent but who did not progress very far. To the question of why were they so negative, they were able to produce from memory, a number of programmes where that had been the case; in their view. Once quality performance is no longer the central criteria for success that means the rules have changed and what should have been explicit becomes ephemeral. For significant numbers of Black young people they start their lives knowing the rules and with a willingness to succeed. However, these rules appear to get changed without notice or rationale. Once these experiences become frequent they opt out and by doing so failure and success become defined on their terms. As important, they may use the materialism which society glorifies to justify their alternative lifestyle. Unconventional economic activities become the norm and their self-destructive journey has resulted in the creation of specific police units such as Operation Trident. This is a special unit established within the Metropolitan Police to combat Black on Black violence and is primarily targeted at gun crimes within the African Caribbean community. Both African Caribbean and Asian young people are concerned about their situation in British society. However, being subject to different ethnic and social classifications has caused them to be more inclined to accentuate their differences rather than unite around their commonalities.

Quality of support

Whatever the circumstances in which Black young people find themselves they need quality support from professionals, parents, peers and society in general. Within the professional arena youth workers should be in the position to provide that support from a position of understanding. The evidence so far indicates that practice is patchy and understanding is shallow. It is hoped that the framework suggested and the brief outlines of the different factors presented will enable youth work professionals to begin the process of re-examining their work with Black young people.

Role of local authority youth work in working with Black young people

The remainder of this chapter will concentrate on how local authority youth services can develop the ideas presented here in devising meaningful work with Black young people. Before that can be done a fundamental shift in thinking is required; in the way that the work is approached and in how greater access to resources is created. Often work with Black young people starts with a focus on additionally i.e. the need for the acquisition of more resources in order to respond effectively to them. However, it might be more appropriate to start the question, why have we excluded them from existing services. If that is a little hard to digest then maybe we could ask, why have we not made our services attractive to Black young people? Users' monitoring figures (2003) in a number of local authority youth services in the Northwest of England revealed the tendency for Black young people to travel longer distances to access youth work activities. Furthermore many did not frequent some of the units that were within easy walking distances. In either case an effective response will require local authority youth services to adopt a more proactive stance in developing services. Recent social policies specifically related to youth work have stressed the need for services to become more inclusive (*Youth Matters*, DfES, 2004). Youth services have been encouraged, and in some instances provided with, financial inducements to increase the participation of young people in decision making processes, including of course Black young people.

Some youth work practitioners, and dare I say some other professionals, are inclined to take the soft option in relation to working with Black young people. This means they are not prepared to challenge Black young people or to provide them with personal challenges. Frequently one sees, for example, initiatives taken to develop stereotypical music or other cultural projects for Black young people. Black young people are presented with interested activities that go no further than cementing their existing interests. Few music projects, for example, provide young people with the opportunity to develop their understanding of music and the arts or to enable them to evidence their learning in future years. We are not suggesting that there should be an abandonment of these types of projects. On the contrary, they provide workers with an opportunity to engage with young people where they are. The betrayal of good youth work practice and Black young people in that process is the concern here because the work should always seek to extend young people's horizons and transport them well beyond their starting point.

An example of good practice, although not located within a local authority structure but nevertheless could be adopted, is the development of a music course at Sheffield College. This programme capitalised on the popularity of Rap and Hip Hop to develop a course designed to improve young people's skills in writing and understanding literature. Programmes of this nature can assist young people to acquire new skills and support them to make linkages with other more established styles. Once the young people have grasped the essential elements of the programme they are able to identify the transferable skills they have acquired.

In one local authority young people were involved in a djing project where they learnt about scratching, toasting and equipment maintenance. Since they arrived on the project with different skills and interest they were asked to self-assess. This enabled them to establish base lines for their levels of skills and to take responsibility for their learning. At the start of each session they would identify through a checklist of core skills those areas they needed to develop. Through a process of instructor input and peer support they worked together to develop their collective skills. Those completing the programme would have their achievement accredited through the Open College Network.

The issue raised earlier concerning identity is of the utmost importance for youth services. Youth workers need to understand their roles as agents of change, not only in the context of big institutions but for the individual. When a young person enters a youth club or an organised youth activity any failure to provide an obviously accurate description of themselves must be challenged sensitively. Workers need to be wary of placing the onus on the young person entirely since they are a product of their environment. Further, the youth work environment might contribute to any feelings of insecurity which that young person may be experiencing.

Education for enterprise

Much emphasis has been placed on the acquisition of a good educational standard for Black young people. The tendency is to accept this as a given without the accompanying question, for what purpose? This, however, is a very important question given the continuing difficulties faced by Black graduates, as alluded to earlier. Clearly, education for employment becomes dysfunctional when Black graduates face similar difficulties in obtaining employment to their less qualified peers. As damaging is the economic necessity to accept positions which are below their ability and skills level. It seems a process of putting their disappointment and frustration higher up the ladder of expectations.

One mistake we often make is to equate enterprise with legal means. This leads to a situation where the enterprise of Black young people is not recognised and valued. However, to survive on the margins of society requires a great deal of entrepreneurial endeavour. Since available anecdotal evidence suggests that a high proportion of Black young people wish to become self-employed the purpose of their education needs to address that desire.

In advocating education for enterprising there are two things to consider. Education for employment only transfers the disappointment and frustration for some Black young people higher up the career ladder. Secondly, enterprise and academic endeavours are not inter-dependent so a move to develop enterprise may motivate them more easily.

Conclusion

Progressive work with Black young people requires services and youth workers to take risks. In this regard the risks referred to are based on innovation and the willingness to try new approaches. If this work is to develop, youth workers must be prepared to challenge Black young people appropriately. They need to leave their comfort zones and take responsibility for their learning since much of the uncertainty experienced was based on them feeling they did not know enough.

As indicated earlier, Black young people are as susceptible to parochialism as the population as a whole. Consequently, the search for difference by youth workers is often misplaced because all young people have their youthfulness in common. Also, because they are young they are naturally at the margins of most decision-making processes although the decisions affect their lives.

Given the fact youth services' priority age range is young people aged 13–19 years old, one has to accept that they come to the youth work situation with a host of previous experiences. Some of these experiences will be both positive and negative and will inform their initial relationship with the youth service. To effectively engage with them a sound understanding of their starting point and the external pressures affecting them is a prerequisite.

References

Baruti, K.B. (2003) *ASAFO A Warriors Guide to Manhood*. Atlanta, GA: Akoben House.

Cheung-Judge, MEE-Yan and Henley, A. (1994) London: NCVO Publications.

Cress-Welsing, F. (1991) *The Isis Papers*. Chicago: Third World Press.

Deosaran, R. (1995) *Cultural Diversity*. Ansa McAL, Psychological Research Centre, University of the West Indies, Trinidad.

DfES (2002) *Transforming Youth Work*. Nottingham: Crown Copyright.

Fanon, F. (1969) *The Wretched of the Earth*. Hammondsworth: Penguin.

Friere, P. (1972) *Pedagogy of the Oppressed*. Hammondsworth: Penguin.

Fryer, P (1984) *Staying Power: History of Black People in Britain*. London: Pluto Press.

Garrison, L. (1983) *Black Youth, Rastafarianism and the Identity Crisis in Britain*. London: ACER Publication.

Gillborn, D. and Mirza, H. (2002) DfES.

Grant, P. (2005) *Blue Skies for Afrikans*. Nottingham: Navigator Press.

Grant, P. (2004) *Niggers, Negroes, Black People and Afrikans*. Nottingham: Navigator Press.

Joseph, J. et al. (2002) *Towards Global Democracy*. DEA.

Mackie, L. (1987) *The Great Marcus Garvey.* Antigua: Hansib Publication.

Madhubuti, H. (1973) *From Plan to Planet.* Chicago: Third World Press.

McWhorter, J. (2006) *Catalyst Magazine*, CRE Publication.

McWhorter, J. (2001) *Internal Constraints.* [cited 12th January 2004] www.reason.com

Morris, S. (1972) *Bogle L'Ouverture.* London.

Richardson, B. (2006) *Tell it Like it is.* Stoke on Trent: Bookmark Publications/Trentham Books.

Ruddock, R. (1972) *Six Approaches to the Person.* London: Routledge and Kegan Paul.

Sangster, D. *Peer Education and Young Black People.* www.drugtext.org/library

Williams, C. (1987) *The Destruction of Black Civilization.* Chicago, Ill: Third World Press.

CHAPTER 14

The Impact of Formal Education on African Caribbean Young People

Richard Kennedy and Leona White-Simmonds

We want education for our people that exposes the true nature of this decadent American society. We want education that teaches us our true history and our role in the present-day society. We believe in an educational system that will give to our people knowledge of self. If a man does not have knowledge of himself and his position in society and the world, then he has little chance to relate to anything else.

The Black Panther Party Platform (October 1966)

As two informal educators employed as youth workers, we believe that formal education is fundamental in order to succeed. Success is often measured in terms of aspirations being met, social status and acquired wealth. There is little doubt that success within education opens many doors in terms of employment which can in turn affect socio-economic positioning in society. Without attaining higher levels of success in education we believe that Black people particularly within Britain will continue to struggle to achieve and invariably succeed. Sewell noted that people in the Caribbean placed a high premium on education, he stated:

Even the most illiterate of farmers in the Caribbean would expect their child to succeed in the education system so that they could better themselves. When we came to Britain we found that there was a fundamental difference.

(Sewell, 1997: 90)

The fundamental difference being that unlike in the Caribbean, there was little evidence to support the notion that the British education system was there to ensure that Black young people succeeded. One could argue that in fact the education system has systematically ensured that Black young people do not succeed (Richardson, 2005). This is not surprising as it has been acknowledged that the British education system has failed or lowered the aspirations of White working class people (Sewell, 1997). The introduction of the 1944 Education Act was primarily designed to address pupils' personal and academic development and ultimately provide a more equitable education for all. We will argue that education for 'all' is merely a concept. A concept which may on the surface provide education for all, however the great variations in the way in which different groups receive a positive form of education, specifically in the case of Black young people, is often less than sufficient.

From this premise it is important to understand the possible effects that failure within formal education can have on Black young people but also how it can prevent them from achieving their full potential and ultimately affect their life chances. How is it that we often have a situation where Black young people enter formal education, often with a higher level of attainment compared with their white peers, but yet leave as the least likely group to achieve five GCSEs? (Majors, 2001). Why it is that Black young people are disproportionately excluded from schools compared to their white peers? (Sewell, 1997; Richardson, 2005). How many times as practitioners have we read or heard Black young people saying 'school is not for me' because they are so turned off with what school signifies to them?

This chapter will seek to explore a range of factors which contribute to Black young people ultimately failing within the formal education system. In order to explore this failure there will be an exploration of how Black young people psychologically develop and the impact this could have on their educational achievements. Throughout this chapter we will highlight the failings of the current formal education system in developing Black young people's full educational potential and also knowledge of self. In addition to this, the chapter will also discuss the role of informal education and examine how informal educators can play an active and positive role in addressing the many issues that Black young people face within the formal educational context.

Within this chapter the term Black will be used to signify young people specifically of African Caribbean origins, inclusive of dual heritage young people (African Caribbean heritage mother or father). We acknowledge and support Black in the political context (signifying people of African, Bangladeshi, Indian and Pakistani origin), but believe that the impact of formal education on young people of African Caribbean origin is significantly different to these specific groups (Wright, Weekes and McGlughlin, 2000).

Historical context

Much of the debate in the past three decades concerning the educational experiences of the Black child, particularly Black young men in Britain, has centred on the concept of underachievement and exclusion. The past fifty years has presented much discussion of the role of school in perpetuating inequalities, particularly in relation to class, gender and race. From the late 1960s neo-Marxists argued that school education was simply there to produce a docile labour force essential to late capitalist relations (Marshall, 1994). In Britain the debate on race and education has fundamentally centred on the notion of 'underachievement' of the Black child (Blair, 2001). The argument has largely been that the educational system, as part of a wider system of structural and institutional racism, has helped to promote the educational failure of the Black child (Gill, Mayor and Blair, 1992). This has in turn determined the future and position of the Black child, within the growing underclass sector of Britain.

The late 1960s and early 1970s saw Black children being classified as educationally subnormal and 'disproportionate numbers of Black children being placed in disciplinary units or 'sin-bins' (Blair, 2001: 2). The debate and research during this time primarily focused on the underachievement of Black young people, as the process of exclusions was not deemed to be a particularly alarming factor within this period (Macan Ghaill, 1988; Rampton Report, 1981; Benskin, 1994). Nonetheless exclusions as a topic of debate certainly came to the forefront in the late 1980s and continues to be of concern into the new millennium.

Attitudes towards the educational needs of the Black child in Britain have, however, undergone a number of changes. Troyna (1990) identified three conceptual models for the 1960s and 1970s, namely; 'assimilation, integration and cultural pluralism' (Gill, Mayor and Blair, 1992: 61). It was initially assumed that Black children would assimilate into British society by accepting and learning British values and traditions. In the mid 1960s Roy Jenkins as Home Secretary made a speech that was to influence a more integrationist phase. The outcome of this was the development of multicultural education (Majors, 2001).

Multicultural education was introduced as a response to what many believed to be a Eurocentric curriculum. In order to combat the underachievement of minority people it was felt by educationalists and policy makers that the curriculum needed to reflect the group's experiences and cultures, in addition to those of the white population (Culture and Education, undated). Despite the new approach much of the work within education continued to trade on superficial 'positive images' and stereotypes, described by Troyna and Carrington as the 3 Ss – saris, samosas and steel bands (Troyna and Carrington, 1990). The concerns were that the celebration of difference was often shallow and ignored the issue of racism within the educational system. As a result it was seen by many as condescending and had very little impact on the real issue of achievement (Culture and Education, undated).

Often a major flaw for many of the models introduced to bring about equality within the education system and to raise achievement was and still is to some extent we believe, the failure to recognise the impact of racism as a structural feature of the British education system. Instead the frameworks and policies that are and have been developed often place the blame of issues such as underachievement faced by Black children within the Black community. For instance, articles arguing that it is the fault of the family, or that parents of Black young people do not get involved in their children's education (Cross, 1977), or that Black young people have bad attitudes (Sewell, 1997), which ultimately leads to them underachieving within the school context. These particular explanations along with many others are often cited as the causes for the failure of Black young people, which are used to almost exonerate schools or the education system. Alongside these, there are, however, a multitude of articles and research that offer opposing perspectives, such as the often negative relationship between white teachers and Black young people and the effect that this has on Black young people's educational achievements (Majors, 2001). Ultimately, it is the failure of Black young people, which we continue to read about, and for those of us who work with Black young people in an educational context, it is a fact we continue to see and question on a daily basis. Therefore this will be the focus of the chapter.

Psychological development of the Black child

In order to explore the impact of formal education on Black young people, we believe that it is necessary to examine and have an understanding of how Black young people develop psychologically. In 1978 Cross outlined in his research, four stages of psychological nigrescence or Black self-actualisation. The research explored the different stages that minority groups (inclusive of Black people) within society move through, these are:

- **Pre-encounter stage**: characterised by partial self-awareness about difference and reliance upon the majority group for sense of value.

  Within this stage a minority group/individual will display an acceptance of the negative stereotypes of their own group and believe that assimilation is the most appropriate method for challenging racism.
- **Encounter stage**: a considerable event creates openness to new identity.

  Within this stage the individual will investigate the culture, history and background of the individual group. The search for identity starts over and above that which is imposed by the oppressive society in which they live.
- **Immersion stage**: there is a shift from the old to a new identity and an emphasis on the obliteration of the old and an elevation of the new.

  The individual will now experience liberation from the wider society's stereotypes and principles. They will start to confront the system and feel a connection to their own group. The strengths and weaknesses of the minority group and the majority group start to become apparent.
- **Internalisation stage**: a new identity is formed and the individual starts a process of discussion with the majority group (Cross, 1978).

  During this stage the individual feels empathy for all minority groups that face oppression within wider society and the person commits to social change.

We now have a perspective of how minority people develop within an oppressive society, where the majority values and beliefs become intrinsically linked with that of oppression.

The education system within any society mirrors the dominant values and beliefs within that society. There is a culture of power played out within wider society and this is also played out within our own educational establishments. Our educational system is based on the principles of a meritocracy; some pupils already come equipped with the necessary tools to enact their role within the power plays in the classroom. This is explained as cultural capital (Apple, 1979) and is easily transmitted between the group members. It can be summarised as ways of talking, writing and interacting (Delpit, 1988). The out group has to develop the necessary skills in order to interact within a predefined role, often linked to stereotypes and oppression. This can start within the classroom as early as pre-school, the point at which children begin to develop an awareness of difference (Clarke, 1950). Black young people quickly realise that they are in what is termed the 'out' group within the wider society and the classroom. Kenneth and Mamie Clark's study of young Black children in 1947 reached the ultimate conclusion that young people overwhelmingly associated being Black with negativity and being White with positive self image (*Journal of Negro Education*, 1950). This study was repeated in the short film 'A Girl Like Me' in 2005 by Kira Davis. The results highlighted that the issues affecting Black young people have not diminished since the study by Clarke in 1950 in which 15 out of the 21 black children preferred the white doll to the black one.

Those in authority i.e. teachers and policy makers, are frequently unable to acknowledge that oppressive systems are in place nor are they able to recognise their role in perpetuating these systems, even if they perceive themselves as multicultural in their approach to the process of education. Delpit (1988) stated:

> The issue of power is enacted in the classroom. There are codes or rules for participating in power; that is, there is a culture of power. The rules of the culture of

power are a reflection of the rules of the culture of those who have power. If you are already a participant in the culture of power being told explicitly the rules of that culture makes acquiring power easier. Those with power are frequently least aware of, or at least willing to acknowledge, its existence. Those with less power are often most aware of its existence.

(282)

Even when teachers are legitimately faithful to equality of opportunity as a goal, they often perceive Black young people as presenting a more frequent and relentless test of their authority. This is largely at odds with the student's intentions and the degree of their motivation (Gillborn, 1990).

To explore the deeper nature of oppression and how it presents within the classroom, Fanon (1967) states that for the Black person, 'every ontology is made unattainable' (109). This is due to the nature of the relationship between Black and White and as Fanon suggests, 'The Black man must not only be Black, but Black in relation to the White man' (ibid. 110). The perception of white society is based on fear and commences at an early age within a white child; 'See the negro I'm frightened' (ibid. 112). This is a manifestation of the subconscious and immediately the issue becomes one of fear and race. Any mutual endeavour is predisposed within this relationship to that of the colonised and the coloniser (Fanon, 1967). These power dynamics and subconscious thoughts affect every interaction between Black and White people. Freud suggested that we operate subconsciously and consciously and he introduced the notion that the subconscious controls the vast majority of our behaviour. It follows that most of our behaviour is controlled by forces of which we are completely unaware (Freud, 1986). Fanon links this exploration of the subconscious directly to the interaction between Black and White and suggests that:

In the remotest depth of the European unconscious an inordinately black hollow has been made in which the most immoral impulses, the most shameful desires, lie dormant. And every man climbs towards the whiteness and light, the European has tried to repudiate this uncivilised self, which has attempted to defend itself. When European Civilisation came into contact with the Black world, with those savage peoples, everyone agreed; those Negroes are the principle of evil.

(Fanon, 1967: 190)

The results of this are that Black people are seen as inferior to White people; this goes beyond the conscious and deep into the subconscious mind.

The question remains, how does this transference develop within the classroom when educating Black students? Black children are entering the education system at a position 20 points higher than the accepted baseline for reading and maths but leaving 20 points below at the age of sixteen (Gillborn and Mirza, Ofsted, 2000). Is this the evidence to suggest that existing systems are not meeting the needs of Black young people and that they are becoming 'stuck' within the early stage of the self-actualisation model?

Why are Black young people failing?

We believe that in order to answer this, there is a need to examine teacher-pupil interaction and the level of support Black young people receive from the national curriculum to help them achieve and progress positively through the model of self-actualisation.

The first point of examination of the national curriculum will consider the rationale behind the recent changes to the education system within Britain. The Conservative Government in 1979 saw falling standards in comparison to other countries and a politicised curriculum based on multiculturalism, sociology and peace studies. This was distracting students from the three Rs and weakening British culture and traditions (Gordon, 1989). The Education Reform Act of 1988 removed control of curriculum content from local authorities and LEAs and produced a centralised model for schools to work within. The aim of these changes was to prepare pupils for the opportunities, responsibilities and experiences of adult life. Kenneth Baker, the then Education Secretary, explained his vision for the future of education:

> *I want to ensure that when our children leave school they will be ready for work in a competitive and technically advanced world.*

> (Hardy and Vieler, 1992)

It could be argued that before this change, the curriculum had the flexibility to meet the needs of groups represented within any given community and in our opinion it is this flexibility which could have been the best prospect of enabling Black young people to self-actualise. Were Black communities asked what they wanted from the education system which was supposedly meant for 'all', and were choices given to them with regards to the nature and the content of the education they would receive? If the choice had been given on the basis of Cross' model or the supply of labour to industry, which would have been chosen? It could be argued that with the current shortage of unskilled labour within Britain that schools and educational systems have a vested interest in failure in order to provide for the needs of these historically low paid industries. Are Black people subconsciously being delivered into low skilled employment by a system that does not reflect their needs and is based on exclusion rather than inclusion? To substantiate these points, the current models employed by society to deal with ethnic difference are outlined below.

There are three perspectives that characterise how the majority group within society interacts with ethnic difference; assimilation, multiculturalism and antiracist.

At the time the National Curriculum was implemented (1988) the general thrust was that Black people should assimilate into the society, fully embracing the norms and values of the dominant group; racism should be ignored and the more Black people assimilated, the less oppression they would feel. This approach we believe is still active today especially in relation to refugees and asylum seekers residing within European countries. The National Curriculum has undergone a number of reviews since its inception. In the review of the National Curriculum in England, the then Secretary of State, David Blunkett said 'Our ambition is to create a nation capable of meeting the challenges of the next millennium (QCA, 1999c Foreword).

At no point during these reviews had there been any discussion about how the curriculum contributed to a multi-ethnic Britain. Crucially, the opportunity to address the needs of Black young people has been missed, as the political elite has moved towards an increasingly multicultural approach in which Black people merely have more freedom to express their own languages and beliefs, but not the more 'sensitive' issues outlined herein.

Through this approach, the mainstays of the British way of life are maintained; contact between different groups and the provision of information, which is the most productive way to challenge oppression, remains unchanged. This has been a tokenistic step to respond to the changing needs of society; conscious racism has been replaced by subconscious racism in the way that it manifests itself in wider society. Black young people continue to fail within the current educational system and White students are twice as likely as Black Students to achieve the bench mark level of five or higher grade passes (Gillborn and Gipps, 1996).

The only way in which Black young people can be allowed to progress through the model of self-actualisation is for the whole education system to adopt an anti-racist perspective; this is over and above the valuing of diversity, which is inextricably linked to the multicultural perspective. This anti-racist approach acknowledges that Black people from the Caribbean came to this country because they were needed for labour purposes. It also acknowledges that racist structures and practices are in place and that there is a need to combat these systems through legislation and direct action. This is the premise for including black history in the curriculum, leading to a programme of cultural education that not only educates young people about different races and cultures but also challenges the colonialist dogma. This must be developed in such a way that the majority group within society could not opt out. For example, under the current system Christian parents can opt out of multi faith religious education and do so, on the basis that they do not want their children to be taught about, or influenced by different religions.

Underachievement remains a problem for the whole of society as we are again in the midst of losing a whole generation of Black young people through an education system that fails to support their particular needs. Moreover, we live in the midst of a consumerist explosion where we are constantly being told that we have choices and it is our right to choose; from health care to education and what we purchase throughout our lives. The reality is that Black young people have very little choice when dealing with the oppression they experience. The subconscious interactions within the educational systems are established to prevent black young people progressing. Within a school context, interaction with teachers is based on oppressive stereotypes. As stated by the Runnymede Trust in 1997:

> *African Caribbean students frequently experience relationships with white teachers that are characterised by relatively high degrees of control and criticism. This finding has been replicated in infant and primary classrooms.*
>
> (Runnymede Trust, 1997: 19)

At this point it is important to acknowledge the Black middle class who have, within an emerging meritocracy, achieved some level of self-actualisation in economic terms and through the education system. This is however, we believe, based on tokenistic achievement and Black people have been deceived into thinking that this is the only model that is acceptable. Some will therefore achieve at the expense of the rest. In our opinion, this new Black middle class has an implicit responsibility to the wider Black society to utilise the power and influence that they have acquired, to challenge the oppression that exists and not to perpetuate a process that reinforces their own self aggrandisement so they can say 'I have achieved, so can you'. This strengthens the oppressive aspects of society and can be used by those in power to emphasise that their policies on multiculturalism are working, using the Black middle class as examples of what can be achieved. In 1999 Sidaneus and Pratto highlighted this within social dominance theory and link dominant and subordinate groups with behavioural asymmetry. The subordinate group's increased level of passive and active collaboration with their personal oppression provides the systems of group-based social hierarchy with significant degrees of resilience, robustness and stability (Sidaneus and Pratto, 1999).

Historically the operation of such systems is not new. During slavery two types of Black people emerged; house Negroes and field Negroes. The house Negroes remained in slavery and were therefore oppressed but felt that they had achieved a higher status through their close interaction with the 'master's' family. The field Negroes however would constantly have to struggle for freedom from their enslavement and their significantly lower status within the hierarchy. When confronted with this fight, the house Negro would suggest what could be better than this (Malcolm X November 28, 1962). Have the new Black middle class been manipulated into thinking that nothing could be better than this?

This is where the link between meritricious achievement and self-actualisation becomes blurred; self-actualisation is not about the attainment of materialistic aims and having a good career at the expense of being oppressed. Self-actualisation is knowledge of the self and demands a commitment to challenge the prevailing norms of society as well as to participate in the struggle and have an understanding that there is no neutral point.

The role of the informal educator

In 1946 Brew described informal education as taking 'philosophy out of closets and libraries, schools and colleges, to dwell in clubs and assemblies at the tea tables and coffee houses' (Brew cited in Jeffs and Smith, 1989). In the 50 or so years that have followed since these words were written, informal education has gone through a transitional period; however the philosophy of educating outside of formal institutions has remained. There is a recognition that the two can work together to fully encourage and support individuals to reach their full potential. Informal education now takes place in a variety of contexts and situations, from bus shelters, coffee bars to the local chip shop and it is this process of informal education which lies at the heart of youth work.

The purpose of youth work is fundamentally to engage with young people in a process of moral philosophising, through which they make sense of themselves and the world in which they live. This in turn should encourage young people to take charge of their lives and ultimately empower them (Young, 1999). Youth work should therefore enable and support young people to:

> . . . explore their values, deliberate on the principles of their own moral judgements; make reasoned choices that can be sustained through committed action. Through this process young people will learn and develop: the skills of critical thinking and rational judgement . . . the ability to engage in moral inquiry.
>
> (Young, 1999: 121)

It is the role of the youth worker as an informal educator to ensure that they foster this process, often without timetables or agendas. However, it is for the skilled youth worker to create and spot opportunities to educate young people, in order to take individuals and groups forward. Success or failure of this process is dependant upon the skills, knowledge base and experience that the youth worker holds.

If the role of the youth worker is that of empowering young people to take charge of their lives, then we believe that they can have a key role to play in working with Black young people and ultimately raising educational achievements. Youth work can be an ideal vehicle to foster and support Black young people through transitional periods, such as that illustrated by Cross' model. As we stated earlier, youth work is fundamentally concerned with equipping young people with the skills to make sense of themselves and the world in which they live, all of which could be related to the stages of self-actualisation. Activities and projects can be tailored to encourage Black young people's positive development, this can range from Black history projects, self-esteem workshops to general discussions about identity. All work undertaken should ultimately aim to encourage Black young people to achieve to their full potential, both in a formal and informal context. Youth workers should be continually encouraging open discussion and challenging the status quo, as well as offering support, guidance and honesty to young people, regardless of race or gender. However, there is also a need to recognise that there are fundamental differences in young people's lives, which are as a direct result of either their 'race' or 'gender'.

Before youth workers can take on this supportive role in relation to Black young people, it is imperative that firstly they have an understanding of 'race' and 'racism' as social constructs. Given that many studies (Weeks and Wright, 1995; Gilborn and Gibbs, 1996; Blair and Bourne, 1998) cite racism as one of the salient features in the underachievement of Black young people within the educational system, it would be irresponsible for any youth worker to begin working with Black young people without fully equipping themselves in terms of knowledge and understanding of how to challenge racism and support young people who are experiencing racism.

An awareness of issues of power and oppression are often core elements for the training of youth workers. There is an expectation, because of their training, that youth workers are able to understand the damaging effects which racism can potentially have on Black young people and recognise the importance of youth work in the struggle against this. However, even equipped with the theory, it is important to recognise that there remain many who still struggle to conceptualise and contextualise the complexities related to the lives of Black young people and the inequalities they face on a daily basis. Only youth workers who develop a critical understanding of inequalities and how they manifest themselves, are in a position to develop tools to support and enable Black young people to begin to positively challenge and attempt to contest the inequalities they face. It is, however, important to acknowledge that even with this critical understanding the work undertaken can still be marginalised and difficulties encountered.

Case study

In 2002 a three-month project was developed within a secondary school, to work with a small group of Black young men, aged 13–14 years through the PSHE (Personal, Social and Health Education) weekly slot. There were 12 young men in total from a year group of approximately 252 students (5.6 per cent).

The group was primarily developed to provide a support mechanism for the Black young men within this year group, as there was recognition by the youth worker that this particular group were experiencing a number of difficulties. These difficulties included some of the group continually being placed in detention and being on a number of report card systems.

The youth worker felt that if these difficulties were merely left it would result in some of the young men ultimately being excluded from the school.

A programme was developed which aimed to explore a number of aspects relating specifically to Black young men and their relationship with the education system, from a historical and present day perspective. It was felt that if the young people were given the opportunity to explore and analyse their experiences within the school context, in a safe and understanding environment, it would not only open the debate of their experiences of racism within school and its impact, but perhaps also alleviate some of their frustrations. Alongside this there was a commitment by the youth worker to support the young people in developing strategies to address the difficulties that they were currently encountering. These strategies were then to be presented to the senior school team responsible for inclusion within the school context.

Over the three months there were many heated discussions, which ranged from teachers using racist language, strategies for dealing with volatile situations within the classroom, to developing a reporting mechanism for what the young people deemed to be racists incidents within school. Throughout the project the Black young men continually articulated their frustrations regarding how teachers treated them, which was often in a negative manner. The majority of the group had an acute understanding of the importance of having a 'decent' education in order to live a particular life style, but there seemed to be a gap in the understanding of how exclusion could impact on their long-term aspirations. Individuals within the group spoke about 'surviving' until their final year, but for some of the group there was almost an acceptance that it was highly unlikely that they would actually survive to year 11.

Within this group of 12 Black young men, the reality was that by year 11 one of the group had been permanently excluded in year 10, two were permanently excluded in year 11, both of which were revoked by the school governors, but one was placed on an alternative curriculum (not on a full timetable). Four other members of the group received a number of fixed exclusions (specific number of days) throughout their time at the school. Out of a group of 12 Black young men, seven of them were excluded at some point within the three years, 2.8 per cent of the total percentage of 5.6 for the year group (Black young men).

One could ask the question as to whether the project was successful, as ultimately a high percentage of the group were prevented from reaching their educational potential in this instance. However, we would argue that the young people were given an opportunity to progress through Cross' stages of self-actualisation, in a supportive and understanding environment. Supportive, as those workers involved not only had an acute understanding of the range of difficulties that the Black young men were facing but were also able to explore appropriate strategies with them. Given the fact that usually very little work is undertaken in a formal context, in relation to developing Black young people's knowledge of self, we believe the project was an extremely important one. The group's evaluations of the project reinforced the importance of providing projects such as these to fully develop young people's potential. It is from this premise that we would argue that the project was a success.

The development of the group offered the Black young men an arena to explore the Encounter stage in an environment in which there was an understanding of the context that these Black young men were currently operating within. At the beginning of the project the majority of the group, were, we believe in Cross' Encounter stage. The Black young men were no longer accepting of the stereotypes that were often levied at them by teachers. Majors (2001) argues that White teachers often enter school to work with Black young people without any reference or understanding of the issues that affect their lives. As a result they often unwittingly prescribe to the negative perceptions of Black young people. The media, which portrays Black young people as violent, disrespectful, unintelligent, threatening, often fuels these perceptions and so Black young people are treated accordingly. It was often the responses to these negative attitudes that continually placed the Black young men in confrontational situations within the school context.

Ultimately the project encouraged the young people to explore and analyse their situation, this was undertaken with adults who had an acute understanding of their experiences and the impact that racism could have on their lives. Time was spent highlighting the positive achievements of Black people and their contribution to society. This method of working supported the Black young men to progress beyond the Encounter stage of the self-actualisation model. It was this same process, which allowed the Black young men to explore constructive mechanisms for challenging oppressive behaviour by adults and most importantly empowered the young people to be pro active rather than reactive within the school context.

Conclusion

In conclusion we would argue that the impact of formal education on African Caribbean young people is all too often a negative experience. In many cases Black young people's education is seriously being stunted in British schools rather than developed, due to negative factors such as streaming, league tables, low school and teacher expectations, racist stereotyping and rigid curricula. Strategies that have been put in place by the government to raise achievement and foster higher levels of educational attainment, have often been merely tokenistic gestures, which have rarely addressed the malice of issues faced by Black young people within the educational system (Gibson and Barrow, 1986). The Black child has instead been expected to learn and achieve within a context which has done very little to foster either elements. Instead, the Black child has been and continues to be subjected to a system which is infected with racist bias, whether it is conscious, unconscious or institutional.

It is important to recognise that some Black young people are able to display great resilience to the conscious and unconscious oppression they face when encountering the formal educational process within Britain and consequently able to succeed. However, the research that we have undertaken has highlighted that many Black young people are unable to cope within the formal educational context and so as a consequence disengage from the process of education. It is from this premise that we advocate for the following in order to redress the current situation:

- Earlier intervention with Black young people in order for them to recognise and combat oppression.
- Provide coping strategies for dealing with the increasing level of subconscious oppression Black young people face.

- Changes to the teacher training programme which places greater emphasis on critical analysis.
- Removal of the cash nexus from the education system, which enhances oppression and competition between individual students and educators.
- Far wider reaching reforms to the national curriculum that would allow students and educators to evaluate their own needs.
- Anti-racist practice as the foundation to all education.
- Independent advocates representing Black young people's views.

These represent only a small step to challenge the oppressive nature of the British education system in relation to Black young people. They are, however, fundamentally based on the principle of support for the individual, in helping them to understand oppression that they may face in order to progress.

Education is our future, for tomorrow belongs to the people who prepare for it today.

(Malcolm X, online)

References

Apple, M.N. (1979) *Ideology and Curriculum*. Boston: Routledge and Kegan Paul.

Benskin, F. (1994) *Black Children and Underachievement in Schools*. London: Minerva Press.

Blair, M. and Bourne, J. (1998) *Making a Difference: Teaching and Learning Strategies in Multi Ethnic Schools*. London: DEE.

Blair, M. (2001) *Why Pick on me: School Exclusion and Black Youth*. Stoke-on-Trent: Trentham Books.

Clarke, K.B. and Clark, M.P. (1950) Emotional Factors in Racial Identification and Preference in Negro Children. *Journal of Negro Education,* 19: 506–13.

Cross, W.E. Jr. (1978) The Cross and Thomas Model on Psychological Nigrescence. *Journal of Black Psychology*, 5: 13–9.

Culture and Education (undated) *Education and Culture*. [cited 19th September 2004] http://www.garysturt.free-online.co.uk/culture.htm

Davis, K. (2005) *A girl like me*. [2nd February 2006] http://www.uthtv.com/umedia/collection/2052

Delpit, L.D. (1988) The Silences Dialogue Power and Pedagogy in Educating Other People's Children. *Harvard Educational Review*, 58.

Fanon, F. (1967) *Black Skin White Masks*. London: Pluto Press.

Freire, P. (1972) *Pedagogy of The Oppressed*. London: Penguin.

Freud, A. (1986) Freud, S. (Ed.) *The Essentials of Psychoanalysis*. London: Penguin.

Gibson, A. and Barrow, J. (1986) *The Unequal Struggle*. London: Centre for Caribbean Studies.

Gill, D., Mayor, B. and Blair, M. (1992) *Racism and Education: Structures and Strategies*. London: The Open University.

Gillborn, D. (1990) *Race, Ethnicity and Education: Teaching and Learning in Multi-Ethnic Schools*. London: Unwin-Hyman/Routledge.

Gillborn, D. and Gipps, C. (1996) *Education and Institutional Racism*. London: Institute of Education.

Gillborn, D. and Gipps, C. (1996) *Recent Research on the Achievements of Ethnic Minority Pupils*. Ofsted.

Gillborn, D. and Mirza, H. (2000) *Educational Inequality: Mapping Race, Class and Gender*. London: Ofsted.

Giroux, H.A. (1995) *Racism and the Aesthetic of Hyperreal Violence: Pulp Fiction and Other Visual Tragedies*. [cited 2nd February 2006] http://www.henryagiroux.com/online_articles/racism_and aesthetic.htm

Gordon, P. (1989) The New Educational Right. *Multicultural Teaching*, 8: 1, Autumn.

Hardy, J. and Vieler-Porter, C. (1992) Race Schooling and the 1988 Educational Reform Act. In Gill, D. et al. (Eds.) *Racism and Educational Structures and Strategies.* London: Sage.

Jeffs, T. and Smith, M. (1992) Putting Youth Work in its Place. Youth and Policy. *Journal of Negro Education*, 36 Spring 1950.

Mac an Ghaill. M. (1988) *Young, Gifted and Black: Student-Teacher Relations in the Schooling of Black Youth.* Milton Keynes: Open University Press.

Majors, R. (2001) *Educating Our Black Children: New Directions and Radical Approaches.* London: Routledge Falmer.

Marshall, G. (1998) *Oxford Dictionary of Sociology.* Oxford University Press.

Rampton Report (1981) *West Indian Children in Our Schools.* London: HMSO.

Sewell, T. (1997) *Black Masculinities and Schooling: How Black Boys Survive Modern Schooling.* Stoke-on-Trent: Trentham Books.

Sidaneus, J. and Pratto, F. (1999) *Social Dominance: An Intergroup Theory of Social Hierarchy and Oppression.* Cambridge: Cambridge University Press.

The Black Panther Party Platform (1966) *What We Want What We believe.* [cited 4th March 2006] http://history.hanover.edu/courses/excerpts/111bppp.html

The Runnymede Trust (1997) *Black and Ethnic Minority Young People and Educational Disadvantage.* London: Runnymede Trust.

Troyna, B. and Carrington, B. (1990) *Education, Racism and Reform.* London: Routledge.

Troyna, B. (1990) Reform or Deform? The 1988 Education Act and Racial Equality in Britain. *New Community,* 16: 3.

Weekes, D., Wright, D. and McGlaughlin, *Race, Class and Gender in Exclusion from School.* London: Routledge Falmer.

Wikiquote (no date) *Malcolm X.* [cited 10th April 2005] http://en.wikiqoute.org/wiki/Malcolm_X

Wright, C. (1985) School Processes: An Ethnographic Study. In Eggleston, J. et al. *Education for Some: The Educational and Vocational Experiences of 15–18 Year Olds Members of Minority Ethnic Groups.* Stoke-on-Trent: Trentham Books.

Wright, C. (1992) *Race Relations in Primary Schools.* London: David Fulton.

Wright, C., Weekes, D. and McGlaughin, A. (2000) *Race, Class and Gender in Exclusion from School.* London: Falmer Press.

Wright, C. et al. (1998) Masculinised Discourses Within Education and The Construction of Black Male Identities Amongst African Caribbean Youth. *British Journal of Sociology of Education*, 19: 1.

Young, K. (1999) *The Art of Youth Work.* Lyme Regis: Russell House Publishing.

CHAPTER 15

The School Mentoring Project

Diane Watt

Introduction

In its broadest sense, the concept of mentoring involves giving advice and support to those who are often younger and less experienced in the areas of education, training and employment. Drawing upon the work of the Manchester based School Mentor Project, this chapter focuses on the effectiveness of mentoring as a strategy for increasing academic performance and reducing levels of exclusion among Black boys of African-Caribbean heritage.

Mentoring is generally regarded as an important strategy in reducing disaffection and increasing attainment amongst Black boys. Majors and Wiener's (1995) research, found that as opposed to punitive measures, mentoring programmes did have a positive impact on the lives of young African-American men. Within the British context, Skinner and Fleming (1999) point to the emergence of three specific models of youth mentoring. First amongst them is the Business Education Partnerships. This model seeks to attract pupils with a good record of attendance and whose behaviour and attitude towards school is generally seen as positive.

The second model is said to consist of mentoring schemes aimed at addressing the educational, personal and career development needs of particular groups as in the case of the City College Manchester Mentor Service. Following Howard Jeffrey's pioneering project at North London College, the college was the second FE institution in the UK to establish a mentor scheme for Black and Asian students (Majors, 2001). This initiative was not only aimed at attracting more ethnic minority students into further education but also to ensure success at the end of their studies. In 1995, the Mentor Service was cited by the Kennedy Report as an example of good practice in widening participation. Given the quality of work undertaken with students of different ages and from a range of social, cultural and ethnic backgrounds, in 1998/99 it was also nominated for the NIACE sponsored New Learning Opportunities Award. This was at a time when Estelle Morris, the then School Standards Minister went so far as to state that 'mentoring can make a world of difference to young people by building their confidence and self-esteem and supporting them at a critical stage in their education' (DfEE, 1999b).

The third model of mentoring has been described in terms of programmes which are a direct response to issues in relation to disaffection and exclusion and which Colley (2003) describes as 'engagement mentoring'. According to Colley, the primary focus of this form of mentoring is to work with young people who are disengaged from the formal system of education and training or those who are at risk of disengaging. Finn (1993) and Wilms (2003) concluded that pupil engagement with the school is more likely to result in academic success and less disruptive behaviour. The reasons for pupils becoming disengaged are varied. Edwards-Kerr (2005) also found that boys usually scored below girls on participation and belonging. These are but some of the factors which influenced the establishment of the School Mentor Project.

This project, an initiative of the City College Manchester Mentor Service was established for the specific purpose of undertaking one-to-one and group mentoring activities within a number of inner city schools. It was also aimed at addressing issues of exclusion and its impact on levels of achievement among Black boys. Throughout the duration of the School Mentoring Project, particular emphasis was thus placed on responding to the educational, cultural and personal development needs of young Black boys within these schools.

Mentoring

In his discussions on the origins of mentoring Jeffrey (1994) stated that although the term 'mentor' was first used in Homer's epic poem *The Odyssey*, mentoring was nevertheless a fundamental aspect of life in African societies.

In traditional African societies . . . the practice was very common:

> . . . *with young people being entrusted to elders, heads of craft associations, societies or extended family members for personal development, job training and general guidance. A mentor is therefore someone who provides guidance and support to a younger or less experienced person over a period of time. Mentors are likely to be sources of inspiration and act as coaches, professional friends, sponsors, facilitators and role models to their mentees.*

(Jeffrey, 1994)

Mentoring has also been described as a complex, interactive process occurring between individuals of differing levels of experience and expertise. It is a relationship which is based on the mentor's ability to empathise, communicate, nurture, support and to respond genuinely to the needs of the mentee. Mentoring involves a range of character building activities and is provided either in one-to-one partnerships or in small groups. Within most mentoring schemes, the development of this relationship is usually in three stages. The first stage is the process of getting to know each other. In other words building trust and establishing rapport. This may involve the mentor sharing with mentees their own experiences of education, training and employment. The second stage is characterised by questions such as what does the mentee want to achieve? In what ways can the mentor help and the ways in which progress will be measured and celebrated. The third stage involves regular meetings to review progress and to plan the next step.

For many of the mentors, the majority of whom were Black men, this was an opportunity to 'give back' to their community. This desire was underpinned by a commitment to principles of self-determination, as well as collective work and responsibility. Given their familiarity with the local community, the mentors were able to relate to the social, cultural and educational experiences of the young people. Overall, the project was aimed at ensuring that high numbers of African-Caribbean, Asian and other inner city school pupils especially those at risk of underachieving or exclusion were given extra support, advice and guidance to increase levels of motivation and confidence. Of particular concern were the levels of achievement among Black boys both locally and on a national scale. For example, a report on the educational experiences of Black boys in

London schools found that for the period 2000–2002, they were the lowest performing group in all of the key stages.

However, one needs to bear in mind Sewell's (1997) book on Black masculinities which points to the difficulties which arise when Black boys are seen as a homogeneous group. In his book *Taking a Stand*, John (2006) argues that there is now a growing acknowledgement of the achievements of young people of African descent. He maintains that these are pupils whose academic successes are not only helping to raise the performance of their schools but are also having a positive influence on the achievement levels of their peers.

The findings of Sewell's study further highlights the complex and often contradictory educational experiences of Black boys. He identified four categories that significantly influenced Blacks boys' attitude towards schooling. The largest group he labelled conformist in that they were committed to the goals of schooling. Edwards-Kerr (2005) also found similar levels of commitments among the African-Caribbean and Asian boys whom she interviewed. However, she went on to state that this was significantly different to that of the white pupils who participated in her study. Many of these young people were in fact quite negative as to the value of school in preparing them for future training and employment opportunities.

The second largest group were made up of the innovators. In other words boys accepted the goals of schooling but opposed the means. In a recent discussion with young men age 18–25, a number of them stated that their failure to achieve at school was in no way a reflection of their ability. Instead, they raised issues in relation to the appropriateness of existing learning and teaching strategies. They drew attention to the fact that it was very often the case of them having to sit and listen to the teacher. This being so, they usually felt unable to creatively participate in the process of learning. It is experiences of this nature which in turn influences their decision as to whether or not to pursue further studies. There was a general fear of being 'talked at'. As opposed to what he terms the 'banking system of education', Paulo Freire the Brazilian educator emphasised the importance of dialogue between the teacher and the learner. In his book *Pedagogy of the Oppressed* (1972) he stressed the need for learning to be directly related to the lived experience of the learner.

Sewell (1997) also identified two further categories of pupils namely the retreatist and rebels. Although small, both these groups rejected the goals and means of schooling. This rejection of schooling on the part of those labelled retreatist was however, not replaced by any significant alternative. For those labelled rebels, Majors (2001) argues that as a strategy for maintaining their cultural identity and gaining the respect of their teachers, Black boys can become engaged in challenging behaviours. As opposed to learning, the school environment thus becomes a battleground for recognition.

One of Majors' strategies for working with both Black and white boys in the UK who are labelled rebels has been the Rites of Passage manhood programme. It is a programme that is based on a concept that originated in African culture whereby village elders would take the boys into the wilderness to instruct them in the skills and responsibilities of manhood. At Kingshill special school for pupils with emotional and behaviour difficulties he developed the Mantra pilot scheme for white working class boys aged from 11 to 13. According to Majors (2000) 'These boys benefit most from work on their self-esteem, rather than issues surrounding race and cultural identity'. However, in his work with City

College Mentor Service he drew extensively on the *Nguzo Saba*, namely the seven principles of *Kwanzaa*.

In the East African language of Kiswahili, the first principle *Umoja* gives emphasis to the importance of unity within the family and the community. This is very much based on the premise of 'I am because we are'. As opposed to becoming victims of racism the second principle *kujichagulia*, is concerned with self-determination and perseverance. *Ujima* focuses on collective action aimed at building and solving problems within the community. In Manchester this is clearly evident in the establishment of organisations such as the Cariocca Education Trust. Instead of a reliance on others especially in areas of employment, the fourth principle *Ujama* , is on the development of businesses based on the collective economic strength of the community. The fifth principle *Nia* is based on the relationship between action and purpose. In her discussion on the sixth principle, *Kuumba*, Riley cites the words of the late Martin Luther King jnr. whereby he stated: 'Potential powers of creativity are within us and we have the duty to work assiduously to discover these powers'. The seventh principle *Imani* places particular emphasis on the importance of having faith. For the young people on the programme the focus was on them having faith in the beliefs that they were valued members of their family and community.

By drawing upon these seven principles, the school pupils and students were able to explore their own self-esteem in terms of personal choices, Black identity and culture. They also had the opportunity to explore attitudes towards school, college and academic performance. This included an identification of educational and professional goals, perceived barriers and how these may be overcome. They talked about events and people that have had a major influence on their lives. The recognition of appropriate and inappropriate masculine roles, skills and responsibilities within the family was a central theme throughout the course. In answer to the question as to his reasons for participating on the programme, one young man stated 'because of wanting to belong to a group and to learn about Black history. It's a sense of identity for me'. The importance of brotherhood and family values were also key areas of learning. Another student pointed to respect for self and others.

Throughout the programme the theme of resiliency by other men in equally difficult circumstances was explored through rap lyrics, poetry and literature. At the end of the programme the young men were given the tasks of identifying their own seven principles in life. The most popular ones included the importance of self-belief and being a role model to other young Black men in their community. One of the young men who participated on the programme has since completed a law degree. In an interview with *Manchester Evening News*, another one stated that: 'I decided to have a go at the Rites of Passage course to give me an extra kick up the backside. Now people who've seen what I've got out of it want to give it a try themselves.' Overall, the Rites of Passage programme highlighted the importance of undertaking culturally specific mentoring activities with young Black men.

Project evaluation

Blecham (1992) points to the importance of mentoring programmes undertaking evaluation which is aimed at measuring its impact on two levels. In the case of the School

Mentoring Project, this involved not only an evaluation of its overall strategy for reducing disaffection and increasing educational attainment, but also its impact on the diverse needs of young people. This included an assessment of personal development issues that were specific to them as individuals. Thus in choosing a qualitative approach, much of the data is a result of one-to-one or group interviews and questionnaires.

Three of the five schools that participated in the evaluation are located in dominantly working class areas with high levels of social deprivation. Over 50 per cent of the young people living in these areas were entitled to free school meals. In one of the schools approximately 45 per cent of the pupils had English as an additional language. This is in stark contrast to that of another participating school. Although pupils at this school are drawn from a range of social, economic and ethnic backgrounds, given its geographical location, it remains a popular choice for white middle class parents. The school is well known for its high academic standards which at times exceeds that of the national average. However, at the time of the study, existing data showed that a significant number of exclusions from this school involved Black boys in year nine.

Approximately 120 male and female pupils completed the 16 point questionnaire. From these questions, information could be elicited as to the pupil's socio-economic position and access to free school meals was one of the strongest indicators. Central to the project's methodology was the importance of enabling the participants to talk openly about their educational experiences, dreams and aspirations. The questionnaire thus allowed for them to give their individual views as to the benefits of the programme. The study was also a means of enabling the Mentor Service team to evaluate the effectiveness of its work from a range of perspectives. Hence semi structured interviews were undertaken with teachers, parents and some of the Black boys who completed the questionnaire.

The data from the questionnaire revealed that almost half the pupils (45.7 per cent) were eligible for schools meals. Approximately 62.9 per cent of them stated that they had been excluded from school. In terms of referral, word of mouth, in particular the recommendation of a friend, appeared the most popular route. In comparison to 21.4 per cent referrals by teachers including heads of year, self-referral was in the region of 32.9 per cent, the majority of whom were Black boys and had attended mentoring sessions for at least half a term.

Amongst the reasons given for attending the mentoring sessions was the opportunity 'to learn life skills'. This was in fact the most popular response which suggest that Black boys perceived mentoring as a process that would contribute to their personal growth and development. In the area of personal development, the mentor usually acts as a critical friend to the young men. This is done by drawing attention in a constructive way to areas of self-presentation, personal communication style and other aspects of character and personality development that are of relevance to the attainment of their stated goals

Where appropriate, the mentor shares with them their own experiences of successfully overcoming barriers to academic success. For some mentors the fact that they are able to make a contribution to others helps to confirm their belief in themselves. One mentor actually stated that it was 'good to be recognised and modelled'. Mentoring has indeed proved to be effective in helping mentors to fine-tune their interpersonal skills. This is of importance not only to the mentoring process but also to the mentor's work with others.

The pupils went on to identify attendance at mentoring sessions as a means of not getting into trouble especially whilst at school. Half of the year seven and eight pupils interviewed had been excluded at least once. The boys reported increased levels of confidence and motivation. This was reflected in the improvement of their schoolwork, relationship with teachers and the fact that they were less likely to be excluded. Of great significance, unlike teachers, they cited mentors as someone whom they could talk with about their feelings.

One pupil went so far as to comment on the fact that in mentoring sessions 'I get respect which I don't get anywhere else in the school'. This comment is not at all surprising in the sense that they did cite a number of situations where they felt teachers had failed to listen to them or had treated them unfairly. The boys in year 11 stated that participation in the mentoring programme had enabled them to 'feel better about themselves'; they got on better with friends and were likely to attend school on mentoring days. Some of them made reference to a growth in confidence and stated that they were better able to control their anger and emotions. They were nevertheless concerned with the fact that teachers did not tell them enough about life and also the tendency among teachers to 'treat you like a kid'.

The feedback from teachers regarding the impact of the mentor programme on Black boys' performance and attitudes towards school was mixed. Although some teachers were positive about the programme, they were concerned as to the extent to which the mentor programme could form part of the day-to-day activities of school life. There were those who reported positive changes in relation to individual pupils but stated that it was difficult to ascertain how effective the programme had been for Black boys on the whole. In one school, teachers reported that although the mentor project had been well utilised, this was only in relation to pupils that have been labelled 'streetwise'. Another teacher also pointed to the association between race and class. He stated that the project's emphasis on personal development was more suited to the needs of working class children. Ironically, the young people whom he labelled middle class were all white when compared to the composition of the working class group. This teacher also argued that the gap in levels of achievements between the two groups was largely due to their social background as opposed to race. His views are based primarily on assumptions as to the socio-economic position of African-Caribbean heritage pupils and their families. There is denial as to the ways in which racism can adversely impact on young people's lives.

Unlike the teachers, the majority of parents welcomed mentoring in schools. On the issue of race and identity, they pointed to the project as the only space in which Black pupils are able to discuss issues of this nature. Another stated that she was very pleased that behavioural problems were being tackled in other ways than just exclusion. As opposed to seeing mentoring as a threat to their authority, parents welcomed the mentors as an ally. 'I was discussing certain issues with my son to try and correct him. I was glad to hear him say that the mentor said the same thing as I said'. Parents also commented on the benefits of the boys having contact with male mentors. They felt that this enabled them to explore issues that they were unlikely to discuss with female mentors. The importance of these encounters between older and younger men is a central theme in Major's Rites of Passage programme. This is based on the notion that manhood is not a birthright but has to be learned. According to some of the parents the benefits of the programme was clearly evidenced by the fact that mentoring was the only lesson that their children would openly discuss with them.

Despite concerns on the part of teachers, the analysis of parents' and pupils' perceptions of mentoring suggest that it is seen as a valid part of Black boys' social and academic development. It also lends support to Miller's (1998) findings on the effectiveness of the different mentoring programmes in schools. During the course of this study, he noted the importance of setting goals, motivating students, improving practice and raising attainment. The comments of their parents and the high participation of boys in the programme is indeed a testimony to the importance of this particular form of mentoring in their lives. The data also suggest that mentors do play an important role in helping Black boys to navigate their way through the schooling process. The college was the first in the country to run a Manchester Open College Network Level 1 accredited Rites of Passage course for African-Caribbean young men.

In his study on the effectiveness of business and community based mentoring in schools, Miller (1998) asserts that participation should involve open discussions with pupils about why they have been selected. The pupils for mentoring should also be volunteers rather than 'conscripts'. There are also issues in relation to the role of mentors within schools. In many cases this is not clearly defined and is often linked to the ways in which schools choose to utilise their mentors. It was therefore not unusual for some schools to place mentors in a 'policing role' or what has been described by youth workers as that of 'glorified baby sitters'.

In terms of teacher-pupil relationships the evidence from this study highlights the fact that Black boys are often subjected to high levels of critique and conflict within school. Despite these experiences, they continued to attend school on a regular basis and place importance on the achievement of good examination results. However, their experiences of expulsion and lack of academic support led some of the boys to conclude that there were teachers who had 'given up' on them. Amidst experiences of racism and negative stereotyping, most of the boys in this study were nevertheless able to positively relate to teachers whom they found friendly and non-judgmental. However, on issues of social justice, some of the Black boys cited examples of unfair treatment on the part of teachers when compared to other groups. One of the boys recalled the time when he and his white friend deliberately shouted out in class as a means of testing the teacher's response. Both were reprimanded, however he was shouted at, and his white classmate was pleasantly told 'don't shout out'.

Research findings point to the fact that Black boys are often singled out as the perpetrators of misbehaviour both in and outside of school. In 2005 Deon Edwards-Kerr also found that in Manchester two thirds of African-Caribbean heritage boys who participated in her study felt they were often treated unfairly in schools. She further stated that nationally, 82 per cent of pupils excluded in 2002/2003 were boys, however, exclusion rates among Black boys remain twice that of white boys and approximately twelve times that of Indian and Chinese pupils.

The findings of this study nevertheless indicate that the work of the School Mentor project was indeed having a positive impact on achievement and levels of exclusion among Black boys. It revealed how important it was for the mentoring team to devise in collaboration with schools a structured programme which takes into account issues relating to pupils' personal, social and academic development. This should involve the utilisation of mentors from differing social, educational and occupational backgrounds. In the light of feedback from parents, there was an obvious need to increase their involvement, in particular, fathers and other male members of the family. Given the ambiguity of the role of mentors, it was important for the project and schools to work towards the development of clearly stated principles and practices.

Furthermore, the role of Black men as mentors in the schools was indeed critical to the project's effectiveness. The 1998 Truancy and Exclusion Report found that their presence in schools often resulted in a decrease in levels of exclusions among Black boys. It is therefore important to recognise the relationship between the old African proverb 'it takes a village to raise a child' and the positive role modelling activities of male mentors in influencing the lives of young Black men. Majors (2001: 208–10) argues that as well as an understanding of racial dynamics and racism, Black mentors' knowledge and familiarity with the cultural values and attitudes of the young men have proved fundamental to the development of meaningful mentoring partnerships. However, he maintains that:

> . . . these mentoring interventions cannot in themselves exact significant changes to the life chances of mentees. Institutions need to change. They need to evolve policies that reflect the cultural diversity of the school and address discriminatory practices.

This statement by Majors points to the need for strategies that are not simply aimed at addressing symptoms of disaffection among Black boys. Sewell (1997) also draws attention to the impact of racism both in terms of levels of exclusions and poor academic performance. It is further argued that this combination of exclusion and under attainment often leads to Black men entering higher education at an older age. Furthermore, their entry qualifications means that they are unable to pursue a wide range of courses hence under-representation in certain career areas. (Edwards-Kerr, 2005). One would therefore argue that initiatives such as the School Mentor Project should not just be seen as a strategy for tackling Black boys experiences of racism in schools.

References

Blechman, E.A. (1992) Mentors For High-Risk Minority Youth: From Effective Communication to Bicultural Competence. In Majors, R. (Ed.) *Educating our Black Children*. London: Routledge.

Colley, H. (2003) *Mentoring for Social Inclusion: A Critical Approach to Nurturing Mentor Relationships*. London: Routledge Falmer.

DEE (1999) Press Release:

Edwards-Keer, D. (2005) *Understanding the Educational Needs of African-Caribbean Young Men and Developing Pathways For Action*. Final Report.

Finn, J.D. (1993) *School Engagement and Students at Risk*. Buffalo: State University of New York.

Freire, P. (1972) *Pedagogy of the Oppressed*. Penguin.

Golden, S. and Sims, D. (1997) Review of Industrial Mentoring in Schools. In Colley, H. (2003) *Mentoring for Social Exclusion*. London: Routledge Falmer.

Jeffrey, H. (1994) *Developing a Mentoring Strategy*. London: CPW Associates.

John, G. (2006) *Taking a Stand: Gus John Speaks on Education, Race, Social Action and Civil Unrest 1980-2005*. Gus John Partnership.

London Development Agency (2004) *The Educational Experiences and Achievements of Black Boys in London Schools 2001-2003*. London Development Agency.

Majors, R. (2001) *Educating Our Black Children, New Directions and Radical Approaches.* London: Routledge.

Majors, R. and Mancini Bilson, J. (1992) *Cool Pose, The Dilemas of Black Manhood in America.* Simon and Schuster.

Majors, R. and Dewar, S.N. (2000) *Lessons from Africa: The Mantra Project.* National Dropout Prevention Centre/Network.

Miller, A. (1998) *Business and Community Mentoring in Schools.* London: DfEE.

Riley, D.W. (2994) *The Complete Kwanzaa, Celebrating Our Cultural Harvest.* Castle Books.

Sewell, T. (1997) *Black, Masculinity and Schooling: How Black Boys Survive Modern Schooling.* Stoke-on-Trent: Trentham Books.

Skinner, A. and Fleming, J. (1999) Mentoring Social Excluded Young People: Lessons from Practice. In Colley, H. (2003) *Mentoring for Social Exclusion.* London: Routledge Falmer.

SEU (1998) *Truancy and School Exclusion Report.* London: SEU.

Wilms, J.D. (2005) *Student Engagement at School: A Sense of Belonging and Participation.* OECD.

CHAPTER 16

Black Young People in the Youth Justice System

Darren Johnson

Introduction

Is it different working with Black young offenders compared to white young offenders? Is there a difference working with Black youth justice professionals compared to working with white youth justice professionals. Youth offending teams are multi-agency and multi-disciplinary; so does the ethnicity of those staff in terms of the similarities of outlook transcend their professional perspective. For example, does a Black police officer within a YOT have more in common with a Black social worker in the YOT than his white police colleague within the YOT when it relates to their approaches to engaging Black offenders and their families or in their understanding of the issues affecting Black people? Are there differences when staff work with Black parents? Is it different from working with white parents? These and other similar questions are ones which those working in and around the youth justice system or those who are stakeholders in the youth justice system should be legitimately asked, as they underpin many of the working assumptions that inform practice and decisions in the youth justice system. They also impinge upon decisions about staff recruitment and the targets set both locally and nationally for addressing the over-representation of Black people in the custodial system and conversely the under-representation of Black people in senior management in all of the criminal justice agencies working in the youth justice system.

There are inevitable differences between Black and White people and the way they experience the youth justice system. These differences occur because of the range of factors and variables such as nature or nurture, personality, professional training, class, gender etc. Even where professionals assert a commonality of outlook, by acknowledging a difference of colour (despite inferring a 'colour blind approach') which ignores the diversity of experiences which people share, some clear perspectives, which are commonly attributed to the way Black people and white people seem to perceive the world and interpret their immediate socio-economic circumstances is evident. This is especially stark in the realm of youth justice and is often brought into sharp focus due to the multi-agency, multi-disciplinary and multi values of the staff who work in the YOTs and broader youth justice sphere.

When a professional in the youth justice sphere, academic or even a parent of a young person uses the term 'Black people', it implies that there are shared experiences or things other than skin colour that are shared by persons for whom the term Black applies. The examination of the extent to which similar outlooks and experiences are shared by the majority of the Black population and an understanding of those shared views or perspectives is key to finding effective ways of engaging Black people who find themselves in the criminal justice system as either offenders or stakeholders.

Hence the identification and finding of what is or are the 'Black perspectives' and the ability to use approaches which are informed by an understanding of the 'Black perspective' is crucial to effective engagement of Black people in the youth justice sphere whether as offenders or as fellow professionals. Caution, however, should be noted as such an approach implies homogeny and thereby may not adequately take account of the diversity of views and perspectives which are held by individuals within the so called 'Black community'. In other words how many Black people would need to be spoken to and their views sought before it was determined that this was a shared perspective amongst the majority of Black people rather than a collection of individual views?

This chapter seeks to assist in informing debate and practice on working with Black young people but does not focus on statistics . . . as a Black worker once remarked when given another questionnaire to complete on race: 'we have been studied, surveyed and questioned to death for the past four hundred years and they still claim not to know what the problems let alone what the solutions are'. Another said:

> . . . *studying Black people is big business and looking at systemic failings is often the solution as it shifts responsibility away from the individual which is often uncomfortable and onto a system which is separate from oneself.*

> (Brown, Black Senior Officers Conference, 1995)

A systemic approach versus individual responsibility

The problems with taking a systemic approach to the issue of race in the criminal and specifically the youth justice system is that Black youths are sentenced individually and not as part of any overtly shared approach towards Black people. A Black young person cannot use as a defence (as legitimate as it may be) 'I only offended because the system as it impacts upon Black people caused me to'. Imagine a young Black person saying to a judge or magistrate: 'I should not be in the dock; you should be prosecuting the system and sentencing the system as this is the real fault . . .'

I would argue that the error many academics and policy makers make when studying this aspect of work is to look for causes of criminality and the solutions to criminality in the system whereas sentencing is based upon punishing or addressing the individual's behaviour. Hence Black people in the youth justice system whilst acknowledging that racism and discrimination contribute to some of the causal factors of why they are in the youth justice system; the need to recognise the role individual responsibility will play in any programme of intervention and indeed in the sentencing process must be clearly understood. It is not logical or possible to divorce the individual from their social setting or context, as every action by an individual arises out of the complex set of daily interactions that occur within their locality. Their ability to make sense of their local environment and their skill in 'negotiating and operating' within their social setting will determine whether they come into contact with the forces of law and order and the way those forces will interact with them. But the crucial point is that the instruments of the state will locate responsibility for a person's actions (however much influenced by other factors) with the individual. This can best be summed up by analysing the Blairite phrase 'tough on crime and tough on the causes of crime' which places at least equal emphasis on being tough on crime i.e. the individual . . . it is debateable whether equal emphasis has yet been placed on being as tough on the causes of crime, as sentencing does not allow causes of crime to be used in mitigation. In fact, it can be argued that causes of crime tend to aggravate sentencing decisions.

The discourse that existed throughout the 1970s and 1980s in many youth justice teams (they were called Intermediate Treatment teams or juvenile justice) was based on a belief and range of interventions that involved working with young offenders and occupying them in a range of activities. These activities were based upon an approach which sought explanations and solutions to their offending behaviour in social, environmental and systemic arenas. Some staff would seek changes in the individual's behaviour but such approaches were spasmodic and not part of any coordinated approach. I can recall working in a North London youth justice team in the 1980s and on my first day I was introduced to my colleagues; I entered a room where a large picture of Bob Marley adorned the walls. He was pictured smoking a 'spliff' and the smoke was billowing around his face. Later that day I couldn't resist asking what message they (the team) felt this sent out to young Black people. I was told that Bob Marley was a positive role model and that young Black males could relate to this 'positive image'. Suffice to say after much arguing the picture came down but it did start a debate in the team about the impact of images on children and Black young men. The poster would have been better sited in some other private venue but not within such an environment. In the same service young Black men would come to their sessions of 'intervention' and be told how racist the system was and how unfair the police were for targeting them and then leave the sessions and go out and commit further quite violent street robberies.

During the late 1980s and early 1990s the social policy of 'individual responsibility' to explain disparities in opportunities and socio-economic outcomes for individuals became very popular. Increasingly, following the introduction of the 1991 Criminal Justice Act (which brought in a range of sentencing options for the new 'Youth Courts' and seemed to capture the prevailing public mood with its emphasis on personal responsibility in the sentences available to young people), the attitudes of staff in the criminal justice system started to change, culminating in the Crime and Disorder Act 1998 which became the embodiment of the 'New Labour' mantra of 'Tough on crime and tough on the causes of crime'.

The change to multi-disciplinary teams and sentences based upon individual assessments (ASSET) and the rise in offender behaviour programmes places most of the responsibility for offending on the offender or their family; parenting orders are an obvious manifestation of sentences designed to engage with parents. This change of emphasis which compelled all parents to take responsibility for their children's actions relied on both Black and white cultures to share this perspective.

Amongst Black young offenders and their families such an approach fails to take account of the view widely held amongst Black people that a contributory factor to them coming into the system was due to their ethnicity. This notion impacts significantly on the extent to which the individual then will take full and complete responsibility for why they are in the youth justice system and more significantly explains why full responsibility cannot be accepted if there is already a view of mitigating circumstances related to one's race or ethnicity. It is often hard for any Black young person to fully accept that they are before the court purely because of their actions. Their whole life experience and indeed the evidence from a range of reports, research papers and Home Office reports would seem to support that being Black does influence the likelihood of being in the youth justice system, irrespective of innocence or seriousness of offending (section 95 CJA, 1991, 2002; *Report on race in the criminal justice system: differences or discrimination* Feilzer and Hood, 2004).

A report published in tandem with *Statistics on Race and the Criminal Justice System 2003* (Home Office, 2004) found that in 2002/03 the search rate per 1,000 population (for searches under section 1 of the 'Police and Criminal Evidence Act' 1984) was six times higher for Black people than for white people. This was even in areas where Black people were less than one per cent of the local population. The search rate for Black and Asian people under section 44 of the Terrorism Act (2000) was between four and five times that for white people. Numbers of arrests per 1,000 population were over three times higher for Black people than for others. Numbers of prison sentences per 1,000 population were over four times higher for Black people than for white people. The picture arising from these statistics supports the views held by many Black people in the youth justice system that the youth justice system and wider criminal justice system is biased against them on the basis of colour. This would give rise to a reason for the homogenous view held in general by Black people and which has justifiably become known as a 'Black perspective'.

The Crime and Disorder Act 1998 was a watershed piece of legislation for children and young people as it restructured the whole youth justice system and placed at the heart of it an ethos of preventing criminal activities occurring within communities. Although the New Labour government stated that it was going to be tough on crime and tough on the causes of crime, many campaigners believed that this would help to reduce the over representative numbers of Black young people in the criminal justice system particularly those in custody. Many social workers and probation officers in the urban centres of London, West Midlands, Manchester and Bristol in the youth justice system believed that the change in law and the change in government would lead to action to address the causes of Black over-representation in the system. Section 95 reports from the Criminal Justice Act (1991) had long since monitored the over-representation of Black young people and NACRO reports published as part of its policy bulletins amongst others had frequently identified some of the causal factors. Yet nearly seven years on since the Macpherson Report (1999), the Race Relations Amendment Act (2000) with its duty to promote race equality and the Youth Justice Board Race Audit (this Audit from 2004 onwards required YOTs to draw up race action plans to address the over-representation and disproportionate sentencing outcomes for Black and minority offenders), no significant shifts in the number of Black young people in the custodial and wider criminal justice system has occurred.

Effective engagement with Black young people

The complexity of the jigsaw of Black young people's experiences of the Youth Justice system and their offending patterns will not be fully explored in this short chapter but some explanation of how the parts fit together is set out.

Again using the jigsaw metaphor, when one approaches a jigsaw with its many pieces, the key decision may be to decide what pieces you believe are the most important ones

. . . yet as anyone who has done a jigsaw soon realises that with any jigsaw every piece is absolutely vital in order to appreciate the whole. In other words when applied to the issue of Black young people in the youth justice system, one needs to not only understand each and every factor but also to understand the relationship and interdependence of each of these factors and their contribution to comprehending the whole picture.

The latest figures from the Youth Justice Board identified that the majority of the workforce of YOTs were white (YJB, 2004), even in those YOTs who had a high ratio of Black clients. Given this fact the majority of Black young people and their cases will be allocated to a white staff member. Therefore, irrespective of arguments which have traditionally centred around 'Black young people being better able to relate to Black staff', the reality is that Black young people will have limited options other than work with white professionals. This then raises the important issue of the quality, type and range of training white workers can undertake in preparation for and prior to working with Black young people.

In 2005, I questioned more than 240 white youth justice professionals from across the country (England and Wales) whilst undertaking a fact finding task for the Association of YOT Managers. Ninety seven per cent of those questioned had worked with Black young people in the past four years. Yet when I asked the question how many had received training or sought advice prior to engaging with Black young people only 19 had done so. When asked a supplementary question 'do you think you can effectively engage Black young men?' The majority said that they could not or did not have the necessary skills. This then challenges the relevance and effectiveness of what exactly the workers are able to achieve with these young people with the aim of preventing further offending. Why then do these professionals and fellow stakeholders in the youth justice system continue doing things that they did not or had not considered would be effective, or of significant benefit to the Black young people?

There is, then, a challenge for managers and staff in relation to the training of staff in working with children from diverse backgrounds and who come from culturally different backgrounds from themselves. This is critical as effective engagement of young people irrespective of their ethnicity is a key part of all the programmes of intervention within the youth justice system. Any professional who engages with young people is aware of the impact their presence has on shaping the way a young person views the world and interprets the role of adults. For a young person still developing a sense of identity and what it is to be a young person in this complex world, is influenced by their contact with those charged with authority over them; whether it be teachers, parents, social workers, youth workers etc. In fact, adults should be aware of the potential for mentoring and role modelling in all encounters with young people . Evidence of this is widespread when one merely looks at the way young people follow fashion trends which are aimed at adults. Therefore, when working with Black young people, it is vitally important that particularly workers from a different cultural background to that of the young offender be made aware of the cultural background within which the young person resides.

Within the worker and the Black young person's interaction, they are both representatives of their existing cultures. When engaging Black young offenders they often adopt a position which they regard as defensive of the so-called 'Black culture'. This defensive posture is extended in relation to the reasons for them coming to the attention of the YOT or similar service, which they may to varying degrees regard as in some part a result of the 'oppression of Black peoples by the "majority white culture"'. Hence, whilst this should not be used as a reason for not engaging by a white worker, it should however be borne in mind in the discourse that will follow any engagement between the Black young person and the worker.

Session work

Black young people coming to the criminal justice system, as had been stated earlier, may use the fact that they are Black as a mitigating factor. How should the worker then approach the situation without falling into the trap of excusing the behaviour that has brought the offender to the attention of the service in the first instance.

During the first meaningful engagement (which may not necessarily be the first session) every effort should be made by the worker to acknowledge to the young person the general fact that Black people are disproportionately represented in the criminal justice system and that this is of concern. The young person should be further informed that time will be found within the programme structure to explore with the young person the impact of this reality upon them and how the work can be tailored to equip them with the necessary skills to minimise the likelihood of repetition. But this subject should not be allowed to become the predominant subject for discussion; as whilst it may be true that Black youths in an area may be particularly or disproportionately targeted, it remains the case that the young person in a session has committed a criminal offence and there are criminogenic behaviours that need to be addressed, such as their values related to right and wrong or law and order. The staff member will need to learn the skills to strike the correct balance within the session. These skills involve the ability to effectively negotiate the balance and tone of the session away from the wider external factors which enabled the offender to be caught and the actual offending that took place and the identified criminogenic factors.

For example, a Black young person may raise the issue during their sessions that they were unfairly stopped and searched by the police who deliberately targeted them because they were Black. This assessment may well be true and maybe evidenced locally by the numbers of stops and searches by the police on Black young people (external drivers). But if following that stop and search illegal substances or a crime is committed by the young person, the causes of that criminal behaviour should be challenged as part of the offending behaviour work by the worker.

To elucidate the point further, let us suppose that a young person comes to the session and is uncooperative when asked questions about why they have offended. A reply may be that they were deliberately targeted by the police because of their colour. Often workers may understand and agree that this is a plausible explanation and contributory factor for their presence or even their incarceration. The worker may then say to the young person that they understand and agree with their reasoning . . . This then can place the worker in a less powerful position to influence the future direction of the sessions, as the young person will then interpret *all* of their behaviour through the prism of racism. The worker is then also unwittingly obliged to do likewise.

However, if the worker adopts the approach of recognising that racism exists and acknowledging that this 'could' have been a factor to the young person committing the offence, without confirming that in this instance the reasons for the young person coming to their attention was to do with their colour, this enables the worker to both acknowledge the part racism plays in targeting offenders but the fact remains the person did commit an offence which needs to be addressed.

In a similar way workers from a similar ethnicity as the Black young person may well understand and have an empathy with the young person. From experience, when working in a particular London Borough, I was working with the police during the day, attending meetings and sharing platforms with senior police officers and then leaving the office and routinely being stopped by police and questioned. My vehicle was also regularly checked by the police. I could, in every way, empathise with the experiences being described by the Black young men at the time, but I was also clear that they nevertheless were committing, in many instances, some very serious offences which needed to be addressed.

It would seem a greater 'pragmatic' necessity for Black young people to acquire a greater 'maturity or sophistication' of approach than their white counterparts when engaging the police and other agents of authority, law and order. The worker will need to acquire the skills to empathise, identify and understand what specific actions or approaches can be taught to enable Black young people to be more effective in their engagements, and refocus the sessions aims on practical steps to prevent re-offending and re-criminalisation.

Addressing criminogenic causal factors

The next phase for the worker once they have acknowledged with the young person that racism does exist and the fact that they may have been targeted and then agree to address the implications of those issues in a separate session; then the task of addressing the criminogenic behaviours can commence. The addressing of the criminogenic causal factors in offending by Black young people must be understood through the prism of their experiences both within their locality and within the race discourse. By this I mean a Black young person who commits an offence similar to a white young person will experience the criminal justice system differently or will have different expectations of the criminal justice system than their white counterparts. Even their motivation for offending will be different from their white counterparts as well as their likelihood of being caught. Therefore, if this is understood by the worker, the programmes that are traditionally used for assessing offenders such as ASSET (the assessment tool used by YOTs to assess the needs of all young people who come to their attention) and the scoring mechanism needs to reflect these differences. Currently the main form of engagement with repeat offenders is by way of a cognitive behavioural programme which is usually delivered through questions and discussions with the offender and eliciting a range of responses through which it is envisaged that the young person will understand and put things in place to change their behaviour. Whilst this methodology appears an appropriate approach suitable for standardisation (applying to all offenders), the ability of the worker to understand the race discourse and apply it to and through the programmes of intervention is essential if one is to prevent the re-offending of Black young offenders.

For example, two young boys, one white and the other Black, go into the local shop to steal cigarettes. The Black young person generally would stand a higher chance of being monitored by staff due to their 'stereotype of Black people's honesty', therefore the Black person has a higher chance of getting caught than the white person. The understanding of these factors will enable a worker to address with the Black young person the 'real risks' for them which lie in a greater risk of being caught. Hence the assessment of the 'risk of offending' for the Black person and the risks associated with re-offending must include an assessment by the worker and exploration of the risks and likelihood of being caught by the police due to increased targeting and focus of the police on offending by Black people.

The worker should therefore also focus any programme of intervention with the Black young person on their increased risk of being caught. This is important as evidence from offenders show that one of the three motivational factors that inhibit re-offending is risk of being caught. This, then, is an ideal opportunity to bring in another factor that influences work with Black young people; namely the role of the 'significant others' in their lives. I have often asked the question 'Why do professionals working with young people believe that their one or two hour session (maybe twice per week) is going to impact upon a young person who is out of their company for at least *164 hours*?'

I am not questioning the validity or effectiveness of spending such little time with a young person, as the Audit Commission report *Misspent Youth* (1996) already covers this ground, but in this context as well as in my experience, the person that a child spends a significant amount of their waking hours with; whether it be peers, parents or others will invariably influence their behaviour, decisions and actions. Within this context the person's attitude to the behaviour (illegal behaviour) of the young person will be significant. Young people who offend therefore tend to associate with other people who offend or who do not disapprove of the behaviour; hence there are no drivers for changing the behaviour from the peer perspective. This leaves parents and teachers as the people who spend significant amounts of time with young people. In the case of a teacher, their influence is affected by the relationship they have with the child. For example, children that tend to spend significant time with the same teacher often cite that person as being significant, whereas particularly in the modern comprehensive school setting, children move from class to class based upon the subject they are having and as such, relationships and influences of teachers are diminished.

The role of the parents

Parents remain the key influential factor in young people's lives. In the case of Black young people in some areas the common perception is that of a single parent, usually female, bringing up the child or children on her own; however, this fails to take into account the role of extended family, church and also the role of the birth father. The father may not live in the family home, yet the way he is viewed by the young person and his status will and can be equal to that of the mother who resides in the home. This factor is important and may enable workers to explore with the young person the question of who are the significant influences in their lives? Workers often establish via the ASSET who lives at home yet fail to explore the role and views of the father or what the young person believes the view of the father would be on their behaviour.

For example, the worker asks the young person about what experience the dad has had, if any, of the criminal justice system or even speaks to the dad. If the father expresses similar feelings about the criminal justice system as their child, then work with the father and the young person should take place together. Otherwise any effective work undertaken by the worker with the young person may be inadvertently undone by a parent who shares and expounds their experience that the criminal justice system treats Black people unfairly, resulting in mitigation of the offending behaviour of their sibling. Professionals will require casework time and good case management to offer a broad service to Black young people.

Treating everyone the same?

A further element that must be considered when working with Black young offenders by workers is the question of 'treating everyone the same'. At a conference I was once told by an expert who had more than 20 years experience of working with young people that she always treated children as individuals. She explained that if two young people had the same antecedents and lived in the same street and were from the same socio-economic groups then the Pre-sentencing Reports PSRs and advice she would give in terms of sentencing outcomes and programmes of interventions would be the same. I asked her a series of questions and to each she answered that the individual circumstances would be the key driver. Finally, I queried 'Why then do we say 'Black young offenders' as the moment we denote an offender by their 'race' then we are implying that there is indeed a 'common' feature shared by all persons belonging to this group which 'homogenises them along "race" lines'. I said, 'If we can identify what this common feature is that all persons who are 'Black' share then we will be in a position to deliver appropriately tailored interventions'.

This is evidenced in the numerous data contained in the reports published under section 95 of the Criminal Justice Act 1991. They continually show Black people over-represented in the criminal justice system. If Black people are truly treated as individuals and come to the criminal justice system on the basis of the 'notoriety' of each case, then either Black people are inherently more dishonest or criminal than their white counterparts, or other factors disproportionately impact upon Black people causing or resulting in them being over-represented in the prison and community sentences population. Their ethnicity clearly is impacting upon professionals working at various stages in the criminal justice process.

We must question whether the factors affecting the initial decision by a police officer to stop, search or arrest a Black person; the decision by the custody officer to charge rather than a final warning or caution; the decision by the CPS to prosecute rather than discontinue; the further decisions by the magistrates to order reports rather than sentence, or remand rather than bail; the decision by the youth justice service to recommend a more intrusive option, rather than a less intrusive option, are all influenced by the ethnicity of the young person. As these stages in the youth justice system all show (from information contained both within the data from the *section 95 report* and the Youth justice board published research on race and discrimination *Youth justice workforce data*) the over-representation of Black young people or more severe sentencing outcomes for Black young offenders when compared to their white counterparts.

In July 2004 the Youth Justice Board produced a report which showed the extent of the over-representation of Black and Minority Ethnic young offenders in the system. The report looked at 17,054 cases, 'while some variation in outcomes could be explained by the nature of certain cases, some differences did indicate discriminatory treatment at various stages in the criminal justice process' (Feilzer and Hood, 2004).

Eight Youth Offending Teams (YOTs) were chosen – seven in urban areas, where there were relatively high concentrations of minority ethnic young people, and one in a rural area with a relatively low concentration. Information was obtained on 17,054 case decisions (14,432 involving males and 2,622 involving females, all aged between 12 and 17) over 15 months in 2001–02 – before the introduction of Referral Orders in April 2002.

This study demonstrated that there are large differences between white and ethnic minority young people of both sexes in the youth justice system as a result of the differential inflow of cases. It has also shown that there are considerable variations in the extent of over- or under-representation of particular ethnic groups in relation to the proportions in the populations served by the eight YOTs included in this study. Notwithstanding, this study did find, at various points of the decision-making processes, differences in outcome in the treatment of white, Black, Asian and mixed-parentage young people, as well as between males and females.

The answers to the approaches for workers in the criminal justice or youth justice system is of course to look at the individual but to understand that a Black young person with the same antecedents as a white young person may not result in them being viewed by the sentencers as the same 'risk' to the community and therefore receiving the same or similar outcome as their white counterpart. The fact is, that every magistrate will defend the way they sentence, which they assert is purely based upon the information in front of them. Yet cumulatively this approach demonstrably results in more Black offenders going to Crown Court and getting not guilty decisions than their white counterparts.

It is not just in the sentencing but also in the provision of reports to the courts, as PSR content should seek to present to the court the full risk factors associated with the offending and in the case of Black offenders a risk factor is their 'visibility' to the law enforcement agencies.

I am mindful of the complexities of arguing such a position as PSR authors would say that they tailor all reports to every individual and can point to a myriad of gate-keeping processes for their reports.

Do Black young people have an 'attitude' making them more difficult to engage than a similarly aged white young person? Given what I have said previously can the same question be posed in relation to the parents of young Black people, 'are the parents of young Black people similarly difficult to engage because of "attitude"?'

I personally cannot find any link between difficult to engage behaviour and Black people, as I have the same difficulties dealing with people who are challenging irrespective of their ethnicity. But my willingness as a professional to engage with an individual is influenced by my patience, views and perceived needs of the person. For example, as a Black person who has been a manager for more than 15 years, I am often reminded of the challenges I face not just as a manager in a complex work setting using my authority to get jobs done; but I am aware that there does on occasion appear to be some 'resistance' at times by staff to accept my authority to require them to do tasks. Sometimes they display what I would consider a 'bad attitude towards me'. On occasions I will think 'is it worth engaging with them . . . I don't need this'. My decision to ignore or engage is influenced by my view of them. So it is that workers, engaging Black young people and their families, who refuse to engage with them on the basis of the difficult or bad attitude they display are as much providing a commentary on their own views of the persons presenting the behaviour and their own responsibilities towards the young offender. I am not arguing that workers should tolerate bad or abusive behaviour as this should be addressed. And that is the point, that 'bad behaviour' should be addressed and challenged so that the person can learn more appropriate ways of engaging.

Recognising diversity

Young Black people may use a combination of their own language, terms and phrases in common use in their locality to explain issues, or as defensive tools to prevent the worker from engaging with them. This form of behaviour is not uncommon when working with white young people and is often typical of teenage behaviour. However, the obvious differences in language between the worker and the young person may serve to emphasise the difference between them and may provide further evidence to both parties to the engagement that the worker does not understand them. For this reason, it is vital that workers working with young Black people learn and understand the 'local terms' and the context within which they are used. Some of these terms may be local to the Black community so emphasising the need to maintain effective and credible contact with the local community from which and within which the young person resides.

One further point of note is to distinguish between cultural practices, perspectives and traditions which the young Black person may espouse and are based upon their religion or heritage and those which are not. An appreciation and understanding of the Black person's culture is therefore vital for any worker. Whilst I am arguing that there are common experiences which Black people share within this society and these are mainly related to their experiences of discrimination, the Black community is not culturally homogenous so these cultural differences should also be recognised by professionals. Increasingly in urban areas Black communities are made up of individuals from all parts of the world who do not share a common cultural heritage or context. Professionals therefore need to keep abreast of the cultural practices of their local communities and ensure that any diversity training is sufficiently robust and informative to enable significant understanding of these issues. However, I am continually dismayed by the common practise amongst professionals working in the youth justice system of either contacting the local race equality council or other similar bodies to answer questions that the worker or service cannot answer.

Such a piecemeal approach misses the point related to the complexities of understanding any culture as *no* culture can be explained in a few question and answer sessions:

> *If the tables were reversed would a one day course explaining the diversity of English culture be sufficient training to understand the needs and issues of English people . . . It needs to be shared and experienced in order to fully understand the perspective.*

Workers who work with children from diverse communities need to be able to spend time within those communities to understand the perspectives and ways members of that community engage with the wider white society.

Current demographic changes have seen in some areas of the country significant increases in the local Black population, many of whom are young families and families with a number of young children. Yet agencies have not responded to the current and future realities of white workers (many of whom reside outside of the areas that the Black families and Black young people live) working in ways which were designed or based upon engaging white young people. The 'factoring in' of the 'race dimension' in all practice, planning and delivery of services is an aspect unfamiliar to many of those working with young people today. Yet this factoring in will increasingly become necessary if the needs of their local youth population, which increasingly may be Black and certainly more diverse, is to be realised.

Section 95 reports came out of the Criminal Justice Act 1991. Its impact appears to have been largely ignored as whilst most public organisations have responded in some way to the Race Relations Amendment Act 2000 with its requirement on public bodies to promote race equality, most criminal justice agencies have focused upon this Act rather than examining their role and contribution into the content of section 95. YOTs are the main vehicles for delivering services to young Black offenders. The Youth Justice Board which is responsible for the youth secure estate (with at least 25 per cent of the population from ethnic minorities) did not from the outset require YOTs and their staff to put in place regimes to work effectively with Black young offenders. The place and status of section 95 within YOT data collection is not evident and continues to not form any significant part of the strategic youth justice plans.

The Youth Justice Board in 2004 published figures on the total workforce of the youth justice sector. Whilst it does effectively monitor the ethnic make up of YOTs, it has no influence or say on how YOT staff are recruited or appointed. This remains locally determined and therefore continues to reflect the 'local market conditions'. This piecemeal approach results in some areas where there is a relatively significant Black adult population having workforces which are multi-cultural, and other areas remaining mainly mono-cultural. This is of concern, given demographic changes in the ethnic make up of local and national populations, and leaves many Black young people and their families receiving services and engaging with staff ill equipped to meet their needs.

A further note of consideration in relation to working with Black young people is to appreciate the different histories which young people from African Caribbean backgrounds have from their Black African counterparts. Therefore a worker will need to establish the cultural heritage that the young person is claiming as theirs and work within the norms of that culture. This factor is further linked to the young person's sense of identity and belonging. For young people identity is important and for Black young people this is even more important yet can be the source of much debate within their peer groups and indeed with the worker. Particularly when completing the ethnic classification monitoring forms, I have found that the range of options may not have an option which the young person is happy to complete and they end up ticking the box 'other'. It is important where this is the case that workers explore with the young person their sense of identity as most people who feel they belong to a society or have a 'stake' in it will have confidence in its laws, rules and institutions.

The level of educational underachievement of Black young people, particularly males, is well documented. People who are well educated generally have more life chances, yet even amongst the Black educated classes the quality of life and other achievements do not mirror that of their white counterparts, as they are still more likely to be stopped and searched if they reside in certain areas, than their white counterparts. They are still therefore by inference more likely to directly know someone who has been or is in the criminal justice system than their white counterparts. This leads to a generally greater interest in what happens and how the system works amongst Black people. When applied to the youth justice system and working with young Black people, Black professionals in this sphere have generally been more vociferous in pushing for the needs of Black children and young people to be met. Indeed, areas that tend to employ Black staff in the youth justice sphere have more policies and procedures in place to address issues of diversity than other places where no Black staff are employed.

Conclusion

Black people in the youth justice system, whether as professionals, young people or other stakeholders, experience the system through a contextual prism that is generally different from that of their white counterparts due to the disproportionate negative outcomes for other Black people that cannot be explained in ways devoid of any reference to race. This reality enables Black people to have a shared interest in how the system works. The documented over-representation of Black young people in custodial settings and the disproportionate use of stops and searches of Black young people only serve to further highlight the unfairness of the justice system.

If disproportionality and over-representation is to be addressed then the focus must be on changing the ways in which professionals make their decisions at every stage of the criminal justice system. The starting point for this change must be effective training of staff. Explicit and specific training should be given to staff working in the youth justice system. Effective training for those who will have direct contact with Black young people should also be regular, rigorous and routine practice.

Staff from YOTs currently receive training in relation to general offending behaviour programmes but the relative usefulness of such programmes if they fail to explicitly tackle how to engage Black young people would render such programmes irrelevant and more significantly would fail to take account of the changing demographics both locally and nationally. It also fails to meet one of the key requirements of the Race Relations Amendment Act which is the duty to 'promote' race equality.

One of the key drivers to preventing offending by offenders is the role and influence of their parents. Staff from all the professions working in the youth justice sphere need to consider how they engage with Black parents. Training on parenting work should incorporate working with parents from diverse cultural backgrounds and take into account their experiences of the criminal justice system. Therefore the advice and support parents will give to their children who become involved in the criminal justice system should be recognised. There are many stereotypes about Black men and parenting. As with any stereotype some individuals fit the stereotype and some do not. However, in relation to parenting, the potential influence of any parent on the actions and values of their birth children should not be underestimated.

Black staff in the youth justice system remain under-represented in senior posts within criminal justice agencies. This under-representation at senior and policy making level contributes to the lack of understanding at senior levels of the factors that not only cause over-representation but the differential outcomes for Black people in the youth justice system. The ability to influence the polices that could bring about significant changes in the way Black young people are dealt with within the youth justice system is therefore limited. Key challenges remain for senior managers of all criminal justice agencies in the youth justice sphere to demonstrate that they understand and are responsive to the needs of Black people in the youth justice sphere. If one indicator or measurement of the level of understanding of diversity is based upon training attended then the absence of regular diversity training and the absence of senior managers on such training is conclusive.

Over the last two decades it is clear that people from Black African Caribbean backgrounds are more likely than the white population and than other BME groups to be:

- stopped and searched
- arrested
- prosecuted
- imprisoned

This fact is irrespective of whether Black people are employed in the youth justice system as professionals, stakeholders or are offenders. Therefore, there remains a challenge to the government, YJB and the YOT managers, to reject this as an effective approach to being tough on crime and the causes of crime. Effective approaches leading to meaningful engagement are the most effective ways of tackling discrimination and over-representation.

References

Brown, K.M. (1995) Black Senior Officers Conference. October. Quinta Centre Weston Rhyn.

Feilzer, M. and Hood, R. (2004) *Differences or Discrimination? Minority Ethnic Young People in The Youth Justice System.* London: HMSO.

Lord Chancellors Department (1992) *Criminal Justice Act 1991.* London: HMSO.

Lord Chancellors Department (2002) *Criminal Justice Act 1991. Report on Race in the Criminal Justice System.* London: HMSO.

Lord Chancellors Department (2003) *Statistics on Race and the Criminal Justice System.* London: HMSO.

NAYJ (2005) *Feedback Form.* NAYJ Annual Conference Sep. Harper Adams College Shropshire.

The Institute for Criminal Policy Research (2004) *Race and The Criminal Justice System: An Overview to The Complete Statistics 2002–2003.* London: King's College School of Law.

Youth Justice Board (2000) *ASSET. Assessment Tool For Young People.* London: YJB.

Index

Russell House Publishing Ltd

We publish a wide range of professional, reference and educational books including:

Anti-racist Work With Young People
by Anna Luffi-Pentini et al.   1996   ISBN 1-898924-01-5

Working With Children of Mixed Parentage
by Toyin Okitikpi   2005   ISBN 1-903855-64-0

For more details on specific books, please visit our website:

www.russellhouse.co.uk

Or we can send you our catalogue if you contact us at:

Russell House Publishing Ltd,
4 St George's House,
Uplyme Road Business Park,
Lyme Regis DT7 3LS,
England.

Tel: 01297 443948.
Fax: 01297 442722.
Email: help@russellhouse.co.uk